# BUY AND HOLD IS STILL DEAD (Again)

# BUY AND HOLD IS STILL DEAD (Again)

## The Case for Active Portfolio Management in Dangerous Markets

### (2nd Edition)

Kenneth R. Solow, CFP®

New York

## BUY AND HOLD IS STILL DEAD (Again)

The Case for Active Portfolio Management in Dangerous Markets (2nd Edition)

Published in New York, New York, by Morgan James Publishing. Morgan James and The Entrepreneurial Publisher are trademarks of Morgan James, LLC.
www.MorganJamesPublishing.com

The Morgan James Speakers Group can bring authors to your live event. For more information or to book an event visit The Morgan James Speakers Group at
www.TheMorganJamesSpeakersGroup.com.

**Shelfie**

A free eBook edition is available
with the purchase of this print book.

CLEARLY PRINT YOUR NAME ABOVE IN UPPER CASE

**Instructions to claim your free eBook edition:**
1. Download the Shelfie app for Android or iOS
2. Write your name in **UPPER CASE** above
3. Use the Shelfie app to submit a photo
4. Download your eBook to any device

ISBN 978-1-63047-210-8  paperback
ISBN 978-1-63047-816-2  eBook
ISBN 978-1-63047-817-9  hardcover
Library of Congress Control Number:
2015916025

**Cover Design by:**
Rachel Lopez
www.r2cdesign.com

**Interior Design by:**
Bonnie Bushman
bonnie@caboodlegraphics.com

In an effort to support local communities, raise awareness and funds, Morgan James Publishing donates a percentage of all book sales for the life of each book to Habitat for Humanity Peninsula and Greater Williamsburg.

Get involved today, visit
www.MorganJamesBuilds.com

**Habitat for Humanity®**
Peninsula and
Greater Williamsburg
Building Partner

# TABLE OF CONTENTS

# LIST OF TABLES AND CHARTS

# ACKNOWLEDGEMENTS

My New Year's resolution at the beginning of 2008 was to write a book about active portfolio management. Step one was to take a Mavis Bacon typing course so that I could learn to type without looking at the keys. Step two was to actually write the book. If my efforts were successful, it was in no small part due to the efforts of many people who provided either emotional or technical support over the course of the project.

I want to thank my fellow Founding Partners at Pinnacle Advisory Group, John Hill and Dwight Mikulis. They have been trusted co-owners since we founded Pinnacle in 1993, and my friends in the financial planning business since I started in 1984. John and Dwight had the courage to join me in steering the company on a course towards active portfolio management after the bear market of 2000- 2002. It must not have been easy to listen to their crazy partner who insisted that there was something terribly wrong with the investment industry status quo. If our efforts at Pinnacle result in better serving our clients, it is in great part due to the untiring efforts of these two men whom I have known for my entire professional life as a financial planner. I have immense respect for both of them. I also want to thank the Junior Partners at the firm, Rick Vollaro, Deb Kreibel, Jake Mason, and Michael Kitces, who have also helped to shape our investment process since they have had to explain it, whatever "it" is, to clients since we first made the change to tactical asset allocation in late 2002.

I also want to thank the investment analysts at Pinnacle: Carl Noble, CFA; Sean Dillon, CMT; and Sauro Locatelli, CFA; along with our Chief Investment

Officer, and Pinnacle partner, Rick Vollaro. They have been involved with the evolution of Pinnacle's active management tactics and strategy since 2002, and their creative and motivated approach to solving the inevitable practical and theoretical problems of actively managing portfolios for a growing number of affluent clients can't be underestimated. If one of the basic responsibilities of being a portfolio analyst is to make the Chief Investment Officer look good, they managed to do so with unfailing enthusiasm on a daily basis while I held the position until January of 2011. I also want to thank the rest of the management team and associates at Pinnacle. Their ongoing efforts on behalf of our clients make it possible for me to have the time to do things like write a book.

My goal in writing was to simplify the theoretical and technical language of portfolio theory and tactical asset management. To that end, I had the kind assistance of several readers who greatly enhanced the quality and the accuracy of each chapter. I want to thank my friend and client, George Drastal, whose background as a scientist was invaluable and whose comments were immensely helpful, especially in writing Part I. My brother, Larry Solow, has an amazing talent for seeing the "big picture" in the writing and provided wonderful insights from the perspective of a "non-investment professional" reader. Former Pinnacle associate Illa Amerson and current Pinnacle Wealth Manager Jeff Troll added helpful insights based on their industry expertise. I could count on both of them to stop by my office and give me their opinions about just about everything that mattered in the text. I thank them for their honesty, and their tact.

I want to give special thanks to Pinnacle Partners, Rick Vollaro and Michael Kitces. Rick is currently the Chief Investment Officer at Pinnacle and his comments and criticisms regarding Part II of the book, which focuses on how to tactically manage portfolios, were invaluable. Michael Kitces is the Director of Financial Planning Research at Pinnacle and has co-authored several professional papers with me on financial planning topics. He is an acknowledged superstar in the world of financial planning. The comments about withdrawal rates in Chapter 2, and basically the entire tax chapter (Chapter 13), reflect Michael's unique and informed guidance regarding both issues. In addition, I owe Michael another note of thanks for suggesting I add *(again)* to the book title. I may never get used to the amount of red ink I receive when Rick and Michael edit my work, but the end result is always better than when they got their hands on it. Finally, I want to thank Pinnacle's former Director of Marketing, Brian Saint-Paul, for working so tirelessly on this second edition. Brian has been a good sport about the whole project, which has taken much more of his time than I would have suspected when we first discussed a second edition.

I also want to thank several academics and financial professionals who took the time to read chapters and correspond with me about the book. Ed Easterling, the author of *Unexpected Returns*, was kind enough to comment on the chapter on secular bear markets, even though he was moving his home and his offices at the time. Professor Mordecai Kurz, from Stanford University, took time out to correspond with me regarding his Rational Beliefs theory of pricing. Woody Brock was especially helpful, contacting me on several different occasions to discuss the logical and academic rationale for actively managing portfolios. I feel honored that these men allowed me some of their valuable time so that I could present their ideas in Chapter 5. Yale professors Antti Petajisto and Martijn Cremers, authors of the important *Active Share* paper discussed in Chapter 7, were also generous enough to share their thoughts about the chapter and offer a few needed clarifications and corrections. I can't thank them enough for taking their time to help. Bill Hester, senior portfolio analyst for the Hussman Growth Fund, was helpful in reviewing the chapters on P/E ratios and secular bear markets. I have huge respect for the analytic powers of both Bill and John Hussman, the fund's manager, and I thank them for their contribution. Finally, I want to thank Bob Veres, a well-known commentator on the financial planning industry, for his comments on the early chapters in the book. Bob is a lightning rod for commentary about active management in the industry, and he has recommended me as a speaker on more than one occasion. If active management becomes more accepted in the financial planning community, I suspect that Bob will have something to do with helping financial planners discuss the matter intelligently.

As a new author with some small knowledge about how to actively manage portfolios, and no knowledge of how to write a book, it may have been an act of divine providence that early in the process I met Cindy Spitzer and somehow knew that she was the right person to edit the book. Cindy is an experienced author with many books to her credit, and the highest compliment that I can give her is that her knowledge and experience about writing has made this a much better book than it would have been otherwise. Aside from her abilities as a writer, I also owe Cindy my gratitude because her friendship and emotional support were invaluable to me in finishing this book.

Finally, I want to thank my wife, Linda, and my two children, Danny and Carly, for putting up with Dad disappearing into his office each evening to write during the first half of 2008. Anyone who is in the business of helping clients reach their financial goals will never forget the 2007—2009 bear market. I don't remember a period that was more stressful for our clients or for their advisors. For me, I can't imagine how I would have dealt with it without the love and support of my family. Thanks gang. I absolutely couldn't have done it without you.

# PREFACE TO THE SECOND EDITION

I must admit that I have been surprised by many of the events that have occurred since *Buy and Hold Is Dead (Again)*, or BAHD, was first published in May of 2009. Most obviously, the date was only two months from the market bottom following the great bear market that began in October 2007 and ended in March 2009 — a bear market that took the S&P 500 Index down by 55%. The rough draft of the book was written in five months and was completed just a few months before Lehman Brothers went bankrupt. Since the market bottomed in March of 2009, the stock market has experienced a powerful cyclical bull market that has seen the market gain more than 200% from the market's March 09 lows (as of this writing.) For those investors firmly committed to the "buy and hold" style of investing, the rally has been a powerful confirmation that trying to "time the markets" is a losers game as diversified portfolio returns continue to make new highs. I would like to say that I saw the current bull market coming as I began writing the book in January of 2008, but I can assure you that wasn't the case. At the time we were in portfolio "lockdown" having made a high conviction forecast of a recession and a bear market. Of course, I couldn't have imagined that Lehman would go bankrupt before the end of the year either.

Investors should not learn the wrong lesson from the current bull market. It does nothing to make the case for buy and hold investing. As I wrote in the first edition of BAHD, "The next bull market will have little to do with efficient markets, Modern Portfolio Theory, and the rest of it, and everything to do with Graham and Dodd and their theories of value-based investing that were originated in the 1930's.

The market will become very inexpensive and that will form the basis for a long-term and profitable bull market at some time in the future."

Alas, once again my crystal ball may have been a little cloudy, because in the opinion of many sophisticated investors the current bull market has little to do with Graham and Dodd and their method of finding value based on studying market fundamentals, and everything to do with an illusion of potential prosperity created by central banks and other policy makers determined to reflate assets and avoid a Great Depression at any cost.

Another relevant quote from the first edition is, "And while forecasting the future is always fraught with risk, it will come as no surprise if buy and hold proponents then attribute its [the next bull market] success to entirely the wrong reasons. Hence, the title of this book contains the parenthesis (again). Buy and hold should be allowed to die, but that doesn't mean that there won't be long periods of time when it is profitable to once again buy and hold stocks. It does mean that the rationale for buying and holding should change, as should the average investor's appreciation of, and strategy for, understanding and managing the portfolio risk that is accepted with its implementation."

Make no mistake. A near six-year cyclical bull says nothing at all about the premise of this book, which is that the traditional paradigm for managing portfolio risk is obsolete. The book was not, and is not, about making a market forecast where the lessons learned are only valid in a bear market and invalidated in a bull market. It is, instead, about a new methodology for managing portfolio risk that promotes the notion of value investing rather than a status-quo approach that essentially claims that there is no such thing as good or bad portfolio (or security) value. Investors must learn the simple rule that cyclical bull markets have a high probability of occurring from a starting point of cheap market values and/or accommodative monetary policy, and cyclical bear markets have the same probability of occurring from expensive valuations and/or restrictive monetary policy.

I personally believe that the 200%+ market move off of the market bottom in 2009 has been propelled by dramatic and unprecedented policy intervention by central bankers around the world. Perhaps just as importantly, but less noticed, is the impact of changing FASB accounting standards so that "mark to model" valuations are allowed for calculating bank balance sheets. The timing of the change was magnificent, magically transforming banks from being virtually insolvent to being healthy in April of 2009, not coincidentally just a few weeks after the 2007-2009 bear market made a bottom.

The reasons for the current bull market matter. Instead of relaxing while the market makes new highs, now is the time to be diligently studying market values. The U.S. stock market is no longer cheap. In Europe and Japan, policy makers appear to be continuing their ride on the quantitative easing bandwagon, while in the U.S. it seems that accommodative monetary policy may be reaching its final plateau. If we are nearing the end of the liquidity wave that has fueled the U.S. stock market rally, at the same time that the U.S. market is getting expensive, it will soon become very clear that the bull market was not the result of the hopes and prayers of buy and hold investors who were desperate for a bull market to bail them out after a decade of underperformance.

The title of the book is called, *Buy and Hold Is Still Dead (Again)* for a reason. Bear markets occur when markets are expensive and monetary policy is restrictive. When we reach the tipping point where shareholders begin to take profits, traditional buy and hold investors are going to be reacquainted with how powerless it feels when there are more sellers than buyers for what inevitably seems like a very long period of time. As greed gives way to fear somewhere near the market bottom, when the pain of the losses are at their peak, the buy and hold mantra will leave a terrible taste in everyone's mouth... again.

## Confusions and High Expectations

I've also been surprised by the amount of confusion there is about the semantics involved in describing active management. For example, I was stunned when an interview with the *Motley Fool* resulted in an article suggesting that I thought Warren Buffett was wrong to buy and hold stocks. The notion that Warren Buffett, *the world's most well-known value investor*, has anything to do with buy and hold strategic asset allocation is absurd. For the record, the "buy and hold" in the title *Buy and Hold Is Still Dead (Again)* does *not* refer to buying and holding securities purchased at a steep discount to fair value, measured by a generous margin of safety, and then holding them as long as it takes for "Mr. Market" to properly recognize franchise value. It *does* refer to the buy, hold, and rebalance, mantra of those who believe in the nonsense of efficient markets.

Another surprise has been the extraordinary expectations investors seem to have about active portfolio management. Where buy and hold investors advance nothing at all in the way of expectations about short-term portfolio performance, it appears that investors have nothing but the highest (sometimes impossible) expectations about active management. The litmus test for active managers seems to be how they performed during the 2007—2009 bear market. For many, the notion that active managers suffered any kind of a decline in asset values during the period means that they were not an effective active manager. In a new chapter, I explain the concepts of core and satellite investment strategies and how alternative (or satellite) strategies often promise to deliver absolute positive returns in a bear market. However, I caution investors that this standard of performance is unnecessary to justify a more active approach to managing risk. In addition, as I will discuss later, such a high level of expectation creates all kinds of mischief in the implementation of active investment strategy. Hopefully, as investors become more educated, they will conclude that the absolute positive return standard for determining the success of active and tactical portfolio management should be combined with other objective methods of determining the success of a tactical strategy, or at least learn to define risk as something other than the amplitude of previous peak to trough returns.

Lastly, it has been interesting to watch investment time horizons collapse as the bull market has continued and active portfolio managers look to trade small corrections in order to add extra value to portfolio returns. BAHD takes the buy and hold investment strategy to task for offering few tools to defend against bear markets, with "patience" being at the top of a very short list. Ironically I now find myself offering the same counsel to active managers, meaning that that they too should be patient. Active and tactical management works best when trying to evaluate the highest probability of investing major turns in the market cycle. Major turns occur infrequently and can be forecast using the tools I offer in the book. But valuation is a useless indicator in the very short-term time frames that active managers are trying to trade. Their activity looks more like day-trading or swing-trading, instead of an investment strategy based on a repeatable and systematic approach to fundamental market analysis. Active and tactical asset allocation should be implemented, and evaluated, over complete market cycles. Investors who try to catch smaller, counter cyclical moves within the larger cyclical pattern will be disappointed. In Part II of the book I describe in great detail how to use valuation, technical analysis, and market cycle analysis to actively change portfolio asset allocation in an attempt to earn excess returns. Excessive reliance on technical analysis to catch short-term market moves will not end well for most investors.

## Late to the Party

All of which brings me to the tidal wave of new tactical portfolio strategies being offered to the public. In Chapter 15 of BAHD, titled "Industry Forecast (An Essay)," I suggest the industry would present consumers with a blizzard of new active management investment choices. "The second major change I see is that the industry will have to create new actively managed investment products to meet the demands of consumers who want a more active approach to managing their wealth." And, "Along the same lines, I see the industry manufacturing new actively managed investment funds for individual investors."

Since the publication of this book, dozens of firms have offered institutional clients "tactical overlays" to quiet the concerns of clients who want to realize historical average portfolio returns when many believe that both U.S. stocks and bonds are overvalued. In the world of broker-dealer platforms offering a variety of investment strategies to advisors who cater to retail investors, the number of active management strategies that are being offered has exploded. Unfortunately, much of what is being sold today is unsuitable as a core holding for investors. (I will better define "core holding" in the new Chapter Eight in Part Two of the book.) The tactics being used to sell these strategies are specifically designed to define (misrepresent) risk as a matter of avoiding the market declines of the past, without any consideration of how these strategies are likely to perform in new investment regimes in the future. Perhaps the most egregious examples are the single asset class strategies that define risk in terms of one asset class that can rotate to 100% cash when needed. Investors flocking to portfolios constructed using 100% US equities, 100% US Junk Bonds, 100% Emerging Markets, or any other single asset class, will be sorely disappointed if future market regimes don't favor that particular choice of risk asset.

From my vantage point, I see that most of the new strategies are technical in nature, and more specifically based on momentum-types of approaches to active management. This is not surprising to me because momentum strategies are:

1. Inexpensive to implement with relatively few technical analysts needed to read the "tea leaves" of a variety of technical indicators.
2. Easy to back-test

Regarding back-testing, since the publication of BAHD I have seen a disturbing number of strategies that are being sold to the public based on hypothetical and back-tested returns, presented as supplemental information within a GIPS compliant presentation. I write about this trend in the new chapter beginning Part Two of the book, and point out that investors must beware. If the Holy Grail is to find an advisor who got totally out of the market in 2008, you can easily find one to show you how their strategy *would* have performed during the period. Unfortunately, many of them weren't in business at the time, and if they were, they certainly weren't actually managing client assets using that specific strategy. Since the publication of the book it has become apparent that both retail and institutional investors need to do a much better job of evaluating strategy, process, people, infrastructure, technology, as well as past performance, in choosing an active portfolio manager.

The investment process at Pinnacle has evolved at an exponential pace since the first edition of the book was published, and it seems like yesterday that we were all glued to our computer screens, watching financial markets implode in the aftermath of the Lehman bankruptcy. After nearly six years I am pleased to offer the second edition of *Buy and Hold Is Still Dead (Again)*. It gives me the opportunity to correct some minor errors that made it through the editing process the first time around, and to hopefully address some of the issues I've raised in this new introduction. I've added a new chapter, called, "Portfolio Strategy in a Post-Lehman World," which shares more details about Pinnacle's approach to tactical asset allocation, and resolves some important questions about managing portfolio volatility. The chapter explores many of the techniques that we have developed since the first edition of the book was published. Perhaps one of the most gratifying surprises with the book is that the content has aged gracefully over the past six years, and the chapters in the original version are as relevant today as they were in May of 2009. I did think it important to add a new opening to Chapter Six, "The Trouble with Quant Models," in light of the fact that Pinnacle introduced two quantitatively-based investment products since the first edition. Finally, I am happy to offer the reader an Index and a Table of Charts and Figures to make it easier to find the material they're looking for.

Astute readers might also note that we have changed the title of the second edition to, "Buy and Hold is *Still* Dead (AGAIN.) The "still" refers to the incorrect notion that the current bull market validates the traditional buy, hold, and rebalance approach to portfolio construction. Hopefully first time readers won't be confused by this play on words in the title.

I would add one final note about this revision. I've left all references to market conditions when the book was originally written intact. It might be instructive for today's readers to consider them in the context of today's cyclical, if not secular, bull market. As indicated above, the case for tactical asset allocation does not depend on current market conditions, then or now. I've also left the final chapter of the book, an essay on the future of the financial planning industry, intact. I thought it was instructive for the reader to see how good (or bad) my forecasting was/is, with the benefit of hindsight.

The investment team at Pinnacle Advisory Group remains fully engaged with the ongoing challenges of tactically managing client portfolios. If we've learned anything in the years since the first version of the book was published, it is that our investment process will have to continue to evolve in challenging financial markets. Hopefully this book will give investors who are interested in a new approach to managing portfolio risk a great foundation to build their own investment process, or to better understand ours.

# INTRODUCTION

The paradigm for what is considered to be a "risky" investment strategy is changing. Perhaps one of the biggest changes in our perception of investment risk is the result of advances in the financial planning industry, where it is now acknowledged that achieving expected average long-term portfolio returns does not ensure that an investor will meet his or her retirement goals. Now we know that it is not only the magnitude of the returns that matter, but it is also the order of the returns that matter. Getting to a properly forecasted 20-year portfolio return of 8% may not achieve an investor's financial goals if they earn 0% for 10 years and then 16% for the next ten years. It is a high probability that even though they achieve the anticipated 8% returns on average, they run a high risk that they will not meet their retirement objectives. Buying and holding stocks and waiting for long-term average returns to appear becomes a high risk strategy for retirees who can't afford less than average returns in the first decade of their retirement.

The definitions of how we measure risk are also changing. We now know that the standard bell curve for measuring risk, known as the standard distribution or Gaussian distribution, is flawed when used to measure financial risk. The idea that randomness increases exponentially as we move away from the average may work well in nature, but it certainly works poorly in modern finance. Today's academics are fully engaged in measuring risk with a new kind of fractal mathematics, where risk increases in a scalable way as you move away from the average. We know that the current measures of risk are wrong because virtually every investment model that measures risk in the traditional way has proved to be a catastrophic failure.

We continue to experience market volatility that is considered to be impossible as measured by standard deviation, so we are left to ponder how we are so lucky to live through events like the 2008 stock market crash, the latest of many such events that should only happen once in many thousands (and in some cases millions) of years, according to the bell curve.

While the academic and financial planning definition of risk is changing at light speed, the notion of what constitutes a risky investment strategy for informed investors is stuck in the dark ages. The underlying assumptions of the models that are used to build modern portfolios are the same as they were 50 years ago, and in many cases were originally "discovered" in the early 20th century. The notion of what constitutes "risk" has certainly not changed for investors who follow the acknowledged, status quo method of investing, which is to buy and hold a diversified portfolio of common stocks and bonds. Using the well-known buy and hold techniques, the biggest risk that an investor can take is to not own stocks, because stocks have offered investors the highest real, or inflation adjusted, rates of return over long periods of time, typically analyzed over ten- to twenty-year time periods. In the buy and hold world, the outperformance of the stock market as an asset class is not free. It comes with a cost of high short-term volatility that presumably cannot be avoided. However, the long-term return premiums offered by equity investing are considered to be a given, a gift, a risk-free bonus of return that is available to investors regardless of *when* they invest, as long as they hold on to stocks for the long run. This gift is theirs for the taking because the buy and hold paradigm of investing also comes packaged with the notion that markets are efficient, and therefore past return premiums for owning stocks will always be available to investors in the future.

As an investor who was thoroughly trained in the modern portfolio theory approach to building buy and hold, diversified, multiple asset class portfolios, I now realize that the old way of investing is a higher risk strategy than most classically trained investors believe it to be. The investment industry still promotes the buy and hold strategy as the most professional methodology to manage portfolio risk, but change is coming very quickly. While there are many roadblocks to change, make no mistake about it, change is inevitable.

Why? Because the notion of efficient markets, as well as virtually all of the other assumptions that provide the academic and philosophical basis for buy and hold investing, are under attack. The ultimate test for any scientific theory is whether or not it works in the real world, and investors are finding out that buy and hold investing is fatally limited because it only works in one market condition, bull markets. Since we are now experiencing the fifth secular, or very long-term, bear market since the 1900's, it is no surprise that once again the idea of buying and holding is being criticized. In fact, I would go so far as to say that buy and hold is dead, at least for the moment, although it may take the investment industry a little while longer to figure it out.

The idea that the buy and hold investment strategy has come to an end may give the buy and hold methodology more credit than it is due. I don't believe that buying and holding asset classes and passively waiting for past returns to magically rematerialize rises to the level of an investment strategy at all. It's almost a religious belief, based more on faith than fact. In practice, the buy and hold strategy asks investors to suspend rational judgment about the current structure of the economy and the value of the investment markets. Instead, this faith-based approach requires investors to believe that the world is a static and unchanging place where the past is guaranteed to eventually repeat itself if we simply wait long enough for past returns to reappear. More accurately, the buy and hold plan is a highly stressful (and unsuccessful) approach to managing money when markets are expensive. In these volatile times, it is not a strategy, it's a prayer.

This book is written to walk the reader through the theoretical background for buy and hold investing, discover why it is flawed, and then to offer an investment alternative that meets the criterion of making sense in a volatile investment world. Let me offer the reader a few observations about the rest of the book. I decided not to rewrite books about the history and nature of risk that have already been written by brilliant writers who have covered the subject much better than I ever could. I highly recommend the books of Nassim Taleb (*Fooled By Randomness* and *The Black Swan*) and Benoit Mandelbrot (*The (mis)Behavior of Markets*) to those who want to learn more about the most current approaches to measuring risk. In addition, read Eric Beinhocker (*The Origin of Wealth*) and Peter Bernstein (*Against the Gods: The Remarkable Story of Risk*)[1] to learn more about the history of risk and how economics and finance have molded our current views about how risk should be managed. I have liberally quoted from these authors throughout the book. I have a tremendous admiration for their work.

Part I of the book answers the questions about investment theory that are so important to investors who have been classically trained in Modern Portfolio Theory. We take a step-by-step approach to learning what the theory tells us, where it came from, what the flaws are, and what modern academia has to say in terms of alternative theories that make a heck of a lot more sense in terms of the reality of

1   Nassim Taleb, *Fooled By Randomness: The Hidden Role of Chance in the Markets and in Life*, TEXERE Publishing, New York, N.Y., 2001; *The Black Swan, The Impact of the Highly Improbable*, Random House, New York, N.Y., 2007; Benoit Mandelbrot and Richard Hudson, *The (Mis)Behavior of Markets, A Fractal View of Risk, Ruin, and Reward*, Basic Books, New York, N.Y., 2004; Eric Beinhocker, *The Origin of Wealth, Evolution, Complexity, and the Radical Remaking of Economics*, Harvard Business School Press, Boston, Mass., 2006; Peter L. Bernstein, *Against the Gods, The Remarkable Story of Risk*, John Wiley and Sons, New York, N.Y., 1998.

financial markets that we face today. Chapter 3 focuses on Modern Portfolio Theory (MPT), the Capital Asset Pricing Model (CAPM), and Fama and French's Three Factor Model. I decided not to address what may be the most important financial model impacting today's derivatives markets, which is the Black-Scholes option pricing model (a model that won the Nobel Prize in Economics for Myron Scholes and Robert Merton, and which is used to price employee stock options, portfolio insurance, mortgage bonds, and other derivatives valued at many times global GDP.) Black-Scholes is the ultimate evolution of complex financial models, and critics are now pointing to it as the cause for the meltdown in our derivatives-based approach to pricing and insuring credit products of all kinds, especially sub-prime mortgages.

I did not focus on Black-Scholes because I don't believe that "average" investors use derivatives to synthetically build long and short equity positions in their portfolios, but instead build "long-only" portfolios of traditional securities that rely on diversification for risk management. Instead of implementing options and futures strategies by themselves, the average investor allocates assets to fund managers, or hedge fund managers, who specialize in using derivative strategies. Therefore, as I will discuss in the book, the Black-Scholes model becomes one of the ultimate causes of "quant" risk, which for institutional investors manifests itself in the "alternative investment" allocation of a diversified portfolio. The problems with the assumptions about how to measure risk that underlie Black-Scholes are the same problems we will discuss with CAPM, which I hopefully cover in some detail. Readers who want to learn more about Black-Scholes should consider the new anthology edited by Michael Lewis called, *Panic! The Story of Modern Financial Insanity.*[2] For those who don't fancy advanced mathematics and arcane academic language, don't worry. I think you will be surprised at the people you will meet and the perspectives that you will gain from reading Part I.

Part II of the book leaves the theoretical realm behind and takes the reader into the practical world of real-life portfolio construction using a methodology for managing portfolio risk that I call tactical asset allocation. Specifically, Part II looks at investment research, top-down and bottom-up portfolio and security analysis, making investment mistakes, dealing with taxes, and the other details that investors need to address if they want to move beyond passive portfolio construction to a more active style of portfolio management.

Part II explains how to actively manage portfolios, using examples from our work at Pinnacle Advisory Group. I do not claim to be an expert on how other Registered Investment Advisors may actively manage portfolios, although I believe that the vast majority are not involved in active management at all, and the ones

---

2    Michael Lewis (editor), *Panic, The Story of Modern Financial Insanity*, W. W. Norton Books, 2008.

who do practice active management do not routinely share information about their methods. I hope readers will forgive my continual references in Part II to how we do things at Pinnacle, but it is my best frame of reference and the only first-hand expertise that I can share. In using Pinnacle as an example, I do not mean to imply that our investment process is "better" than any other. It is simply the only one that I know enough to write about. I fervently hope that individual investors and financial advisors will use these examples to advance their own exploration of active management.

I am the first to acknowledge that there are many useful and successful ways to actively manage portfolios. The method proposed here meets the criteria of someone who was trained as a buy and hold investor and therefore had to overcome an overwhelming and almost pathological fear of market timing. The strategy and tactics presented are also limited by the necessity of being able to employ them for a large number of portfolios since my company is in the business of managing money for affluent investors. The need to evolve a process of portfolio risk management that is not market timing and that can be practically implemented in transparent client portfolios provides the framework for the tactical asset allocation strategy found within Part II. I believe that some or all of the techniques discussed here should be of interest to any investor looking to actively manage their portfolio, regardless of the details of how they actually manage money.

Buy and hold investing, like virtually all other portfolio strategies that are "long only" and require investors to own stocks and other risk assets, works well in secular bull markets. While this book was being written, by virtually any measure, stock market values have become more favorable. It would not be surprising if within the next few years we lay the foundation for the next long-term bull market. If this is the case, then the reason that buy and hold investing will work will have little to do with the academic dogma that currently forms the basis for our belief in buy and hold, and everything to do with a powerful force for stock returns that is completely ignored in today's theory and in the education of professional investors, and that is the idea that investors who buy low should be able to sell high with a high probability of success. The next bull market will have little to do with efficient markets, Modern Portfolio Theory, and the rest of it, and everything to do with Graham and Dodd[3] and their theories of value-based investing that were originated in the 1930's. The market will become very inexpensive and that will form the basis for a long-term and profitable bull market at some time in the future.

Ironically, the belief in the buy and hold approach will probably die at just about the time it deserves to be reborn. Buy and hold investors will lose faith because the expected returns that they anticipated did not occur over a prolonged period of

---

3    Benjamin Graham and David Dodd, *Security Analysis*, McGraw-Hill, 1934.

time, and because the theory underlying buy and hold investing offers no legitimate reason for why these surprisingly low returns should have materialized in the first place. Predictably, investors will conclude that buying and holding has no merit at the exact time that it offers the highest probability of success. And while forecasting the future is always fraught with risk, it will come as no surprise if buy and hold proponents then attribute its success to entirely the wrong reasons. Hence, the title of this book contains the parenthesis (again). Buy and hold should be allowed to die, but that doesn't mean that there won't be long periods of time when it is profitable to once again buy and hold stocks. It does mean that the rationale for buying and holding should change, as should the average investor's appreciation of, and strategy for, understanding and managing the portfolio risk that is accepted with its implementation.

While the nuances of applying the ideas of value investing to constructing multiple asset class, globally diversified portfolios, are difficult, the basic idea remains: There are two basic methods for managing portfolio risk—diversification and valuation. Until investors come to understand how to apply valuation to the portfolio construction process, they will be stuck in a high-risk paradigm for portfolio construction that they can't escape. As long as buy and hold investing ignores the idea of valuation, it deserves to meet an ignominious end.

# PART ONE

# BUY AND HOLD
# IS DEAD

# 1  WE'RE ALL INVESTMENT GENIUSES IN BULL MARKETS

Any investor can feel like a genius in a bull market. During those highly profitable times when asset values are rising, virtually anyone can prove their investment acumen by the appreciation of their portfolio values. During bull markets, the notion of investment risk is flipped on its head, redefined as being "out of the market" and missing out on the capital appreciation that is available to all while stock prices move higher. The notion that risk management is about protecting one's capital becomes lost as people who don't yet own the market wallow in self-pity and wonder if it is too late to jump in and buy. We are taught that bull markets are the natural order of things in a capitalistic system where economic growth is predicated on the "animal spirits" of market participants trying to further their own self-interests, and where ever-expanding corporate profits are the reliable result of human enterprise, ingenuity, creativity, and the drive to succeed. It is no wonder then, that investors believe that given enough time and enough patience, buying and holding stocks for the long run is a low-risk strategy. In today's Internet-connected, high-technology, and increasingly democratic and capitalistic world, where equity ownership allows investors to participate in the profits of corporations around the globe, choosing to be anything other than an equity owner as stock prices increase over time is just plain foolish.

Of course, there are those times when stock prices move significantly lower for short periods. This condition, called a bear market, is acknowledged to occur on occasion and investors are taught that the associated fear and anxiety that accompanies bear markets are simply the "cost of doing business" in the world of buy and hold investing. For the past forty years the investment industry's message has been that stock returns will always "eventually" outperform bond and cash returns over the long-term because equity ownership always offers investors a premium return for the risk (volatility) that they are willing to accept. Therefore, the industry's accepted strategy for dealing with bear markets has been simple: Just ignore them.

For years, professional and non-professional investors alike who thought there must be a better investment strategy for dealing with portfolio risk and volatility than simply waiting until things get better have been routinely ostracized and ignored. The status quo thinking about risk reduction techniques in portfolio construction and management has not changed for a generation of investors, schooled in the buy and hold strategy of investing during the great secular bull market that began in 1982 and ended in early 2000. There can be no doubt that buy and hold investing does work quite well in bull markets—as does just about every other investment technique when stocks are charging ahead.

Historic long-term bull markets with record breaking returns create lasting impressions for those who participate in and profit from them, but the secular bull market of 1982-2000 was only one of the reasons that buy and hold investing became the only acceptable methodology for building portfolios and creating wealth. The buy and hold strategy—known in the professional investment world as "strategic asset allocation"—was born out of a series of academic papers that eventually earned Nobel Prizes for their authors, who are now considered the fathers of modern finance. Their theories of Modern Portfolio Theory (MPT), The Capital Asset Pricing Model (CAPM), and the Efficient Markets Hypothesis all rely on a series of assumptions about risk and the nature of how prices change in financial markets which assert that current market prices are always rational, that investors are nearly perfect in their ability to forecast future changes in prices, and that risk premiums afforded to stocks (the added returns that investors earn by owning stocks versus owning cash) are relatively stable over long periods of time. These assumptions led to mathematical models for portfolio construction that promised investors the highest possible returns for a given level of risk. The army of finance professors teaching this one approach to portfolio construction was overwhelming, and all other approaches to portfolio construction were simply ignored. Virtually every MBA, Chartered Financial Analyst®(CFA®), and Certified Financial Planner® (CFP®) was taught this one methodology of money management to the virtual exclusion of all others.

And if this powerful combination of academic endorsement along with a reinforcing secular bull market wasn't enough to calcify the investment world's reliance on buy and hold investing, the ascendance of this status quo approach was also driven by one other important motivation in the investment world: the desire by the professional financial planning industry for a consistent, mathematically-based approach to investing that they could sell to their clients. The professional financial planning industry, as we know it today, was in its infancy in the mid-1970's. Exhausted from the secular bear market that lasted from 1965 to 1982, the investment industry needed a strategy of managing money that offered clients a more "scientific" methodology for reaching their financial goals. Strategic asset allocation (aka, buy and hold) met the industry's requirement for a systematic and scientific approach to portfolio construction, and provided the entire money management industry with a consistent strategy that could be "mass produced," duplicated by thousands of financial advisors and institutional investors at every level of experience. The popularity of buy and hold investing grew along with the growth of the financial planning industry, with financial professionals and industry pundits singing its praises for decades.

As a result of these three powerful forces—a long-term secular bull market that confirmed the value of buying stocks for the long run, a Nobel Prize–winning theory that provided academic support, and the financial industry's business model that was greatly enhanced by an easy, duplicable, buy and hold message—the strategy of buy and hold investing became the single most powerful and popular investment philosophy of the last 50 years.

That is, until now.

## Buy And Hold Is Dead

At the time of this writing, investors are facing a financial crisis that threatens to overwhelm the entire global banking system and drive governments to the brink of bankruptcy. Investor panic, as measured by the amount of volatility in the options markets, as well as by the extent of recent price declines, is at record highs. Virtually all risk-oriented asset classes, including stocks, commodities, and real estate, have plunged in value, and serious pundits are talking about the possibility of another Great Depression.

As frightening as the current bear market feels to investors, the current market trauma is not an isolated event, but comes after a prolonged period of genuine market upheaval. The bursting of the Internet bubble at the beginning of this decade completely destroyed leveraged investors in the technology sector and saddled non-leveraged NASDAQ investors with 75% declines. The bursting of the dot. com bubble helped to create the conditions for a mammoth bubble in real estate prices that was aided and abetted by stimulative fiscal and monetary government policy. And now the real estate bubble has burst, which has resulted in the end (for now, anyway) of a 30-year cycle of credit creation that was built on the back of lax regulation of the banking sector, impossibly complicated financial products, changing social values about thrift, and policy makers of all political persuasions agreeing that asset inflation had to be maintained at all costs in order for the system to perpetuate itself and prosperity to continue.

The results for long-term, buy and hold investors have been catastrophic, or not, depending on your point of view and your approach to risk. For 10 years, from 10/30/1998 to 10/30/2008 the S&P 500 Index has essentially broken even. The index traded at 1098 in 1998, and it traded at 954 on October of 2008, a loss of 13.1%. If an investor owned the S&P 500 market index and reinvested the dividends, then their return would have "skyrocketed" to an annual return of only 0.38% per year. Those who view risk in terms of a decline in the value of their assets should feel comforted in knowing that they haven't "lost" a lot of money in that period. However, for those who take a slightly more sophisticated view of market returns, they would observe that cash (in this case measured by the return of 90-day T-Bills) returned a total of 43%, or an annualized return of 3.60% per year for the same period that stocks essentially earned zero. For an investor with a $1 million portfolio, the "cost" of owning the stock market over that period was approximately $400,000. From a financial planning point of view, if an investor relied on the appreciation of the stock market to offset the impact of inflation on his portfolio, then unfortunately the buying power of their portfolio has been dramatically reduced, even though we have experienced a relatively low rate of inflation at the same time. Inflation was 2.8% per year for the decade and cash returned 3.6% for the same period. (That is, if you believe the government statistics on inflation. For skeptics, the loss of buying power for investors over the past decade has been even higher.) Obviously, earning 0.38% per year in the stock market while inflation grew at 2.8% constituted a real or inflation-adjusted annual *loss* of 2.42%.

Perhaps the most unfortunate group of investors are those who retired in the late 1990's expecting that the stock market would deliver its historical average return of about 11% per year in a 3% inflation environment. For those who either invested in a balanced portfolio of stocks and bonds on their own, or who relied on the advice of professional financial advisors, and who have subsequently systematically withdrawn their capital in order to maintain their standard of living in retirement, the resulting decade of less than expected portfolio performance has been potentially catastrophic. Depending on the amount that these investors have withdrawn from their portfolios, and depending on the details of the asset classes used to build their portfolios, those ten years of flat returns from the stock market have forced retirees either to significantly reduce their standards of living, or to go back to work. In many cases, neither of these negative possibilities was considered to be a risk when they retired.

Unbelievably, according to the buy and hold approach, the most widely followed theory of investing, absolutely none of the above should have happened at all. Buy and hold, or strategic asset allocation as the professionals call it, was supposed to best manage the risk of the current market problems because, according to the theory that justifies it, investors and other "economic agents" are supposed to have a perfect (or a close to perfect) ability to know what the correct or "equilibrium" price of stocks should be in the future, given any change in today's news. Therefore, bubbles in the stock market, the real estate market, the commodities market, and the credit market, simply should not happen, and therefore investors don't need a portfolio strategy that allows them to manage the risk that these events could actually occur. According to the theory that supports strategic asset allocation, all asset classes should eventually generate average returns for investors in the future equal to their *average past returns* (mathematicians would call this approach to past data static, non-linear programming), and therefore, all we need to do is wait patiently for the returns to materialize over a long enough period of time. As we will learn, unfortunately the period of time may be too long for most investors to be able to afford to wait.

Strategic (buy and hold) investing, the investment strategy adhered to by most professional financial advisors, and the strategy that is taught to all CFP® practitioners and CFA®s presumes that the market mechanism governing day-to-day price movements is perfectly random, and that there is no such thing as momentum or any other movement in price caused by investors themselves. In the theory, all risk is "exogenous," meaning that forces outside of the market cause price changes to occur. We can call this type of exogenous risk "the news." But investor panics, or the risk of market participants actually causing changes in market prices due to emotion, or plain old investor mistakes, simply cannot happen.

Nonetheless, for the second time in a decade, investors who follow the rules of buy and hold investing are watching their portfolios plummet in value. It is very difficult to make the case that the best way to manage portfolio risk is to own the stock market and ignore short-term volatility when the stock market delivered 10 years of returns that are less than cash returns. All of the sudden, informed investors are taking a hard look at strategic asset allocation and questioning why it is that no other methods of portfolio construction are considered to be acceptable at a time when the financial markets are experiencing the greatest volatility since the Great Depression.

## A Fantastic Business Model

I began my career as a financial professional in 1984, and for the first sixteen years of my career as a professional investor I invested according to the principles that I was taught as a CFP® practitioner and as a Chartered Financial Consultant® (ChFC®), meaning that I religiously followed the teachings of Modern Portfolio Theory. For those who don't know, Modern Portfolio Theory (MPT) is the Nobel

Prize–winning theory of portfolio construction given to us by Harry Markowitz in 1952[4], which proposes that investors can use the laws of chance and probability to construct a portfolio that is the most "efficient" mix of the various asset classes that are used to build it. In this case, efficient means crafting a portfolio that will give us the most return for any given level of risk.

In addition to Modern Portfolio Theory, I, along with all other informed investors, was also taught the basics of William Sharpe's Nobel Prize–winning Capital Asset Pricing Model (CAPM), which teaches us that there are two kinds of risk: unsystematic or business risk that we can diversify away in our portfolio, and systematic or market risk that we cannot. The measure of systematic risk is something called beta, and once we know what it is we can measure the risk of our portfolio by comparing the volatility of our portfolio to the volatility of the market. I learned to evaluate my success or failure as an investor by trying to achieve portfolio "alpha," which is the amount of return actually earned over and above the expected return of the portfolio, as measured by the risk relationship between cash and the stock market in the CAPM model.

As discussed earlier in this chapter, the strategic model of portfolio construction also relies on something called the Efficient Market Hypothesis, which was popularized by Eugene Fama in the 1970's, but can be traced back to a French economist named Louis Bachelier[5] who originally developed the mathematics of efficient pricing models in the early 1900's. As it is commonly used today, the theory proposes that a large group of investors can either perfectly (or at least imperfectly) know what market prices will be in the future given the news of today. The theory teaches us that the market so efficiently prices changes in the news that it is not possible to "beat" the market's performance, and so the conclusion that rational investors much reach is that they should simply own the market in the aggregate.

As a professional financial planner, adhering to this theory of portfolio construction was a godsend in terms of a model for doing business. Using MPT and CAPM to construct efficient portfolios was easy using modern software tools that allow investors to build a portfolio using Markowitz's algorithms with a push of a button. To this day, investors can easily invest in a globally diversified, multiple asset class portfolio, using a variety of mutual funds that can be reviewed once or twice each year, with ease. The financial planning industry taught me, as the financial media continues to teach all investors, that any other method of portfolio construction is unprofessional, or at least, "retail," meaning that only non-professional investors would ignore the theories behind strategic investing.

---

4    We will discuss Markowitz, Modern Portfolio Theory (MPT), Sharpe, Capital Asset Pricing Model (CAPM), and Fama, Three Factor Model, in some detail in Chapter 3.

5    Louis Bachelier, Foreword by Paul Samuelson, *Theorie De La Speculation: The Origins of Modern Finance*, Princeton University Press, 2006

Therefore, no matter how the portfolio actually performed, I was always "right" in the eyes of my clients who knew I was following the status quo of the professional money management industry. In fact, the accepted wisdom about how to best manage a portfolio became so ubiquitous that portfolio management came to be considered a commodity product within the planning industry, where financial advisors are encouraged to spend most of their time managing client expectations as a business model, as opposed to spending valuable time in a portfolio construction process that presumably has no hope of differentiating investment management services within an industry where everyone pretty much manages money the same way.

Not only was I almost entirely released from the need to think about how to construct and manage the portfolio, I was also the beneficiary of another great perk of adhering to the rules of MPT, CAPM and efficient markets. By following the status quo, strategic asset allocation protected me, as an investment professional, from ever being "wrong" throughout the entire length of my engagement with my clients.

The status quo theory allows for only one method of managing portfolio risk or volatility, namely portfolio diversification. From the financial industry's business point of view, the beauty of diversification is that its benefits are likely to occur over *long periods of time*, just like the historic average returns of the asset classes that are used to build the portfolio. This is so because risk premiums, or the relative returns between various risk assets and cash, are presumed to be mean reverting (meaning they revert to their long-term averages) over time. Therefore, investors are taught that they must completely ignore whatever portfolio volatility occurs in the short-term, a rather hazy time horizon that is best defined as something shorter than long-term. As a result, once we have built the most efficient possible portfolio of diversified asset classes, the only risk reduction tool left to investors is to rebalance the portfolio on a regular basis back to the original percentage allocations that we determined were efficient in the first place, and then to simply *wait*. Rebalancing forces investors to sell appreciated securities and buy underperforming securities, therefore allowing strategic investors to claim that they are professionally and unemotionally engaging in securities transactions that force them to buy low and sell high.

The bottom line is that once the portfolio is diversified and rebalanced, there is literally nothing else to be done but wait long enough for the hoped-for returns. In some cases, if the portfolio is constructed using active managers to invest each asset class (mutual funds or separate accounts), an investor can analyze the fund manager performance to see if they are still generating benchmark returns. But for all intents and purposes, the main skill needed by professional financial advisors and investors is the ability to teach their clients to be patient and wait for the magic of investing for "the long haul." Regardless of current market conditions or portfolio returns, most professional advisors see their role as making sure their clients stay "in the market," because any other strategy implies that they are engaging in the heretical tactic of market timing, which is considered ridiculous and frightful by most buy and hold investors. The beauty of this for the financial industry is that portfolio returns can theoretically always be achieved *sometime in the future*, and therefore, professional advisors and investors can *never* be wrong in the present. How many other professions can make such a career-protective claim?

## Becoming an Investment Heretic

The record-breaking bull market that occurred in the S&P 500 Index during the five-year period from 1995 to 2000 was extraordinary in that the "market" was entirely led by the performance of about 50 large-cap growth stocks. The valuations of these companies went through the roof as investors who wanted to earn the returns of the "market" were forced to buy the same 50 stocks that were driving the index returns. This self-reinforcing behavior of more and more investors being forced to buy the same companies, regardless of the fundamental metrics of valuation that were being applied, resulted in the S&P 500 Index finishing the decade with the most spectacularly high price-to-earnings multiple on record. At the time, investors rationalized the absurdly high multiple with a belief in the so-called "New Economy." The New Economy was the Internet-driven, technology-based, global, post–Cold War, productivity-miracle economy that promised above-average global growth for years to come. Coupled once again with lax regulation by global central bankers and promiscuous policies regarding credit creation and interest rates, the bubble in stock prices wasn't difficult to see, for those who were trained to look.

But for most classically trained investors, the best they could do to manage risk in a period of frightening valuations was to rebalance their passive, strategically allocated portfolios, and to be certain that the portfolio was properly diversified. To be fair, remaining diversified wasn't easy at the time because the only asset class that was "working" was large-cap growth, and remaining invested in small-cap stocks, value stocks of any kind, and international stocks, as well as real estate and commodities, was difficult for investors trying to keep pace with the market index. Nevertheless, when the dot.com bubble burst in 2000, and the subsequent news of corporate malfeasance and then the events of 9/11 shook the market over the next two years, the resulting declines in portfolio value were catastrophic. Even the most diversified portfolios declined by 20%. These declines occurred in a market environment where diversification actually worked and correlations for many asset classes remained fairly low. Value-tilted portfolios performed quite well relatively during the period, but investors who owned "market" weightings in the technology and U.S. large-growth sector realized portfolio declines of 30% - 40%, or more. Investors didn't know it at the time, but the price lows of 775 on the S&P 500 Index that were made in October of 2002, after a 48% decline in value from the highs set in March of 2000, would be retested and broken almost exactly six years later.

For me, the bear market of 2000-2002 was an eye-opening event. Amid the wreckage of the bear market, I felt betrayed and depressed that I had adhered to a strategy that didn't make a lot of sense in the run up to the market top, and failed so miserably to protect wealth during the steep market decline that followed. Those feelings led me to ask many questions about the investment strategy that I had followed so faithfully for my entire career. Specifically, I wanted to know the following:

- What value is an investment strategy that is based on the idea that obscene market valuations don't matter, and worse, theoretically can't occur?
- Where did the theory of efficient markets actually come from? Did these guys Markowitz, Sharpe, and Fama just appear out of nowhere with the "Holy Grail" of investment theories?
- Does the "scientific" nature of discussing efficient frontiers, alpha, beta, and the other mystifying language of Modern Portfolio Theory, create the illusion of professional money management when in fact the underlying investment strategy is embarrassingly simple to implement, and embarrassingly ineffective in bear markets?
- Is the investment industry so hooked on quantitative methods of portfolio design that investors will do almost anything to avoid having to make a qualitative decision about portfolio construction? In other words, would we follow a flawed strategy in order to avoid being put in the position of making an investment mistake?
- Why are investors taught that there is only one "correct" way to invest when there is ample evidence that investors use dramatically different tactics other than "buy and hold?" For example, why do advertisers spend so much to support the financial media on TV and why do people buy investment research if markets are efficient and current prices don't matter?
- If selling large-cap stocks in the year 2000 constituted "market timing," then what is so wrong with market timing? Is the industry's preoccupation with demonizing market timers completely misplaced?
- Is it possible that the passive, buy and hold portfolio strategy that is so beneficial to the financial planning industry is not being properly evaluated? What constituency within the industry would be interested in destroying a

model of portfolio management that generates fantastic profits and can be implemented with so little time and cost?

- Is there any academic evidence supporting the practice of active management? Is it possible that investors just don't hear about the "state of the art" in academic research because the money management industry has no interest in promoting it, or because the financial planning industry has no interest in hearing it?
- If active management requires a subjective element in the portfolio construction process, doesn't that imply that certain investors will be better at it than others? If so, would the industry standard bearers ever promote such a strategy considering that they have an interest in promoting the idea that all CFP® certificants are equally qualified as financial planners?
- If investors shouldn't build strategic, passive, globally diversified portfolios, then what strategy should they implement?
- Are there ways to manage portfolio risk other than solely relying on the traditional method of portfolio diversification? If the strategy involves active management, can it be done in a way that is systematic, effective, and repeatable, and can pass the test of common sense?
- How can individual investors and small institutional financial advisors compete with massive money management companies that have nearly limitless budgets and a global network of analysts?

Searching for the answers to these questions took me and my colleagues at Pinnacle Advisory Group more than eight years of brutally hard work, and the truth is we still don't have all the answers. We spent thousands of hours reading both theoretical and industry research in our quest to determine whether strategic investing made any sense for investors who are vitally concerned about risk, and then to determine what other tactics should be employed for portfolio construction, and how to implement them. Our work led us to a very simple, yet shockingly ignored idea: Investors should avoid buying overvalued assets. Overvalued assets will not deliver average annual returns to investors in a time horizon that is short enough to help them achieve their financial goals.

From this, we decided there were two unbreakable rules for managing risk:

1. Do diversify
2. Don't buy overvalued assets

These two investment rules are simple and absolute. However, following them is certainly not easy for investors who are determined to use them in the construction of their portfolios. The problem with diversification is correlation, or the way in which the performance of different asset classes can "zig" and "zag" in different directions under the same market conditions. To have a well-diversified portfolio, investors want to own assets that have a low correlation to each other, so that they don't all move in the same direction, at the same time, in their portfolio. As we are experiencing in today's markets, the problem with correlations is that they change over time, and tend to rise to a peak in bear markets, just when investors need the low-correlation benefits of the portfolio to work. The old saying that "the only thing that goes up in bear markets is correlation" is correct. Relying on diversification in bear markets can be a very risky proposition.

The problem with valuation is that market valuation is a notoriously poor market-timing device. Here the old saw is John Maynard Keynes famous saying, "markets can remain irrationally priced for longer than you can remain solvent." Markets tend to "overshoot" their fair values both to the upside and the downside, making valuation a difficult tool for investing for any time frame other than the intermediate term, which many analysts loosely define as seven to ten years. In addition, determining market value is a subjective process at best, causing investors to reach different conclusions about market values at the same time using the same data, but looking at it in different ways. Much of Part II of this book is devoted to better understanding the nuances of investing portfolios in a way that tries to take advantage of the implications of the second rule of investing.

If investors believe that both of these laws are true, it follows that strategic investing becomes a potentially high-risk strategy since the theory, as it is applied in practice by most strategic asset allocators, denies the possibility that current market valuations should matter in building a portfolio. The almost religious belief that markets will reward investors with historical average returns within a time frame that is useful to their financial plan, regardless of their purchase price, fails the test of common sense. While both laws of portfolio construction mentioned above offer challenges that investors must deal with, strategic investing ignores one of the laws entirely, and that makes it a potentially high-risk strategy that should be used with caution by intelligent and risk-averse investors in bear markets.

The active portfolio management strategy that we outline for investors in this book, tactical asset allocation, is a strategy that incorporates both unbreakable rules of investing mentioned above, and then goes well beyond them to offer a nuanced and common sense approach to portfolio construction. The questions that we posed after the 2000-2002 bear market (listed above) are just as relevant today as they were then, and perhaps even more so. Investors who don't wish to spend thousands of hours doing the research will find the answers to these questions and more in the following chapters.

## The Buy and Hold Alternative: Tactical Asset Allocation

For lack of a better term, we call the portfolio strategy that we recommend "tactical asset allocation." Tactical asset allocation incorporates both of the unbreakable rules of investing. It is an investment strategy in which the asset allocation of the portfolio is not fixed as the result of a strategic or long-term buy and hold methodology, but instead is *actively managed* to own asset classes that have the best value characteristics at any point in time. Therefore, the asset allocation of the portfolio will change.

The active management of asset classes in the portfolio should not be confused with the decision to invest each asset class either passively by owning index funds or exchange traded funds (ETFs), or actively by owning active fund managers or separate account managers. Regardless of whether or not each asset class is passively or actively managed, the evaluation of the value characteristics of the asset class itself, either on an absolute basis, or on a relative basis when compared to other asset classes, will determine the percentage ownership of the asset class in the total portfolio.

**Figure 1.1** shows the difference between the two management styles. The strategic asset allocation portfolio is passively managed in terms of the asset allocations of the portfolio. We construct the portfolios using three asset classes consisting of stocks, bonds, and cash. Next we illustrate the portfolio construction in two different (admittedly simplified) environments. In the first regime the equity asset class in the portfolio is considered to be inexpensive (which implies higher future equity returns) based on its low P/E (price to earnings) ratio. In the second regime the equity asset class is considered to be expensive (indicating lower future returns) based on its high P/E ratio. In both cases, the percentage allocation to each asset class is the same. For the strategic investor, the future long-term returns

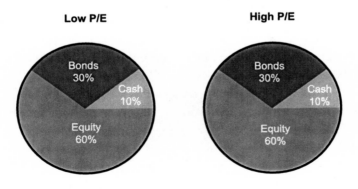

**Figure 1.1—Strategic Portfolio**

Source: Pinnacle Advisory Group, Inc.

are presumed to be the same, regardless of the value characteristics of each asset class in different regimes, so there is no need to change the portfolio allocations to these securities. At most, a strategic investor will rebalance the portfolio in order to stay within the target allocations shown, which does have the impact of selling the expensive securities as they go up in value in order to buy the inexpensive securities at low prices. However, the impact is relatively minor compared to the tactical approach.

In the tactical asset allocation approach shown in **Figure 1.2**, we show the same three asset classes in the same two regimes. Notice that in the regime where stocks are considered to be inexpensive, the asset allocation has been changed to reflect the favorable valuation characteristics and anticipated future returns of the stock market. Now look at the high P/E portfolio that is considered to be expensive based on the investor's analysis of the underlying value of the U.S. stock market. The portfolio construction has been changed to reflect the change in underlying value of the securities in the portfolio. Tactical investors believe that reducing exposure to expensive asset classes is an essential form of risk management that is completely missing in the strategic approach. Note that both the strategic and tactical portfolio constructions remain diversified and own percentage allocations to all three asset classes, regardless of the valuation environment. Obviously the difference between the two strategies is the investor's willingness to change the asset allocation for the equity allocation in the tactical portfolio.

Strategic investors often describe themselves as "active" if they choose to invest each asset class with managed funds or separate accounts. In our example, each asset class, stocks, bonds, and cash, could be invested in an actively managed fund or an index fund. As we previously observed, the asset allocation of the portfolio doesn't change even though the value characteristics of the asset classes have changed.

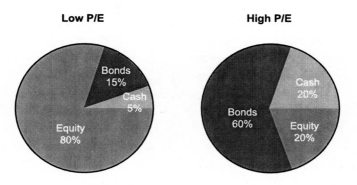

**Figure 1.2—Tactical Portfolio**
Source: Pinnacle Advisory Group, Inc.

However, if strategic investors choose to use an active fund manager to invest in each asset class, they might claim to be an active portfolio manager. For professional financial advisors, the debate about active versus passive management is a critical detail that often defines their worth in a competitive market for financial advisors.

On the other hand, the tactical portfolio is actively managed at the asset class level. The decision about whether or not to own an asset class is made based on the value characteristics of each asset class *on an ongoing basis*. As we will see, *how* tactical investors make the decision to change their asset allocations in changing market conditions will differ from one tactical investor to another. For quantitative-oriented investors there is no need for "art" in making the portfolio changes. They will simply input new assumptions for asset class returns into their quantitative model and derive a new portfolio construction whose value characteristics make sense in the current economic regime. On the other hand, investors who add qualitative aspects of decision-making to the process will use both quantitative and qualitative methods to change the portfolio construction. In this case judgment and experience are needed to assess market values, and an element of "art" is added to the science of asset allocation.

In either case, tactical investors may choose either active managers or passive indexes to invest each asset class in the portfolio. The important point is that the portfolio is actively managed regardless of the active fund versus passive index decision. The "value added" or alpha (we will discuss alpha in Chapter 3) comes from the tactical asset allocation decisions made by the investor, as well as any additional returns generated by an actively managed fund chosen to invest in some or all of the asset classes in the portfolio.

Tactical asset allocation is similar to strategic asset allocation in that both strategies benefit from owning multiple asset classes that have low correlations to each other. The difference between the two management styles is that for strategic, buy and hold investors, diversification is the only risk management tactic that they can employ. It is used in a "scientific" fashion where the mathematics of standard deviation and correlation work together to presumably allow the total portfolio to be less volatile than the individual securities that are owned in it. On the other hand, tactical investors think of diversification as a hedge to their point of view about market conditions. Diversification is a simple expression of not being 100% certain about an investment forecast. The amount of diversification in the portfolio at any point in time is a function of the investor's conviction about their forecast, as opposed to the buy and hold approach where the amount of diversification is based on the average historical performance of asset classes. As we will see, tactical investors can employ a second, more powerful method of managing portfolio risk and volatility that has little to do with diversification.

For both tactical and strategic investors, the traditional secret of diversification is that by building the portfolio so that asset classes have low correlations to each other, then it is possible to systematically add volatile high-return assets to the portfolio where the portfolio volatility actually falls for each incremental addition of risk. This occurs because a single asset class may be volatile, but it is often "zigging and zagging" at different times from the other asset classes in the portfolio, and the result is a smoother portfolio total return. It is much like putting two high handicap golfers together in a scramble golf tournament. Even though they may both shoot a high score, if they happen to do well on alternating holes their team score may actually be a lot better than the sum of their individual scorecards. We have discussed the problems with diversification earlier in this chapter.

Strategic asset allocators determine the fixed allocations for the asset classes that will be included in their portfolio at the beginning of the investment process. Portfolios with higher targeted returns tend to have higher allocations to stocks and portfolios with lower targeted returns tend to have higher allocations to fixed income. Once the allocation is fixed, the only timing consideration for the investor is how often they should rebalance the portfolio to the initial or target allocation. Many strategic investors advocate rebalancing on a calendar basis, although the most recent studies suggest that investors may benefit from rebalancing using a "decision rule" based on how much an asset class varies from its target percentage. For example, if the target allocation were 10% for real estate, and significant outperformance caused the allocation to rise to 11%, the position would be sold back to the target allocation if the rebalancing rule applied any time the asset class was at least 1% away from the target level.

Tactical asset allocation takes a completely different approach to portfolio construction. While there are countless methods for actively and tactically managing portfolios, one strategy used by some tactical asset allocators is to create a range for the target weightings of the asset classes in the portfolio. For example, if the target allocation for real estate is 10%, then they might establish a portfolio policy that allows for the real estate allocation to be as low as 5% and as high as 15%, which is a range of 5% above and below the original target of 10%. This methodology, when applied to each asset class in the portfolio, allows the investor to exercise his judgment regarding the current and forecasted performance of each asset class. However, it creates some policy limitations as to which asset classes will be included in the portfolio and what the minimum investment in each asset class can be at any point in time.

A less constrained methodology for tactical asset allocation is to construct the portfolio without any constrained ranges for the target allocations. The asset allocations are strictly determined by the value characteristics of the asset classes themselves, as well as the volatility constraints that are contained in portfolio policy statements that are agreed to by the investor. The determination of asset class value is a multiple-step process that typically includes both top-down macroeconomic analysis, and bottom-up industry analysis. Tactical investors believe that observation, judgment, and experience, combined with quantitative analysis, are the best methods to determine the percentage weightings of the asset classes that are owned in the portfolio.

Either tactical methodology results in a portfolio that offers many of the diversification benefits of a strategic portfolio, yet also offers a more robust method for managing risk. *While diversification is the only risk management tool available for the strategic investor, the tactical investor can also rely on his assessment of the valuation of asset classes to reduce the portfolio exposure to overvalued securities.* This second level of risk management is critically important for investors who don't want to rely merely on the hope that historical average returns will magically appear in the future regardless of the price level of securities. Instead of a "fixed-mix" of asset classes, the tactical asset allocation approach involves actively changing the "recipe" of the asset class mix to maximize returns and minimize risk, based on agreed-upon constraints.

This may be easier to picture if you imagine a portfolio in which each asset class represents a slice of the total portfolio pie. Now imagine that the pie, rather than being fixed in time, is animated with the relative sizes of each pie slice constantly changing as the investor's views of economic and financial conditions change. Particular pie slices will become larger or smaller as tactical investors trim or add to portfolio positions. Occasionally, a pie slice might disappear altogether if the investor no longer likes the value story for a particular asset class, or perhaps a new pie slice will appear if they find a new investment opportunity to add to the portfolio.

The changes that tactical investors make to the portfolio asset allocation involve deciding when to buy and sell asset classes in the portfolio, and that process obviously involves an element of timing the transactions. However, in no way does tactical asset allocation resemble an effort to "market time" in the traditional sense of the term. The differences are subtle, but important to investors who believe that market timing is a high-risk portfolio strategy. A typical market timing tactic is to invest 100% of portfolio assets in cash until technical market indicators signal that you can move 100% of your assets to stocks. Market timers usually use technical analysis techniques like trend lines, relative strength, MACD (Moving Average Convergence Divergence Indicator) and other price oscillators, candlestick charts, and other well-known charting methods to make their decisions. (Tactical investors use many of the same tools, but as we will see, in a different context.) They can do several transactions into and out of a stock or an asset class per day, depending on which technical indicators they use and their proclivity for trading. Classic market timers have no use for diversification, and are happy to only own one or two asset classes at a time. In addition, they typically have little use for valuation because their work is based on technical analysis of market prices versus a fundamental assessment of market value.

In contrast, tactical investors believe in both diversification as well as fundamental assessments of market values as the best means to manage risk. While tactical investing does involve an element of market timing, as would any strategy that involves something other than buying and holding asset classes, the resulting tactical portfolio is much more diversified, and the holding period for the asset classes in the portfolio is much longer than a typical market timing strategy.

Tactical and active portfolio managers can rely heavily on qualitative, fundamental analysis when making asset allocation decisions. However, they can also utilize many elements of technical analysis as part of the overall consideration of the value characteristics of an asset class. In addition, technical analysis is undeniably useful in determining the entry and exit points for individual portfolio positions, and technical analysis tools can be helpful in timing individual transactions. As stated earlier, these are the same technical tools used by market timers, but they are used within the context of a diversified portfolio of rationally valued assets.

**Table 1.1**

| COMPARISON | STRATEGIC | TACTICAL |
|---|---|---|
| **Asset Classes** | Passive allocation | Active allocation |
| **Fund Managers vs. Index funds** | 40-year debate over which is better | Choose either based on investment merit only |
| **Selection Criteria** | Past Performance | Value Characteristics |
| **Time Horizon** | Life-expectancy | Market Cycles |
| **Market Philosophy** | Efficient markets | Inefficient markets |
| **Market Timing** | Rebalancing only | Only in the context of diversified portfolios |
| **Technical Analysis** | No | Varies by investor |
| **Ingredient for success** | Investor patience | Investor skill |

Source: Pinnacle Advisory Group, Inc.

**Table 1.1** compares several of the basic differences between tactical and strategic asset allocation. These differences in portfolio tactics and strategy will be discussed throughout the succeeding chapters of this book.

There is a time to buy and hold, and that is when there is a powerful case to be made for a long-term bull market due to extremely low market valuations. In virtually all other market conditions, buy and hold is simply not the best investment strategy for investors who would like to earn higher returns with less risk. Unfortunately for those who still follow the mantra of buy and hold, it has been many years since we could make the case for a powerful new long-term bull market. Ironically, as the current bear market grinds on the case for buy and hold investing will be easier to make. For many, its arrival will come too late for them to achieve their financial goals. Until the next long-term bull market comes along and allows us all to once again become bull market geniuses, it's time to put the notion of strategic, buy and hold investing aside and move on.

# 2 THE RISKS OF BUY AND HOLD INVESTING IN BEAR MARKETS

## (or, Why You May Never Be Able To Retire)

M r. and Mrs. Financial Planning Client, if we look at the past performance of stocks versus bonds and cash, we can clearly see that stocks always earn significantly higher returns over long periods of time. The trade-off is that if you want the extra returns you get from owning stocks, you have to be willing to accept the short-term portfolio volatility that comes with investing in the stock market. No one knows what the risk to your principal will be if you invest in stocks for a short period of time, like one or two years. But if you hold stocks for at least five years or longer, the chances of losing money during that time frame are very, very small. In fact, stocks delivered positive returns more than 90% of the time in the 75 rolling five-year periods beginning in 1926 and ending in 2006. The data clearly show that if you will just be patient, the risk of owning stocks in your portfolio is negligible.

In terms of your retirement, this same data shows us that if we build a balanced portfolio of stocks and bonds that earns its expected average long-term return, you can plan on your money earning somewhere around a 5% - 6% premium over inflation. This means that if we assume inflation averages 3% annually, your portfolio should earn the 3% annual inflation rate plus the 5% annual inflation premium, which adds up to 8% per year. As long as your balanced portfolio earns an average of 8% per year during your retirement, it is perfectly fine for you to enjoy the standard of living that you are used to in retirement. Trust me, you can count on these long-term historical relationships between the performance of stocks and bonds, which means that the longer you own your diversified portfolio, the higher your probability of retirement success. The biggest risk to your retirement is that you will sell your stocks in a bear market. If you can just be patient, Mr. and Mrs. Client, you will succeed.

So goes the typical conversation about portfolio performance in the world of private wealth management. Investors routinely accept the risks of short-term portfolio volatility in exchange for the promise of nearly guaranteed long-term portfolio returns. While this hypothetical discussion is steeped in terminology that today's financial planning industry deems to be correct, once a high P/E ratio for the stock market is included in the analysis, the risks to a successful retirement plan escalate dramatically. (Note: The price to earnings ratio is an accepted measure of the value of a stock or the stock market where the higher the ratio, or multiple, the more expensive the stock market is considered to be.) Unfortunately, and without realizing it, investors who believe that stocks will outperform bonds and cash over long periods of time, regardless of the valuation of the stock market at the start of the retirement period, are engaging in a high-risk investment strategy that has a high probability of delivering less than expected returns over the first decade of their retirement. As we will see, these years are often the most critically important to a successful retirement plan.

Traditional investors make the tradeoff between risk, reward, and time by relying on one of the most basic tenets of modern finance, which is that portfolio risk is defined in terms of asset volatility. The theory says that as long as investors are patient enough to utilize the wonderful tools of time and diversification—the magic elixir that allows expected returns to eventually materialize in the future—then their portfolio risk is actually quite small. While investors are offered no comfort regarding whether or not a portfolio will "lose money" over short time periods, they are assured, based on overwhelming historical data, that if they will just hang on for five years or longer, the odds of actually getting a negative return are very small. If you also diversify the portfolio into a variety of asset classes, as suggested by Modern Portfolio Theory, then the odds of a negative return over long time periods falls even further.

This level of "certainty" about long-term returns makes the job of portfolio risk management much easier for all concerned. If portfolio risk is defined as the risk of loss in portfolio value, and time allows for a high probability that portfolio returns will be positive, then investors can conclude that risk has been effectively managed, that returns should appear like clockwork on a long-term schedule, and that long-term retirement plans which depend on long-term portfolio returns should be safe.

## Figure 2.1

| Year | Annual | Year-end |
|------|--------|----------|
| 1972 | 13.82 | $113,817 |
| 1973 | -4.55 | $104,084 |
| 1974 | -12.36 | $91,216 |
| 1975 | 26.72 | $115,591 |
| 1976 | 18.85 | $137,378 |
| 1977 | 2.97 | $141,458 |
| 1978 | 10.56 | $156,403 |
| 1979 | 14.71 | $179,412 |
| 1980 | 22.31 | $219,445 |
| 1981 | 2.82 | $225,629 |
| 1982 | 19.43 | $269,477 |
| 1983 | 17.66 | $317,079 |
| 1984 | 8.03 | $342,531 |
| 1985 | 27.60 | $437,749 |
| 1986 | 20.02 | $525,383 |
| 1987 | 7.08 | $562,580 |
| 1988 | 14.86 | $646,165 |
| 1989 | 19.57 | $772,645 |
| 1990 | -2.26 | $755,148 |
| 1991 | 22.35 | $923,894 |
| 1992 | 5.72 | $976,776 |
| 1993 | 12.39 | $1,097,773 |
| 1994 | 1.26 | $1,111,598 |
| 1995 | 22.95 | $1,366,680 |
| 1996 | 12.78 | $1,541,379 |
| 1997 | 17.70 | $1,814,172 |
| 1998 | 16.39 | $2,111,425 |
| 1999 | 13.82 | $2,403,189 |
| 2000 | -1.55 | $2,365,902 |
| 2001 | -3.94 | $2,272,571 |
| 2002 | -9.66 | $2,053,096 |
| 2003 | 20.27 | $2,469,275 |
| 2004 | 9.57 | $2,696,229 |
| 2005 | 5.09 | $2,830,679 |
| 2006 | 13.08 | $3,190,046 |
| 2007 | 5.94 | $3,380,632 |
| 2008 | -22.65 | $2,615,082 |

Selected chart annotations:

- Jan $100,000
- Jan 1980 $185,927
- Jan 1982 -5.7% 4m
- Feb 1981 -7.6% 2m $171,335
- Mar 1981 $171,335
- Mar 1982 $216,761
- Feb 1982 $216,761
- Apr +13.8% 12m
- Apr 1974 -24.1% 21m
- Apr 1998 +37.2% 24m
- May 1981 $224,695
- Jun +196.6% 65m
- Jun 1999 $2,001,578
- Jul $783,599
- Jul 1994 +183.3% 93m
- Aug +115.2% 64m
- Aug 1987 $643,087
- Aug 1990 -9.8% 2m
- Aug 1998 $1,818,154
- Aug 1999 $2,493,738
- Sep 1974 $95,393
- Sep 1981 $208,617
- Sep 1987 -16.2% 3m
- Sep 1990 $706,845
- Sep 2000 $1,954,234
- Oct 2007 $3,468,998
- Nov 1980 +31.1% 14m
- Nov 1981 $229,762
- Nov 1987 $538,910
- Dec $113,817
- Jun 1989 +45.4% 32m
- Feb 2001 -21.6% 25m
- Jul 1998 -9.2% 2m
- Jan 1980 $185,927

Statistics:

- Standard Deviation 8.99

| | Risk | Time Period |
|---|------|-------------|
| Worst Decline | 24.0% | 25 months |
| Average Decline | 12.7% | 8 months |
| Number of Declines | 8 | |
| Average Recovery | | 6.9 months |

| | Reward |
|---|--------|
| Annual Return | 9.29% |
| Annual Inflation | 4.65% |
| Annual Reward | 4.64% |

Source: Pinnacle Advisory Group, Inc.[1]

1 I first saw this method of charting portfolio returns years ago in an excellent book called *Beyond Stocks, A Guide to the Best Performing Complete Portfolios...*, by John F. Merrill, 1997, Tanglewood Publishing. Merrill uses this methodology to chart several different portfolio constructions in his book. Pinnacle has changed the asset class mix in the chart and updated the data, but the rest of the chart construction is borrowed from *Beyond Stocks*. Readers who are interested in a thorough and fascinating exploration of a variety of different asset allocations should read this highly recommended book.

To test the premise that a diversified, balanced portfolio should earn a 5% premium over inflation over time, we can measure the risk and return of owning such a portfolio by constructing a simple indexed, five-asset-class portfolio of U.S. and International stocks, bonds, and cash, and then looking at its performance over various time periods. Our portfolio is a "moderate risk" portfolio consisting of 60% stocks and 40% fixed income assets, where the stock allocation is 38% U.S. large-cap stocks (S&P 500 Index), 12% International stocks (EAFE Index), and 10% U.S. small-cap stocks (Russell 2000 Index). The fixed income asset allocation is 30% diversified bonds (Barclay's Capital Bond Index) and 10% cash (90-day U.S. Treasury Bills).

**Figure 2.1**[6] shows an investment of $100,000 in a portfolio with a 60% equity and 40% fixed income asset allocation where the portfolio is rebalanced to the target asset allocation on a monthly basis. For simplicity, no taxes or transaction charges are included in this illustration. The up and down arrows show whether or not the portfolio's return was positive or negative for each month, which is an interesting time frame considering that investors get their portfolio statements from their custodians on a monthly basis. The time periods in the chart that are dark gray are periods in which the portfolio return declined by at least 5% from month-end to month-end. In a bear market, even if the portfolio's return rallies for a short period within the bear cycle, as long as the portfolio makes a new low, the entire period is shaded dark gray and included in the ongoing bear market. The light gray color shows the number of months that it takes for the portfolio to recover in value back to the pre-bear market peak. The sum of both the dark gray and light gray months shows how long it takes for the portfolio to go through an entire cycle from peak to trough and back to peak, assuming that there are no additions or withdrawals from the portfolio.

In addition, the bottom of the chart shows the return of the portfolio expressed as a premium over inflation for the entire period. For the period beginning in 1972 and ending in October 2008, the annual portfolio return was 9.29% and annual inflation was 4.65%, so the inflation premium earned by the portfolio was 4.64%, just below the 5% premium in our hypothetical conversation. (Readers should note that this premium was 5.8% over inflation

---

6    I first saw this method of charting portfolio returns years ago in an excellent book called *Beyond Stocks: A Guide to the Best Performing Complete Portfolios...*, by John F. Merrill, 1997, Tanglewood Publishing. Merrill uses this methodology to chart several different portfolio constructions in his book. Pinnacle has changed the asset class mix in the chart and updated the data, but the rest of the chart construction is borrowed from *Beyond Stocks*. Readers who are interested in a thorough and fascinating exploration of a variety of different asset allocations should read this highly recommended book.

before the 2008 market decline.) For those who are unimpressed with compounding wealth at that rate, our $100,000 investment in 1972 is now worth $2.615 million. The risk of the portfolio is expressed in terms of peak to trough declines in portfolio value. This moderate portfolio asset allocation had a worst-case decline of 24% from peak to trough that occurred in the 1972-1973 bear market, closely followed by the 22% decline in the 2000-2002 bear market. Once again, readers who like to keep score should note that the current bear market will soon take its place as the most severe market decline during the period. We just don't know where the dark gray bars of this bear market will stop and the light gray bars of the recovery will begin. The chart also shows the average number of months that it takes to recover to the pre-bear market peak portfolio value. In this case, the average portfolio recovery time is 6.9 months for the entire period, with the longest recovery from a bear market trough back to the prior peak taking 16 months after the 2000-2002 bear market.

This chart provides an enormous amount of information, but for our purposes the main point is that the worst top to bottom decline for this conservatively built, strategically managed, portfolio, is 24%. In addition, the longest complete cycle of peak to trough to peak values is 41 months. The entire cycle included the 2000-2002 bear market that lasted 25 months, and the subsequent 16-month recovery back to the peak. If a retiree is fearful of an event where the portfolio suddenly "blows up" and the investor unexpectedly loses all of his or her money, it would appear that our non-leveraged, diversified portfolio delivered as promised. The best example of this is to focus on the October 19, 1987 market crash where the S&P 500 Index fell more than 27% in one day. Here is how Benoit Mandelbrot, author of *The (mis)Behavior of Markets*, describes the mathematical odds of such an occurrence using traditional statistical methods:

> On October 19, 1987, the worst day of trading in at least a century, the index fell 29.2 percent. (He is referring to the Dow Jones Industrial Average.) The probability of that happening, based on the standard reckoning of financial theorists, was less than one in 1050 power, odds so small they have no meaning. It is a number outside the scale of nature. You could span the measurable universe—and still never meet such a number.

Yet look at our chart. This statistically impossible event shows up as a relatively benign 16% 3-month portfolio decline with a rather long recovery period. One can only guess how many super-sophisticated, highly-leveraged, quantitative model–

driven investors lost (or made) their entire fortune on that one unprecedented day in the stock market. However, our boring, non-leveraged, simple five-asset-class portfolio didn't do that badly at all. Good news.

**Table 2.1** shows a different look at the returns by focusing on the returns of each individual asset class of our hypothetical portfolio from the inception date in January 1972 to October of 2008. For the entire period, small-cap U.S. stocks were clearly the best performing single asset class with nominal returns of 11.2% per year and real or after-inflation returns of 6.55%. U.S. large-cap and international stock returns were almost exactly the same for the entire period with nominal returns of 9.67% and 9.62% respectively. The nominal and real returns for fixed income investments including both bonds and cash lag far behind the equity returns, with bonds earning a premium of 2.95% more than inflation and cash only earning 1.17% over inflation. These relationships between asset class returns, portfolio returns, and inflation are the same investment assumptions that are used by most investors to estimate future portfolio returns and to analyze their retirement plan. It would seem entirely rational to take comfort from these seemingly clear and incontestable statistics.

| ASSET CLASS | NOMINAL RETURN | INFLATION | REAL RETURN |
|---|---|---|---|
| T-Bill | 6% | 5% | 1% |
| U.S. Bonds | 7.60% | 5% | 3% |
| U.S. Large Stocks | 10% | 5% | 5% |
| U.S. Small Stocks | 11.20% | 5% | 7% |
| International Stock | 10% | 5% | 5% |
| Portfolio | 9% | 5% | 5% |

**Table 2.1—Five Asset Class Portfolio
from January 1972 to October 2008**

Source: Pinnacle Advisory Group, Inc.

We have now discovered for ourselves two of the main assumptions of strategic investing.

1. Returns for stocks are always projected to be higher than the returns of fixed income over long periods of time.

2. Higher portfolio returns are available for investors willing to accept the higher portfolio volatility that is the result of greater allocations to stocks. As noted earlier, in our example investors who invested $100,000 in 1972 saw their wealth grow to $2.615 million at the end of the time period, clearly an excellent reward for being patient and allowing the compounding of stock investments to do their work.

But the question is can we count on passive, strategic portfolio asset allocation to deliver these kinds of returns to investors all the time? And if not, what impact do the subsequent unanticipated returns have on retirement plans?

## Secular Bear Markets

Stock market cycles are measured over different time horizons. Short-term, or cyclical market cycles tend to last 2 to 7 years. They are typically thought to be closely tied to economic cycles. As the economy gradually moves from boom to bust to boom again, stock prices often lead the economy through the cycle, which is why the stock market is considered a leading economic indicator.

Unlike short-term market cycles, long-term secular market cycles can last up to 10 to 20 years. Secular markets are often composed of a series of cyclical markets that trend higher in bull markets and sideways in bear markets over time. As the series of bullish and bearish short-term cycles follow each other, the stock market develops a longer-term, over-arching secular trend. If the overall trend of several cyclical markets is higher, then we are considered to be in a secular bull market. On the other hand, if the cyclical markets are moving sideways or trending lower as they move from cycle to cycle, then we are considered to be in a secular bear market.

**Figure 2.2** shows the major cyclical market moves within the 1965 to 1982 long-term secular bear market. Note that these peak to trough moves in market price take place over a period of years, as opposed to days or months.

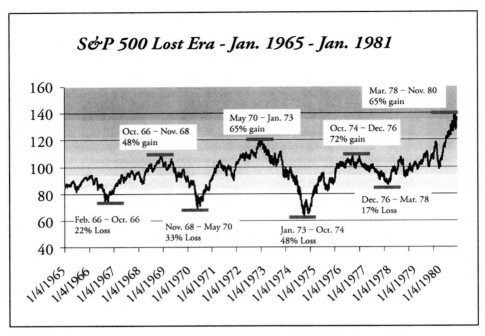

**Figure 2.2—S&P 500 Lost Era: Jan. 1965 to Jan. 1981**

Subcaption: "Source: Pinnacle Advisory Group, Inc.

One of the best ways to learn about secular market cycles is to turn to the work of Ed Easterling at Crestmont Research[7], who is a leading expert on the subject of market cycles and the author of a highly recommended book with the excellent title, *Unexpected Returns*. **Table 2.2** from Crestmont Research shows the secular bull and bear markets since 1901:

Easterling's table shows that since 1901, investors have enjoyed four secular bull markets and endured five secular bear markets. Historically, secular bull markets have run as long as 24 years (1942—1965) and as short as just four years (1933—1936). On average, they have lasted 13.5 years in length. On the other hand, secular bear markets have averaged 11.3 years and have ranged from four years (1929—1932) to 20 years (1901—1920). The trends in stock market performance are driven by trends in the peaks and troughs of the stock market's P/E (price to earnings) ratios. The highest long-term returns occur when the P/E multiple is low at the beginning of the period and expands from the beginning to the end of the period. **Table 2.3** from Crestmont Research, presents a different view of stock market returns than the view we saw in the previous chart.

---

7    Ed Easterling, *Unexpected Returns: Understanding Secular Stock Market Cycles*, Cypress House, Fort Bragg, CA., 2005

| MARKET CYCLE | | TOTAL YEARS | MARKET | P/E RATIO | |
|---|---|---|---|---|---|
| From | To | | | Beginning | End |
| 1901 | 1920 | 20 | Bear | 23 | 5 |
| 1921 | 1928 | 8 | Bull | 5 | 22 |
| 1929 | 1932 | 4 | Bear | 28 | 8 |
| 1933 | 1936 | 4 | Bull | 11 | 19 |
| 1937 | 1941 | 5 | Bear | 19 | 12 |
| 1942 | 1965 | 24 | Bull | 9 | 23 |
| 1966 | 1981 | 16 | Bear | 21 | 9 |
| 1982 | 1999 | 18 | Bull | 7 | 42 |
| 2000 | ??? | ??? | Bear | 42 | ??? |

**Table 2.2—Secular Market Cycles from 1901**

Source: Crestmont Research

| DECILE | FROM | TO | AVERAGE | AVERAGE BEGINNING P/E | AVERAGE ENDING P/E |
|---|---|---|---|---|---|
| 1 | 1.20% | 4.50% | 3.20% | 19 | 9 |
| 2 | 4.50% | 5.20% | 4.90% | 18 | 9 |
| 3 | 5.20% | 5.40% | 5.30% | 12 | 12 |
| 4 | 5.40% | 5.80% | 5.60% | 14 | 12 |
| 5 | 5.90% | 7.20% | 6.70% | 14 | 14 |
| 6 | 7.20% | 8.80% | 8.30% | 17 | 18 |
| 7 | 9.00% | 9.30% | 9.20% | 15 | 17 |
| 8 | 9.40% | 10.80% | 10.40% | 11 | 20 |
| 9 | 11.00% | 11.90% | 11.70% | 12 | 22 |
| | | | | | |

**Table 2.3—20 Year Returns Ending 1919-2005 (87 Periods)**

Source: Crestmont Research—Total returns shown net of gains, dividends, and transaction cost of 2%.

In this analysis, the returns for the S&P 500 Index are grouped by their 20-year returns. This time period is long enough to do two important things. First, it is long enough to be considered long-term by the most ardent strategic investors who insist that stock market returns are only predictable over long time periods. Second, the twenty-year period represents a significant amount of the remaining life expectancy for a retiree who is worried about running out of money during his or her retirement. As we will show, for an investor who is currently retiring at age 60, the stock market's return, and the investor's subsequent portfolio return, over the next 20 years is critical. Easterling divides the 87 20-year periods that begin in 1919 and end in 1995 into 10 groups (or deciles), ranked from the lowest 20-year returns to the highest 20-year returns. He then gives us the range of returns for each of these 10 deciles, as well as the median return for each decile.

Finally, we get to the "secret sauce" of Easterling's insights about long-term stock market returns. For each of the ten performance deciles he gives us the average beginning and average ending P/E ratio for the stock market. The results of this chart are startling to say the least. If we consider the median returns for stocks in the fifth and sixth decile of performance, we can see that the average returns are similar to investor expectations. If you add in Easterling's assumption of 2% annual expenses to these numbers, the median returns are 8.7% and 10.3% respectively (6.7% +2% and 8.3% + 2%). No surprise here. However, once we analyze the returns from either high or low beginning P/E ratios the numbers may be surprising for investors who expect to earn historical average returns from any purchase price. It is easy to observe that the highest 20-year market returns historically occur when the average P/E ratio at the beginning of the period is low, and expand during the holding period, and the lowest 20-year average returns occur when the average P/E ratio at the beginning of the period is high, and falls during the holding period. The historical data shows that buying the stock market at P/E ratios of 19 or higher results in median returns, net of expenses, of only 3.2%. On the other hand, the data shows that investors buying at the lowest P/E ratios should expect the highest or tenth decile median returns of 13.4% annually for the next twenty years. Investors who insist that expected returns have little to do with market valuations when P/E multiples are high are obviously pursuing a high-risk investment strategy over both short-term and long-term time horizons.

We will study the mysteries of calculating the P/E ratio in great detail in Chapter 10. For now, investors should be content with the not-so-startling conclusion that the valuation of the stock market matters greatly when forecasting long-term returns. It is definitely not true that investors who follow the "rules" by building strategic, buy and hold portfolios, should expect to achieve average stock market returns for the 10- to 20-year period following their retirement, regardless of the valuation of the stock market when they retire. What is true is that buying and holding stocks when P/E ratios are low is likely to result in higher than average portfolio returns over long time periods and buying and holding stocks when P/E ratios are high is likely to deliver lower than average portfolio returns over longer time horizons. In short, we are faced with the inescapable conclusion that buying when prices are low leads to higher returns in the future. As I am fond of saying (in a tongue in cheek manner) when I'm invited to speak to industry groups, "Don't let anyone else know about this secret buy-low/sell-high methodology."

## Components of Stock Market Returns

It is important to examine the components of stock market returns to understand why they behave the way they do.[8] John P. Hussman, manager of the Hussman Growth Fund, shows how nominal stock market returns can be broken down into two components, the dividend yield and the amount of capital gain or appreciation in the market price. The dividend yield is impacted by the growth of corporate earnings over time since increases in corporate cash flow tend to lead to increasing dividend payouts over time. Over shorter periods of time, changes in dividend yields have more to do with changes in the price of the stock market index. As the price of the stock market changes up and down, the dividend yield moves inversely to the change in price. As an example, the current S&P 500 dividend is $27, so if the S&P 500 Index were at 1565 (its peak level) the dividend yield would be 1.7% ($27/1565). However, if the S&P 500 value falls to 900 then the dividend yield rises to 3 percent ($27/900).

The capital gain portion of the return is determined by the rate of earnings growth that the stock market will achieve in the future, as well as the earnings multiple or amount that investors are willing to pay for those earnings in the future. Many forces in the economy, including inflation, monetary policy, corporate taxes, productivity growth, and corporate profit margins impact the amount of earnings as well as the rate of earnings growth for the stock market over time. Over long-term time horizons, corporate earnings growth tends to oscillate around the long-term growth of the economy as measured by Gross Domestic Product (GDP). A large component of nominal (before considering the impact of inflation) earnings growth is inflation, so higher rates of future inflation imply higher earnings growth rates, which presumably implies higher stock prices in the future. Falling rates of inflation would imply slower rates of earnings growth and subsequent lower stock prices. Interestingly, nominal GDP growth, and consequently nominal earnings growth rates, remain relatively constant throughout secular bull markets and bear markets. According to Easterling, over the past 100 years, stocks fell by an average of 4.2% per year during bear markets while nominal GDP grew an average of 6.9% during the same bear market periods. During bull markets, however, stocks gained an

---

8   For an excellent discussion about calculating long-term market returns, see a February 22, 2005 research report written by John P. Hussman, Ph.D. of the Hussman Funds titled *The Likely Range of Market Returns in the Coming Decade* (which can be found at www. hussmanfunds.com).

average of 14.6% per year, while nominal GDP grew an average of 6.3% per year during these periods. It is obviously the change in P/E ratios, as opposed to changes in the growth rate of earnings that is the more powerful force that dictates stock market returns over long bull and bear markets.

The market P/E multiple (price to earnings ratio) is a simple ratio that tells us how much investors are willing to pay in aggregate for the earnings that are generated by the total of all the stocks that make up the S&P 500 Index. Similar to earnings growth rates, the P/E ratio that investors are willing to pay for earnings seems to be highly correlated to both inflation and deflation (or disinflation.) However, where higher inflation drives earnings growth rates higher on a nominal basis and becomes a tailwind for stock prices, the impact of inflation on P/E ratios is devastating and results in significantly lower stock prices over long periods of time. During periods of rising inflation and rising interest rates, investors are not likely to reward corporations by paying higher P/E ratios for stocks since the real (post-inflation) present value of their future earnings will be less in a high interest rate and high inflation economy. The reverse is also true. In normal economic conditions, investors are likely to pay higher multiples for corporate earnings if inflation and interest rates are expected to fall. However, today's economy, which is characterized by a deep recession, 0% short-term interest rates and record low longer-term rates, has resulted in falling rather than rising P/E ratios. In fact, the rule for investors is that both inflation and deflation may cause P/E multiples to contract.

The forces that cause the P/E multiple to expand and contract are actually the subject of some debate.[9] In any event, it is important that investors realize that changing P/E multiples have a major impact on stock market returns over time. There is no dispute that buying stocks at cheap multiples results in higher than average returns in the future.

In addition to these fundamental indicators, P/E ratios can be highly impacted by the psychology of the financial markets. In bull markets investors are likely to award high valuations to stocks based on their enthusiastic outlook for future earning growth based on bullish assumptions that good news will continue in the future. And of course, once again the reverse is true in bear markets. At market peaks and troughs P/E ratios tend to overshoot or undershoot the levels of valuation that might be implied by only looking at economic fundamentals.

---

9    John Hussman's research asserts that in years following periods of low year-over-year inflation, stock market returns are actually disappointing. He contends that low inflation may be given too much credit for subsequent high P/E multiples. His feeling is that low inflation may be correlated with high multiples but low inflation shouldn't justify high multiples. For Hussman's views on P/E multiples in low inflation environments read http://www.hussmanfunds.com/wmc/wmc070529.htm.

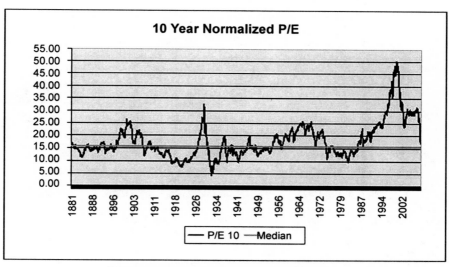

**Figure 2.3—10 Year Normalized P/E**
Source: Pinnacle Advisory Group, Inc.

One method of calculating the E in P/E ratios that accounts for the cyclicality of stock market earnings is to "normalize" or average the actual earnings of the stock market for the past ten years. To do so, we use an average of the previous ten years of stock market "as reported" or GAAP (Generally Accepted Accounting Principles) earnings in order to determine the "E" in the P/E ratio. The "P" in the ratio is simply the current market price of the Index. By calculating the P/E ratio using the average of ten years of trailing earnings, we "normalize" or smooth out the volatility of the earnings assumptions by using a long-term average that includes several shorter-term market cycles. Happily, this is a similar methodology to the one used by Easterling in his research. **Figure 2.3**[10] shows the December 2008 P/E ratio of the S&P 500 using the "Normalized-10" methodology. Readers will immediately notice how high the P/E ratio was at the top of the market in 2000 reaching levels that were clearly unprecedented going all the way back to 1881. The chart also shows how dramatic the valuation adjustment has been in the stock market over a very short time horizon. For example, the normalized P/E fell from 27 in January of 2008 to 17 in November of 2008, testimony to the violence of the market crash that took place over that period of time.

---

10  There are differences in how analysts treat historical inflation data in calculating normalized earnings multiples. Pinnacle's PE-10 calculations use the nominal earnings data with no adjustments for inflation.

| Earnings Growth: | 6% | | |
|---|---|---|---|
| Time: | 20 Years | | |
| Inflation: | 3% | | |
| Ending P/E: | 15.8 | | |
| | **P/E 50** | **P/E 31** | **P/E 17** | **P/E 10** |
|---|---|---|---|---|
| Expected Capital Gain | 0% | 2% | 6% | 8% |
| Initial Dividend | 1% | 2% | 3% | 4% |
| Average Dividend | 2.10% | 3% | 3.10% | 3.30% |
| Total Return | 2% | 5% | 9% | 12% |
| Net After Inflation | -1% | 2% | 6% | 9% |

**Table 2.4—Components of Return**

Source: Pinnacle Advisory Group, Inc.

**Table 2.4** uses a simple calculator suggested by Hussman to illustrate how our equation of expected capital gains plus the dividend yield can be used to estimate long-term returns. We can use the calculator to show the results of four different market scenarios where we buy the market at different price levels and current dividend yields and then hold for twenty years, after which we assume that the stock market will be priced at its long-term median P/E ratio of 15.8 times earnings. In the first scenario we buy and hold the stock market at the market top in the year 2000 and pay 50 times earnings. In the second scenario we buy and hold the stock market at a P/E ratio of 31, the market valuation on 10/2007, after the five year bull market that began in 10/2002 and saw the S&P 500 index double in value. In the third scenario we purchase the stock market at the 11/2008 P/E multiple of 17, after a record breaking crash in market prices, and in the fourth scenario we purchase the stock market at a future P/E multiple of 10, a price multiple consistent with the beginning of secular bull markets in the past. In the periods beginning in 2002, 2007, and 2008 we use the actual dividend yield of the stock market for our return calculation, and in the scenario where we buy the index at a P/E ratio of 10 we assume a dividend yield of 4%.[11]

Because we want to focus on the impact of P/E ratios and dividend yields, we are making the simplifying assumption that earnings growth rates remain fixed

---

11   Our review of nominal and real calculations of PE-10 data reveal there is little difference in the conclusions about market valuation between the different approaches to the data.

at 6% in both high and low P/E scenarios. We are also using a fixed inflation assumption for all of the scenarios using the historical average inflation rate of 3%. Finally, we assume that P/E ratios won't overshoot or undershoot their historical averages at the end of each holding period, and use the historical average P/E of 15.8 in each scenario. Astute readers will remember that the P/E ratio at the end of secular market cycles tends to move well beyond the average in either direction. They might also ask if inflation will average more than 3% from today's rather depressed levels over the next twenty years. Readers should be properly skeptical of all three of these assumptions.

Retirees who had the misfortune to retire in the year 2000 when the stock market was valued at a 50 P/E ratio had little reason to believe that they would achieve historical average returns if they bought and held stocks for the long run at such high prices. The calculator shows the expected capital gain or price appreciation of the stock market, *after 20 years*, is only 0.7% per year. Combined with an average dividend yield of 2.1%, the projected annualized total return for the stock market was only 2.15% per year. If we consider an inflation assumption for the following twenty years of 3%, the net after inflation return for holding stocks was a negative -1.15%. Rebalancing to a fixed percentage stock allocation from these price levels would hardly resolve the overwhelming problem of buying at such high prices. Retirees who expected to achieve historical average returns by buying and holding stocks in the euphoric days of late 2007 after a five year stock market rally are also likely to be disappointed. Even if corporate earnings grow at the trend rate of 6% per year over the next twenty years, buying and holding when the stock market is purchased at 31 times earnings results in a projected total return of 5.45%, and an inflation adjusted annualized return of only 2.24%.

Interestingly, buying and holding at November 2008's market valuation of 17 offers some hope that the strategy will actually deliver the returns that investors might expect from studying historical average returns. Because the P/E multiple does not significantly contract from the current multiple to our assumed future average multiple of 15.8 times earnings, the forecasted buy and hold return is 8.68% per year, and the net after inflation returns is 5.68%, much closer to expectations. And finally, if the stock market declines in value to a normalized P/E ratio of 10, the result is much higher than expected returns over the twenty year holding period. In this case, investors get the benefit of a significant tailwind to expected returns because the stock market P/E multiple expands over time, which combined with our assumption of 6% earnings growth drives a total return forecast of 11.75% and an inflation adjusted return of 8.75%. Clearly, the fundamentals of market price have a dramatic impact on the results of a buy and hold strategy. Investors who believe that they "should put their money to work," regardless of market prices, do so at their peril.

Of course the data that we have been analyzing pertains to just one asset class, U.S. large-cap stocks. Investors might wonder if the results would be materially different if we consider the returns of a diversified portfolio, as opposed to just one asset class. We can use the data from our 5-asset class portfolio to test the past returns of a simple, diversified, balanced 60-40 portfolio during secular bear markets. The first period to study is the secular bear market period from 1965 to 1981, a period of 16 years. **Table 2.5**[12] shows the returns of each asset class in the portfolio as well as the total portfolio performance for the 16 year period:

| ASSET CLASS | NOMINAL RETURN | INFLATION | REAL RETURN |
|---|---|---|---|
| T-Bill | 7% | 7% | 0% |
| U.S. Bonds | 6% | 7% | -1% |
| U.S. Large Stocks | 6% | 7% | 0% |
| U.S. Small Stocks | 15% | 7% | 8% |
| International Stock | 8% | 7% | 1% |
| Portfolio | 8% | 7% | 1% |
|  |  |  |  |

**Table 2.5—Five Asset Class Portfolio from 1965-1981 (16 Years)**
Source: Pinnacle Advisory Group, Inc.

The performance results for the total portfolio are a testimony to the power of diversification. The total portfolio annualized return of 7.86% exceeded the return for large-cap U.S. stocks, which was 6.25%. More importantly, on an inflation-adjusted basis, and despite the fact that U.S. stocks returned a *negative* real return of -0.44%, the portfolio still managed to earn a small but positive inflation premium of 1.17%. Most analysts would agree that the fact that inflation averaged 6.69% for the period resulted in lower stock and bond returns. The normalized P/E ratio for the U.S. stock market fell during the period from 25 to less than 10. This is an interesting point for investors who have never managed money in an inflationary environment to consider. After all, the past 26 years from 1982 to the

---

12   Note: Because the Morgan Stanley EAFE Index was unavailable prior to 1970, the table relies on Large-U.S. stock data for the period from 1965 through 1970 for the model, while the returns from 1970 through 1981 include international stock performance.

present have been characterized by a falling rate of inflation. If recent government intervention in the financial markets is the catalyst for a structural change where inflation becomes persistent, then that could be a significant headwind for P/E ratio expansion in the future. Looking at the returns, it is clear that small-cap U.S. stocks had a disproportionate impact on the portfolio results. The nominal small-cap stock return of 14.72% and the real return of 8.03% rescued investors from an even worse fate over this time frame.

The next secular bear market to examine is the one that we are currently experiencing. **Table 2.6** shows the returns for our familiar 5-asset class portfolio from March of 2000 through November of 2008. Once again, it appears that portfolio diversification is helpful for investors, but doesn't result in anywhere near the forecasted returns for the portfolio over a long holding period of 8 years.

Here we see that once again, large-cap U.S. stocks actually earned a negative inflation adjusted return of -6.91% for the 8-year period, while the portfolio managed a smaller loss of -1.87%. Unlike the previous secular bear that was characterized by higher inflation, the current bear market is characterized by a period of disinflation. The resulting environment of falling interest rates resulted in higher bond prices. Bonds were the biggest contributor to portfolio returns with nominal returns of 5.91% per year and inflation-adjusted returns of 3.11% for the period. Remember that in the 1965-1981 secular bear period, small-cap stocks were the best performing asset class. Unfortunately, over the past 8 years, small-caps have not performed nearly as well with nominal returns of 0.23% per year and real returns of only -3.03% per year. Once again, investors should conclude that diversified portfolios composed of traditional asset classes are not immune to the dangers of secular bear markets. Instead, investors should consider that the current secular bear market began when the normalized P/E for the S&P 500 Index was at an unprecedented 50 times earnings. There is little to suggest that

| ASSET CLASS | NOMINAL RETURN | INFLATION | REAL RETURN |
|---|---|---|---|
| T-Bill | 2.90% | 2.80% | 0.10% |
| U.S. Bonds | 6% | 2.80% | 3% |
| U.S. Large Stocks | -4% | 2.80% | -7% |
| U.S. Small Stocks | 0% | 2.80% | -3% |
| International Stock | -2% | 2.80% | -5% |
| Portfolio | 1% | 2.80% | -2% |

**Table 2.6—Secular Bear Market: March 2000-November 2008**

Source: Pinnacle Advisory Group, Inc.

traditional diversification alone can manage portfolio risk and volatility from such elevated valuation levels.

Having explored the realities of secular bear markets and the resulting less-than-expected portfolio returns that occur during these periods of falling P/E multiples, it is time to move on to the most important point of this chapter, which is to better understand how secular market cycles can impact a seemingly well-crafted retirement plan.

## Retirement Planning and Secular Bear Markets

Planning for a successful retirement has long been an important focus for all investors and for the financial planning profession. In most retirement studies, the moving parts in the equation of retirement planning include:

- The future inflation rate
- The amount of spending needed for the retiree
- The future tax rate
- The amount of social security or other pension income available
- Any additional earnings or sales in the future that will impact the client's balance sheet
- The long-term return on the retiree's assets

Of these variables, the one that is typically given the least attention in retirement studies is the long-term return on assets. This is because the return projections are based on an ample amount of detailed historical data that explains the relative performance of stocks, bonds, and cash and the subsequent past performance of portfolios composed of those asset classes. Not surprisingly, in these studies, long-term portfolio returns depend entirely on the amount of stocks in the asset allocation of the portfolio. In virtually every study, adding to the percentage of stocks in the asset allocation mix results in a higher portfolio return over the client's life expectancy because, *on average*, stocks outperform other assets over long-term time periods. These studies do not analyze market valuations at the beginning of the retirement period.

In addition, investors are taught that the best way to assure that long-term portfolio returns are actually realized over the retirement period is to stick with what I call the strategic portfolio management "playbook." The rules for successful strategic portfolio management are:

- The portfolio should not be leveraged in any way, meaning that no money is borrowed in order to invest.

- The portfolio should be properly diversified in a variety of asset classes that have low correlations to each other.
- The mix of asset classes should generate an "optimal" level of portfolio return for the amount of expected portfolio volatility according to Modern Portfolio Theory, based on the past performance of the asset classes used to build the portfolio. (Note: we will explore optimal portfolios in detail in the next chapter.)
- Each asset class should be invested either passively by owning index funds or exchange traded funds, or actively by using managed funds that are either mutual funds or separate accounts.
- The portfolio should be rebalanced to the asset allocation targets established at the portfolio inception date, usually on a calendar basis.
- The portfolio is allowed a long-term time horizon to deliver expected returns, usually ten years or longer.
- The investor should not engage in market timing that would invalidate the risk/reward characteristics of the portfolio at any given time.

We have already discovered the very good news that the evidence seems to show that a catastrophic loss of principal over three- to five-year time horizons is highly unlikely for investors with unleveraged, well-diversified portfolios. The problem for retirees, and for investors in general, is that we have set the bar far too high about what constitutes an investment event that can "blow up" a retirement plan for less than super-affluent investors. *Portfolio returns don't have to be negative in order for a retirement plan to fail, they simply have to be less than expected.* While most investors with passively managed portfolios remain focused on the preservation of their capital as the most important investment risk that they should be concerned with over long time periods, *it is the inflation-adjusted return on their capital over time that they actually need to worry about.*

Peter Bernstein, in his book *Against the Gods*, addresses the nature of risk for retirees when he offers the following quote from Robert Jeffrey, a former manufacturing executive who now manages a substantial family trust. Jeffrey offers an interesting observation about portfolio volatility being used as the primary measure of risk for portfolio managers and financial planners: "Volatility fails as a proxy for risk because volatility *per se*, be it related to weather, portfolio returns, or the timing of one's morning newspaper delivery, is simply a benign statistical probability factor that tells us nothing about risk until coupled with a consequence." Jeffrey sums the matter up with these words: "The real risk in holding a portfolio is that it might not provide its owner, either during the interim or at some terminal date or both, with the cash he (or she) requires to make essential outlays."

Bravo to Mr. Jeffrey. He has helped us to identify a fundamental problem with the industry's definition of risk. While modern financial theory teaches that risk is the measure of portfolio volatility, Jeffrey correctly points out that risk is actually the potential that a retiree won't be able to make his "essential outlays" during retirement. The entire industry seems to have taken their eye off the ball as it relates to portfolio returns in the retirement planning equation. Far from being a "given" as the average of long-term past returns, the future portfolio return is closely tied to the valuation of financial markets at the beginning of the retirement period. For most people, the notion of portfolio risk in retirement being tied to the long-term risk of losing their portfolio principal is simply incorrect. They should be focused on whether or not the stock market, and their portfolio, is likely to deliver needed returns over a specific time period, which happens to be the first decade of their retirement.

Perhaps a simple illustration would be helpful. **Table 2.7** shows a sample 30-year retirement scenario where the portfolio value is $1 million at the beginning of the retirement period and the payment or portfolio withdrawal made by the retiree is 5% of $1 million, or $50,000 at the end of year 1. In our retirement model, the portfolio grows at 10.43% each year and the payment to maintain the retiree's standard of living grows at the rate of inflation, which is assumed to be 5.38% per year (don't worry, we'll explain why we are using these numbers in just a second.). The "real" annual rate of return for the portfolio, after considering the inflation rate, is 5.05%, which is very close to the 5% inflation premium that our hypothetical retiree was led to expect at the beginning of this chapter.

The resulting retirement projection for this investor looks terrific. The portfolio continues to grow in value every year, even though the retiree's withdrawal to support his or her standard of living in retirement continues to grow every year by the 5.38% rate of inflation. The $52,690 retirement withdrawal at the end of year 1 grows to $240,833 by the end of the thirty-year period, yet the portfolio value still grows from the initial $1 million to a whopping $4,183,628. Clearly everyone (the retiree and or the retiree and his financial advisor) is feeling very comfortable about the recommendation that the client should go ahead and retire. There seems to be little risk that the retiree would have to change his or her lifestyle, or run out of money during their life expectancy.

But what if we are in a secular bear market? How would that change things? In the secular bear scenario, **Table 2.8** illustrates what happens if the portfolio still earns the same average annual return of 10.43% over the 30-year period from our first example, but instead of earning 10.43% each and every year, the portfolio earns the actual annual returns that we generated for our 5 asset class strategic model portfolio during the secular bear market that began in 1966. In other words,

| YEAR | BEG. VALUE | GROWTH% | END VALUE | CPI% | PAYMENT | VALUE |
|---|---|---|---|---|---|---|
| 1 | $1,000,000 | 10% | $1,104,331 | 5% | $52,690 | $1,051,641 |
| 2 | $1,051,641 | 10% | $1,161,360 | 5% | $55,525 | $1,105,835 |
| 3 | $1,105,835 | 10% | $1,221,208 | 5% | $58,512 | $1,162,696 |
| 4 | $1,162,696 | 10% | $1,284,001 | 5% | $61,660 | $1,222,341 |
| 5 | $1,222,341 | 10% | $1,349,869 | 5% | $64,977 | $1,284,892 |
| 6 | $1,284,892 | 10% | $1,418,946 | 5% | $68,473 | $1,350,473 |
| 7 | $1,350,473 | 10% | $1,491,370 | 5% | $72,157 | $1,419,213 |
| 8 | $1,419,213 | 10% | $1,567,281 | 5% | $76,039 | $1,491,242 |
| 9 | $1,491,242 | 10% | $1,646,824 | 5% | $80,130 | $1,566,695 |
| 10 | $1,566,695 | 10% | $1,730,150 | 5% | $84,441 | $1,645,709 |
| 11 | $1,645,709 | 10% | $1,817,407 | 5% | $88,984 | $1,728,424 |
| 12 | $1,728,424 | 10% | $1,908,752 | 5% | $93,771 | $1,814,981 |
| 13 | $1,814,981 | 10% | $2,004,340 | 5% | $98,816 | $1,905,524 |
| 14 | $1,905,524 | 10% | $2,104,329 | 5% | $104,132 | $2,000,197 |
| 15 | $2,000,197 | 10% | $2,208,879 | 5% | $109,734 | $2,099,145 |
| 16 | $2,099,145 | 10% | $2,318,151 | 5% | $115,638 | $2,202,513 |
| 17 | $2,202,513 | 10% | $2,432,303 | 5% | $121,859 | $2,310,444 |
| 18 | $2,310,444 | 10% | $2,551,495 | 5% | $128,416 | $2,423,079 |
| 19 | $2,423,079 | 10% | $2,675,881 | 5% | $135,324 | $2,540,557 |
| 20 | $2,540,557 | 10% | $2,805,616 | 5% | $142,605 | $2,663,011 |
| 21 | $2,663,011 | 10% | $2,940,846 | 5% | $150,277 | $2,790,569 |
| 22 | $2,790,569 | 10% | $3,081,712 | 5% | $158,362 | $2,923,350 |
| 23 | $2,923,350 | 10% | $3,228,346 | 5% | $166,882 | $3,061,464 |
| 24 | $3,061,464 | 10% | $3,380,870 | 5% | $175,860 | $3,205,010 |
| 25 | $3,205,010 | 10% | $3,539,392 | 5% | $185,321 | $3,354,071 |
| 26 | $3,354,071 | 10% | $3,704,005 | 5% | $195,291 | $3,508,713 |
| 27 | $3,508,713 | 10% | $3,874,781 | 5% | $205,798 | $3,668,983 |
| 28 | $3,668,983 | 10% | $4,051,771 | 5% | $216,870 | $3,834,902 |
| 29 | $3,834,902 | 10% | $4,235,001 | 5% | $228,538 | $4,006,463 |
| 30 | $4,006,463 | 10% | $4,424,461 | 5% | $240,833 | $4,183,628 |

### Table 2.7—Sample Retirement Scenario #1
Source: Pinnacle Advisory Group, Inc.

what happens if we experience a secular bear market in the early years of this retirement scenario, but still have the same average annual portfolio return for the entire period? Likewise, even though the average inflation rate for the retirement period will be the same 5.38% annual rate that we used in our first example, in this second scenario the inflation rate used to inflate the client's spending each and

| YEAR | BEG. VALUE | GROWTH% | END VALUE | CPI% | PAYMENT | VALUE |
|------|-----------|---------|-----------|------|---------|-------|
| 1 | $1,000,000 | -4% | $961,600 | 3% | $51,675 | $909,925 |
| 2 | $909,925 | 21.00% | $1,101,009 | 3% | $53,246 | $1,047,763 |
| 3 | $1,047,763 | 11.00% | $1,163,017 | 5% | $55,759 | $1,107,258 |
| 4 | $1,107,258 | -6.30% | $1,037,501 | 6.10% | $59,160 | $978,340 |
| 5 | $978,340 | 3.80% | $1,015,517 | 5% | $62,402 | $953,115 |
| 6 | $953,115 | 13.30% | $1,079,879 | 3% | $64,493 | $1,015,386 |
| 7 | $1,015,386 | 14.10% | $1,158,556 | 3% | $66,647 | $1,091,909 |
| 8 | $1,091,909 | -8% | $1,000,734 | 9% | $72,452 | $928,283 |
| 9 | $928,283 | -11.70% | $819,674 | 12% | $81,392 | $738,281 |
| 10 | $738,281 | 27.00% | $937,617 | 7% | $87,041 | $850,576 |
| 11 | $850,576 | 19.00% | $1,012,185 | 5% | $91,271 | $920,914 |
| 12 | $920,914 | 3% | $951,580 | 7% | $97,405 | $854,175 |
| 13 | $854,175 | 10% | $940,618 | 9% | $106,200 | $834,418 |
| 14 | $834,418 | 15% | $958,662 | 13% | $120,314 | $838,348 |
| 15 | $838,348 | 22% | $1,023,455 | 13% | $135,378 | $888,077 |
| 16 | $888,077 | 3% | $912,855 | 9% | $147,440 | $765,415 |
| 17 | $765,415 | 19% | $912,604 | 4% | $153,087 | $759,517 |
| 18 | $759,517 | 18% | $893,876 | 4% | $158,874 | $735,002 |
| 19 | $735,002 | 8% | $792,773 | 4% | $165,165 | $627,608 |
| 20 | $627,608 | 28.10% | $803,966 | 4% | $171,458 | $632,508 |
| 21 | $632,508 | 21% | $762,489 | 1.10% | $173,344 | $589,145 |
| 22 | $589,145 | 6% | $623,139 | 4% | $181,023 | $442,116 |
| 23 | $442,116 | 15% | $507,682 | 4% | $189,006 | $318,675 |
| 24 | $318,675 | 19.60% | $381,136 | 5% | $197,776 | $183,360 |
| 25 | $183,360 | -2% | $179,161 | 6.10% | $209,840 | -$30,679 |
| 26 | -$30,679 | 22% | -$37,564 | 3% | $216,303 | -$253,867 |
| 27 | -$253,867 | 6% | -$268,363 | 3% | $222,533 | -$490,896 |
| 28 | -$490,896 | 12% | -$551,865 | 3% | $228,653 | -$780,518 |
| 29 | -$780,518 | 1% | -$789,650 | 3% | $234,758 | -$1,024,407 |
| 30 | -$1,024,407 | 23% | -$1,263,709 | 3% | $240,720 | -$1,504,429 |

### Table 2.8—Sample Retirement Scenario #2
Source: Pinnacle Advisory Group, Inc.

every year is the actual yearly change in the Consumer Price Index for the 30-year period beginning in 1966.

The results are startling. Even though this portfolio has the same average portfolio return and inflation rate for the period as our first example, the portfolio begins to decline precipitously in value after year 15 of the retirement period. By year 20, the portfolio value has fallen to $632,508, and the next year's withdrawal to meet retirement expenses is projected to be $173,344, a full 27% of the portfolio value! And, even though the portfolio delivers an excellent return in year 21 of 20.55%, the portfolio value still declines from $632,508 to $589,145. If our 60 year old retiree is now 80 years old, what must he or she be thinking when their projected retirement value in year 21 was supposed to be $2.79 million dollars but is actually $589,000, and instead of living a carefree retirement they are retaining the services of a financial advisor who is asking how they can significantly cut back expenses so that they don't run out of money?

*In this secular bear scenario, despite the fact that for the last 20 years of retirement the portfolio delivered an outstanding annual return of 13.7%, and despite the fact that there was only one calendar year out of the last twenty years where the portfolio delivered a negative return (-2.29% in year 25), the portfolio blows up in year 25 of the retirement plan.*

How is this possible? How could two retirement plans with the same average portfolio return and the same inflation rate over a 30-year period have such different outcomes? The answer is found in the order of the returns, not the magnitude of the returns. Because the retiree experienced less than expected returns in the early years of his or her retirement, the retirement plan was doomed to fail, even though the returns for the last 20 years of retirement were outstanding. The preceding retirement scenarios serve to illustrate the case that for retirees, portfolio risk should not be defined as the potential for catastrophic short-term portfolio losses or even the risk that capital won't be preserved over relatively long periods of time. Instead, the real portfolio risks are:

1. A well-diversified portfolio with no leverage significantly underperforms expected returns over a significant percentage of the client's remaining life expectancy, usually 20 years or longer.
2. The portfolio does deliver expected long-term returns, but delivers them in the wrong order where the portfolio returns during the first decade or more of retirement are much lower than expected.

Although the financial planning industry typically ignores the problem of market valuation and the subsequent risk of actually achieving projected future portfolio returns, planning professionals do use some sophisticated planning techniques to analyze the probability of retirement success. When modeling the probability that the portfolio will be able to meet a client's cash flow objectives in retirement, perhaps the most celebrated and useful analytical tool for financial planners is called "Monte Carlo" analysis, which is essentially a random number generator capable of modeling thousands of retirement scenarios. Today, Monte

Carlo analysis is offered directly to investors through a variety of custodians and other online resources.

## Monte Carlo Analysis and Withdrawal Rates

In many respects, Monte Carlo analysis uses the same methodology for modeling portfolio volatility as Modern Portfolio Theory. In Monte Carlo models, the volatility of portfolio returns is measured as the standard deviation of the returns around the expected average portfolio returns in the future. Investors input the average expected return of their portfolio (the mean return) and the volatility of the portfolio around the mean (the standard deviation), as well as their expectations of future spending and inflation into the Monte Carlo model. The simulation then begins to pull random portfolio returns out of a statistically constructed hat, where approximately two-thirds of the returns fall within a specified range from the average. The two-thirds range is measured as plus or minus one standard deviation, and the graph of those returns forms a perfect bell curve where the probability of positive portfolio returns is exactly equal to the probability of negative portfolio returns. About one-third of the returns fall outside of the one standard deviation range (1/6 on the positive side of the range and 1/6 on the negative side of the range) and they, too, are theoretically equally distributed between positive and negative returns.

The computer simulation then runs thousands of retirement scenarios where each year's portfolio return is randomly drawn from the statistically defined pool of possible returns. If the investor has a 30-year life expectancy, then 30 different random portfolio returns are used to fund future expenses, one random draw for each year of the investor's retirement. Once the computer model determines how much capital the retiree has at the end of the first retirement simulation, based on the random portfolio returns it picked each year from our statistically defined pool of possible returns, it stores the result and begins again, picking another 30 different portfolio returns out of the hat, each one conforming to the rules we established with the inputs to our model.

The results of the simulation are expressed as probabilities. If we set the computer to run 3000 or more retirement scenarios, the output is very useful.

As an example, the simulation might show that 90% of the time, or in 2,700 of our random retirement scenarios, the retiree didn't run out of money during retirement. However, the other 300 scenarios were not so successful and the retiree spends all of the liquid investable assets in the model, leaving only personal assets to fund future retirement expenses.

With this information, the retiree now has a way to deal with the challenge that Robert Jeffrey posed above, which is the probability that "the portfolio will be able to provide its owner, either during the interim or at some terminal date or both, with the cash he requires to make essential outlays." In this case the answer is that the retiree would not run out of money 90% of the time. Most investors (and their advisors) would view this answer as a very high probability of success and the retiree could then go on to a life of golf, travel, leisure, and whatever other spending assumptions that were built into his plan. If on the other hand, if 1,500 of the 3,000 retirement scenarios were unsuccessful and the retiree ran out of money before the end of his or her life expectancy, then they would only have a 50% probability of a successful retirement, and an alternative plan would be in order.

There is no doubt that this type of probability-based analysis is a huge improvement over using an Excel spreadsheet to analyze a retiree's retirement plan. Instead of the obviously silly assumption that the portfolio will grow at a fixed percentage growth rate each and every year, investors can now model a potentially volatile portfolio where the computer randomly chooses annual returns from a carefully specified range of possible outcomes. However, retirees must be careful to understand the limitations of Monte Carlo analysis. Like all quantitative models, the output is only as good as the input to the model and any problems with the assumptions used in building the model in the first place.

In using standard deviation as the measure of risk in the model, the analysis makes the assumption that the distribution of future portfolio returns will be "normal." As we discussed earlier, two-thirds of future returns will dutifully fall in a well-defined range around the average return, and one-third of the returns will be equally divided on either side of the 1 standard deviation range, 1/6 below the range and 1/6 above. When the model pulls random portfolio returns from the hat holding possible returns, it is possible, but unlikely, that it will pull a secular bear market from the possible choices. The rules governing how the returns are selected will limit the number of negative returns that are likely to be chosen, and to pull a secular bear market from the hat would mean that the model randomly chose 20 years of returns that in aggregate earned significantly less than average returns in the early years of retirement. *At the very least, the rules of standard deviation will not allow the probability of negative returns to equal the "real world" probability of negative returns following a regime of high P/E ratios.* The data indicates that long periods of lower than average returns following high P/E multiples are a virtual statistical certainty, but the Monte Carlo analysis still suggests that lower than average returns only occur 50% of the time, and lower than one standard deviation returns only occur 17% of the time.

Another problem with Monte Carlo analysis is that the inputs for the average return and standard deviation of the portfolio are usually based on the long-term average past returns of stocks and bonds. If average returns for the entire retirement period do not materialize for any reason, the model will not reflect this reality.

Finally, most Monte Carlo models only allow for one input of average return and standard deviation. If stock market P/E ratios dramatically change from the first decade of retirement to the second, it is unlikely that the Monte Carlo analysis will accurately model this scenario. Unless it is programmed to do so, the simulation will randomly choose returns based on only one set of inputs for average return and standard deviation that was determined at the beginning of the simulation.

The best defense against the inability of Monte Carlo analysis to properly model secular bear markets is to choose a portfolio withdrawal rate that is "safe." There have been many studies completed recently that determine the safe withdrawal rate, which is the amount of dollars that can be withdrawn from the portfolio, adjusted for inflation, on an annual basis, without the portfolio being completely liquidated. To date, one of the best-known studies on the subject is by Bill Bengen, who in his important article in the *Journal of Financial Planning* in October of 1994, cleverly back-tested different portfolio withdrawal rates using *actual* past portfolio returns that date back to 1871. The methodology calculates the amount of the first retirement payment as a percentage of the portfolio value at the beginning of the retirement period, and then inflates the payment in the future in much the same way that a pension plan payment is subject to a cost of living adjustment. In the Bengen study, once the first "payment" is determined, it is then inflated using the actual inflation rates of the period studied. The inflated payment is then subtracted from the back-tested portfolio value each year, and the results tell us how different withdrawal rates fare against actual past market returns, as opposed to model returns. The withdrawal rate studies include the Great Depression of the 1930's and the Great Inflation of the late 1960's and 1970's. As a result, the study includes the secular bear markets that we have been discussing in this chapter.

The results of the studies are clear. In all market conditions, the safe inflation-adjusted withdrawal rate from a portfolio for a 30-year retirement period is 4% - 4.4%. This means that if you have a $1 million portfolio, you can withdraw up to $40,000 in your first year of retirement, and then inflate your $40,000 payment each year by the inflation rate in each future year of retirement. There are no 30-year periods where the 4% withdrawal rate failed to provide income for the entire period. However, for retirees who are using Monte Carlo analysis with withdrawal rates higher than 4.0%, some caution is in order. The probabilities of success shown by the analysis are likely to be overstated in a high P/E ratio market.

An important study by Michael Kitces, a partner and the Director of Financial Planning Research at Pinnacle Advisory Group, and author of the financial

| QUINTILE | LOWER P/E | UPPER P/E | LOWEST SWR | HIGHEST SWR | AVERAGE SWR |
|----------|-----------|-----------|------------|-------------|-------------|
| 1 | 5.4 | 12 | 6% | 11% | 8% |
| 2 | 12 | 14.7 | 5% | 8% | 7% |
| 3 | 14.7 | 17.6 | 5% | 8% | 6% |
| 4 | 17.6 | 19.9 | 5% | 7% | 6% |
| 5 | 19.9 | 28.7 | 4% | 6% | 5% |

**Table 2.9—Safe Withdrawal Rates Based on
P/E10 Quintiles (60/40 Portfolio)**
Source: The Kitces Report

planning newsletter *The Kitces Report*[13], revisited Bengen's methodology of studying withdrawal rates using actual past market returns in his May 2008 newsletter. Kitces studied the same time period as Bengen, but looked more deeply into how market valuations impact withdrawal rates. His findings are conclusive, and in the context of this chapter, not surprising. After discussing the long-term relationship between P/E ratios and market returns and seeing that there are long, 30-year cycles where returns can be considerably less than average, Kitces concludes:

> The data show that when the real returns are elevated for the first 15 years, significantly higher withdrawal rates are sustainable. On the other hand, when real returns are depressed for the first 15 years, the result is typically a lower safe initial withdrawal rate. In point of fact, in virtually every instance where the safe withdrawal rate was below 6%, it was associated with a time period where the annualized real return of the portfolio was 4% or less for the first 15 years.

Kitces goes on to test different portfolio constructions for safe withdrawal rates based on the P/E multiple of the stock market at the beginning of each 30-year retirement period. Not surprisingly, he finds that adding stocks to the portfolio asset allocation does not result in a higher safe withdrawal rate when the stock market is expensive at the beginning of the retirement period. The asset allocation that allowed the highest safe withdrawal rates was a 60- 40 mix of stocks and fixed income. **Table 2.9** shows the safe withdrawal rates for a 60-40 portfolio grouped by the P/E multiple at the beginning of each 30-year period.

**Table 2.9** clearly shows that investors must be cautious about their retirement spending when market P/E ratios based on 10-year normalized earnings are high.

13   Kitces Report, May 2008, http://kitces.com/retirementwhaitepaper.php

The good news is that the severe market decline in September and October of 2008 has reduced the P/E ratio from a very high 27 to a more reasonable 17 times earnings. According to this study, the safe withdrawal rate based on historical data dating back to the late 1800's is currently between 4.9% and 8.1%, with the average being 6.3%. Investors who fear that market valuations will move significantly lower in the future and who spend more than 4.4% of their initial portfolio value adjusted for inflation should do so with caution. On the other hand, if P/E ratios fall to the first quintile of valuation, the withdrawal rates can be much higher, from 5.7% to 10.6%, with the average being 8.1%.

## The Bottom Line

The possibility that we are mired in a secular bear market, which if history is any guide, could last for several more years, should give every investor pause. The important question becomes, if buying and holding for the long-term won't generate the returns that are needed for today's investors, then what strategy is appropriate? We have learned that there is little to gain from adding to stock allocations when stock market P/E ratios are high. Unfortunately, adding to equity exposure in high P/E ratio environments will not add to expected returns, regardless of what is implied by looking at the historical average returns for the asset class. If stocks are added at high P/E ratios, then investors will significantly add to the volatility of their portfolio without any appreciable difference in additional returns over time.

It seems fair to ask how in the world we got into this mess in the first place. How is it that buying low and selling high is considered to be an unprofessional approach to portfolio management by classically trained investors, even though ignoring valuation clearly puts investor retirement plans at risk? In the next chapter we will discuss the basic investment theory that guides the money management industry today, beginning with the work of Markowitz, Sharpe, and Fama.

# 3 WHY THE FINANCIAL INDUSTRY BELIEVES IN BUY AND HOLD INVESTING

The accepted strategy and tactics for managing portfolios have not changed for fifty years, and that should be a matter of great concern for today's investors. Classically educated investors are taught only one scientific and academically accepted methodology for managing wealth which is based on a handful of theoretical constructs about how to quantify risk and return that were developed many decades ago. Whether they realize it or not, investors use these traditional theories in very practical ways when constructing strategic, buy and hold portfolios. The ideas of asset allocation, correlation, diversification, and the familiar terms of alpha, beta, and investment risk premium, are the result of this one body of investment theory. The investment industry, with few exceptions, has fully embraced the fundamental ideas advanced by the pioneers of modern finance that we are about to meet.

Understanding the basic principles that guide modern portfolio construction is necessary for any investor who wants to fully understand the theoretical rationale for moving from a strategic/passive portfolio strategy to a more productive tactical/active style of portfolio management. This chapter intends to give a brief summary of the academic theory that is responsible for the strategic, buy and hold strategy of investment management that dominates our industry today. The three papers discussed here are part of a huge body of academic work within the current field of modern finance. However, if the curriculum for Certified Financial Planner® practitioners and Chartered Financial Analysts® is any guide, these papers are the most important.

## Markowitz and Portfolio Selection

Prior to the 1952 publication of Harry Markowitz's article, "Portfolio Selection," in *The Journal of Finance*, investors did not think of managing portfolio risk the way they do today. Prior to Markowitz, investors were primarily focused on the individual securities in their portfolio, and to the extent that they owned stocks, they were typically more interested in return than risk. The name of the game was security selection. Those who attempted to manage risk did so by analyzing each individual stock in their portfolio. For individual and institutional investors, their portfolio returns were, for the most part, in the hands of stockbrokers and other security analysts who seemed to have a gift for stock picking.

When John Burr Williams (1933, *Theory of Investment Value*) and Benjamin Graham (1934, *Security Analysis*), first published their famous books about how to analyze individual stocks, investors were still trying to figure out the lessons of buying and selling stocks after the market crash in 1929 and during the Great Depression. Managing risk, according to Graham and Williams, meant that investors should exhaustively analyze individual companies in order to determine their "intrinsic value." The intrinsic value of the company should then be reflected in the price of the shares. According to Graham, if an investor could purchase shares at a considerable discount to their intrinsic value, then the investor had purchased the stock with what Graham called a "margin of safety." The margin of safety meant that investors had allowed for the possibility that they had made errors in their evaluation of intrinsic value, which meant that it was less likely that share prices would fall significantly from their purchase price. It was a way to minimize downside risk at the individual security level.

In practice, the calculation of intrinsic value was completely subjective and different investors would arrive at different conclusions about what it might be for a particular security. The analysis was about finding the intrinsic value of an individual business, and not about the value of the stock market as a whole. Graham was fond of discussing "Mr. Market" who was always offering shares for purchase to discriminating investors. Sometimes the shares were fairly priced and sometimes they were not. It was up to the investor to determine which was the bargain. At a time when stocks were bought and sold on a good story or tip, this style of investing where investors analyzed a company's current financial statements and future cash flows was a new innovation.

Yet, even with the best possible analysis, it seemed that the returns of individual stocks were subject to enormous risk and volatility. Investing was more like taking a chance at a casino than relying on a mathematically precise science. While the industry waited for a better solution, portfolio construction was done on a security-by-security basis and if only one stock passed muster as having a large enough margin of safety, then presumably a one-stock portfolio would have to suffice.

Harry Markowitz provided a remarkable leap forward for the investment industry with the publication of his paper. One of many insights that Markowitz offered was his idea that risk should be analyzed at the *portfolio level* as opposed to only focusing on the individual securities in the portfolio. For the first time, a theory acknowledged that investors were interested in the behavior of the entire portfolio of individual securities, and not just the performance of any one individual security.

Another great insight was that the process of constructing an investment portfolio should consider both risk and returns. It may be hard for us to imagine now, but back in the 1950's, Markowitz's insight that portfolios should be constructed so that investors would achieve the highest possible returns combined with the least possible risk, was a new and innovative idea. Portfolio risk had never been quantified prior to Markowitz, who also gave the world of finance a mathematical basis for determining the trade-off between risk and return. Markowitz's idea that the mathematics of probability could be used to model "efficient portfolios" was so revolutionary that in 1990 he earned a Nobel Prize in economic science for his paper and book of the same name. Markowitz's insights about the trade-off between risks and returns came to be known as Modern Portfolio Theory (MPT).

Markowitz assumed that the return on an investment was its expected average return, or mean return, in the future. He considered risk to be the fluctuation or variance of those future returns around the expected average return in the future. In fact, Markowitz was so wedded to the idea of risk as the fluctuation of price around a mean, he actually never used the word risk in his paper. He simply identified it using the statistical term, "variance." This identification of return with the mean or average of returns, and risk with the variance of the returns, which is so familiar to investors today, was a brand new concept when his paper was published. Using variance as a definition of risk allowed Markowitz to use the mathematics of algebra and statistics for the study of portfolio selection. In statistics, variance is equal to the square of standard deviation, and standard deviation had been identified as a measure of risk way back in 1730 when Abraham de Moivre suggested the structure of the normal distribution—also known as the bell curve—and subsequently discovered standard deviation. The idea that price distributions are symmetrical and that the random nature of portfolio gains and losses are best measured by standard deviation has deep roots in the history of finance, and Markowitz incorporated these ideas about risk in his paper.

According to Peter Bernstein, in his discussion about Markowitz in his book, *Against The Gods: The Remarkable Story of Risk*, the most important insight that Markowitz gave us is the concept of diversification:

The mathematics of diversification helps to explain its attraction. While the return on a diversified portfolio will be equal to the average of the rate of return on its individual holdings, its volatility will be less than the average volatility of its individual holdings. This means that diversification is a kind of free lunch at which you can combine a group of risky securities with high-expected returns into a relatively low-risk portfolio so long as you minimize the covariances, or correlations, among the returns of the individual securities.

In other words, if the prices of the securities in the portfolio tend to zig and zag at different times in response to changing expectations of investors, the overall portfolio volatility will be less than the total average volatility of the individual securities in the portfolio. The object is to minimize the amount that the securities zig and zag together. If Security A tends to rise in a particular economic environment and Security B tends to fall in the same environment, the net result is a portfolio that has total volatility which is less volatile than the average of the volatility of securities A and B. By continuing to add securities, or asset classes, that have low correlations to each other but that each earn high average returns, investors can build an efficient portfolio, with the best trade-off of mean (return) for each amount of variance (risk). The concept of diversification is so ubiquitous to professional investors today that it is difficult to imagine how revolutionary this idea was in the 1950's.

The process that Markowitz gave us for building efficient portfolios is called mean-variance optimization, and today virtually anyone can optimize a portfolio with optimization software available at a reasonable price, or they can find an optimizer on the Internet for free. The programs typically come preloaded with the historic mean returns, standard deviations, and cross correlations for about 20 to 30 asset classes. With a click of a mouse, the software will determine the efficient frontier of possible portfolios based on the asset classes that the investor chooses to optimize. As Bernstein describes it:

> By substituting a statistical stand-in for crude intuitions about uncertainty, Markowitz transformed traditional stock picking into a procedure for selecting what he termed "efficient" portfolios. Efficiency, a term adopted from engineering by economists and statisticians, means maximizing output relative to input, or minimizing input relative to output. Efficient portfolios minimize that "undesirable thing" called variance while simultaneously maximizing that "desirable thing" called getting rich." "Markowitz reserved the term "efficient" for portfolios that combine the best holdings at the

price with the least of the variance—optimization is the technical word. The approach combines two clichés that investors learn early in the game: nothing ventured, nothing gained, but don't put all your eggs in one basket.

The result of the optimization process is a line that represents all of the possible efficient portfolios that can be built from the asset classes selected for analysis. The line is plotted on a graph where the vertical Y-axis represents return and the horizontal X-axis represents risk. Today's investors can click their mouse at any point along the efficient frontier generated by their means-variance software, and the program will show them the optimized portfolio that has either the lowest risk for a given level of return, or the highest return for a given level of risk.

**Figures 3.1** and **3.2** illustrate the concept of the efficient frontier. **Figure 3.1** shows four different portfolios along the efficient frontier where risk is measured on the horizontal axis and return is measured on the vertical axis. **Figure 3.2** shows the four associated stylized portfolio constructions along the efficient frontier, where the allocation to U.S. stocks increases along with targeted return and expected volatility.

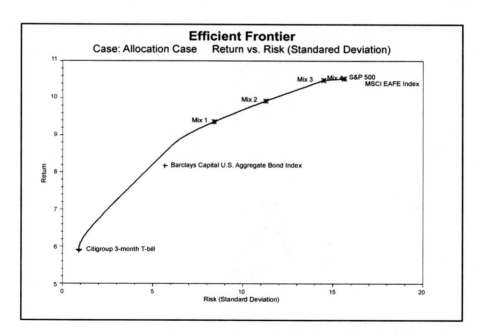

### Figure 3.1—Efficient Frontier

**Figure 3.2**

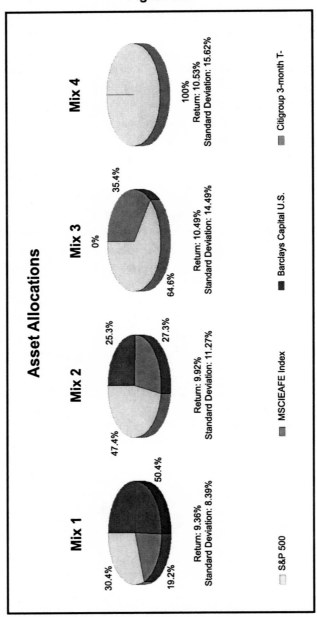

The output of the program in **Figure 3.2** yields instantly recognizable portfolios where the asset allocation for "moderate risk" portfolios targeted to earn 10% to 11% per year is approximately 50% to 70% in stocks and 30% to 50% in fixed income. In this example Mix 2 owns a somewhat growth tilted portfolio of 47.4% S&P 500 Index and 27.3% MSCI EAFE Index, a total of 74.7% in stocks. In this case the investor also owns 25.3% in Barclays Capital US Aggregate Bond Index. Lower return targets get smaller allocations to stocks and higher return targets get larger allocations to stocks. These allocations, regardless of what optimization program you use, have stayed roughly the same for decades because every program runs the same algorithms with roughly the same historical data. This method of portfolio construction is the only one taught to industry professionals, so naturally many investors have been indoctrinated into this world of Modern Portfolio Theory and efficient frontiers of portfolios based on means-variance optimization. It is truly a testimony to the genius of Markowitz that MPT is still the bible of the investment management business after more than half a century.

The next important step in the development of the contemporary money management industry came when a brilliant graduate student named William Sharpe attempted to simplify Markowitz's portfolio process, and ended up changing the fundamental mission of financial planners and investment professionals.

## William Sharpe and the Capital Asset Pricing Model

Markowitz gave the financial world the concept of maximizing portfolio reward and minimizing risk in the most efficient manner, and quantified the benefits of portfolio diversification. His work set the stage for William Sharpe, who provided a new and equally important set of mathematical tools for portfolio construction. In the years following the publication of Sharpe's Capital Asset Pricing Model (CAPM), investors began to not only build diversified, efficient portfolios according to Markowitz and Modern Portfolio Theory, they also became focused on a new idea, whether or not active fund managers could beat the expected return of the market portfolio.

Sharpe gave investors the first workable model for forecasting portfolio returns based on the systematic risk of the portfolio. Ultimately his work, and the work of two other academics, John V. Lintner, Jr. of Harvard Business School (1965) and Fischer S. Black, University of Chicago (1972), set the academic community on a seemingly never-ending quest to prove or disprove the Efficient Market Hypothesis by comparing the returns of active fund managers to the returns predicted by Sharpe's CAPM. In 1990, Sharpe received the Nobel Prize, along with Markowitz and Merton Miller. Forty years and hundreds of studies after its introduction, academics are still debating the usefulness of Sharpe's theory.

To understand this better, it helps to dig a little deeper into why Sharpe proposed CAPM in the first place, and what it can and cannot do.

Sharpe introduced himself to Markowitz while Markowitz was working for the Rand Corporation. Sharpe was looking for a good thesis for his Ph.D. and Markowitz suggested that a good topic would be to simplify his Modern Portfolio Theory (MPT) model. The problem with MPT was that in order to arrive at the correct answer for the model you had to complete a large number of calculations. For a small portfolio of stocks, determining the average returns, average volatility, and the average amount that the securities varied with each other could take a few hundred calculations. But to calculate the same data for all of the stocks on the stock exchange required millions of calculations. Before the invention of the personal computer, this was an impossible task.

In 1964 Sharpe published "Capital Asset Prices: A Theory of Market Equilibrium Under Conditions of Risk," in the *Journal of Finance*. His paper offered an elegant solution to Markowitz's problem and then went on to explain how to model expected returns for managed portfolios. Sharpe's solution to simplifying the math necessary to calculate Markowitz's' efficient portfolio was to imagine that every investor invested according to the rules of MPT. As Mandelbrot states in *The (mis)Behavior of Markets*:

> What happens if everybody in the market plays by Markowitz's rules? The answer was surprising. There would not be as many efficient portfolios as people in the market, but just one for all. If fluctuations in stock prices suggested a second, better investment palette, then everybody would start moving their money into that new portfolio and abandoning the first. Soon, there would again be just one portfolio, the "market portfolio." The market itself was doing the Markowitz calculations. It was the most powerful computer of all, producing tick-by-tick the optimum investment fund. Thus was born the notion of a stock-index fund: a big pool of money, from thousands of investors, holding shares in exactly the same proportion as the market overall.

Sharpe posited that in Markowitz's world of efficient portfolios, a certain type of risk, called non-systematic risk, could be diversified away by owning the market portfolio. We tend to think of non-systematic risk as the business risk or financial risk associated with an individual security. In Sharpe's model, investors are not compensated for taking non-systematic risk because it can be diversified away.

However, investors who take risk that cannot be diversified away by owning the market portfolio expect to be compensated for doing so. Systematic risk is the risk inherent in owning the market as a whole. Every security has some element of market risk as well as non-systematic risk or the risk associated with the individual security. Sharpe developed a measure of the amount of systematic risk in an investor's portfolio by comparing the volatility of a security to the volatility of the market portfolio.

The measure for this relative volatility is called beta. The performance of a security (or a portfolio) with a beta of 1 is exactly the same as the market portfolio. If the S&P 500 Index were used as a proxy for the stock market, then a 10% change in price for the index would result in a 10% change in price for the security. But if the security has a beta of 0.9, then a 10% change in the market portfolio would only equal a 9% change in the security value. Similarly, a security with a beta of 1.1 would return 11% versus the market return of 10%. With the invention of beta, investors could measure the risk of individual securities, and just as importantly, the risk of their portfolio, *relative* to the risk of the market. Investors who accept a beta greater than 1 in their portfolio expect to be rewarded with returns greater than the market portfolio.

Sharpe imagined a portfolio with a beta of zero to have no volatility and no risk, and the return of a zero beta portfolio was called the risk-free rate of return. Today the risk-free rate of return is usually considered to be the return of 90-day Treasury Bills. He then imagined the market portfolio to deliver returns in excess of the risk-free rate. This excess return is known as the equity-risk premium. Armed with a series of historical data that included beta, the risk-free rate of return, and the equity-risk premium, Sharpe could now calculate the future expected return of a security or a portfolio based on the security's beta. His formula states that a portfolio's excess expected return over the risk-free rate equals its beta times the market's expected excess return over the risk-free rate (or stated differently, the market's beta multiplied by the investment risk premium). The resulting pricing model is known as the Capital Asset Pricing Model (CAPM). The CAPM implies that returns for all risky assets are a linear function of only one factor, which is the relative risk of the security to the market portfolio. Sharpe's measure of relative risk, beta, is now accepted by the industry as the standard measure of portfolio or security risk.

**Figure 3.3**[14] shows the point where the market portfolio lies on what Sharpe calls the Security Market Line. The market portfolio has a beta of 1. As the amount of beta in the portfolio is reduced the expected return decreases until it is ultimately reduced to the risk-free rate of return, shown as the intercept of the security market line with the vertical Y-axis.

14  *Understanding Risk and Return, the CAPM, and the Fama-French Three-Factor Model,* Tuck
    Business School, Kent Womack and Ying Zhang, 2003. Case 03-111

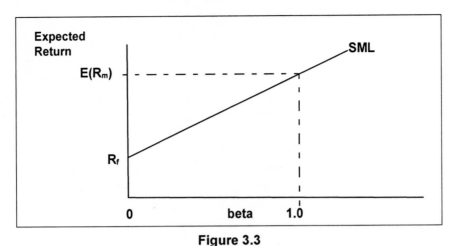

**Figure 3.3**
Source: Tuck Business School

In addition to being a useful tool for predicting the expected return of an asset in the future, by manipulating the mathematical equations the CAPM model can also be used to evaluate the performance of active fund managers relative to the market portfolio. More accurately, CAPM allows investors to determine whether the returns of an actively managed portfolio exceed the returns that should be expected given the risk taken by the fund manager. CAPM states that fund managers can increase the expected return of a given fund by investing in positions that embody greater systematic risk. In effect, by accepting more volatility, the manager can increase the beta (and thus the portfolio risk) of a fund and thereby increase the expected returns.

While some investors may choose to accept greater risk to increase expected returns, real value comes from a fund manager who is able to deliver higher returns for the same level of risk. The term for the excess return earned by an active fund manager, over and above the expected return for the market for a given level of risk, is called alpha. A positive alpha gives investors confidence that a fund manager is adding value to fund performance and is justifying his or her management fees.

Analysts can perform a regression analysis for a managed portfolio that best represents the portfolio's past returns. A regression line represents the one line that best "fits" many points on a graph. **Figure 3.4** shows the data points that represent the fund returns plotted on a graph where the vertical Y-axis represents excess asset or portfolio returns, the horizontal X-axis represents excess market returns, and the slope of the line represents beta. Alpha is the point where the regression line intercepts the Y-axis. Given enough data about the past performance of a fund manager, analysts now had a tool to determine whether or not the manager was adding value compared to the broad market.

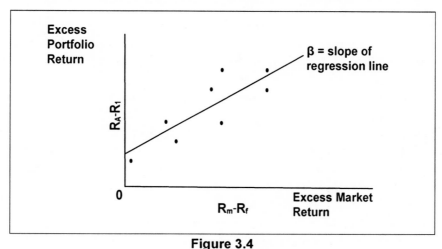

**Figure 3.4**

Source: Tuck Business School

Viewed another way, alpha is the amount that a managed portfolio sits above the security market line, which predicts the returns for a portfolio for any given amount of volatility or beta. **Figure 3.5** once again manipulates the CAPM equation so that the horizontal axis is beta, the vertical axis is expected return, and the slope of the line is the security market line, or the difference in risk and return between the risk-free rate and the market portfolio. In this example the managed portfolio is earning higher returns with the same volatility that is predicted by the CAPM model, so the manager is earning positive alpha.

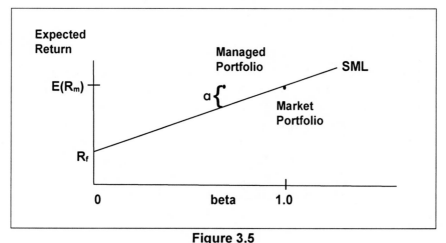

**Figure 3.5**

Source: Tuck Business School

Today the statistical terms used in CAPM form the essential language of modern finance and traditional money management. Investors compare the betas of individual securities and managed portfolios without a second thought. To generate portfolio alpha is the holy grail of every investment manager. Remarkably, the idea that returns for all risky assets are a function of only one factor, which is the relative risk of the asset to the market portfolio, stood without serious challenge for decades.

Perhaps most importantly, the results of Sharpe's CAPM model set the academic community on a 40-year quest to prove or disprove the Efficient Markets Hypothesis, which was originally proposed by Eugene Fama in his doctoral thesis in 1965.[15] Fama famously described efficient markets as follows:

> An 'efficient' market is defined as a market where there are large numbers of rational, profit-maximizers actively competing, with each trying to predict future market values of individual securities, and where important current information is almost freely available to all participants. In an efficient market, competition among the many intelligent participants leads to a situation where, at any point in time, actual prices of individual securities already reflect the effects of information based both on events that have already occurred and on events which, as of now, the market expects to take place in the future. In other words, in an efficient market at any point in time the actual price of a security will be a good estimate of its intrinsic value.

Institutional portfolio construction now began to take on the form that we know today. Efficient portfolios were constructed using diversified asset classes based on the work of Markowitz, and Sharpe's CAPM model was used to determine whether or not the active fund managers who invested the various asset allocations in the portfolio were adding value over and above their expected returns. Since virtually all of the early studies suggested that they did not add value, the industry created the ability to own the market portfolio through a new product: market index mutual funds. These funds allowed investors to own the market portfolio, or a capitalization-weighted index of each asset class in the portfolio, without worrying about whether or not an active manager was generating positive alpha. Since the publication of CAPM, there has been a furious debate in the academic community and in the financial planning industry about whether active management can actually add value for investors. Bill Sharpe and

---

15   Eugene F. Fama, "Random Walks in Stock Market Prices," *Financial Analysts Journal,* September/ October 1965 (reprinted January-February 1995).

CAPM gave us the tools to compare the performance of active managers to the performance of passive indexes.

The next important players further refined the process of choosing portfolio managers. They suggested the idea that perhaps beta, or risk, wasn't the only factor to use when doing a regression analysis to explain fund manager returns. For a more accurate model to explain fund returns, we next turn our attention to Eugene F. Fama and Kenneth R. French and the Three Factor Model.

## Fama-French and the Three Factor Model

Twenty-five years after the publication of CAPM, it became increasingly obvious that factors other than beta might be at work in determining portfolio returns. There were several "anomalies" in market returns that CAPM could not explain.[16] Several academic papers indicated that something other than beta was at work in influencing stock prices. These studies showed that beta was lower than it should be for factors that seemed to be associated with high returns. Remember that the fundamental assumption in CAPM is that low beta should lead to lower returns, not higher returns. In these studies, the opposite was being observed: low betas were in fact associated with higher returns. Beta didn't seem to adequately explain empirical observations of actual market performance.

The definitive study on the problem was conducted by Eugene Fama and Kenneth French and published in the *Journal of Finance* in 1992. This was the same Eugene Fama who became famous in the 1970's for his views on market dynamics that he called The Efficient Markets Hypothesis. Fama believed that published prices contain all of the information about a particular stock price, and represent all of the market's wisdom regarding what the stock's likely return would be in the future. According to the Efficient Markets Hypothesis, investors were unlikely to obtain information about an individual security that would allow them to earn excess returns over the market. The theory said that even if investors did have information that would allow them to outperform, the market would quickly discount that information and arbitrage away any opportunities for excess returns. However, according to Sharpe's CAPM, none of the factors impacting market prices that were being studied by academics, including market-capitalization, price-to-book value, leverage or debt to equity, or price-to-earnings ratios, should have any impact on prices. In fact, as we have

---

16  In Fama's paper he specifically mentions that prior studies on market capitalization (Banz 1981), leverage (Bhandari, 1988), book–to–market value (Stattman (1980) Rosenberg, Reid, and Lanstein (1985)), and earnings-to-price ratios (Basu 1983) all indicated that CAPM was inaccurate.

already seen, since 1964 the assumption was that the only factor that should explain returns was beta.

Fama and French devised an ingenious methodology for testing these anomalies. They began by analyzing all of the 2,000+ stocks that were listed at the time on the NYSE, AMEX, and NASDAQ indexes from 1962 to 1989. Price data was available to them from the Center for Research in Security Prices (CSRP) and income statement and balance sheet information was available from the COMPUSTAT annual industrial files. Next they grouped all of the stocks into different portfolios ranked by size and other characteristics depending on which factor they were testing. After sorting and grouping the returns data, they conducted a series of regression experiments to determine which factors had the highest relationship to subsequent one-year returns during the period.

Their results were shocking. Fama and French described them as a *"shot to the heart of the Sharpe-Lintner-Black (CAPM) model."* First they found that the market capitalization of the companies in the study was more important than beta in modeling returns. In fact, they found that beta had no explanatory power at all.

> The proper inference seems to be that there is a relation between size and average return, but controlling for size, there is no relation between beta and average return. The regressions show that when one allows for variation in beta that is unrelated to size, the relation between beta and average return is flat, even when beta is the only explanatory variable.

Next they turned their attention to the other anomalies under consideration, namely book-to-market, P/E ratios, and leverage. Their results were equally startling. They found that all of these factors were more predictive of future price changes than beta, but they also found that book-to-value was a more important factor than either leverage or P/E.

> We show that there is also a strong cross-sectional relation between average returns and book-to-market equity. If anything, this book-to-market effect is more powerful than the size effect. We also find that the combination of size and book-to-market equity absorbs the apparent roles of leverage and E/P in average stock returns.

Critics of the Efficient Markets Hypothesis had a field day. The fact that small-cap, value-tilted portfolios consistently achieved higher returns in the study seemed to disprove Fama's ideas about efficient markets. In fact, the academic community is still hotly debating why these factors have such an impact on returns, and there seems to be no sign that either the EMH theorists or their critics are about to give in anytime soon.

As a result of this groundbreaking work, investors now had scientific "proof" that the most important factors in generating portfolio returns were the size (market capitalization) of the stocks in the portfolios they owned, and the price-to-book value (value characteristics) of the stocks in their portfolio. Including beta with these two factors, the model became known as The Three Factor Model. Investors started to think about fund managers in terms of their investment style. Were they large-cap or small-cap managers? Were they value managers or growth managers? In many ways, Fama and French laid the groundwork for evaluating manager style using the well-known Morningstar Style Boxes[17], where mutual funds are divided into a 9-factor grid based on the size and value characteristics of managed funds. Fund managers found it easier to raise money from institutional investors if they clearly invested in only one investment style. A fund manager guilty of "style drift" was likely to be fired by the institutional investors who were responsible for the overall asset allocation of the portfolio. In addition, by demanding that fund managers stick to one investment style, as defined by the style boxes, performance comparisons could be done on an "apples to apples" basis. Today the methodology of grouping managed funds by investment style is fundamental to how most institutional money is managed.

## An Industry Frozen In Time

MPT, CAPM and the Three Factor Model remain the foundation for much of the status quo thinking about the best way to construct institutional quality portfolios. The practical application of these studies is strategic, buy and hold investing. The idea of building diversified, multi-asset class portfolios populated by active managers that are constrained to manage style-specific portfolios is so strongly ingrained in the popular investment culture that there seems to be little room for discussion or criticism of the theory or its application. However, the failure of the status quo to deliver expected returns and the resulting pain for retirees and other investors who are failing to meet their investment objectives is changing the climate for debate. In the next several chapters we will discuss many of the problems and criticisms with buy and hold, strategic investing, and

---

17  Readers can learn about Morningstar Style boxes at Morningstar.com. A specific PDF regarding the Morningstar Style Box methodology can be found at: *Fact Sheet, The New Morningstar Style Box Methodology*, news.Morningstar.com/pdfs/FactSheet_StyleBox_Final.pdf

give some insights into new investment theories that do a much better job of describing the practical realities of the investment landscape that we must deal with today.

# 4    HOGS, COBWEBS, AND OTHER IMPERFECT ASSUMPTIONS

---

To become a Certified Financial Planner® practitioner or a Chartered Financial Analyst®, investors must memorize the formulas and learn the language of statistics and finance that form the foundation of Modern Portfolio Theory and that give validity to the practice of strategic asset allocation. The fundamental concepts of MPT and CAPM are taught as though Harry Markowitz and William Sharpe descended from a mountaintop with sacred texts about how to properly manage risk and build portfolios. There is little in the curriculum that puts any of Markowitz and Sharpe's work in historical perspective, or highlights the ongoing academic debate about MPT and CAPM. To fully understand the criticisms of the theory, and in order to make the case for active portfolio management, we must first understand the problems with the assumptions that are the foundation of MPT and the Efficient Markets Hypothesis.

Markowitz's genius was to brilliantly use the mathematical tools of risk and probability to build portfolio models. He did this by drawing on the ideas of many remarkable thinkers that came before him. For those who wish to learn about the innovators who built the foundation for Markowitz and Sharpe, I recommend the seminal book by Peter Bernstein, *Against the Gods, the Remarkable Story of Risk*. In his discussion of Markowitz's famous paper called "Portfolio Selection," Bernstein points out that the paper contained dense amounts of mathematics but lacked footnotes and bibliography. In fact, he notes that Markowitz only makes three references to other writers in his Nobel Prize–winning paper:

This failure to credit his intellectual forebears is curious: Markowitz's methodology is a synthesis of the ideas of Pascal, de Moivre, Bayes, Laplace, Gauss, Galton, Daniel Bernoulli, Jevons, and von Neumann and Morgenstern. It draws on probability theory, on sampling, on the bell curve and the dispersion around the mean, on regression to the mean, and on utility theory. Markowitz has told me that he knew all these ideas but was not familiar with their authors, though he had invested a good deal of time studying von Neumann and Morgenstern's book on economic behavior and utility.

Clearly Modern Portfolio Theory is built on the discoveries and assumptions of others about the nature of risk, the nature of human behavior, and the workings of the economy.

## Assumptions and Economics

In a paper called "The History of Finance: An eyewitness account," published in *The Journal of Portfolio Management* in 1999[18], Nobel Laureate Merton Miller described how in the United States the huge body of academic research in finance falls into either the business school approach to finance or the economics department approach. In the U.S., the huge majority of academics in finance teach in business schools and not in economics departments. At the same time, in the elite schools, a substantial number of the finance faculty have been trained and received their Ph.D.'s from the economics departments. This is relevant because, as Miller puts it, "Habits of thought acquired in graduate school tend to stay with you."

Many of the important assumptions in finance, and hence the important assumptions of Modern Portfolio Theory, the Efficient Markets Hypothesis, and the Capital Asset Pricing Model have their roots in the history of economics, long before Markowitz published his paper in 1952. As we will see, the "science" of economics and finance is very different from the physical sciences in terms of how economists treat the basic assumptions for economic and financial models. Critics believe that in the case of MPT and the other traditional finance models, the problems with the assumptions are so great that the theory that underlies the models cannot withstand the test of scientific rigor.

Although Miller and others credit Markowitz as being the father of modern finance (Miller goes so far as to call him the "Big Bang" of the profession), I agree with many others who consider Louis Bachelier to be the true forefather of modern finance. His major work on the subject was published in the early 1900's and

---

18    The paper was actually a modified version of an address delivered at the Fifth Annual Meeting of the German Finance Association in Hamburg on September 25, 1998.

was not rediscovered until the 1950's by MIT professor Paul Samuelson, and the assumptions in his work are still used by strategic asset allocators today.[19]

Bachelier was an expert at trading bonds (called rents) and options on rents in the French financial markets in the late 1890's. Bachelier's Ph.D. thesis, *Theorie de la Speculation*, presented in 1900, was an attempt to mathematically predict the direction of option prices. To do so, Bachelier applied the mathematics and physics of his time to create a remarkably prescient model to estimate the probable direction of price movements. He made two important assumptions about the behavior of security prices in his model that are still used in modern portfolio theory.

Bachelier's first assumption was that the movement of securities prices was like tossing a coin. In a fair game the distribution of heads and tails would be the same, and the nature of the distribution could be measured by a bell curve. By the early 1900's, the mathematics of measuring probability as a normal distribution had been firmly established. As early as 1733, in his treatise called *The Doctrine of Chance*, Abraham de Moivre, (1667-1754) studied numerous problems about throwing dice and drawing balls of different colors from a bag, as well as questions relating to life annuities. He is credited as being the first to analyze normal distributions. The scientist who is given the most credit for the mathematics of normal distributions is Friedrich Gauss (1777-1855). Gauss was one of the most brilliant mathematicians and astronomers of his day, and used normal distributions as a methodology for predicting the orbits of planets. Today we call normal distributions Gaussian distributions. Most of us who struggled through basic statistics remember that the middle of the bell curve represents the average measurement for a series of observations, and the side tails of the curve depict the amount that the series of observations vary from the mean. In terms of mathematics, the bell curve gives us mean and variance as measures of risk. In using the assumption of a normal distribution and the bell curve in his model, Bachelier introduced mean and variance to the still unborn discipline of modern finance.

The second assumption that Bachelier borrowed from 19th century physical science is a method to predict the motion of price movements, called Brownian motion. As Mandelbrot describes it,

Nearly a century before, the great French mathematician Jean Baptiste Joseph Fourier had devised equations to describe the way heat spreads. Bachelier knew the formulae well from his physics lectures. He adapted them to calculate the probability of bond prices moving up or down,

---

19   For an excellent account of Bachelier and his work I recommend Benoit Mandelbrot's book, *The (mis) Behavior of Markets*, in which the author devotes an entire chapter to this important historical figure in finance and economics.

and called the technique "radiation of probability." Strangely, it worked. Also, as fate would have it, very different motivations had sent other scientists on this trail. Long before, the invention of the microscope led to observations of the erratic way that tiny pollen grains jiggled about in a sample of water. A Scottish botanist, Robert Brown, studied this motion, observed that it is not a manifestation of life but a physical phenomenon, and received (possibly inflated) credit for the discovery through the term "Brownian motion.

The idea that the distribution of price movements can be measured the same way as a fair toss of a coin is central to the methodology of contemporary pricing models, as is the notion that prices move with a constant drift and volatility like grains of pollen dropped into a sample of water. Today's critics argue that the true nature of the randomness of price movements does not fit the bell curve, and that empirical observation leads us to conclude that the "tails" of a bell curve are not fat enough. I recommend Nassim Taleb's books, *Fooled By Randomness* and *The Black Swan*, as well as Mandelbrot's book *The (mis)Behavior of Markets*, for anyone interested in better understanding the problems with normal distributions. Both authors argue that financial risk is exponentially more "wild" than a normal distribution might suggest that it is—meaning that the financial world is far riskier than a standard bell curve would suggest. Mandelbrot explains that risk should be measured using fractal mathematics, and that the problem with normal distributions is that they are not scalable, meaning that normal distributions severely underestimate the probability of unlikely events. Normal distributions work well to measure randomness in nature, but fractals work much better to measure the risk of financial markets.

Today the industry routinely discusses "Black Swan" events, which Taleb describes as an occurrence that lies outside the realm of regular expectations, has extreme impact, and can only be explained *after the fact*. These events shouldn't occur if investment risks are properly measured by normal distributions, but in fact today's investors are almost routinely experiencing market volatility that is virtually impossible to explain under the current theory. For now, it is enough to recognize that the basic assumption of normal distributions in MPT is considered controversial.

In addition, the idea of constant drift and volatility in price movements that are mathematically modeled as Brownian motion is also under attack by contemporary researchers. The geometric Brownian motion assumption implies that the volatility of a stock will stay the same through time. Today it is acknowledged that price movements are subject to momentum and that price volatility tends to bunch up at certain times and not at others. Once again, contemporary researchers take issue with Bachelier, and by extension, with the assumptions underlying Modern Portfolio Theory.

Beyond the difficulties with the assumptions of normal distribution and Brownian motion, there are many other problematic assumptions that are integral to the MPT and CAPM model, including:

- There are no transaction costs in buying and selling securities. There are no brokerage fees, no spreads, and no taxes of any kind. (False)
- An investor can take a position in any security he wishes of any size without moving the market. Liquidity is infinite. (False)
- Investors are indifferent to the tax consequences of investing and don't care about dividends and capital gains. (True for institutional investors of pensions and foundations, but not for most individual investors)
- Investors are rational and risk-averse. (False—completely disproved in behavioral finance)
- Investors, as a group, have the same investment time horizon. A short-term speculator and a long-term investor have the exact same motivation to invest. (False)
- Investors all measure risk the same way. All investors have the same information and will buy or sell based on an identical assessment of the investment and all expect the same thing from the investment. (False)
- Investors seek to control risk only by the diversification of their holdings. (True for proponents of MPT and strategic asset allocation but not true for tactical asset allocators, actively managed fund managers, hedge fund managers, and any other proponents of active management.)
- Investors can lend or borrow at the risk-free rate, and can also sell short without restriction. (False)
- Politics and investor psychology have no effect on the market. (False; see studies on price momentum and the herd behavior of investors.)

## Do Incorrect Assumptions Matter?

How can academics in finance, and the practitioners of Modern Portfolio Theory, accept a theory based on so many assumptions that, at the very least are controversial, and in most cases have been disproved by a variety of academic studies? For the answer, it is important to understand how some economists use assumptions in their economic models.

Eric Beinhocker's book, *The Origin of Wealth*, offers a unique perspective into the history of economic theory. Beinhocker provides insights into the economists who built the foundations on which traditional economic theory has been built and then explains what he calls Complexity Economics. Complexity economics, the latest in economic theory, acknowledges that the economy is a super-complex system that is not easily modeled using simplifying assumptions. Beinhocker has much to say about how unrealistic assumptions are used in economic theory. Economists seem to be unique in that, unlike most physical scientists, they conclude that unrealistic assumptions do not matter as long as the resulting economic theories create accurate predictions.

The modern notion that unrealistic assumptions don't matter in economics can be credited to the University of Chicago's Milton Friedman. In 1953 he published a highly controversial essay titled, "The Methodology of Positive Economics."[20] According to Beinhocker, "the essay argued that unrealistic assumptions in economic theory simply do not matter so long as the theories make correct predictions. If the economy behaves "as if" people were perfectly rational, then it really doesn't matter whether people are perfectly rational or not. Assumptions need no further justification as long as the results are correct. In other words, as long as there's no "garbage out," it doesn't matter if there's "garbage in."

In his speech to the German Finance Association, Merton Miller spoke about how Friedman's view permeated the world of finance:

> The realism or lack of realism of the assumptions underlying the Sharpe CAPM has never been a subject of serious debate within the profession, unlike the case of the Modigliani and Miller propositions to be considered later. The profession, from the outset, wholeheartedly adopted the Friedman positivist view: that what counts is not the literal accuracy of the assumptions, but the predictions of the model.

He goes on to further discuss the assumptions in the CAPM model:

> …the tendency of many at first was to dismiss the assumptions underlying M&M's then-novel arbitrage proof as unrealistic. The assumptions underlying the CAPM, of course, are equally or even more implausible, as noted earlier, but the profession seemed far more willing to accept Friedman's "the assumptions don't matter" position for the CAPM than for the M&M propositions.[21]

---

20 Milton Friedman, *Essays in Positive Economics, Part I, The Methodology of Positive Economics*, University of Chicago Press, 1953.

21 The M&M propositions refer to the work of Franco Modigliani and Merton Miller. The Modigliani- Miller Theorem is a Nobel Prize winning financial theory that states that the market value of a firm is determined by its earnings power and the risk of its underlying assets,

I presume that for most reasonable investors, the idea that accurate assumptions shouldn't matter in formulating economic theories seems as outrageous to them as it does to me. Beinhocker gives a simple example to make the point that underlying assumptions do matter very much in scientific theory. He suggests that one could offer a theory to explain that the sky is blue by assuming the existence of giants who paint the sky blue every night while we are sleeping. Taken to an extreme, Friedman's logic would say that the assumption of giants is irrelevant as long as the theory makes the correct prediction, that the sky is blue, which it does. However, Beinhocker points out that to accept such a theory, one would have to observe the giants in action. He quotes economic philosopher Daniel Haussman who says that one must look "under the hood" of a theory to see that the causal chain of explanation is valid as well.

It is worth noting that other branches of science seem quite bemused about the insistence of economists that there is validity to Friedman's positivist views. In Miller's speech before the German Finance Association, he relates a story that gives some insights into how other branches of science view financial assumptions:

> I still remember the teasing we financial economists, Harry Markowitz, William Sharpe, and I, had to put up with from the physicists and chemists in Stockholm when we conceded that the basic unit of our research, the expected rate of return, was not actually observable. I tried to parry by reminding them of their neutrino—a particle with no mass whose presence is inferred only as a missing residual from the interactions of other particles. But that was eight years ago. In the meantime, the neutrino has been detected.

Perhaps the best story about how other scientists feel about the use of poor assumptions in economic models comes from Beinhocker[22], who recalls a conference hosted by the Santa Fe Institute, a nonprofit research organization created to pursue the study of complex systems across different scientific disciplines. Some of the country's top economists met with top physicists, biologists, and computer scientists, to discuss a very complex system, the global economy. Both sides had the best experts in their field in attendance, including Nobel Prize winners and captains of industry. Each side presented the current state of its field and then spent ten days debating economic behavior, technological innovation, business cycles, and

---

and is independent of the way it chooses to finance its investments or distribute dividends. Readers interested in a further introduction to the Modigliani-Miller Theorem can read: http://en.wickopedia.org/wiki/Modigliani-Miller_theorem.

22   Eric Beinhocker, *The Origin of Wealth, Evolution, Complexity, and the Radical Remaking of Economics*, Harvard Business School Press, 2006, pages 46-48.

the working of capital markets. According to Beinhocker, the physical scientists were shocked at how the science of economics seemed like a throwback to another era. Economists appeared to be out of touch with several decades of intellectual progress. The physicists were equally surprised by the way the economists used simplifying assumptions to justify their models.

> One assumption that got the scientists particularly exercised was what economists refer to as perfect rationality. Traditional economics simplifies human behavior by assuming that people know everything possible about the future and crunch all that information through incredibly complex calculations to make such basic decisions as where to buy a pint of milk. Even without being fully aware of the long history of debate on this subject, the physical scientists vociferously objected to the use of a model so clearly at odds with day-to-day reality.

Science writer Mitch Waldrop quotes one of the economists, Brian Arthur, who describes the exchange.

> The physicists were shocked at the assumptions the economists were making—that the test was not a match against reality, but whether the assumptions were the common currency of the field. I can just see Phil Anderson (note: A Nobel Laureate from Princeton University), laid back with a smile on his face, saying, "You guys really believe that?" The economists backed into a corner would reply, "Yeah, but this allows us to solve these problems. If you don't make these assumptions, then you can't do anything." And the physicists would come right back, "Yeah, but where does that get you—you're solving the wrong problem if that's not reality."

Investors, who believe that asset classes are not always perfectly valued, and express that belief by actively managing the asset allocation of the portfolios they manage, can certainly understand the vexation of the physical scientists who attended the conference at the Santa Fe Institute. The inability of industry pundits to acknowledge the obvious problems with the assumptions that are used as the basis for strategic, buy and hold investing can be, to say the least, very frustrating.

For many investors, the idea of perfectly rational investors is attributed to Eugene Fama and his Efficient Markets Hypothesis. It is lumped in with Modern Portfolio Theory and the Capital Asset Pricing Model as one of the pillars of thought that support the house of modern finance. Perhaps many investors would be surprised to learn that although we credit Fama with the idea of Efficient Markets, the modern concept of applying perfect rationality to pricing models is to a large extent the result of the work of a little-known economist named John Muth. While few in the financial industry seem to know Muth and his work, it has indirectly resulted in a titanic shift in the way that today's investors approach portfolio construction.

It is one of those ironic twists in history that Muth was not at all interested in resolving the problems of modeling the capital markets. In fact, Robert Lucas won a Nobel Prize for the further application of Muth's work, which also had little to do with managing portfolios. Lucas's work used rational expectations to refute the Keynesian approach to macroeconomics. Investors who are interested in the history of the investment profession may be interested to know that one of the most important assumptions used in contemporary economics, and even more importantly for us, one of the most important assumptions needed for MPT, CAPM, and the Efficient Markets Hypothesis, is credited to a man whose Ph.D. thesis was about the study of hog prices.

## John Muth and Perfect Rationality

So far in this chapter we have discussed how finance is usually taught by professors who did their graduate work in economics departments, and we have seen that Nobel Prize–winning economist Milton Friedman's positivist view on the use of poor assumptions in economic theory is aptly demonstrated in MPT and CAPM. We have briefly reviewed the simplifying assumptions needed for the theory to work, and we have found that many of them are unrealistic and under serious academic attack. We paid special attention to the assumptions regarding normal distributions and Brownian motion. We learned that both assumptions are based on 19th century science, and that recent evidence suggests that both of these fundamental and important assumptions are also subject to considerable debate.

However, one of my favorite stories about the history of the assumptions that are so important to how we build our portfolios is the story of a little-known contemporary mathematical genius who didn't even think of himself as an economist. Since the physical scientists at the Santa Fe Institute seemed to have so much difficulty with the economic concept of perfect rationality, it seems fitting to end this chapter with the story of the man credited with inventing the rational expectation equilibrium pricing theory, John Muth. Compared to other giants in the field, there is relatively little in the popular literature about Muth. However, Ike Brannon published a beautiful memoriam about Muth called "Remembering the Man Behind Rational Expectations"[23], which gives us some wonderful insights into

---

23    Ike Brannon has worked as an economic adviser for Sen. Orrin Hatch, the Senate Finance
      Committee, the Department of the Treasury, John McCain, and others in Washington,
      D.C. His article, "Remembering The Man Behind Rational Expectations," was published in
      *Regulation*, Vol. 29, No. 1, pp. 18-22, Spring 2006.

the person who would later have so much influence over how most financial advisors construct portfolios.

Muth grew up in the Midwest and in 1952 he went to Carnegie Tech in Pittsburgh to study mathematical economics. At the time, some of the most important future Nobel Laureates in finance were on the faculty, including Herb Simon, Merton Miller, and Franco Modigliani. Future Nobel Prize winners Ed Prescott and Robert Lucas arrived later in Muth's tenure there. Muth quickly went from graduate student to professor before taking his Ph.D., and his doctoral thesis was on rational expectations. His paper, titled "Rational Expectations and the Theory of Price Movements," was published in *Econometrica* in 1961, and a companion piece was published in *The Journal of the American Statistical Association* at about the same time. The paper was little noted at the time and one of the referees fought against it being published at all. Muth left Carnegie Tech and abandoned his work on Rational Expectations, and eventually ended up teaching at Indiana University, where he pursued a variety of topics. He did important work in the field of operations management and spent much of the 1970's pondering artificial intelligence, another topic he abandoned before it became an important area of research. According to Brannon, Muth's work on non-convex cost curves generated interest from other economists as well.

Muth felt that when his article on Rational Expectations was published, he would be able to go anywhere he wanted. But when no publisher would publish a third article on the subject and his colleagues didn't muster a lot of enthusiasm for his ideas, he moved on to other pursuits. Brannon quotes Donald McCloskey's book, *The Rhetoric of Economics*, where McCloskey argued that Muth's paper wasn't popular for several very good reasons. First, he argued that the paper was poorly written and the writing was very dense. Second, the technical aspects of the paper were simply too far ahead of most readers of the day. While today's economics papers are full of sophisticated math, back in the 1960's Muth was one of the few economists comfortable with such a technical approach. Finally, Muth suffered from bad timing. While economics departments were consumed with macroeconomic issues like inflation, Muth was writing about an obscure microeconomic issue: the volatility of commodity prices, and specifically, hog prices. Muth apparently didn't think of himself as a true economist and scarcely thought about macroeconomic problems. When Muth did his research on rational expectations, no one was questioning the Keynesian macroeconomic model that was working so well at the time.

After Muth left Carnegie Tech he taught at Indiana University's Kelly School of Business for many years. Apparently his MBA students disliked him for his chaotic, research-oriented approach to his classes. According to Brannon, they once delivered a petition demanding his removal from the classroom. As the story goes, the administrator who received the petition from MBA students demanding Muth's removal ripped it up in front of the students. "All of you should be giving him your signing bonus for your first job for what he's done for this school's reputation," he admonished them. A friend of Brannon happened to be part of the petition delegation and asked what the dean was referring to. After Muth's contributions were explained to him, the friend asked plaintively, "Why on earth didn't they let us know about this?" Now that I know a bit about Muth, myself, I think we should all be asking the same question.

Brannon tells us that Muth apparently didn't mind the lack of recognition for his achievements. Eventually, the bulk of what came to be considered as mainstream "Keynesian" economics, with its emphasis on the need for government to play an active role in the economy, was jettisoned. (Of course we now live in a Keynesian world of government intervention in the economy that was unimaginable at the time.) Robert Lucas, the economist who popularized the idea of rational expectations, received the Nobel Prize for his efforts. Brannon writes:

> Despite the impact of Muth's idea, the honor and glory ultimately accorded by the profession for this titanic idea skipped by him with nary a nod in his direction. John Muth passed away on October 25, 2005, at the age of 75, and if the lack of honor and glory bothered him, he never let on. Muth, a shy and socially awkward man, would have found the attention and fuss that goes with a Nobel Prize pure torture.
> Rational Expectations and the Cobweb Model

If titanic new ideas are needed to resolve titanic problems, then what exactly was the titanic problem that Muth set out to solve? In a nutshell, the problem was with the cobweb model.

The cobweb model referred to a problem that economists had been trying for years to solve regarding how to model commodity prices that never seemed to reach equilibrium. As shown in the chart below, theoretically, low quantities of a commodity lead to higher prices, which encourage farmers to plant more crops, which in turn increase supply. The higher quantity leads to decreasing demand, which is met by falling prices. The low prices then lead to an increase in demand and the cycle starts over again. The see-saw fluctuation of rising and falling supply and demand and the resulting price volatility of commodities were difficult to model because the market theoretically never reached equilibrium.

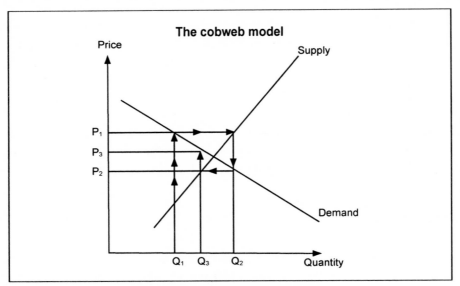

**Figure 4.1—The Cobweb Model**
Source: The Oil Drum

The graphing of this behavior appeared similar to a cobweb, hence the name, as seen in **Figure 4.1**.[24]

The classic paper on the cobweb theorem was published by Mordecai Ezekiel in 1938.[25] In that paper, Ezekiel pointed out that the basic idea of a cobweb model was implied by the work of several prior researchers in the 1920's. As early as 1917, an economist, Henry Moore, had demonstrated that the current price of cotton was determined by the size of the current crop; while the current crop was influenced by the previous year's crop.

American economist, Irving Fisher, is credited with first use of the error-learning hypothesis in the 1930's to explain the cobweb problem. During the 1950's, economists like Milton Friedman wrestled with the problem and expanded Fisher's ideas in a theory of pricing called the Adaptive Expectations pricing model, which assumes that changes in immediate past prices impact economic agents' predictions of immediate future prices. In this view, all economic forecasts are based

24  I found this image on Google on a site called, *The Oil Drum, Discussions about Energy and Our Future.* The posts were on the subject of "Predator-Prey Dynamics and Demand Destruction in Oil Prices. A post from drillo, August 2008, about the predator-prey economic model compared the oil market to the pork market, and hence the illustration of the Cobweb Model.

25  These references come from a paper I found online by Frederick Waugh, a research advisor in the Economic Research Service. You can find the paper at aem.cornell.edu/courses/415/articles/JOFA.Pdf. The other sources are Mordecai Ezekiel, *The Cobweb Theorem*, Quar. *J. Econ* Vol. 53, February, 1938, and Henry Moore, *Forecasting the Yield of Cotton*, Macmillan, NY, 1917.

on past price performance. Forecasters then use new price data to incrementally change forecasts of future price movements. In essence, it was assumed that economic agents could not and did not anticipate future price changes, but only extrapolated future prices from changes in past data. Another problem with the adaptive expectations model was that the math was cumbersome. The equations did not neatly fall into equilibrium.

Muth studied the cobweb price problem by analyzing the hog market. If the adaptive expectations theory was correct, then the hog market should have been rife with wild fluctuations in price and quantity as farmers reacted poorly to price changes. As Brannon put it, "If hog prices were low in a given year, people would react by not raising as many hogs the next year, pushing prices higher. Then, seeing the higher prices, farmers would raise a lot of hogs, pushing prices lower the following year. The idea was that farmers would never catch on to such a cycle because they were too busy looking only at the current prices."

Muth's theory of rational expectations said that the hog market was much more efficient than the cobweb model implied. If farmers consistently made such mistakes they would go out of business. In fact, he hypothesized that farmers look ahead and analyze the changes in the hog markets to determine what is likely to happen to hog prices in the future. As rational economic agents they then plan their supply of hogs in a way that mutes the price changes. Muth found little evidence of hog price volatility from year to year as if farmers irrationally only looked at current prices. In simple terms, in his Rational Expectations paper, Muth resolved the problem of farmers who couldn't anticipate future price changes by creating super-farmers that had perfect economic foresight and instantly knew what future prices would be. It turns out that Muth's super-farmers, who were capable of perfectly predicting future hog prices, are in many ways responsible for one of the most important notions of modern finance, which is that investors have perfect knowledge of future security prices. Sound familiar? We know this theory as the Efficient Markets Hypothesis.

At the time when Muth was publishing his paper on Rational Expectations, the economics profession was celebrating the works of John Maynard Keynes. In his *General Theory of Income and Employment*, published in 1936, Keynes introduced the concept that the neoclassical approach to economic rationality was wrong. Basically Keynes and his followers believed that government policies were necessary to keep the economy out of recessions. The ideas of using tax cuts and active monetary policy to stimulate spending were essentially Keynesian views that are still in vogue today. But as the 1970's progressed and the U.S. economy fell into a combination of high unemployment and high inflation at the same time, economists began to look for new ways that government policy could influence the economy. The answer came in the form of the Rational Expectations pricing model, but the author was not John Muth. It was, instead, a colleague of Muth's from his earlier days at Carnegie Tech, Robert Lucas.

Robert Lucas received his undergraduate and graduate degrees from the University of Chicago. He taught at Carnegie Tech from 1963 to 1974, overlapping some of the time that Muth was a teacher there, and then returned to the University of Chicago to become a professor in 1974. In the 1970's, along with Thomas Sargent, the David A. Rockefeller Professor in Economics and also an economist at the Hoover Institution at Stanford, Lucas applied Muth's concept of Rational Expectations to macroeconomic policy. The core aspect of Lucas's theory was that the expectations of economic agents play a large part in the success of government economic policy. Because economic agents anticipate the result of government policy, often the policies themselves are counterproductive.

Lucas's work was dramatic in its timing and importance, coming as it did just prior to and then during the great inflation of the 1970's. His papers suggested that economic policy had to deal with the inflation expectations of economic agents if the government was to be successful in taming the raging inflation of the 1970's. Today's central bankers recognize that inflation expectations are hugely important in the implementation of central bank policy, and it is widely recognized that an increase in inflation expectations must be met with dramatic policy action by the government and the central bank.

Commenting on Lucas's Nobel Prize in the *University of Chicago Chronicle* in 1995, Sherwin Rosen, a distinguished service professor of economics at the University said of Lucas and Rational Expectations:

> Conventional macroeconomists only thought about what was happening at the current time, and not what effect macroeconomic policies might have on the future. Lucas' model of rational expectations says that if citizens anticipate the reactions of policy-makers in the future, then they are going to change their behavior now in a way that could make those policies less effective—or completely nullify a policy's effect.
>
> The effect of his work is to really change the way economists think about macroeconomics. It kind of destroyed the Keynesian model. This really took a lot of the thunder out of the Keynesian way of thinking.

Rational Expectations became a sensation in the economics community and the reappearance of the idea of economic rationality was expressed in a new school of economic thought called New Classical Economics. Lucas was awarded the Nobel Prize for Rational Expectations in 1995. Apparently there was little controversy about whether Lucas deserved the acclaim more than Muth. As the Nobel committee stated when they made the award to Lucas:

John Muth (1961) was the first to formulate the rational expectations hypothesis in a precise way. He used it in a study of the classic cobweb phenomenon. Muth's analysis was restricted to a single market in partial equilibrium. The importance of the rational expectations hypothesis became apparent when Lucas extended the hypothesis to macroeconomic models and to the analysis of economic policy.

## Summary

The story of Muth and hog prices should resonate with investors for several reasons. One lesson from the story is that economists are human and their theories are often interpreted differently within the economics profession. It is important to understand that the heated debate between Keynesian and non-Keynesian schools of economic thought has been going on since the 1930's with no signs of slowing down anytime soon. Clearly the academic profession does not turn professors into deities that cannot be questioned. The lesson for investors is that they need to be more skeptical of the buy and hold approach to portfolio construction that has been presented to them as unassailable and above debate. If finance theory is tied to traditional economic theory, then investors deserve to be skeptical, if for no other reason than some economists have a remarkably unusual approach to the assumptions that go into economic models. For example, I love the fact that the cherished notions of efficient markets and rational investors, that are so necessary to justify the use of strategic asset allocation and buy and hold investing, are at least partially based on a study of hog prices and cobweb models. Who knew?

Now that we have analyzed some of the problems with the assumptions behind the most cherished theories of modern finance, it is time to meet two men who have provided some very powerful academic justification for a new way of thinking: Professor Mordecai Kurz and H. "Woody" Brock, Ph.D.

# 5 THE THEORETICAL CASE FOR ACTIVE PORTFOLIO MANAGEMENT

I f someone hadn't invented Modern Portfolio Theory and the Efficient Markets Hypothesis, upon which the strategic or passive approach to portfolio management has been based for half a century, what other theory might have taken its place to govern the construction of contemporary portfolios?

If we were to come up with a new rational approach for building successful portfolios, surely our new theory would not rely on the existence of investors who had perfect knowledge of future securities prices. It's hard to believe anyone would seriously suggest that even though none of us, individually, knows the future, if we put millions of us together, we can magically discern what future prices will be. It's true that we can see market prices adjust to the latest news with incredible speed on our Bloomberg machines and on CNBC, but in this day and age where market bubbles appear and pop at a frightening pace, does anyone really believe that investors know the exact "correct price" for securities as we watch prices change throughout the day? Perhaps, from a statistical point of view, we could justify our transformation from one uncertain investor into a large market of perfectly prescient investors by applying the Law of Large Numbers, which says that if you flip a fair coin ten times, even though there is a 50% probability of heads for each flip, it is still possible to get 10 tails in a row. It is unlikely, but certainly possible. But flipping the coin many thousands of times yields very close to 50% heads and 50% tails. As the number of coin tosses increases, so does the likelihood of getting to the true probability of 50/50. So in our zeal to provide a mathematical proof for our model of investor behavior, we could twist this concept to mean that one investor doesn't know the future, but large numbers of investors know the true probability law for future market prices. In designing our new theory for building portfolios, we might be able to sell the idea that market prices are the same as coin tosses—except for the small problem that they are not. The truth is that we have no rational reason to assume that if one investor does not know the future, then a football field full of uncertain investors will somehow become brilliant future-tellers.

Maybe, our new theory of portfolio construction should be based on the idea that investors themselves have nothing to do with the movement of prices. If that were the case, there would be no such thing as price momentum and no need to worry about investor psychology. And we'd have no need for Charles Mackay's amazing book *Extraordinary Popular Delusions and the Madness of Crowds*[26], originally published in 1841, which details several financial panics throughout history, all caused by the herd behavior of investors. We could just ignore financial manias and panics because our theory would say that crowd behavior has nothing to do with the markets, other than being a perfect pricing mechanism that instantly knows what future prices should be based on perfect analysis of the news. The only problem with this is that there is an overwhelming amount of empirical evidence that investor psychology has much to do with changing market prices.

In creating our new theory for successful portfolio management, would we choose to assert the idea that there is no such thing as structural change in the economy, therefore leading to the assumption that the average price changes of the past would always repeat in the future? We might run into a little difficulty selling people on the idea that the end of the Cold War, the birth of the baby boomers, and the rise of the BRIC countries (Brazil, Russia, India, and China) all had no impact on security prices.

I suppose that if some brilliant mathematicians were able to cobble together all of these fatally flawed ideas into a mathematical model that could be "proved" by other mathematicians, then our new theory might gain some traction in the academic community. You would think that such a model would be subject to the closest scrutiny by investors and academics alike, because the underlying assumptions are so outrageous that any empirical evidence that didn't support the theory would render it useless. But sophisticated and complex mathematical models tend to be very persuasive to the uninformed, regardless of the validity of the underlying assumptions in the model or the empirical evidence of the markets. Who knows, a theory like this just might catch on.

On the other hand, what would happen if we built a new theory to govern portfolio construction and investment strategy based on a completely different set of

26   Charles Mackay, *Extraordinary Popular Delusions and the Madness of Crowds*, Richard Bentley, New Burlington St., Publisher in Ordinary to Her Majesty, London, 1841. More recently published by Three Rivers Press, New York, N.Y., 1980.

assumptions? What if we got rid of the idea that investors somehow magically know the true probability law that governs future prices, and we also dismiss the notion that the probability law that governs prices never changes? In fact, let's build our new theory on the "radical" idea that the economy gradually changes over time, and so even if investors think they have figured out what variables will cause prices to change in the present, they cannot be certain that they are correct. Only in retrospect could they discern how changes in the economy actually affected market prices. In our new theory, investors would be left to their own devices to figure out how and why events cause prices to change. They would form their own separate theories about how economic variables impact prices, and they would all make mistakes in applying their beliefs about price changes in the construction of their portfolios. This is because, like it or not, no one can perfectly predict the future. As obvious as this may seem to most rational people, using these assumptions to build a new theory for portfolio construction and management would be considered a radically new idea. Think of it: investors make mistakes! Instead of a market being made up of perfect investors who instantly process today's news and correctly project future prices, we would have a marketplace of uncertain investors whose definition of risk is that they can't rely on past market prices in order to predict prices in the future. In this new investment paradigm, investors would understand that the economy is not stationary, and that "past performance does not guarantee future returns." In this new theoretical approach to managing money, what need would we have for this well-known disclaimer about past performance and future results? Any other notion would be considered just plain silly.

I hope by now you recognized that our first hypothetical new portfolio theory is, in fact, a description of the assumptions that form the basis for Modern Portfolio Theory and the resulting strategy of buy and hold strategic asset allocation. Shocking, isn't it? As we discussed in Chapter 4, the assumptions underlying the current investment community status quo are the subject of a vigorous debate in the academic community. And as we discussed in our chapter on secular bear markets, the argument that the practical implementation of the theory is "good enough most of the time," is a high-risk proposition when the market multiple for the S&P 500 Index, based on normalized 10-year trailing GAAP earnings, is expensive. The empirical evidence simply does not appear to support the strategy of strategic asset allocation, unless of course, we start out with the proposition that we are in a secular bull market. In a bull market, all theories that include buying and holding stocks will, by definition, allow investors to meet their long-term retirement objectives. Bear markets are not so generous.

This chapter is about the second portfolio theory that we hypothetically created in the previous discussion. The very good news for investors is that this new theory is not hypothetical at all. It is based on the work of Professor Mordecai Kurz and H. "Woody" Brock, Ph.D. Because Kurz and Brock's work provides an academic justification for active portfolio management, and because it actually meets the tests of common sense, I believe it is well worth our attention. Readers should know that there is the usual amount of complicated mathematical proofs in Kurz and Brock's papers. For our purposes, we will leave the mathematics aside, and concentrate on the fundamental ideas that drive their theories.

## Kurz Discusses Rational Expectations

Professor Mordecai Kurz is currently the Joan Kenney Professor of Economics at Stanford University. He received his Ph.D. and M.A. in Economics from Yale University and has published many papers on the subject of Rational Beliefs and Endogenous Risk. The paper that we will concern ourselves with is *Endogenous Uncertainty and Rational Belief Equilibrium: A Unified Theory of Market Volatility*[27], which was presented at the International School of Economic Research, July 5-11, 1999. In his words, this was a "non-academic paper," and his work has progressed since this paper was published. However, it will suffice for our purposes in order to understand the basics of a new school of economic thought.

With this paper, Kurz directly and forcefully challenges the academic status quo, especially with regard to the Rational Expectations theory of pricing.

In the last chapter, we saw that the rational expectations pricing theory, first published by John Muth and later popularized by Robert Lucas, came to us via Muth's attempt to resolve a long-standing economic riddle known as the cobweb problem, where economists were trying to model commodity prices that theoretically would never reach equilibrium. Muth tackled the problem by studying lean hog prices and observing that the price volatility of the market was actually much lower than the current theory would suggest it should be. Muth's solution to the problem was to propose a new theory of pricing called the Rational Expectations pricing theory. His insight was that farmers were anticipating changes in market conditions and therefore, were adjusting their hog harvest to stabilize prices. Muth's work theorized that farmers were perfectly rational and had perfect knowledge of what hog prices would be in the future.

Robert Lucas popularized the Rational Expectations theory as a tool for macroeconomics, using it to explain why Keynesian economics didn't seem to work during the inflationary 1960's and 1970's. For this, Lucas won the Nobel Prize and his ideas about the expectations of economic agents have been widely incorporated into our national economic policy. To this day, the inflation

---

27  Mordecai Kurz, *Endogenous Uncertainty: A Unified View of Market Volatility*, Stanford University, September 9, 1997 (updated November 28, 1998)

expectations of investors are at the top of the list of concerns of the Federal Reserve when setting monetary policy.

Understanding rational expectations is important to us as investors because Modern Portfolio Theory and the Efficient Markets Hypothesis rely on the underlying assumptions of rational expectations. Although most investors have never heard of rational expectations, it is one of the core theories that supports the concepts and assumptions of strategic asset allocation—which we have all been taught is the only academically accepted methodology for managing money.

Mordecai Kurz proposed a dramatically different approach to modeling economic behavior than the rational expectations model. Kurz begins his paper by reminding us that rational expectations theory is based on the traditional idea we all learned in college about how prices are determined at the intersection of supply and demand. He then describes the three basic assumptions about the true probability law that are fundamental to the theory of Rational Expectations, and goes on to further explain the flaws of each basic assumption.

The first assumption is that the true probability law is stationary. This is a very important concept. Not only are price changes independent of each other, but also the forces that govern price changes (true probability law) are unchanging and fixed forever.

The second assumption is that all economic agents (for the purposes of this book, "economic agents" will be called "investors" from this point forward) know the true probability law. This is a component of "structural knowledge" that investors are assumed to possess, which we learned about with Muth's super-farmers that knew the future of hog prices.

The third assumption regarding the true probability law in the Rational Expectations theory is that investors can compute fair prices in the present and the future whenever there is any news that could impact future prices. This is another part of the "structural knowledge" that investors are assumed to possess. It is the same structural knowledge that Muth's super-farmers used to instantly know how changes in hog harvests would impact future hog prices. Instantly knowing how the news will impact future prices makes them "super" farmers, indeed.

Kurz then tackles the important issue of exogenous risk. Everything outside of the economic system that investors are uncertain about is called exogenous "state space." Remember that the economy is supposedly a closed system where nothing can disturb economic equilibrium except events that happen external to the economy. Examples of external risks include weather, health conditions, earthquakes, fire destruction, and mortality risk. "News" is typically considered an exogenous event. In the Rational Expectations theory, all economic changes vary with and depend on the news. In other words, if there is no news, there is no change in prices. The amount of news impacts the amount of price changes.

Investors are assumed to agree on the meaning and interpretation of the news, and all investors are assumed to agree about the current state of the economy. Rational Expectations theory assumes we are all super-investors who agree on the state of the economy and can interpret the meaning of the news in exactly the same way.

Kurz calls the financial risks and volatility that arise from outside of the economic system, "exogenous uncertainty." Under the Rational Expectations theory, no risk can be created from within the economic system due to human beliefs or actions. In other words, investors themselves have no impact on price changes within the system. In this mythical world, there can be no stock market bubbles or irrational investor behavior affecting the markets. Price momentum, therefore, cannot exist. Because investors know the impact of the news, or the new equilibrium price for all securities based on exogenous risks, all price uncertainty is magically resolved. This is, of course, why many institutional investors prefer to use indexes for investing in the stock market. When individual investors can perfectly predict prices, there are no pricing uncertainties for active managers to exploit. Let's hear it once again for Muth's super hog farmers!

Kurz concludes that under the Rational Expectations theory, active asset management is not needed since the only services that are needed to be provided to investors so they can properly construct portfolios are *diversification and information gathering.* This conclusion rings true considering the message delivered by today's financial planning community that our role is more about managing client relationships than worrying about any changes in market fundamentals. Investors who even think about how the news may impact risks and returns are assumed to be unprofessional. Professionals and amateurs, alike, have been trained to believe that the news is nothing more than market "noise" we need to ignore. Under the Rational Expectations theory, it is clear that investors know the true probability law and agree on the meaning and interpretation of the news, and so there is no need to worry about the news at all. What a relief!

Of course, as Kurz wisely observes, Rational Expectations theory fails to properly model empirical reality. Over the years, many people have pointed out the flaws, paradoxes, and anomalies of these assumptions in many different academic papers. Kurz reviews many of these, discussing some of the theories about why Rational Expectations does not work. For example, he explores the idea that the financial markets are dominated by investors subject to fads and mass psychology, which is being addressed more and more by the field of behavioral finance. He also mentions some academic work suggesting that markets are only partially rational. In these models, markets are assumed to be fairly priced most of the time, but not all of the time.

## Kurz Proposes Something Better: Rational Beliefs Equilibrium Theory

Having thoroughly reviewed the rational expectations pricing theory, and commenting on the current academic debate about its flawed assumptions, Kurz then proposes an alternative theory called the Rational Beliefs Equilibrium theory. Kurz presents a number of alternative assumptions for his Rational Beliefs theory. First, he tells us that in Rational Beliefs, the economic universe is stable, but not stationary. Remember that under Rational Expectations the conditions that create price changes do not ever change. In Kurz's view, structural change is possible. However, although the economy experiences technological and other structural changes, the P/E ratios of major indexes have well-known "normal" ranges and securities have well-known long-term means, variances, and covariances (average returns, volatility, and correlations).

In today's Internet-driven world, there is an enormous amount of data about past market performance available to any investor who is interested in researching past returns. Perhaps the best-known source of past market data is the popular *Ibbotson Yearbook*[28], which gives the returns for stocks, bonds, bills, and inflation dating back to 1926. Clearly, the long-term historical returns and volatility of most institutional quality asset classes are available to everyone.

Under Rational Beliefs, investors do not know the true probability law underlying current prices and additionally, investors do not know how changes in the news (exogenous variables) will impact current and future market prices. Kurz essentially "fires" the perfect farmers first imagined by Muth and later turned into super-investors by Lucas and Fama. In Kurz's theory, investors don't know exactly what prices should be today based on yesterday's news and they don't know exactly what prices should be in the future based on today's news. However, they do have access to large amounts of past data to statistically test their own theories or beliefs against the "normal" market returns of the past.

One of the important ideas that Kurz gives us in his Rational Beliefs theory is the idea of regime change. He states that a system that experiences new technologies, new production methods, and new social organizations, is not likely to be stationary, as is claimed in the Rational Expectations theory, but it may be stable. While a technology or social organization is in place, the economy appears to have a fixed structure (stationary) until the next change. Kurz calls each episode of change

---

28  "Stocks, Bonds, Bills, and Inflation" is published by Ibbotson Associates, Chicago, Ill. and is a respected source of historical asset class data.

a regime change. In real time, investors don't know the exact parameters of the prevailing regime or its starting or ending dates. They only discover the nature of regimes in retrospect. Having learned about the nature of a regime in *retrospect*, they cannot correctly predict the next regime.

To me, this is an accurate representation of the behavior of investors and market pundits who are always correct in their analysis of economic change, *after the fact*. This seems to be a lot more sensible than any assumptions that technology and social change have no impact on the economy and market prices.

Kurz offers us some interesting observations about the true probability law in Rational Beliefs and how it differs from the assumptions about the true probability law in the theory of Rational Expectations. He theorizes that the true probability law cannot be learned, and even if investors discover it, they cannot be sure that they are right about it. Investors cannot know the map between market prices and those variables that determine prices. Investors cannot know with certainty how all of the many factors that impact price changes will actually determine the market's values in the future. In Kurz's Rational Beliefs theory, investors don't know the true probability law and must form their own individual ideas about how prices will change. In other words, *every investor uses his or her own judgment about the fair price of a security*—a method of determining value that will fail the test of those demanding scientific "certainty" in pricing models. Unlike Rational Expectations theory, where investors agree on how news (exogenous uncertainty) will impact prices, in Rational Beliefs theory, in every regime, investors will disagree both about their forecasts of the future as well as their interpretation of the news.

So what exactly is a "rational belief" anyway? Kurz says that a theory is rational if it cannot be contradicted by past data. In other words, economic models must generate statistics that are the same as the historical record. If a model generates long-term statistics that differ from past empirical evidence, it is judged wrong and the underlying belief is judged to be irrational. This is the argument that is used to populate means-variance optimizing models with past data in order to generate efficient asset allocations in strategically constructed portfolios. Doing so absolutely meets the test of being rational in your approach to model building. Unfortunately, as we will see, it also results in something else: *Being wrong!*

## Investors Make Mistakes

If you are an investor who relies on the quantitative methods of strategic asset allocation to ensure that you can't make a mistake in your forecasts of future price behavior, Kurz's views of how investors behave under Rational Beliefs theory is especially interesting.

Kurz's model suggests that investors cannot help but make mistakes. All investors know that the long-term averages of past returns represent the "normal" probability of events. An investor who adopts the "normal" empirical data as his belief is entirely rational, but to maintain such a view indefinitely requires that the investor believe that no structural change can ever take place. To put this in the context of investors who cling to the strategic asset allocation approach to portfolio management, over very long periods of time investors should expect to achieve historical long-term average returns. This expectation is entirely rational. Furthermore, an investor who expects to achieve the "normal" probability of returns has to believe that the economy will be exactly the same in the future as it was in the past. However, according to Kurz's Rational Beliefs theory, *"the process of structural change is the central building block of its complexity and the root cause of diversity of beliefs. In this system, the past is not an entirely satisfactory basis for assessing risk in the future."*

It is inconceivable to me that this conclusion could be considered controversial by just about anybody. Nevertheless, it is resisted mightily by the powers that be in the financial planning industry and in academia. Fifty years after Markowitz, and 40 years after Sharpe, we finally have an academic model that concludes that past performance does not guarantee future results. If past performance really doesn't guarantee the future, then how in the world can investors avoid mistakes? Clearly, they cannot.

Kurz explains for us how mistakes happen and why. An investor who believes that the market does change can't support his theory about what prices should be in the future by relying on long-run statistics of the past. His theory about future prices may not be acceptable to other investors. In addition, his theory may sometimes be right and sometimes be wrong. Investors may hold different theories both about the nature and intensity of changes in the economy as well as their timing. Above all, investors will have different opinions regarding the significance of "news."

According to Kurz:

> If there is a true and unknown equilibrium probabilistic law underlying the dynamics of the market, and if rational agents have different beliefs about the future, then most may be holding wrong beliefs, leading to forecasting mistakes. A mistake is the difference between an agent's forecast at a particular date versus the forecast that would be made with the correct model, were it known."

A mistake is a rule by which rational agents utilize information efficiently, but fail to make the correct forecast. There is no statistical way agents can avoid mistakes. However, agents know that without committing to an investment program that takes advantage of changing conditions of the market, they cannot earn excess returns.

Here we reach the crux of the argument. It may not be obvious to readers, but the investment industry status quo teaches that it is impossible to earn excess returns because the markets are efficient, and therefore there is no need to even try to take advantage of changing market conditions. Kurz, on the other hand, tells us that investors do try to earn excess returns. However, to earn them, investors must make forecasts, and if investors don't know the future, and if they have different beliefs about the future, then someone is going to be wrong in their beliefs, which will lead to forecasting mistakes. A mistake is simply the difference between the forecast of what would happen to prices in the future and what actually occurs once the future becomes the past. Since they cannot know the future, investors cannot avoid mistakes. However, without implementing an active management strategy to take advantage of changing market conditions, they have no way of earning more than market returns. This is, of course, exactly what investors must conclude if they are to make the transition from passive or strategic asset allocation to active or tactical asset allocation. If market returns are going to be less than average in the future, and investors want the opportunity to outperform the market averages, then they have no choice but to consider a more active approach.

## Risk and Uncertainty

Kurz defines risk by stating that for investors, the market is an arena for the competition among investment ideas that seek to capture excess returns. Once again it is worth noting that Kurz assumes that 1) there is such a thing as excess returns, and 2) that investors behave in the real world as though they want to capture them. Risk is committing to an investment idea without having statistically reliable evidence to support the investment idea. As we have seen, if the economy is subject to structural change then there cannot be a statistically reliable way to model the future. Kurz advances the idea that investors must use their *judgment and expertise* in order to interpret existing information about future security returns. This is precisely what the money management industry hoped to avoid with the creation of quantitative models that do not require investors to exercise their judgment in making assumptions about future asset class returns and the strategic asset allocation decisions that result from them. We will examine the problems with quantitative models in more detail in the next chapter.

As we have discovered, in the Rational Beliefs system, where all investors hold rational beliefs, then all investment, consumption, production, and portfolio decisions are, in part, determined by the mistakes of investors. If individual investors can make mistakes in assessing market values, then the market as a whole can assess value incorrectly. Price levels may overshoot above fundamental values or undershoot below fundamental values. An important component of volatility is due to the mistakes of investors arising from differences in their states of belief. According to Kurz, "That component of volatility above and beyond the level justified by exogenous variables is said to be internally propagated. This type of uncertainty is called "endogenous uncertainty."

Kurz thus gives us a second type of uncertainty that affects market prices, and I might add, a couple of new words that will impress your friends at your next cocktail party. In Rational Expectations, exogenous uncertainty refers to risk that comes from outside of the economic system and is often referred to as "news." It is instantly discounted by investors who not only know the true probability of the news, but also know the true impact of the news on market prices. Endogenous risk, on the other hand, is what we often call "market misbehavior." It takes the form of price overshoot that results from the mistakes of investors. These mistakes reflect their inability to know the true probability of news and its impact on future prices.

In Rational Beliefs theory, the Law of Large Numbers cannot rescue investors who are doomed to make mistakes. If one investor can make a mistake then the market as a whole can assess value incorrectly. I wonder if investors who bought the NASDAQ at the height of the tech bubble can relate to this idea. Kurz believes as much as 60% of the market's volatility can be ascribed to endogenous uncertainty. Remember that there is no such thing as endogenous risk in classical economic theory (think "super-farmers"). According to Kurz, endogenous risk varies due to:

**Dynamics of beliefs of investors:** The frequency of change in their outlook and the intensity or amount of change from their normal forecasts.

**Distribution of beliefs of investors:** Market sentiment has an important impact on endogenous risk. If 5% of investors are bullish, 5% are bearish, and 90% are neutral about the prospects for the market, that is potentially less volatile than if 50% of investors are bullish and 50% are bearish. This is because there is more potential for major changes in sentiment from a polarized market.

**Correlation of beliefs of investors:** If the forecasts of all investors shift at the same time, then volatility can be drastically affected.

Kurz sees price momentum as a major manifestation of endogenous uncertainty. It is created in the market by three different investor behaviors—the similarity in the *direction* of investors' deviation from past data, the similarity in the *intensity* of investors' deviation from past data, and the similarity in investors' *interpretation* of the news. In short, once the "herd mentality" takes over the market, prices can swing much further than the fundamentals might indicate that they should, depending on the direction of market prices, the intensity of price changes, and how much fear and greed are motivating investors to not get left out of a crowded trade.

With my apologies for summarizing and simplifying Dr. Kurz's important contribution, I think readers who have stuck with me this far will agree that the Rational Beliefs theory meets the requirements of an econometric model that fits the objective reality of the market as we know it. Unlike the currently accepted model of Rational Expectations, in Kurz's model the economy can change and these changes have an impact on how prices change. It's hard to believe that such a claim could be considered so radical, and yet it is. In this changing world, investors can and do make mistakes while trying to earn excess returns. And the mistakes of large numbers of investors constitute a new risk, called endogenous risk, which is caused by investors as opposed to exogenous events that occur with the news. It is possible for the madness of crowds to create market bubbles, and it is possible that prices will deviate from their fundamental values, perhaps offering opportunities for tactical investors to exploit the mispricing of securities to earn above market returns.

If this is true, then how can investors continue to justify sticking with the old, passive strategic approach to asset allocation? To me, not making the transition to a more active, tactical asset allocation approach—especially if we are in a long-term secular bear market—is fraught with risk for all investors. In any case, Professor Kurz certainly has given us a wonderful academic foundation for actively managing portfolios and rejecting several of the fundamental assumptions of strategic asset allocation.

How can we best profit from this new theoretical view of the financial markets? For that, we now turn to the work of H. "Woody" Brock.

## Woody Brock and the Justification for Active Management

Horace W. Brock, Ph.D., (widely known as "Woody") is the president and founder of a research firm called Strategic Economic Decisions, Inc. (SED). Dr. Brock earned his B.A., M.B.A., and M.S. from Harvard University, and his M.A. and Ph.D. from Princeton University (mathematical economics and political philosophy). Brock studied under Kenneth J. Arrow, Professor of Economics, and John C. Harsanyi, Professor of Economics, at the University of California, Berkeley. Both are winners of the Nobel Prize in Economics. In short, Woody Brock is a really smart guy.

I first heard Brock speak at the Schwab Impact Conference in Washington, D.C. in 2006. Having never heard of him before, I was surprised that his talk was filled with references to physics and Brownian motion and several other theoretical ideas that I couldn't understand at the time. While I contemplated how to escape the lecture, Brock suddenly produced a simple slide illustrating the difference between Markowitz's buy and hold method of investing on the efficient frontier and what he called "optimal" asset allocation. I thought the graphic perfectly illustrated what we were attempting to do at Pinnacle, and the encounter led me to begin a three-month saga of trying to learn more about Woody Brock and optimal asset allocation. The result of my research was a two-hour, 81 slide PowerPoint presentation that I inflicted on the Pinnacle Advisory Group investment committee that to this day lives in infamy. (I doubt that anyone who was there will ever forgive me for making them sit through the last 50 slides.)

Brock has written several important papers about the justification for active management, and he also worked closely with Kurz on his theories regarding endogenous risk. One paper of interest to investors is *The Logical Justification for "Active" Investment Management*.[29]

The paper reviews the shortcomings of the two main axioms of the Rational Expectations pricing model, and supports the work of Kurz, which we just discussed above. Brock points out that the two axioms of the Rational Expectations theory (specifically, that the economic environment is stationary and that investors magically know what future prices will be given any future news) are both highly problematic.

Axioms 1 & 2 create such a loss of explanatory power that they have never been able to explain or predict real-world asset market behavior. When the respective axioms do not hold true, then the theory is not robust with respect to reality.

Brock ponders how the financial industry could embrace a theory that was so flawed for so long, saying:

Financial economists, pension consultants, and the *Journal of Portfolio Management* have endorsed the CAPM as if it were descriptive of reality. Having canonized it, they urged its adoption in practice, and this occurred in the pension consulting and financial planning communities... Now, two decades after the coronation of the efficient markets and rational expectations paradigm, it is crumbling due to: Empirical attacks by Robert Shiller and others, the rise of behavioral finance, and most recently the rise of the theory of Rational Beliefs by Kurz.

Brock then gets to the good news for investors interested in actively managing portfolios:

---

29 Horace Woody Brock, The Logical Justification for "Active" Investment Management, Strategic Economic Decisions, Inc., NY. 2006

The axioms that underlie Kurz's Rational Beliefs Equilibrium theory not only make possible a satisfactory descriptive theory of asset markets, but also a normative prescriptive theory of how investors can and should legitimately outperform the market.

Brock's recipe for active management is surprisingly simple and in my opinion its importance cannot be overstated: *"Investment managers must be less wrong than the consensus in forecasting future prices."* The idea of being "less wrong" is based on the idea that all economic agents make mistakes under Kurz's theory of Rational Beliefs. Since no one can know the true probability law, and the only way to rationally utilize past data in making price forecasts is to assume that the economic environment is stationary, which it clearly is not, then all investors will be wrong. The best investors will be wrong, as well. However, they will be *less wrong* than the consensus.

The second idea is also critical. Like Kurz, Brock assumes that the best investors will be engaged in the process of forecasting future prices. This is, of course, one of the most taboo activities for an investment manager to pursue under the current strategic, buy and hold paradigm of investment management.

A second paper by Brock of great interest to investors is, *The Ability to Outperform the Market-Logical Foundations based on the Theory of Rational Beliefs*.[30] In the paper Brock expands on his earlier work and gives us three logically defensible strategies as a basis for superior price forecasting. The three strategies meet the following two criteria: First, they must be consistent with a satisfactory descriptive and explanatory theory of how the markets work in reality. And second, they must be defensible so that an investor can claim, after the fact, "I was right for the right reason." Both criteria follow from the observation that price changes have two components: 1) News of some kind, and 2) The quantitative reaction of price, over time, to the news. Therefore, superior price forecasting requires expertise in either better anticipating the timing and nature of the news than others, or better anticipating how prices will react to the news.

There are three generic strategies that meet Brock's criteria for being descriptive of reality and for being defensible after the fact. The first strategy is to exploit structural change in the economic environment (non-stationarity.) Brock says:

An investor who invests time and money to understand (forecast) structural change should possess and will possess an edge. Specifically, he will better forecast future news than will other investors, in particular those who stick their head in the sand and ignore structural change.

30   Horace W. Brock, Ph.D., The Ability to Outperform the Market—Logical Foundations Based on the Theory of Rational Beliefs, *Revista Internazionale di Science*, 2007, n.3, 365-402.

Of course, most strategic asset allocators are terrified of being accused of trying to forecast anything, and the MPT/CAPM/rational expectations paradigm teaches them that there is no such thing as structural change anyway; so the good news for active managers is that beating the consensus at forecasting structural change is possible. After all, the majority of strategic buy and hold investors aren't even in the game. Brock says that an investor who successfully hones these skills can claim, after the fact, to have been right for the right reason. Some well-known investment strategies that take advantage of structural change include fundamental analysis, sector rotation, and demographic and political "macro" bets.

The second strategy suggested by Brock is to exploit endogenous risk. You may remember that endogenous risk refers to the degree to which asset prices over respond to the news. Since the new theory of Rational Beliefs has finally clarified the reasons for different kinds of price overshoot and market misbehavior, Brock proposes that investors exploit this new knowledge to gain a competitive edge regarding asset price movements. Successful investment strategies that are based on the idea of exploiting endogenous risk include many familiar hedge fund strategies, including arbitrage strategies and all market-timing strategies that exploit long-term bull and bear markets.

The third strategy for successful price forecasting is to "exploit logical errors of inference." In essence, Brock maintains that many of the basic relationships that govern change in our economy are counterintuitive and that investors often simply misunderstand how the markets work. What is important about this third strategy is that investors don't need to properly forecast structural change to use it. As Brock says, "investors who choose to educate themselves about the counterintuitive aspects of economic and market behavior end up less wrong in their forecasts than those who do not." Brock gives seven different examples of errors of inference in his paper.

Brock's first and most simple example is the Birthday Paradox. Suppose you ask a group of well educated people the probability that some pair of people out of a group of 50 randomly selected people will share a common birthday. The typical response is 8% probability whereas the true probability exceeds 98%. Brock's point here is that people who possess all of the correct data to reach a correct conclusion will not always know how to do so. In this case, the answer requires that the question be inverted to, "what is the probability that some pair does not share the same birthday?" In addition, it requires that normal people understand compound conditional probability calculations. He goes on to give other examples of errors of inference including widespread misunderstandings about the true impact of shifts in foreign investor asset preferences on U.S. capital flows and interest rates.

Brock's seventh and final example of exploiting errors of inference is particularly relevant to the thesis of this book: Logical Fallacies about Modern Portfolio Theory and its implications for asset allocation.

## Optimal Asset Allocation and Beyond

In an earlier chapter we discussed at great length the problems with the tortured assumptions that are required for MPT and CAPM to work. Readers may recall that Markowitz's work allows investors to create an "efficient frontier" of possible portfolios that contain all of the possible portfolios that can be most efficiently constructed from a given set of asset classes. Investors then pick the one efficient portfolio that best meets their requirements for the trade-off between return and risk. Brock's paper, *The Concept of Outperforming the Market—Logical Foundations based on the Theory of Rational Beliefs*, gives us two instructive charts that help us to understand the fallacy of having only one efficient frontier and only one portfolio construction (asset allocation) that best meets an investor's goals.

**Figure 5.1** shows two triangles that represent the possible portfolios that can be constructed from three asset classes, stocks, bonds, and cash. The chart on the left has only one dot, or one asset allocation, and it represents the traditional Markowitz approach to the efficient frontier. There is only one efficient portfolio that meets an investor's long-term goals and objectives. The triangle on the right shows a case

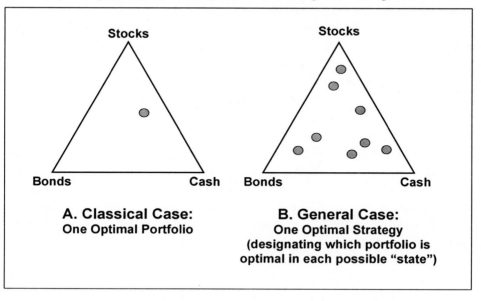

**Figure 5.1—Efficient Frontier**

Source: Horace Woody Brock, Strategic Economic Decisions, Inc.

where there are several optimal portfolios. To understand the differences between the two cases shown, it is best to resort to one of Brock's favorite metaphors, in which he constructs an analogy between portfolio construction and crop rotation and farming.

Imagine that you are a farmer in New England. You must deal with the weather at different times of the year as you plant your crops, and you must rotate your crops so as to best take advantage of the seasonal weather changes. Extensive historical data for the weather in each season is available to all. Therefore, farmers who wish to do so can compute the *conditional* (season— dependent) means and variances of the weather for each season. Having done so, they can compute an optimal mix of crops for each season. The right triangle captures this logic: think of each dot as representing the optimal mix of crops (portfolio) for each of the eight planting seasons.

In contrast, in the classical world of Markowitz and Sharpe, the farmer would ignore the existence of seasons and would only use the unconditional mean and variance of the weather throughout the entire year, as opposed to each season of the year. The single dot appearing in the left triangle corresponds to the best mix of crops that result from optimization with respect to this mean and variance. The problem, of course, is that unless the farmer lives in Tahiti where the seasons never change and a single mix of crops is optimal, the optimal portfolio will bankrupt the farmer both in summer and winter.

Brock stresses the importance of understanding that the optimal portfolios computed within the two triangles are all computed on the basis of objectively true historical data about the weather. No subjective forecasts need be used at all. The only difference lies in the type of portfolio optimization model used in each case. In the left triangle, static nonlinear programming suffices—the classical static models familiar from textbooks. More advanced theories of stochastic dynamic programming are required to determine the optimal portfolios in the right hand triangle. While executing the seasonally-dependent strategy in the right triangle *appears* to represent "active" as opposed to "passive" management, it does not. That's because a robot (Brock's term for an optimizing model) can be utilized in both cases to determine the optimal portfolios. In particular, no subjective "market timing" decisions need be made at all within the right hand triangle. Rather, the robotic solution to the dynamic programming problem will determine exactly when to rotate the crops.

In **Figure 5.2**[31], Brock relates the forgoing discussion to the concept of the efficient frontier. In particular, he shows that there are three fundamental types of efficient frontiers. The first and lowest frontier, marked Classical,

---

31   Horace W. Brock, Ph.D., Strategic Economic Decisions, Inc.

relates to the classical portfolio in the left triangle. The intermediate frontier marked True, corresponds to the triangle on the right. The True efficient frontier is "higher," meaning that investors can earn higher returns for less risk, because the farmer is able to use seasonal data to rotate his crops in a profit maximizing manner.

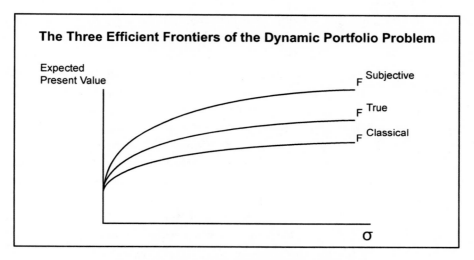

**Figure 5.2—The Three Efficient Frontiers
of the Dynamic Portfolio Problem**
Source: Horace Woody Brock, Strategic Economic Decisions, Inc.

It is the third and highest frontier that represents something completely novel and it deserves the attention of all investors. The third frontier, called the subjective frontier, provides the justification for the kind of active management that I promote in this book. In this third set of possible portfolio constructions, the data is based on the *subjective forecasts* assumed by the investor. In this case the portfolio will be the most efficient, *in the eyes of the investor*. This portfolio construction cannot be proved by past data, because the investor is making assumptions about future asset class returns and risk based on his or her own investment in time and research to make better inferences about the market than the consensus. And, it is on this third efficient frontier that the portfolio reflects the impact of non-stationarity and structural change as defined by Kurz.

To use Brock's metaphor again, in both of the triangles in **Figure 5.1**, every investor can find the data for rainfall and temperatures in the summer months in New England. They may or may not choose to invest by dynamically using this information, which is the difference between having one dot and many dots.

However, what if they want to consider the impact on future weather patterns from global warming? This would represent a structural change whose implications for weather and crop prices cannot be known from historical data. In this case it is the superior judgment and skill of the farmer (or the investor) as to which theory of global warming, out of many, is the best. Suppose the farmer adopts a particular theory of global warming that he thinks is best after spending time and money to consult with leading experts. Using his beliefs about future crop prices based upon this theory, he will able to create the third and highest frontier in the diagram in **Figure 5.2**. Note that this frontier will always be "higher" in *his eyes* than the True or Classical frontier. This perfectly captures the true meaning of "beating the market" or "adding alpha." This is because, for any given level of risk on the horizontal axis, the expected return will always be higher in his eyes. Assuming that his theory of global warming ends up to be correct *ex-post*, he will have added value by having been right for the right reason. Achieving excess returns in this manner—whether for the farmer or the investor—is "theoretically legitimate" according to Brock because the endeavor is completely consistent with Kurz's descriptive theory of how markets work (Rational Beliefs Theory).

Note that Brock labels the lowest efficient frontier as "classical" since it represents the risk-return tradeoffs using the single fixed portfolio of the left triangle as recommended by the Markowitz theory. The middle frontier is called the "true" frontier since it is the highest frontier that can be obtained in a completely passive manner using generally available statistical data—data reflecting that the means and variances in summer versus winter are very different. Taking these differences into account, which Markowitz did not, permits an identification of the optimal mix of crops on a season by season basis. Each season-dependent optimal crop mix (portfolio) is represented by a dot within the right side triangle, and the risk return possibilities generated by using this more refined seasoned-dependent data is captured by the middle frontier. It is very important to understand that the payoffs achievable by this more general and flexible approach do not require any subjective inputs by the investor at all since it is assumed ("stationarity") that historical data alone accurately reveal the true probabilities of future weather, crop prices, and returns. The way you obtain the best portfolio of crops for each season (the dots within the right triangle) is to use the mathematical theory of stochastic dynamic programming.[32]

Brock stresses one final point about the dots in the right triangle and the corresponding "true frontier." The logic involved obliterates the traditional

---

32  Note that this is not an original insight of Brock who stresses that it was logically implied by Paul Samuelson, America's first winner of the Nobel Memorial Prize in Economics. His paper on the subject is *Samuelson, Lifetime Portfolio Selection by Dynamic Stochastic Programming, The Review of Economics and Statistics*, 1969.

distinction between strategic and tactical asset allocation. This is because, according to the logic of dynamic programming used to solve for the correct set of dots in the triangle, being strategically rational *requires* being tactically rational. Strategic rationality in this context refers to the utilization of each of the dots in its proper season, but the switch from crop mix to crop mix is what most of us think as being tactical. The logic fully fuses the confusing distinction between strategic and tactical and shows that the one requires the other.

The highest frontier (subjective) is the only frontier where the investor chooses to go beyond the generally available data about past weather patterns to invoke his own theory of how global warming will change matters.

In many ways, **Figure 5.2** illustrates the philosophy of active management that we employ at Pinnacle Advisory Group, and the philosophy that I want to introduce to investors in this book. Investors should consider the obvious benefits of moving to the subjective (highest) efficient frontier based on a more qualitative, subjective, decision-making process, which is a function of their skill and judgment. This process can be implemented alongside of a quantitative approach, as long as the investor moves from the classical frontier of statically using past data to a more dynamic approach to past data illustrated in the right hand triangle in **Figure 5.1**.

The implications of Kurz and Brock's work are enormous for professional investment advisors and individual investors. Their papers provide the academic foundation and justification for active management, and give us a theory of the markets and the role of investors and investment advisors that rings true based on my experience in managing portfolios for affluent clients. We no longer have to apologize for trying to earn excess returns. Instead, we now have legitimate grounds for studying the markets in order to discover those times when value opportunities present themselves with the objective of earning higher returns with less risk on a new "subjective" efficient frontier.

It is important to note there is no need for an investor to be "contrarian" in seeking higher risk adjusted returns in the Brock paradigm. Indeed, Brock admits that he quite often agrees with the consensus forecast. It is only when he feels that he has good reason not to that he will attempt to construct the third frontier using his own hopefully superior analysis. We will discuss high conviction and low conviction "points of view" and how to invest them in Part II of this book.

After decades of relying on MPT to construct portfolios without having to think about portfolio construction, Kurz and Brock have finally given us the academically based permission to use our best judgment and skill in constructing portfolios, and as importantly, they have given us permission to make mistakes in the exercise of that judgment. Active portfolio managers can now make market forecasts without apology. In addition, we now better understand the nature of the forecasts made by strategic, buy and hold investors. Their forecasts assume that the markets are stationary and economic regimes never change. Buy and hold is an irrational strategy in a world where the changes of the seasons can be forecast, as can the cycles of earnings or the economy. In this case, investors should at a minimum strive to be on the True efficient frontier by rotating their crops, or changing the asset allocation of the portfolio, and foregoing the simplicity of a fixed buy and hold portfolio. I believe they should then aspire to the subjective or highest frontier by making better forecasts then the consensus. The buy and hold approach corresponds to the single dot in the left triangle which only makes sense for the farmer living in Tahiti where there is only one season all year round.

It is now time to better understand our industry's infatuation with quantitative models, and how our insistence that our beliefs be derived from the application of advanced statistical models do not necessarily lead to better decision-making. In the next chapter, as we continue to explore the science of financial decision-making, we will discover that as much as we try to avoid it, quantitative decisions still have many of the attributes of fine art.

# 6 THE TROUBLE WITH QUANT MODELS

When current Pinnacle Advisory Group Chief Investment Officer, Rick Vollaro, read the original chapter six years ago, he offered the criticism that it was well written but poorly named. His point was that much of the chapter is a commentary and criticism of Modern Portfolio Theory and the Capital Asset Pricing Model (CAPM), where I point out that using these Nobel Prize winning economic models to build portfolios is far from the risk-free strategy their proponents would claim. Rick suggested that most of the industry does not consider MPT to be a quantitative strategy in the way that the term is commonly used today. I gratefully accepted his criticism and then proceeded to ignore it; hence the title of the chapter remains, "The Trouble with Quant Models."

Perhaps I should have taken his advice. In the years since the first edition of the book was published, quantitative portfolio strategies have swamped the investing public. All quantitative approaches to portfolio construction are similar in that they offer objective and unemotional portfolio decision-making that is not subject to human biases and heuristics. Like MPT and CAPM before them, current quant-based strategies mathematically program a variety of rules for making portfolio decisions. The major difference between the two is MPT offers us a relatively simple quantitative model for determining the single most efficient portfolio asset allocation. The model is based on the notion that markets are efficiently priced so there is one correct asset allocation that should rarely be changed. In contrast, many of today's quantitative strategies imply that markets are so inefficient that we need quantitative rules for dramatically changing portfolio allocations to what are often extreme positions. So while I was correct that MPT is truly the Granddaddy of all quantitative portfolio strategies and serves as an excellent example of how quant can be misused by investors, I wish I had been more prescient about the poorly designed quant-based products that were soon to take over the investing world.

My firm has been integrating quantitative decision-making into our investment process for years, and even introduced two investment strategies that utilize quant as part of a core and satellite portfolio construction. I mention them because this chapter concludes with a section called, "The Solution: Use Both Methods." Here I advocate using common sense and good judgment in combination with the quantitative decisions of portfolio optimization software. However, using both methods means that value can be also be gained by adding a quantitative dimension to qualitative or judgment-based investment decisions. After all, value investing is inherently subjective; good investment value lies strictly in the eyes of the beholder. Relying on the common sense and good judgment of portfolio managers without adding the ingredient of quantitative, rules-based, decision-making would seem to unnecessarily add to investor risk.

Pinnacle's quant strategies offer a different solution to the problems with quantitative portfolio construction that I describe in this chapter. To better manage quant risk, we've simply appended a quant strategy as a satellite allocation to the rest of the portfolio. In this way, we believe we are avoiding the problem of relying 100% on quantitative decision-making. In one strategy, called the Dynamic Market Strategy, we utilize a core allocation that is 70% of the total portfolio that is designed as a classic, globally diversified, buy and hold portfolio, exactly as suggested by MPT. However, the 30% of the remaining portfolio, or the satellite portfolio, is a quantitatively driven strategy based on Pinnacle's proprietary valuation model. In building the quant allocation as a smaller, satellite allocation within the total portfolio, investors can manage the risks of buying and holding in overvalued markets in the core portfolio, and at the same time manage the risks of quant decision-making by limiting the amount of assets invested in the quantitatively managed satellite.

Our second quant-related investment product, called Dynamic Quant, is also a core and satellite construction, where 37.5% of the total portfolio is allocated to a quantitative, rules-based, satellite strategy. But the remaining 63.5% of the portfolio is invested in an actively managed tactical "core" portfolio strategy that is qualitatively managed using the skill, judgment, and informed intuition of Pinnacle's investment team. In both cases we believe we are managing quant risk by combining a quant satellite position with a strategic or tactical core allocation.

I encourage you to consider the benefits of quantitative, rules-based decision-making, as well as the unavoidable problems with quant that I detail in this chapter. As always, be careful of back-tested quantitative strategies that only delivered spectacular results in a computer simulation as opposed to real world investment performance delivered in real time. Note: See Chapter eight for an in-depth discussion of how backtested results can be abused. Also beware of trend-following strategies that make large asset allocation bets based solely on markets breaking above or below long or short-term trend lines. And finally, remember that any strategy that makes extreme asset allocation bets is probably not suitable as a stand-alone core holding for most investors. In that regard, if a quantitative strategy allows the portfolio to go to 100% cash in a bear market, it is probably suitable as a satellite strategy you should only consider for a small percentage of your investable assets.

On the other hand, remember that rules-based decision-making *can* add value when you consider that actively managed portfolios ask investors to accept manager risk—the risk that a portfolio manager with a long and distinguished track record is still human, and subject to biases and heuristics that are genetically programmed into all of us.

I've made no changes to the original text in the remainder of this chapter, because the case to be cautious about quant remains the same as ever.

## Looking at Quant

Quant models are the turbo-charged workhorses of the financial world. These mathematical models often use the science of statistics and probability to determine the construction of investment products and investment portfolios. Not only do quant models make portfolio investment decisions faster and easier, they do so with all the power and comforts of relying on "real science" rather than mere human judgment. Quantitative models are so vital for keeping the financial industry running; it's hard to imagine how professional investors would conduct themselves each day if they did not have them. But perhaps the greatest benefit of quantitative models is slightly less obvious. By relying on quant models, investors are relieved of the one thing that many would prefer to avoid: responsibility for being wrong about investment decisions that they make.

The advent of quant has become a necessary ingredient for the growth of the financial planning industry, which requires that planners be "generalists" with regard to the value proposition they offer their clients. Many planners simply do not have the time to follow all of the complicated micro- and macroeconomic variables needed to manage a portfolio by any other methodology. Quant models are also necessary for the institutional money management industry. Corporate and foundation investment officers, as well as the investment industry consultants that advise them, need a scientific and foolproof methodology for the asset allocation decisions they make. For professional planners and institutional money managers, like all investors, quantitative models relieve them from the responsibility of having to make subjective judgments about portfolio strategy, which of course also relieves them from ever being "wrong." It is hard to imagine a better tool for protecting an investment career than one that allows you to deny responsibility for poor portfolio performance.

But as useful as quant models are, they do have one major flaw. No quantitative model—no matter how sophisticated or complex—is better than the accuracy of the assumptions on which it rests or the relevance of the data used for its inputs. Quant models offer the promise of consistently delivering better results than fallible human judgment alone, but despite its promise of increased productivity, each quant model is ultimately only as good as the judgment of the mathematician who produced the model in the first place. As we will see, their judgment often is questionable to the point of putting an investor's portfolio at great risk.

To see convincing evidence that quant models are only as good as the subjective judgment of the people who create them, one only needs to look at the headlines. When 2008 came to a close, the U.S. financial markets were in a state of near panic, with banks, brokerages, hedge funds, monoline insurers, municipalities, and money market fund managers facing multi-billion dollar write-offs due to the miscalculation of the value of structured investment products. The rating agencies, having adjusted the quantitative models they used to evaluate the risk of default of subprime mortgages, were busy downgrading most of the RMBS (residential mortgaged backed securities), which were owned by banks, insurers, brokerages, hedge funds, and pension plans, and which were "wrapped" in other structured products, like CDOs (credit default obligations and CDO squareds.) These ratings downgrades had a dramatic negative impact on the financial industry and many worried that they put the capital structure of the entire global banking system at risk.

The reason that the rating agencies were adjusting their models is because they apparently assumed (incorrectly) that there was little risk of default in mortgages that had virtually no underwriting requirements. It was also assumed (again, incorrectly) that real estate values would continue to rise indefinitely into the future, just as they had risen in the recent past, which was a primary factor in the low default rates in subprime mortgages. We can only imagine the mathematical complexity of the powerful quantitative models that are used to evaluate the default rates of these complicated derivative securities, but in retrospect it seems easy to question how anyone creating a model for evaluating default risk would use such silly assumptions in the first place. Given that this is not the first time quantitative models have brought the banking system to the edge of a crisis (think Long-Term Capital Management), why does the investment industry persist in relying so heavily on these models without more thought to their underlying (sometimes dead wrong) assumptions?

The short answer is that it's easier to rely on quant models to make investment decisions than to make them ourselves. Unfortunately, we are seeing that relying entirely on quantitative models to make investment decisions is leading to catastrophic portfolio results. The objective of this chapter is not to convince investors to abandon quantitative decision-making, but to encourage them to consider adding an additional ingredient to the decision-making process: their own good sense.

Investors who are considering making the leap from strategic (passive) portfolio management to tactical (active) portfolio management will inevitably find themselves face to face with the difficult issue of choosing an investment strategy that allows them to be "wrong" in their own eyes, or in the eyes of their clients or their employers. This uncomfortable predicament is so different from the industry's status quo, where quant models are presumed to give us scientifically accurate investment recommendations, that it seems worthwhile to more fully explore the benefits and drawbacks of quantitative methodologies for decision-making. As we will see, there is strong evidence that making decisions based on quantitative methods is superior in many ways to decisions that are based on human judgment alone. However, as we will also discover, there are serious drawbacks to relying on any quantitative model, which means there is room for more than one approach to making investment decisions. In the end, there really is no foolproof way to resolve the fundamental problem that faces anyone who manages money. No matter what decision-making strategy you use, forecasting the future is fraught with uncertainty.

## The Nature of Black Boxes

Over the years, many great minds have poured lifetimes of effort into developing the powerful quantitative investment tools that we use today. It could be argued that the era of modern finance began with Bachelier's invention of the first quantitative model for pricing options in 1900, and that the entire modern industry of institutional money management and financial planning depends on quantitative methods of portfolio construction. Most investors think of "quant models" as super advanced mathematical models that are used to implement complicated long-short, market neutral, bond arbitrage, and other hedge fund strategies. However, the first quantitative model to be generally accepted by the money management industry was the model for means-variance portfolio optimization proposed by Harry Markowitz more than fifty years ago. This formula for portfolio construction, known as Modern Portfolio Theory, allows investors to "engineer" the construction of portfolios without any fundamental knowledge of financial markets. Anyone with access to the data necessary to run the model can build a scientifically accurate, perfectly efficient portfolio that will deliver the best possible returns for a given level of risk. Today, of course, historic market data is available to all as is the software needed to run this particular quant model.

The reasons for using quantitative models go back to the very basics of how we use science and mathematics to solve problems in the world. In his book, *The (mis)Behavior of Markets*, Benoit Mandelbrot gives an elegant explanation for why quantitative methods are so useful in science. He first describes how scientists in the 19th century believed that if only we had the vast knowledge of God, everything could be understood and predicted. He tells how the great French mathematician, the Marquis Pierre-Simon de Laplace, asserted that he could predict the future of the cosmos—if only he knew the present position and velocity of every particle in it. 19th century economists, called economic Marginalists, believed that they could theoretically construct a model for the one "true" mathematical explanation for the economy with their adaptation of the theory of marginal utility from the world of physics. This "cause and effect" way of looking at the world is what Mandelbrot describes as the deterministic approach. If we only had enough data, we could safely predict everything, including the future of the financial markets.

Of course we can't know everything, and scientists have long acknowledged that there is no way to perfectly model all cause and effect because the universe is a place of unimaginable complexity. Instead, science utilizes a different technique to model reality. Mandelbrot describes it like this:

> They (scientists) learned to think of the world in the second way, as a black box. We can see what goes into the box and what comes out of it, but not what happens inside; we can only draw inferences about the odds of input A producing output Z. Seeing nature through the lens of probability theory is what mathematicians call the stochastic view. The word comes from the Greek *stochastes*, a diviner, which in turn comes from *stokhos*, a pointed stake used as a target by archers. We cannot follow the path of every molecule in a gas; but we can work out its average energy and probable behavior, and thereby design a very useful pipeline to transport natural gas across a continent to fuel a city of millions.

We can think of the quantitative models that investors use today to construct investment portfolios as the investment industry's own "black box." The box, which is built from the assumptions and resulting mathematical equations of Modern Portfolio Theory and the Capital Asset Pricing Model, generates output based on the historical asset class performance data that investors enter into it. Because the investment industry relies on a probabilistic, stochastic view of the financial markets, investors do not need to understand the fundamental investment relationships between price, currency, interest rates, economic cycles, etc., that goes on inside the box. Instead they only need to make useful inferences about the probability of what comes out of it. In the case of MPT and CAPM, they can infer what constitutes the best mix of asset classes per any level of risk. Or, if you are (were) an investment banker, you can use Value at Risk (VaR) models to assess what the impact would be to your capital structure if portfolio volatility was more than you expected. The black box approach to portfolio construction resolves the problem of investors needing to understand the fundamental causes of market movements, because the causes are considered to be so complex that they are unknowable. Allowing academia to quantify the probabilities of future price movements using stochastic methods makes value investing, in the traditional sense of trying to analyze why a stock or a market is cheap or expensive, irrelevant.

Prior to the acceptance of Modern Portfolio Theory, it was accepted that earnings, dividends, cash flow, management, competition, interest rates, and a host of other factors needed to be analyzed by investors in order to determine the "value" of a security. The most well-known proponents of this type of analysis were Graham and Dodd, whose book, *Security Analysis*, is still considered to be the bible of value investing. It was assumed that the fair value of a security was the present value of the long-term future cash flows of a company. Investors who purchased the security at a price below its fair value would profit as other investors eventually recognized the same value proposition, buying the security until it reached "fair" value. Unfortunately, the entire process of determining fair value involves making many subjective judgments about future earnings, cash flows, competition, interest rates, etc. Investors presented with the same set of data would reach different conclusions about fair value. Graham and Dodd's methodology was as much art as it was science. Value (like beauty) resided in the eyes of the beholder.

The advent of Modern Portfolio Theory and CAPM made the Graham and Dodd methodology completely obsolete in the eyes of institutional investors, who were liberated from the work of determining whether a security or an asset class represented good value. This was possible because the underlying assumptions of the efficient market hypothesis assured investors that every asset class is always properly valued! In the most fundamental way the stochastic, scientific method had caught up to the money management industry. Valuation was deemed to be unimportant; as was all of the other aspects of security analysis necessary to determine fair value. MPT and CAPM became the investment industry's black box. *Investors no longer needed to know why prices move, they only needed to know that they did move.* By putting the details of past price movements into a black box, investors get a "scientific" solution to portfolio construction without the risk of misunderstanding or misperceiving the reasons for why prices move in the first place. In short, traditional value investing is based on cause and effect, and MPT and CAPM is based on a black box. Or, put another way, value investing is art, and MPT and CAPM is science. Since the perception is that the average investor has little desire to base their portfolio construction on "art," it is not hard to figure out which methodology became the investment industry's status quo.

## Behavioral Finance and Quantitative Models

The Nobel Prize–winning field of Behavioral Finance gives investors another good reason to embrace quantitative decision-making. In their groundbreaking work, *Judgment Under Uncertainty: Heuristics and Biases*[33], Daniel Kahneman and Amos Tversky showed that human beings are often not genetically "wired" to use good judgment in making financial decisions. They conducted a number of clever experiments to prove that humans are subject to many biases and heuristics in making choices about gains and losses. (Note: we will discuss these problems in more detail in Chapter 12.) They conclude that investors are far from being "rational" in their decisions about money, and instead are likely to make decisions that are based on basic human instincts and emotion. The results of this Nobel Prize–winning work have been confirmed repeatedly by researchers over the years, who continue to find quantitative decision-making superior to decisions that rely on skill or judgment in carefully controlled experiments.

James Montier, the Director of Global Strategy at Dresdner Kleinwort Watterstein, a London and Frankfurt based investment bank, in his article, "Painting by Numbers: An Ode to Quant,"[34] gives us an overview of some of the recent literature on the subject. Montier shows how in such diverse fields as baseball, wine, medical diagnosis, university admissions, and criminal recidivism, simple statistical models have outperformed so-called experts. Here is what Montier discovered about criminal recidivism:

> Between October 1977 and May 1987, 1035 convicts became eligible for parole in Pennsylvania. They were interviewed by a parole specialist who assigned them a score on a five point scale based on the prognosis for supervision, risk of future crime, etc. 743 of these cases were then put before a parole board. 85% of those appearing before the board were granted parole, the decisions (bar one) following the recommendation

33  Daniel Kahneman and Amos Tversky, *Judgment Under Uncertainty, Heuristics and Biases*, Cambridge University Press, Cambridge, UK, 1982.
34  John Mauldin published this essay in his e-letter, *Outside the Box*, Investors Insight Publishing, August 26, 2006, www.investorsinsight.com

of the parole specialist. 25% of the parolees were recommitted to prison, absconded, or arrested for another crime with the year. The parole board predicted none of these. Caroll et al compared the accuracy of prediction from the parole board's ranking, with that of a prediction based on a three factor model driven by the type of offence, the number of past convictions and the number of violations of prison rules. The parole board's ranking was correlated 6% with recidivism. The three factor model had a correlation of 22%.

In this case, the quantitative approach was clearly superior to the experts. Another example of quantitative modeling in Montier's paper had to do with purchasing managers:

> Professor Chris Snijders has been examining the behavior of models versus purchasing managers. He has examined purchasing managers at 300 different organizations. The results will not be surprising to those reading this note. Snijders concludes, "We find that (a) judgments of professional managers are meager at best, and (b) certainly not better than the judgments by less experienced managers or even amateurs. Furthermore, (c) neither general nor specific human capital of managers has an impact on their performance, and (d) a simple formula outperforms the average (and the above average) manager even when the formula only has half of the information as compared to the manager.

Montier's paper, and indeed the entire field of Behavioral Finance, seems to make a strong case for using quant models like MPT and CAPM to determine portfolio construction. The obvious conclusion is that the Nobel Prize–winning black boxes built by Markowitz and Sharpe are better models for making financial decisions than any subjective, deterministic approach that relies on investor judgment. How can investors determine good value when they are genetically programmed to make a whole host of mistakes in their analysis? Montier concludes that even the simplest statistical models outperform expert human judgment in many diverse fields, and that investors would do well to consider using them to properly construct portfolios.

## The Limitations of the Black Box
Paul Volcker (former Chairman of the U.S. Federal Reserve) on the Charlie Rose Show in February 2008:

Charlie Rose: Somebody said to me that we entered a period in which they were worshiping mathematical models… And mathematical models had no business sense.

Paul Volker: The market was being run by mathematicians that didn't know financial markets. And you keep hearing, you know, god, that event should only happen once every hundred years, according to my model. But those every hundred years events are coming along every two or three years, which should raise some questions.[35]

Indeed, when models of the financial markets completely fail to forecast real world events, then as Paul Volcker says, it should raise some questions. If investors are to view the world through the lens of the stochastic method, where we don't need to understand the cause of future price changes, but only the probability that they will occur, then it's vitally important that we consider the limitations of the magical black boxes that give us the answers we need to construct portfolios. If we are to concede that humans are terribly flawed decision-makers, subject to all of the biases and heuristics revealed to us by behavioral finance research, then we also must also recognize that our black boxes (quantitative models) are subject to the same flaws. After all, it is humans who build these quantitative models, and it is humans who select the data that goes into these models. As we will see, there are multiple problems with the quantitative models that we rely on to manage assets. Based on the empirical evidence, it seems that our reliance on "scientific" quant models as the only methodology for reaching decisions about portfolio construction may be a higher-risk proposition than many investors bargained for. At a time when our mightiest financial institutions are trying to avoid disaster in part because they relied too heavily on flawed quant models, shouldn't investors be doubly concerned about the financial industry's blind faith in the black box approach to portfolio construction?

To understand the basic problem with relying entirely on quantitative models for making decisions about portfolio construction, we need to look at three core issues:

- How data is chosen to input into the quantitative model
- How mathematics determines what happens outside the model
- And most importantly, the accuracy of the output of quantitative models

---

35   This small excerpt of the Charlie Rose and Paul Volcker discussion can be found online at http://video. google.com/videoplay?docid=1047202915400865465

## Data, Data Everywhere

The world is awash in potential information. What distinguishes the golden nuggets of relevant data from the huge background of less useful noise? In other words, based on what you are trying to achieve, how do you know what information is important and what isn't?

Nassim Nicholas Taleb's wonderful books, *Fooled By Randomness* and *The Black Swan*, provide rare insights into the data-selection process that can create false beliefs about the correct inputs for quantitative models. In *The Black Swan*, Taleb describes what might be the data selection process of a Thanksgiving-bound turkey being raised on a farm. (Taleb notes that his turkey tale comes from the great philosopher Bertrand Russell, who used a chicken in the original story.)

> Consider a turkey that is fed every day. Every single feeding will firm up the bird's belief that it is the general rule of life is to be fed every day by friendly members of the human race "looking out for its best interests," as a politician would say. On the afternoon of the Wednesday before Thanksgiving, something unexpected will happen to the turkey. It will incur a revision of belief.

Not only was the turkey's data selection process fatally flawed and of no value, it turned out to be worse than worthless because it created a false sense of security that convinced the poor bird not to invest any time in attempting to escape. In this case, relying on past data created a false set of beliefs that unfortunately had to be "revised." Taleb points out this very real problem of inductive reasoning:

> Let us go one step further and consider induction's most worrisome aspect: learning backward. Consider that the turkey's experience may have, rather than no value, a negative value. It learned from observation, as we are all advised to do (hey, after all, this is what is believed to be the scientific method). Its confidence increased as the number of friendly feedings grew, and it felt increasingly safe even though the slaughter was more and more imminent. Consider that the feeling of safety reached its maximum when the risk was at the highest! But the problem is even more general than that; it strikes at the nature of empirical knowledge itself. Something has worked in the past, until—well, it unexpectedly no longer does, and what we have learned from the past turns out to be at best irrelevant or false, at worst viciously misleading.

There are many useful lessons to learn from Taleb's turkey. Whenever investors use past data to populate black boxes, they must be very careful not to build a model that elevates past data to objective truth about the future. Clearly, various hedge funds have blown up due to making mistakes of this kind. The same can be said of the MPT/CAPM model, which is often misused in a manner that assumes that the means and variances of the past will be realized with certainty in the future. Professor Kurz teaches us that while this assumption is rational, unless the world never changes it most certainly will be wrong. And as we saw in the chapter on secular bear markets, these kinds of incorrect assumptions lead many investors to the same revision of belief as Taleb's Thanksgiving turkey. Fortunately, they will be not be served for dinner. However, their retirement plan may very well end up in shambles.

When choosing the data to input into a quantitative model, how do investors know that they are not making the same mistake as the turkey? Investors who subscribe to the MPT methodology should know that most optimizing software programs come preloaded with asset class data going back to the 1970's. One fundamental question for investors to answer is how we are using this data to populate our black box. For example, the oldest past data series that are typically used in mean-variance models goes back as far as 1928. Ibbotson Associates publishes the total return data for stocks, bonds, bills, and inflation for every year for that entire time frame. They also publish the standard deviation and correlations of the data for the entire period. In addition, they offer the data for one year, five-year, ten-year, and twenty-year holding periods, and they give us the average return for each of these holding periods calculated as the arithmetic and geometric mean. The Yearbook also uses inflation statistics to give us the historic risk premium for stocks since 1928.

Using the data in this way is the methodology described by Woody Brock as being static, non-linear programming. Most investors using Ibbottson data are simply using arithmetic or geometric averages of past data in order to determine the inputs for the MPT model. According to modern probability theorists, there is a better and more dynamic approach to using data. The new methodology, known as the non-i.i.d. method (non-independent and identically distributed random variables), results in different and more optimal results for quantitative models. In other words, our black boxes give us more useful output because we use a different approach to the data. Or, as we saw in the last chapter, if stated in the context of MPT, the non-i.i.d. approach gives us the potential to build more efficient portfolios, the highest being the "true" efficient frontier as proposed by Brock. It is only when we add a subjective element in our decision-making that can't be found in the past data that we elevate to the most efficient of all portfolio constructions, found on the "subjective" efficient frontier.

Regardless of the choices that are knowingly or unknowingly being made by investors who use the MPT and CAPM models, it seems to me to be unassailably true that presenting the past data in the form of color graphics and charts is very persuasive. For investors who are the true believers in buy and hold investing, viewing color mountain charts of past performance gives the strong impression that the historical data must lead to meaningful and scientific conclusions about portfolio construction. Furthermore, most financial planners present the data as if it were a certainty that the data will repeat in the future, rather than merely being a forecast of how these assets will perform in the future based on a flawed, static, non-linear programming approach to data. Ibbotson's mountain charts showing the cumulative returns of the markets are well-known to most investors, and unfortunately many investment advisors use them to improperly "sell" the idea of buying and holding stocks for the long run. These are the investors who will continually have a "revision of belief" about the meaning of past data.

The bottom line for investors is that relying on average past performance data for inputs into our black box is rational, but wrong unless nothing ever changes in the future. The static, non-linear approach to data offers all of the trappings of certainty about the future when the model gives us its "scientific" answer for how to construct a portfolio. By now, investors should realize that these black boxes offer no certainty whatsoever in forecasting future portfolio performance, and in fact offer a lower probability of being correct than most investors realize. Investors should understand that while quant solutions offer a valuable piece to the puzzle of portfolio construction, relying too much on a black box approach to investing may be adding a new type of risk to their investment strategy.

## What Happens Inside the Black Box?

During the week of August 6, 2007, a number of quantitative long/ short equity hedge funds experienced unprecedented losses. Based on TASS hedge fund data and simulations of a specific long/short equity strategy, we hypothesize that the losses were initiated by the rapid "unwind" of one or more sizable quantitative equity market-neutral portfolios. Given the speed and price impact with which this occurred, it was likely the result of a forced liquidation by a multi-strategy fund or proprietary-trading desk, possibly due to a margin call or a risk reduction. These initial losses then put pressure on a broader set of long/short and long-only equity portfolios, causing further losses by triggering stop/loss and de-leveraging policies. A significant rebound of these strategies occurred on August 10th, which is also consistent with the unwind hypothesis. This dislocation was apparently caused by forces outside the long/short equity sector—in a completely unrelated set of markets and instruments suggesting that systematic risk in the hedge-fund industry may have increased in recent years.[36]

One of the biggest problems with quantitative strategies is that even the brilliant Ph.D.'s who construct them are no more capable of modeling reality than the rest of us. In their paper, *What Happened to the Quants in August 2007?*, MIT graduate students Khandani and Lo discuss the many causes of the meltdown that occurred in quantitative portfolios during the month of August 2007. Clearly, in this case, the models did not predict the speed of the "unwind" of sizeable quantitative market-neutral funds. They also failed to model the cascading impact that these unwinds had on other types of hedge fund strategies, causing even more forced selling. The authors of the paper conclude that forces outside of the long/short sector in completely unrelated markets might have been responsible for the unusual and unexpected returns, which of course, no one was able to model before the fact. The events of 2008 have certainly confirmed that the systematic risk in the hedge fund industry has dramatically increased in recent years. As we have discussed, the systematic risk is in no small part attributed to the industry's determined reliance on quantitative decision-making.

For the average investor who is required to memorize the mathematical equations for MPT and CAPM in order to pass the CFP® practitioner and CFA® exams, the nuances of the mathematics are completely lost in the massive overload of information that needs to be learned in order to pass the tests. These mathematical black boxes are ancient in terms of their complexity, compared to modern day quantitative models used to manage long/short, market-neutral, convertible arbitrage, distressed security, and other contemporary hedge fund strategies. While MPT and CAPM are more than 40 years old, it is fair to observe that many investors have difficulty understanding the mathematics of these older quantitative models, not to mention the extraordinary mathematical gymnastics of the more current quantitative approaches. Today's highly advanced quant models have become the playgrounds for the very brightest students from leading business schools, leaving the internal workings of these black boxes a complete mystery to most investors.

I call this new kind of risk, which is the risk of not fully understanding the complexities of quantitative models, "quant risk." It is an acknowledgment that there is a certain kind of systematic risk that occurs when investors invest in quant model–driven portfolio strategies that they will never completely understand. While investors can clearly understand the theoretical benefits of investing in quant-driven portfolios, and are more than capable of analyzing the past returns of these types of managed accounts (assuming that the past returns are not distorted by survivorship

---

36   Amir E. Khandani and Andrew W. Lo, *What Happened to the Quants in August 2007?*, Latest Revision November 4, 2007.

bias and other problems with studying past hedge fund returns), they should own quantitatively managed mutual funds, hedge funds, and separate accounts, fully understanding that one morning they may wake up and experience a "revision of belief" similar to Taleb's Thanksgiving turkey. If and when the unexpected meltdown comes, they can attribute it to quant risk, which is a type of risk that seems to be unavoidable in today's derivative-driven markets.

Of course, the fact that investors can't understand the complexity of the models may be moot because modern quantitative models are proprietary in nature. Unlike the formulas for MPT, CAPM, and their successor pricing models, today's quantitative models are privately owned and guarded with the greatest secrecy. The underlying mathematics and subsequent computer models are the result of huge investments of time and money by the investment firms who own them, and the best quant models presumably give investment firms a competitive edge that is worth millions of dollars to investment professionals, whether they understand them or not.

In an increasingly complicated and uncertain investment climate, it's understandable that all investors yearn for a quantitative model that works. Quant models offer the Holy Grail for investing money "correctly," while releasing investors from a large degree of personal accountability for investment decisions. If the portfolio loses money, then something must be wrong with the model, the computer, or the math geeks—anything and anyone but me! But as much as we would love for these magic black boxes to work perfectly, the fact is that the very construction of quant models, from the simplest to the most complex, is fraught with human misunderstandings and errors in judgment. The irony is that while only the anointed few can understand and explain the mathematics in today's complex world of quantitative decision-making, it is readily apparent that the underlying assumptions of some these models are as flawed as the false hopes of a Thanksgiving turkey.

Unfortunately, the investment community still leaps to the defense of the two quant models that drive so many of our portfolio construction decisions, MPT and CAPM. It would be nice to believe that the lack of critical discussion about our reliance on these quant models is due to their impressive accuracy over the years. Unfortunately, based on actual results, that has not always been the case.

## The Bottom Line: Is the Output Any Good?

As we discussed earlier, investors who rely on quantitative models are not required to understand *why* prices change, only that they do. Price changes are assumed to be the result of stochastic processes driven by probability theory that occur inside of a black box, and the ultimate test of the usefulness of the black box is whether or not the output of the box is accurate. In other words, did its predictions about the future become true in reality? Because investors are taught that the quantitative method for portfolio construction is the only true and "scientific" method for reliable decision-making, it is only fair to evaluate how these models perform in meeting the standard of explaining or predicting actual market behavior.

We don't have to look far to find obvious examples of quantitative models that completely failed to accurately model market behavior. For example, Long-Term Capital Management LP was a hedge fund that used the best quantitative models of the day.[37] At one point they employed 25 Ph.D.'s, including Nobel Prize winners Merton and Scholes, and managed more than $7 billion using leverage as high as 50-1. Unfortunately, in 1998 the Russian government defaulted on its bonds and the fund "blew up" in one of the most spectacular financial disasters of our time. Another example occurred in August 2007, when much of the hedge fund industry suffered completely unexpected losses due to rapid "unwinds" of certain quant strategies. In a preview of one of the biggest financial meltdowns of all time, in July of 2007, two Bear Stearns hedge funds that owned structured products based on sub-prime mortgages went belly-up when their risk models failed to properly forecast the default risk of sub-prime and Alt-A mortgages.

The Bear Stearns meltdown was just the beginning. It could be argued that the entire investment banking business in the U.S. has been vaporized because of the industry's reliance on poorly constructed quantitative risk models. These models are at least partially responsible for the AAA investment ratings for high-risk financial products, lax regulation, and the now well-known chain of events that has led to trillions of dollars of Federal bailouts of the financial system itself. The recalibration of valuation models by rating agencies and the resulting problems with "mark to model" versus "mark to market" accounting has resulted in billions of dollars of downgrades in financial securities. The whole idea of "model-based pricing" for non-liquid structured products has produced an ongoing crisis in confidence in the valuation of mortgage-backed products. Whether or not financial institutions will be allowed to price non-liquid mortgaged-backed and other asset-backed securities on a "mark to market" basis versus a "mark to model" basis will have a huge and direct impact on the solvency of U.S. banks. The irony is, of course, that everyone realizes that the models being used for "mark to model" accounting are completely inaccurate and have nothing to do with the actual market value of the structured products that are currently residing on bank, and now the Federal Reserve, balance sheets. It is clear that quantitative analysis has come under heavy fire lately as bad judgment in building quant models has trumped any benefit they may have added

---

37 For an excellent discussion of the demise of Long-Term Capital Management, read Roger Lowenstein's book, *When Genius Failed, The Rise and Fall of Long-Term Capital Management*, Random House Publishing, New York, N.Y., 2000

by offering the promise of eliminating subjective mistakes that individual investors may make in security analysis.

If there is one model to blame for the tsunami of financial problems that is overwhelming the U.S. financial system, and the global economy, critics would contend that it is the Black-Scholes model for pricing options. The Black-Scholes pricing model uses advanced mathematics to forecast how time and the underlying volatility of stocks that options are written on, impact the price of stock options. Critics contend that the industry's reliance on this model is responsible for the growth of the derivatives industry in the U.S. and around the world. If financial participants like investment banks, hedge funds, monoline insurers, pension funds, mortgage companies, etc., used extreme leverage in the pursuit of profits, it was at least partially due to the fact that risk was presumed to be hedged in the derivatives markets through a variety of complex financial securities that acted as risk insurance. According to critics, the idea that extreme market events can be insured by using derivatives is directly related to Black-Scholes. Yet the model is flawed because, like MPT and CAPM, it uses standard deviation as the measure of volatility for securities. And in financial panics, we know that market prices for the underlying securities do not behave "normally" as standard deviation would suggest. Instead, in a selling panic, markets simply stop functioning as buyers disappear. As Paul Volcker complained to Charlie Rose, at that point the mathematicians who were running the models were completely lost, because actual market volatility spiked to levels that can't be modeled using antiquated tools that rely on normal measures of risk. The result for the institutional investors has been catastrophic.

While it is unfortunate that large institutional investors relied on poor quantitative methods to try to achieve superior investment returns by investing in complicated structured financial products that ultimately failed, the average investor had little to do with the financial calamities mentioned above. The quant model that most investors are familiar with and that guides the portfolio construction for most institutional money managers is the MPT and CAPM means-variance quantitative methodology. We have already seen that the inputs that go into the model have an enormous impact on the output of the model, and that investors have to use their judgment in deciding how data should be used for inputs. And we have learned in previous chapters that many of the assumptions used to describe what goes on inside the black box of MPT and CAPM have been disproved over the past 40 years since the models were first published. But despite these problems, is it possible that the models are still useful in accurately describing the reality of financial markets?

Unfortunately the answer is no. In the business world, corporate MBA's who learned CAPM as a methodology for forecasting future business values recognize that the model is very limited in its real world application. In addition, there are many academic studies that have found CAPM to be inaccurate. For example, in Chapter 3, we discussed Fama's Three Factor Model and his findings that market capitalization and book-to-price ratios are more important than beta in predicting future prices. Remember that CAPM concludes that beta is the only factor that drives future security prices.

There are several other studies (by Kurz and others) identifying "anomalies" or paradoxes in which CAPM appears to be in conflict with theoretical and empirical observations, as well as with common experience. These problems include:

- The standard deviation of returns of the stock market is 4 times that predicted by CAPM.
- The standard deviation of the P/E ratio of the S&P 500 is 50 times that predicted by CAPM.
- The paradoxical existence of GARCH phenomena (momentum) should be impossible under CAPM.
- The existence of forward-bias in the FOREX (foreign exchange) markets should not occur in CAPM.
- The market equity risk premium is 10 times higher than what is predicted in classic CAPM.
- Cash yields are 1/10th that predicted by classical CAPM theory.

Clearly, investors should be wary of the accuracy of the quantitative models that are the fundamental basis for modern portfolio construction.[38]

## The Ultimate Solution: Use Both Methods

Clearly, quantitative methods are useful in making decisions about portfolio construction. Anyone who has had to exercise their judgment in making a decision about security selection or asset allocation knows that the human decision-making process is flawed. In fact, later in this book there is an entire chapter about the psychology of making mistakes.

Human beings are not computers. Psychologists tell us that we tend to oversimplify the facts in order to make a decision. We build mental narratives that might not be accurate in order to justify our decisions. We don't want to be wrong, which influences our judgment when we know what the consensus thinks. Other investors tend to overestimate their own expertise and tend to underestimate the conclusions of others. Investors don't want to lose money, and at the same time they

---

38   Note: For a more complete list of the proper references for the academic and theoretical work on these subjects, see Mordecai Kurz, *Endogenous Uncertainty: A Unified View of Market Volatility*, Stanford University, 1997.

worry about trailing their performance benchmarks for an extended period of time. Clearly, qualitative, human, judgment-driven decision-making is fraught with flaws.

But as imperfect as qualitative decision-making may be, we have seen that decisions based on quantitative models can be much worse. Perhaps as science progresses, quantitative models will become so accurate that we can justify abandoning our best judgment in making investment decisions. However, the current evidence shows that quantitative models are still burdened with so many human errors that every serious investor should question how these models are used in the investment process. Certainly in the case with MPT and CAPM, the models have failed to accurately model empirical reality. Since these models are used to justify the strategic, buy and hold methodology for portfolio construction, it follows that investors need to finally leave their blind adherence to this one investment strategy behind.

So what's the best solution for serious investors? I believe the best strategy is to combine a more deterministic, cause and effect approach to understanding why prices move, with a quantitative approach to decision-making. After 50 years of the pendulum swinging towards the black box methodology, the time has come to consider a more *qualitative*, value-oriented decision-making process, not to replace but to enhance the quantitative process. This new value-driven decision process need not be overly complicated, and could start with the simplest possible statement of cause and effect. For example, investors could start with the premise that buying securities when they are undervalued is associated with a high probability of achieving above-average returns in the future, and of course, buying securities when they are overvalued will result in a high probability of achieving lower than expected returns. In the case of undervalued securities, the cause of future above-average returns is attractive valuation, however it is defined. The returns are not the result of stochastic probability models, but are determined by how individual investors derive the characteristic of good value.

If this assumption is correct, you no longer need MPT and CAPM to model future returns. All you need is to learn how to make a careful and systematic evaluation of good value. Of course, the bad news is that determining good value is not easy. It takes time and effort. It takes experience. It requires that investors utilize their expertise and good judgment in a qualitative as well as a quantitative process, making it as much of an art as it is a science. Naturally, not every investor will be an equally good artist—a message that the financial planning industry may be reluctant to embrace.

However, the good news is that the process of determining good value has been around for a very long time. Graham and Dodd were writing in great detail about the subject long before Harry Markowitz thought to apply means-variance to portfolio construction. For the past 40 years the financial industry has only taught quantitative methods as the proper way to manage portfolios. For investors moving from strategic, passive portfolio construction to active, tactical portfolio management, art, as well as science, will become an integral part of the investment process. This change requires a different skill set for investors who are schooled in MPT and CAPM, which is why the entire second half of this book is devoted to putting active portfolio management into successful action.

In the next chapter, we address the ultimate nagging question for any portfolio manager considering the switch from the passive to active approach: Does it actually work in the real world?

# 7 COMPELLING EVIDENCE THAT ACTIVE MANAGEMENT REALLY WORKS

The first half of this book offers a new way of looking at passive, strategic buy and hold investing. So far, we've seen that the passive approach, rather than limiting risk, actually puts investors at increasing risk, especially as they near retirement, because the buy and hold strategy falsely presumes that the stock market will continue to yield historical average returns even when the stock market is expensive and experiencing a long-term secular bear market. Part One also reveals that many of the key ideas that justify the passive, buy and hold approach—including Modern Portfolio Theory, the Capital Asset Pricing Model, and the Three Factor Model—depend on tortured assumptions that are simply untrue. And despite the investment industry's relentless desire to find a scientific, mathematically driven "black box" formula for successful portfolio construction, it seems that many quantitative models have their own significant problems. Fortunately, for those who are willing to think outside the black box, there is a growing body of cutting-edge academic work that now gives real credence to the practice of active portfolio management and tactical asset allocation.

But before we explore the many practical, day-to-day issues of implementing tactical asset allocation, there is still a nagging issue that must be addressed: Can you prove that an active approach will actually outperform passive portfolio management, either at the asset class level (tactical asset allocation), or at the money manager level (mutual funds or separate accounts)? Even casual students of money management know the conventional wisdom: Active money managers *cannot* outperform the passive indexes. Studies consistently show that markets are efficient and managers, on average, cannot outperform. So even though the underlying assumptions that justify passive investing are doubtful, this pesky notion of efficient markets remains. Tactical asset allocation seems like a good idea in theory, but if the universe of fund managers can't beat their benchmarks, how can a tactical investor identify "good value?" Won't the market of asset classes quickly identify value and arbitrage it away, proving that value is no easier to find at the asset class level than it is to find at the security level of portfolio construction? Put another way, if managers of individual stocks can't beat their style-specific benchmarks; is it reasonable to think that a portfolio manager can add value at the asset class level?

Surprisingly, two researchers at Yale University say "yes." Instead of looking at the performance of fund managers based on tracking error (which is the difference between managed portfolio performance and the benchmark portfolio), they came up with a second metric for comparison that throws a whole new light on the issue. Based on this way of evaluating the differences in performance, the Yale researchers found conclusive evidence that active management consistently and significantly does add value over and above the returns generated by passive portfolio management.

## Understanding the Debate

There is no debate more heated in the investment community than the dispute about active versus passive management. However, the context for the debate is somewhat limited. The vast majority of investors are buy and hold, strategic (passive) asset allocators, meaning they devise asset allocations for their portfolios that typically do not change over time. Usually the modifications made are called "lifestyle" changes, which typically occur as an investor gets closer to retirement and their portfolio asset allocation is altered to be more conservative to provide a more stable asset base for anticipated portfolio withdrawals. Once the portfolio is reallocated for retirement, there may be no further changes to asset allocation policy for the lifetime of the investor.

The portfolio asset allocation becomes the "target" allocation for the portfolio, and most investors are taught to rebalance the portfolio back to the fixed target percentages for each asset class based on either a calendar method or a rules-based method. As we have seen in earlier chapters, the academic and theoretical basis for this strategic, buy and hold approach has its roots in Modern Portfolio Theory and the Capital Asset Pricing Model. Because markets are considered to be efficient, and investors are considered to have perfect economic foresight, there is no need to change the asset allocation of client portfolios because the assumption is that today's capitalization-weighted allocation of global markets is always efficiently priced.

However, it is somewhat baffling that in the practical world of individual investors and investment professionals, this insistence on buying and holding asset classes due to efficient markets does not translate to the level of investing each asset class in the portfolio. The majority of investment advisors choose to use active fund managers when they invest the asset classes they have selected for their clients, as opposed to passively investing in index funds for each asset class. Apparently financial advisors believe that active fund managers, in the form of mutual fund or separate account managers can outperform their specific asset allocation benchmarks, which ironically is a strong statement that markets are not, in fact, efficient.

Therefore, one conclusion that can be reached about this inconsistent state of affairs is that many investors believe that fund managers can beat the performance of efficient markets, but they, themselves, cannot. Why? Perhaps the two groups are somehow genetically wired so that only one can actively manage money. It is very ironic that many financial advisors will vehemently deny that they are active managers when it comes to asset allocation strategy, while at the same time vehemently defend their use of the active fund managers that they use to invest client portfolios. It is possible that in the case of some investment advisors their insistence on using active managers for the investment of asset classes is due to a very practical need to differentiate their services from other advisors. After all, if everyone is a passive, buy and hold, strategic asset allocator, then being able to sell "better" active managers at the asset-class level to prospective new clients becomes very important.

There is a further irony to the insistence of investors on using active fund managers for the investment of asset classes, while also insisting that they (the investors) should be passive in their asset allocation decisions regarding asset classes. The academic world has been studying the ability of active fund managers to outperform passive indexes since the late 1960's, and the results have not been kind to the idea that active managers can outperform. In fact, dozens of studies have shown that the average active fund manager cannot outperform either the Capital Asset Pricing Model, or a passive benchmark of stocks. The results of these studies have been well publicized in the media, and informed investors are well aware of them. In addition, the proponents of index fund investing often repeat the message that active management does not add value compared to passive management. These venerable and wise investment sages (John Bogle, the founder of Vanguard Investment Group, is a good example) are held up to be friends of the consumer who understand, better than the rest of us, why active management does not work. Over and over again, the message is that active management is a waste of time and money, and investors should simply own the market itself. It is a message that permeates the consciousness of professional and non-professional investors alike. Yet, the majority of investors still utilize active managers to invest the various asset classes in their strategically asset-allocated portfolios. Clearly, while the *average* fund manager may trail the passive indexes for each asset class, investors feel that *their* fund manager will not.

It is true that the majority of academic studies conclude that active management does not add value for investors. However, a closer look at how many studies were conducted reveals several flaws in their methodology that are not as well-known as the accepted conclusion about active versus passive management. For example, many of the earlier studies were based on a small universe of actively managed funds, probably because the databases to analyze large amounts of fund data were not yet available. The earliest studies evaluated less than 200 funds, hardly enough to be a meaningful sample. Another problem with the studies had to do with choosing a benchmark. Large groups of style-specific funds were often compared to a broad market benchmark like the S&P 500 Index, which often led to conclusions that were colored by investment style as opposed to active management itself. Perhaps the biggest problem with the historical studies that attempt to answer the question of whether or not active managers can add value to portfolio performance above the expected returns as determined by the CAPM model, or broad market benchmarks, is that these studies look at one dimension of return, which is called tracking error. They compare portfolio and index performance without making any qualitative assessment about the securities that are owned in each.

What if there were an academic study that proved that individual fund managers actually do outperform their benchmarks with persistence in a statistically significant way? If truly active fund managers, as opposed to closet indexers, were shown to be able to beat their style-specific benchmarks, then perhaps the idea that investors should put their brains to sleep because markets are efficient would become less attractive. As it happens, two researchers at Yale University have conclusively shown that the most active fund managers actually do significantly outperform their style-specific benchmarks. Their study is important because it helps to allay the fear that using judgment and experience in constructing portfolios is futile.

### "Active Share"

In 2007, the Yale University School of Management published an important paper called "How Active Is Your Fund Manager? A New Measure That Predicts Performance,"[39] by Martijn Cremers and Antti Petajisto, which has taken the air out of previous studies that say active management doesn't work. As the authors explain, the other studies comparing fund managers to benchmarks rely on the traditional method of evaluating how funds perform compared to benchmark returns, which is to use tracking error (the amount of the volatility between a

---

39   K.J. Martijn Cremers, Antti Petajisto, *How Active is Your Fund Manager? A New Measure That Predicts Performance*, Yale School of Management, October 3, 2007.

fund's return and its passive benchmark return) as a guide. But tracking error does not explain whether fund performance is impacted by stock selection or by sector or industry selection.

Instead of merely analyzing tracking error, the authors of the Yale study did something entirely different: They compared the active fund portfolio *holdings* to its benchmark index holdings. Based on this comparison, they concluded that if a fund overweights a fund holding relative to the benchmark holding, it is considered to have an active long position in the stock. If a fund underweights an index stock or doesn't own it at all it implicitly has a short position in that stock. With this methodology they then show that funds own 100% of the benchmark index stocks, plus or minus the implied long and short positions. They call the net total of the implied long and short positions the "Active Share" of a fund. Since mutual funds almost never take actual short positions, they find that the Active Share of funds is always between 0% and 100%. Funds with Active Share greater than 80% are considered "stock pickers." Funds that are non-index funds with an Active Share less than 60% are considered to be closet indexers. Funds with Active Shares less than 20% are Index funds.

Cremers and Petajisto came to these conclusions after analyzing massive amounts of data. They analyzed individual stock holdings and monthly and daily returns for three different families of index funds, including the S&P/ Barra, Russell, and Wilshire Indexes. They then collected an exhaustive amount of data on the universe of mutual funds, including the individual holdings of each fund and the monthly and daily returns of the funds from a variety of databases. In the end, after thoroughly scrubbing the fund data to make sure that they had a reliable sample of funds, they studied the Active Share of 2,650 funds in the period 1980-2003. Because they compared the individual holdings of the funds to the individual holdings of the benchmark indexes, they were able to choose the best possible benchmark for each fund by coming up with the closest match between fund holdings and benchmark holdings. This resolved the problems with similar studies where critics argued that active managers were not being compared to an accurate benchmark, thereby invalidating the results of the study.

The Yale study's conclusions about active management are startling. They show that active management should be measured in two dimensions: tracking error and Active Share.[40] Tracking error measures the volatility of portfolio return around a

---

40   Source: Yale School of Management. Note: **Figure 7.1** shows different types of active and passive management, as revealed by a two-dimensional picture. Active Share represents the fraction of portfolio holdings that differ from the benchmark index, thus emphasizing stock selection. Tracking error is the volatility of fund return in excess of the benchmark, so it emphasizes bets on systematic risk. Active funds with concentrated portfolios of individual stocks have the highest exposure to Active Share and tracking error. Factor bets represent active

benchmark index, whereas Active Share measures the deviation of portfolio *holdings* from the holding of the benchmark index. The study's methodology identifies different types of active management: diversified stock picks, concentrated stock picks, sector rotators (factor bets), closet indexing, and pure indexing.

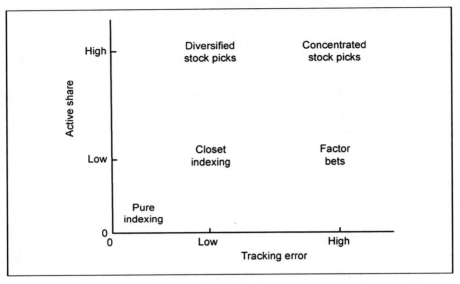

**Figure 7.1**

Source: Yale School of Management

The study confirms the popular belief that small funds are more actively managed than large funds. They also found that a significant percentage of large funds were closet indexers after their size increased over $1 billion in assets. In fact, the active share of "active" all-equity mutual funds in the U.S. ranges from 30% to 100%, with an average of 66% for large-cap funds. This means that the average large-cap fund essentially indexes one third of its assets, while the worst closet indexers index two thirds of their assets. The study found that there has been a significant shift from active to passive management in the 1990's. Prior to the 1990's most mutual funds were truly active, while in recent years the number of actively managed funds has dropped to 20% - 30% of all funds. This is partly due to index funds, but "an even larger part is due to closet indexers and a general tendency of funds to mimic the holding of benchmark indexes more closely," say the study's authors. They also found that half of the active positions at the fund level cancel out within the mutual fund sector, so that the entire mutual fund industry is less actively managed.

managers who make bets on systematic risk relative to the index. They could be overweighting value versus growth, large versus small-cap stocks, or have an index beta different from 1.

But here's the truly earth-shattering conclusion from this study. They find that not only does Active Share predict fund returns, but that funds with the highest Active Shares significantly outperform their benchmarks both before and after expenses, while funds with the lowest Active Share underperform after expenses. On average, funds with the highest Active Share exhibit some skill and pick portfolios which outperform their benchmarks by 2.00—2.71% per year. After fees and transaction costs, this outperformance decreases to 1.49—1.59% per year. However, the highest performing group of funds was the group with the highest Active Share, smallest assets, and the best prior one-year performance. This group outperformed their benchmarks by 6% per year, even after deducting fees and transaction costs. In addition, the study finds that active management, as measured by Active Share, is persistent, where tracking error is not. In other words, ranking funds by their relative performance versus a benchmark alone is not likely to predict winning funds in the future, but adding active management to the analysis does.

While Cremers and Petajisto excluded pure index funds from their study, they did find that the funds with the lowest Active Share (closet indexers) underperformed. These funds actually had lower returns than actual index funds because of their higher fees. Importantly, however, funds that were the most actively managed showed persistently higher returns, even after considering fees and expenses. In fact, they found no correlation between fund returns and fees and expenses when studying Active Share. This is an important discovery since one of the biggest objections to active management is that the added transactions involved create additional fees that are presumed to be an insurmountable headwind to beating index performance. The 6% alpha or outperformance of the best performing group, consisting of small funds that had the best performance in the prior year and the highest active share, after fees and expenses, is staggering. It gives credence to those investors who have said that while fund managers on average may not be able to outperform, the particular mutual fund manager that they own in their portfolio is simply superior to the average.

It appears that the reason that active managers couldn't outperform passive benchmarks is because they weren't really actively managing the portfolios in the first place. With the publication of Fama and French's Three Factor Model and the subsequent overwhelming concern about manager style, it is now clear that 70% of funds became either indexed or became closet indexers in their zeal to stay within their Morningstar Style Box. In such a world, the passive funds with the lowest fees would relatively outperform. It is only recently, using the methodology of Cremers and Petajisto's 2007 Yale study that we can now focus on the 30% of funds that are truly actively managed. The results show that active management does, in fact, add significant value.

Enlightened readers will realize the question of whether an active manager investing in one asset class can beat a single passive benchmark has little to do with the question of whether or not asset classes themselves are always efficiently priced on an absolute or relative basis, and whether or not it is prudent to rely on past performance rather than judgment and experience to forecast asset class returns. However, if answering that sticky question about why active fund managers can't outperform their style-specific benchmarks is a critical issue for those who are considering tactical asset allocation, they can now rest a little easier.

## Moving On

Given the tremendous global palette of asset classes now available to today's investors, it is pure nonsense to assume that all asset classes are fairly valued all of the time, either absolutely, based on their past metrics for value, or based on their relative value to other asset classes. Now that Cremers and Petajisto have shown us that active managers can outperform their benchmarks, and Kurz and Brock have given us the academic and theoretical reasons why we should spend time and money to attempt to earn excess returns, we're almost ready to begin the practical discussion of how we can find value at the asset class level. It is one thing to say that we should be active, tactical asset allocators, but it is entirely another thing to understand how to best execute such a strategy.

# PART TWO

## ACTIVE PORTFOLIO MANAGEMENT

# 8  PORTFOLIO STRATEGY IN A POST-LEHMAN WORLD

W hen Lehman Brothers declared bankruptcy on September 15, 2008, it ushered in a new era for portfolio managers. Prior to Lehman investors were familiar with market risk — or systematic risk — as one component of total portfolio risk explained in William Sharpe's CAPM pricing model (discussed in Chapter 3). In CAPM, portfolio risk is divided into two parts, non-systematic risk, or business risk, and systematic risk, or market risk. By diversifying within asset classes, investors are presumed to be able to eliminate business risk, so the risk that is left to be managed is market risk. As we have discussed, using the tools of mean-variance optimization and Modern Portfolio Theory, a diversified multi-asset class portfolio was considered to be the best method for managing market risk and portfolio volatility. Prior to Lehman, investors concentrated on finding asset classes where the correlation of returns was low versus one another (cross-correlation) and predictable. As long as correlations stayed low (meaning returns zigged and zagged at different times across the entire portfolio of asset classes), then investors were doing all they could to manage volatility within the limits of MPT. Since for many financial advisors correlations, variances, and returns, are presumed to be mean reverting, the historical average of asset class returns was used to build the MPT model and the resulting portfolio was presumed to be efficient in terms of earning the highest returns for each unit of risk.

However, in the post Lehman investment climate, market risk has taken on a whole new meaning. Instead of discussing systematic risk in the context of CAPM where market risk is tame and manageable through portfolio diversification, investors now discuss systemic risk in a more ominous context for risk where risk means the possible meltdown of the entire financial system. During the October 2007 to March 2009 bear market, investors with diversified portfolios watched with horror as *all* risk assets suffered dramatic declines at the same time. When liquidity dried up and investors lost confidence in the banking system around the world, stocks, commodities, real estate, and a variety of alternative investment strategies like hedge funds and private equity, all suffered dramatic losses.

Having already experienced two major market declines in the past fourteen years, the first from March of 2000 to October of 2002, and the second that included the Lehman bankruptcy, individual investors are worried that another major bear market will permanently impact their lifestyle and ability to achieve their financial goals. Institutional investors worry that a continued period of less than expected returns will result in underfunded pension plans falling further into the red, and endowments having to severely curtail their annual giving. The fear is that policy makers have not understood, much less solved, the many systemic problems facing today's investors, and that subsequent bear markets may not be the 'normal' bear markets that are closely tied to historically average fluctuations in the global business cycle, but more like the frightening bear market declines we have experienced since the year 2000. As a result of Lehman, investors have become more focused on tools and techniques that will defend portfolio values in the event of another major and drastic systemic portfolio decline like the 2007-2009 bear market, a period when diversification did *not* properly manage risk. Prior to the Lehman bankruptcy, those overly concerned about systemic risk seemed like conspiracy theorists who were not to be taken seriously. Today, however, the opposite is true. Those who are unconcerned about systemic risk seem out of touch with the grim realities of today's financial system. A few of the more well-known systemic problems facing the world's financial markets include:

## Too Much Sovereign Debt

Global growth has been supported by forty years of debt creation described by some as the "debt super-cycle." As we near the end of this super-cycle, the solvency of the countries that issued the debt will become a major risk to investors. In fact, consumers, corporations, and sovereigns have all extended their balance sheets to levels that require an extended period of deleveraging. In the past, deleveraging has resulted in numerous debt-related financial crises that consequently resulted in decades of poor economic growth and relatively low returns on risk assets.

## Aggressive Central Banks

Central banks around the world have adopted a policy of trying to enhance global growth through aggressive monetary policy. These policies have resulted in zero interest rate policies and an expansion of central bank balance sheets that is unprecedented in modern times. Unfortunately, the long-term implications of these policies is unknown. Past examples of profligate central bank monetary expansion have resulted in hyper-inflation and decades of lower than average economic growth, both of which result in the destruction of real returns.

## Fiat Money

The world's economy is no longer tied to a gold standard, but instead rests on a system of fiat money that is not backed by any identifiable standard of value. A fiat monetary system is completely reliant on the trust and confidence of the economic participants in the system. Aggressive central bank policies implementing "quantitative easing" may well test the trust and confidence of investors on a global basis. There are no guidelines about how far central bankers can push their policy of creating money out of thin air without destroying investor confidence, but the current scale of monetary expansion is unprecedented (again) in modern times.

## Derivatives

Warren Buffet has described derivatives as "financial weapons of mass destruction." The use of derivatives as a means to create additional profit centers for the banking system, as opposed to having any purpose in properly allocating capital in our economic system, has added an unnecessary and non-quantifiable layer of financial leverage and risk to the entire system. The bailout of AIG is but one example of what occurs when derivative investing goes wrong. Had AIG gone under a number of remaining financial institutions would have met the same fate as Lehman. Estimates of the notional value of derivatives owned by both the traditional banking system, and the shadow banking system of hedge funds and other large financial institutions, vary widely. However, the number is so large as to constitute a significant systemic risk for investors contemplating how to manage their portfolios. Critics maintain that recent legislation has been watered down to the point where it will do little to minimize the risks related to derivative investing.

## Too-Big-To-Fail Banks

The Lehman bankruptcy highlighted the risk of today's too-Big-To-Fail money center banks. With the repeal of the Glass-Steagall Act in 1999, the Chinese wall that was set up to prevent banks from speculating with consumer deposits was destroyed. The resulting series of mega-mergers and acquisitions in the investment banking industry created bank supermarkets that were so large that regulators had to bail them out at tax payer expense when speculative investments and large amounts of leverage resulted in insolvency. Consequently the entire investment banking industry has been merged out of existence or morphed into traditional banks where deposits are backed by government guarantees. What remains are money center banks that are so large that a new round of bank failures could result in another Great Depression. While more recent legislation (namely the Dodd Frank Wall Street Reform and Consumer Protection Act) attempted to remedy the "Too Big to Fail" threat, many critics maintain that it falls far short of actually resolving the problem of banks that are so large that they create systemic risks for investors. In fact, today's bank supermarkets are actually *bigger* than the banks were prior to Lehman.

I could go further. Lax accounting standards allow for bad loans (synthetic derivative credit instruments) not to be marked to market, creating the possibility that we have "zombie-banks" with no real net worth being supported by explicit government subsidies and where existing accounting standards are inappropriately applied. Perhaps even worse, the central bank has purchased billions of these synthetic debt instruments and may never realize their model values. In addition, the "Flash Crash" in the summer of 2010 gave us an insight into the extent that proprietary high-frequency traders may be distorting the financial markets. Many maintain that computer driven trading may create systemic investment hazards that are not properly appreciated by regulators and are not properly understood by investors. Third-party rating agencies that are financially supported by the very institutions they are designed to regulate create the perception that there is no credible source for investors to turn to in order to determine the risk of debt-instruments issued around the world. There is growing concern about the health of the U.S. municipal bond market as municipalities faced with overwhelming pressures to fund pension plans and retiree health care costs look to bankruptcy as a viable financial alternative for restructuring their debt.

Clearly we live in a world where risk is being redefined. Prudent investors are taking another look at the notion of systemic risk and are reaching the conclusion that it must be managed differently than in the past. The MPT paradigm that diversification is the only tool needed to manage systemic risk is being reconsidered, and sophisticated investors are implementing strategies to manage the problems posed by today's difficult markets in an entirely different way.

One of the symptoms of this problem is the ongoing confusion among individual and institutional investors, as well as the media, about the definition of "active management." As we discussed in Chapter 7, the debate about active management has traditionally been framed as a discussion about whether a style-constrained money manager investing in one asset class can beat the performance of a market index that is suitable as a benchmark for the money manager's investment style. As pointed out in the discussion about Active Share, many of the tracking error studies show that, on average, active managers can't outperform an index. While this may be true due to the fees and expenses charged by active managers, the Active Share study pointed out that many of the active managers are closet indexers who actually own many of the index stocks.

However, in the current market environment of wild investment risk that can't be managed by diversification alone, the debate about active money managers versus indexes should be obsolete. Unfortunately, as we will soon see, the debate is alive and well due to the paradigm of "manager search" in the buy and hold industry status quo. What *should* be the most important question for investors today is not *how* you invest in any particular asset class, but *should* you invest in any particular asset class. When it is clear that traditional asset classes do not offer good value, and that systemic risks create an environment where risk is wild and cannot be managed by diversification alone, then non-traditional investment solutions must be found.

Perhaps the most popular solution to the problem lies in the class of investments known as alternative investments. These investments include hedge funds, private equity, managed futures, real estate, commodities, and other eclectic approaches to active management. The question for sophisticated portfolio managers is how to integrate these alternative investments into a traditional portfolio.

## Core and Satellite

The most well known strategy for constructing modern, sophisticated, institutional quality portfolios is called "core and satellite." Most corporate pension plans, endowments, and state pension plans use some version of this formula.

The core portfolio is simply the part of the portfolio invested in traditional asset classes using Modern Portfolio Theory. Part One of this book describes in detail the issues and problems with traditional buy and hold investing. The underlying premise for building multi-asset class, diversified portfolios, is that the returns, variances, and correlations, of the underlying asset classes are mean reverting. This means that over time the past historical average returns of each asset class will be earned, allowing investors to use the algorithms given to us by Markowitz and Sharpe in Modern Portfolio Theory to construct portfolios that efficiently earn returns for each unit of risk.

Unfortunately, the data clearly shows that when markets are overvalued, long-term average returns will not be earned for long periods of time (measured in decades). As markets become more overvalued, and as systemic risks become more prevalent, markets are prone to riot. Instead of an orderly process of earning returns within well-defined parameters that seem statistically significant, today's investors have been dealing with markets where returns have little to do with mean reverting long-term fundamentals, and much to do with day-to-day monetary intervention by central banks. Investors in core portfolios that are invested in traditional asset classes find themselves exposed to policy maker risks that are unprecedented.

In addition, new research continues to point out that below average long-term returns should be expected from today's high U.S. equity and U.S. bond market valuations. The recent six-year bull market in stocks and bonds has erased any valuation advantage after the prior decade of low single-digit stock market returns. Many experts are projecting S&P 500 total returns, including dividends, for the next decade to fall in the 2% annual to 6% annual range. Few experts are projecting more than 2% positive returns from today's prices in government bonds, and some are projecting negative returns. It's no wonder that investors are looking for a new approach.

It should be no surprise that Wall Street and its related army of portfolio consultants have been providing a solution to the problems with traditional core portfolio construction for many years. And even though the strategy didn't work during the 2007-2009 bear market, Wall Street is undeterred and neither are their institutional clients. Pension funds and endowments simply can't afford another lost decade of S&P 500 returns as well as the new threat of lost bond market returns in the future. The solution to the core portfolio problem is to create an additional portfolio allocation that is invested in non-traditional securities and asset classes, called "alternative investments," that are meant to hedge the returns of the core portfolio. The resulting allocation to alternative investments is called the satellite portfolio, and it has the singular mission of delivering positive and non-correlated returns compared to the returns of traditional asset classes.

## Manager Search

Before discussing the securities and strategies that make up the satellite portfolio, it's important to note that the core and satellite strategy works neatly within the "manager search" model of portfolio construction that has been the paradigm for building institutional portfolios for decades. In the core and satellite model, percentage allocations to the core and satellite are assigned after analyzing the likely returns, correlations, and variances of both the core and satellite positions. Consultants put each strategy into a style-box so that they can be easily compared to a benchmark and to each other. In the past equity managers were relegated to the traditional Morningstar style boxes. Today, however, even hedge fund managers are assigned their own style category (for example, market-neutral, long-short, event-driven, convertible arbitrage, global-macro, equity arbitrage, etc.) so they can be compared on an "apples to apples" basis using a variety of new hedge fund indexes. In fact, the fastest growing Morningstar mutual fund style category is called "liquid alternatives."

Positions in both the core and satellite allocation are then invested in a fixed percentage that is quantitatively determined to be the best mix to obtain high returns with minimum risk for the entire portfolio. Consultants diligently sell the notion that they can search for and find active managers in either the core or satellite portfolio, based on their own sophisticated and proprietary techniques, which can reliably outperform the unmanaged benchmark that is appropriate for each segment of the portfolio allocation.

This manager search paradigm implies that when asset allocations are fixed in either the core or satellite part of the portfolio, extra returns (or alpha, in the parlance of CAPM) can be earned when above average managers deliver above average returns in each asset class. It is interesting how this consulting model has been applied over many decades so that it is relevant even though portfolio construction has moved beyond simple core portfolios. The big difference today is that consultants are searching for managers who can beat the benchmarks for non-traditional, as well as traditional, investments. The combination of core and satellite portfolio construction and the industry paradigm of manager search allow the strategy of buying and holding to remain popular. Buy and hold is invested using quantitative methods that seem scientifically sound. The strategy does not require the portfolio manager to tactically and actively change the portfolio asset allocation. And the strategy seems very sophisticated based on the innovative and non-traditional investment strategies found in the satellite portfolio.

So what are satellite holdings? Satellite holdings generally include real estate, commodities, hedge funds, managed futures, private equity, venture capital, and other non-traditional asset classes like collectibles or timber. I suggest thinking of satellite holdings by dividing them into alternative asset classes, alternative investment strategies, and alternative superstar managers, all having the same objective of outperforming traditional investments in the core portfolio while at the same time having presumably predictable low correlation to the core portfolio. Let's look at each of these categories.

## Alternative/Satellite Asset Classes

Satellite, or alternative, asset classes are those asset classes that are presumed to have a low correlation to stocks and bonds. The two most popular are real estate and commodities. Real estate is by far the elder statesmen of the two in terms of being considered an institutional quality asset class and many investment advisors would claim that owning commercial real estate is so essential to a professionally constructed portfolio that it should be considered a core holding. Commercial real estate is rationally priced based on the cash flow generated by the rental income of the building's tenants. Rental income, like the dividend income from stocks, tends to rise in strong economic environments and fall in poor economic environments. The big difference, as we have seen in earlier chapters, is that in inflationary environments investors tend to penalize stock prices with a lower P/E ratio as the future value of earnings is worth less in the present when interest rates are increasing in the future. In addition, corporate profits are presumed to suffer when costs increase due to inflation. On the other hand, real estate rents (including commercial, multi-family residential, and retail) tend to adjust upwards in an inflationary environment making the cash flow from institutional quality properties something of an inflation hedge. In addition, real estate is much less liquid than stocks and bonds, so the pricing tends to be more rational in volatile markets. The result is an institutional quality asset class that offers the promise of a low correlation to stocks and bonds, especially in a rising interest rate environment, and the ability to earn excess returns in inflationary market environments.

Commodities are similar to commercial real estate in that the value of commodities can run counter-cyclical to common stocks for long secular periods of time. Commodities such as precious metals, industrial metals, oil and gas, as well as soft commodities like corn, soy beans, wheat, etc., represent real assets that do not generate an ongoing stream of cash flow, and consequently tend to be valued differently from stocks and bonds. Additionally, high commodity prices may lead to lower corporate profits since commodities are one of the major costs of production for many industries. Commodities are now available to be purchased by institutional investors in a variety of managed funds and partnerships, as well as exchange-traded funds (ETF's) based on a variety of commodity indices. Again, by owning commodities as a satellite holding an investor can expect to own an asset class with historically low correlations to stocks and bonds, yet can potentially earn excess returns compared to traditional asset classes over long periods of time.

## Alternative / Satellite Strategies

Satellite strategies are predominately found in the hedge fund universe of active managers. Hedge funds are typically divided into several sub-categories including long-short, market neutral, event-driven, convertible arbitrage, global-macro, and others. Many hedge funds take a long position in equities with a large percentage of the portfolio and then borrow against the long positions to take short positions with an equal percentage of the portfolio. When the manager owns equal amounts of his or her best long and short positions at the same time, the portfolio is considered to be market neutral, where the overall direction of the broad financial markets theoretically no longer matters. The returns from this strategy are generated by the manager's ability to select winning, and if short, losing stocks. Therefore, if the broad market suffers a steep decline, a market neutral strategy has an equally good chance of making money for investors as when the market makes outsized gains.

In both cases, it is the manager's ability and not the market's direction that will be the key to earning positive returns. While the manager may or may not earn excess returns with this strategy, the point is that the portfolio should have a very low correlation to the stock market, even if the manager is a poor stock picker. Many hedge fund strategies involving the use of leverage to earn returns based on arbitraging market inefficiencies come under the category of satellite strategies. Additionally, market-timing strategies based on quantitative, rules-based trading are another example of alternative, or satellite strategies. In these cases it is not an alternative asset class, but an alternative trading strategy, which holds the key to reducing or minimizing market risk.

### Alternative / Superstar Managers

A third type of satellite strategy is superstar managers. Superstar managers are given the discretion to make large asset allocation or security selection bets. At times managers are given the discretion to take the portfolio "long" or "short" at their discretion. When superstar managers take very concentrated positions in securities they reintroduce the notion of business risk, or non-systematic risk, to the return equation. If the manager is correct in the evaluation of the underlying stocks in the portfolio, investment gains can soar above benchmark returns. If a superstar manager is allowed to take the portfolio to 100% cash, the portfolio offers the advantage of allowing the manager to completely neutralize the impact of a bear market on portfolio values. That's a wonderful contrast to a core holding, because core investors *want* to capture the risk and reward of the market. The distinction between satellite *strategies* and satellite *superstar managers* is that, for the most part, satellite strategies reduce market risk by implementing the strategy itself, where superstar managers use their judgment and experience to make large directional portfolio bets in order to either embrace or obliterate market risk and earn returns that have low correlations to the broader market.

The benefit of alternative, or satellite, investments is that they are exciting. Instead of being limited to the returns of markets, which is the fate of core managers who buy traditional asset classes, the satellite allocation can potentially earn positive returns in bear markets. Wow! On the other hand, investing in traditional core investments limited to earning market returns is comparatively boring. The market's return is out of an individual investor's control so the best he or she can do is diversify the core portfolio and hope for the best. In a bear market, when traditional core investors feel helpless as markets are falling in value, the satellite allocation offers the promise that it could earn positive returns providing a tremendous hedge against the falling values in the core portfolio. If and when this happens headlines are made and managers get featured on the cover of magazines. In summary, while core investment strategies are based on capturing the risk and reward of markets, alternative, satellite strategies are trying to *eliminate* the risk of markets by capturing the returns available through non-correlated asset classes, strategies, and superstar managers.

**Table 8.1** shows the core and satellite allocation of three state pension funds: Maryland, New York, and California. These large institutional portfolios are useful examples of typical core and satellite allocations.

| ASSET CLASS | CALIFORNIA | MARYLAND | NEW YORK | AVERAGE |
|:---:|:---:|:---:|:---:|:---:|
| EQUITY | 50% | 47% | 43% | |
| INCOME | 17% | 25% | 22% | 71% Core |
| CASH | 4% | 2% | 3% | |
| REAL ESTATE | 8% | 6% | 6% | |
| FORESTLAND | 2% | | | |
| PRIVATE EQUITY | 14% | 5% | 10% | |
| INFLATION | 3% | 10% | 8% | |
| OPPORTUNISTIC PORTFOLIO | | | 4% | 29% Satellite |
| ABSOLUTE RETURN | 2% | 5% | 4% | |
| | 100% | 100% | 100% | |

**Table 8.1—Maryland, New York, and California State Pension Funds**
Source: Pinnacle Advisory Group, Inc.

You can see that the satellite holdings are typically 20% to 40% of the total portfolio. (NOTE: The exception to this allocation to the satellite allocation is found in the "endowment model" of portfolio construction made popular by Yale and Harvard University where 80% or more of the portfolio is allocated to non-traditional alternative assets. For our purposes we will consider the endowment model as the exception and move on with our narrative.) Why not more? I believe there are two reasons: First, core holdings have the advantage of years of data that can be parsed and analyzed by the consultant, client, and financial advisor. The parameters for risk and reward for stocks, bonds, and cash are well known. In many cases there are more than one hundred years of data to be analyzed that span many different investment regimes. This adds to the validity of identifying the likely parameters of future returns, variances, and correlations. In contrast, alternative investments have comparatively short track records and rational investors will question the efficacy of using limited data to forecast future returns. In many cases, investors also question the accuracy of reporting alternative investment returns, where the lack of liquidity and the prevalence of derivative-based securities create problems in accurate reporting.

Second, the status quo of investing tells us that the past parameters of risk and return are the only rational data that can be used for long-term forecasts of future returns. As long as the consumer of financial advice and the provider of financial advice agree that short-term future returns are unknowable, but long-term returns can be safely estimated based on past data, then the worst thing that a core manager can do is to change the portfolio asset allocation. It is the portfolio policy itself, or the asset allocation of the portfolio, which dictates future risk and return. The portfolio manager is jeopardizing the agreement he or she has with his or her client about portfolio policy if he or she changes the asset allocation, or if they hire investment managers that "style drift" within any individual asset class in the portfolio.

In other words, the core portfolio is actually the low risk allocation for both parties, because both parties understand that they are not at risk to returns in the short-term. To use a term from Jeremy Grantham, one of my favorite portfolio managers and observers of the financial industry, the core holding has little "career risk." As strange as it may seem, for many investors it is acceptable to lose money, as long as they lose it at the same time and for the same reason as everyone else. Because core portfolios are tied to risks related to the markets, and the universe of investors *are* the market, then core portfolio investors are all in the same boat. With everyone winning and losing together, it is a psychologically safe place for all concerned. To be blunt, for professional investors the core portfolio, if properly sold to a client, represents a place where they are far less likely to be fired.

In addition to the fundamental benefits of core portfolios mentioned above, the satellite portfolio allocation is far from the risk-free solution to core portfolio concerns that alternative investment fans might hope for. Risks to the satellite portfolio include, but are not limited to, the following:

## Asset Class Correlation Risk

This is the risk that owning asset classes that are presumed to offer low correlation to traditional markets don't perform as expected in bear markets. As noted above, in the 2007—2009 bear market virtually *all* asset classes lost money at the same time. Satellite portfolios with large positions in non-correlated asset classes did little to hedge the core portfolio when liquidity concerns destroyed virtually every risk market. In the post-Lehman world, where investors fear the impact of a serious deflationary event, real estate and commodities may once again do little to offset declines you might expect from the stock market.

## Strategy Risk

Satellite strategies are at risk of having all of the possible excess returns from the strategy arbitraged away by other investors. This occurs when too many investors chase too few investment opportunities. The hedge fund community is notorious for having a strategy be identified by other hedge fund managers who then try to exploit the same market inefficiencies that led to profits for the investors in the original funds. As millions (or more likely, billions) of additional dollars are invested in the same type of securities attempting to execute the same type of strategy, excess returns suddenly disappear, as investors can no longer find good values. New investors who are attracted to hedge fund managers with brilliant track records are disappointed when subsequent returns are lower than expected. We like to say, "strategies work until they don't work." Experienced investors keep that in mind when investing in satellite strategies.

## Superstar Manager Risk

Perhaps the best-known risk for satellite, or alternative strategies, is manager risk. In this case a superstar manager with a long and successful track record suddenly begins to consistently under perform. Investors who invested in the manager's earliest funds made fortunes, but investors who invest after the initial track record becomes well known find themselves losing money. This could be because the manager is investing in an asset class that isn't liquid enough to allow for much larger positions needed for a hugely successful fund. Or, it could be because the manager specializes in investing in only one part of the market cycle. Or, as would be claimed by efficient markets believers, it could simply be because the manager got lucky the first time around. Earning huge returns that are not correlated to the market means that managers can also earn large losses that are not correlated to the market. If the manager is leveraging his or her portfolio to double and triple their bets, then let the buyer beware.

## Performance Reporting Risk

This risk isn't well known to the public and deserves a thorough explanation. Performance reporting risk refers to the fact that many alternative strategies are based on quantitative methods that have been developed over the past few years. As the demand for satellite strategies has grown, the industry has rushed to provide new and innovative solutions. Knowledgeable investors want to see the performance track record for satellite managers as part of doing their due diligence. Unfortunately the industry has not made the due diligence process easy for consumers. It is generally acknowledged that the institutional standard for performance reporting is the Global Investment Performance Standards (GIPS), and virtually every publicly traded fund meets the GIPS requirements. Managers who claim GIPS compliance are saying that they're reporting their performance in a way that allows consumers of investment advice to be confident that the track record they're studying meets a standard of "fair representation and full disclosure" that is accepted by the investment community.

Unfortunately there are many ways that an investment track record can be distorted so that investors make decisions based on misleading evidence. The key to understanding how the deception usually works is to understand an element of GIPS reporting called Supplemental Information. Supplemental Information is defined as "any performance-related information included as part of a compliant performance presentation that supplements or enhances the required and/or recommended disclosure and presentation provisions of the GIPS requirements." Supplemental returns are considered to be misleading if they include:

1. Model, hypothetical, back-tested, or simulated results *linked* to actual performance results.
2. Non-portable performance from a prior firm *linked* to current ongoing performance result.

This seems reasonable. However, the following are *not* considered misleading and are allowed as Supplemental Information:

- Carve out returns that exclude cash
- Non-portable returns
- Model, hypothetical, back-tested, or simulated returns
- Representative account information, such as portfolio-level country weightings, portfolio-level sector weightings, and portfolio-level risk measures
- Attribution
- Composite or portfolio-level specific holdings
- Peer group comparisons
- Risk-adjusted performance

A discussion of each of these bullets is beyond the scope of this chapter. However, consumers do need to be especially wary of model, hypothetical, and back-tested or simulated returns, where firms can literally conjure up an investment track record out of thin air, as long as the fine print calls it supplemental information. Of course, GIPS guidance doesn't call it fine print, but requires "the standard of reporting to be clearly labeled and identified."

Let's review an example of how this is commonly abused.

Imagine that you want to manage money using a quantitative, momentum-based investment strategy that is all the rage with today's investors. You have hired a fabulous quantitative analyst in the past year who has been tinkering with several investment models that would have delivered excellent returns over the past decade based on back-testing the results. You are allowed to publish those *completely fictional* returns as supplemental information as long as you disclose to investors that the returns are fictional... or supplemental. You then put together a glossy, five-page marketing brochure, which shows how you neatly sidestepped down markets over the past ten years and earned investors fabulous returns with little risk. The supplemental track record is in large, bold print with multicolored explanatory graphs. The actual six-month GIPS compliant track record and the statement that the large print multi-year track record is hypothetical and back-tested is found in small print at the bottom of page five. You then assemble a sales force that does a terrific job of simplifying the "complex," "proprietary," and "scientific" investment process behind the amazing returns, using language effective with both retail and institutional investors yearning for mystical success in dangerous markets, and you raise a few billion dollars of assets under management before lunch. This is a terrific way to make a living... except for the fact that you never actually managed money using the fictional strategy!

The best investors avoid hypothetical back-tested returns when possible. They know that investing in a strategy that is only successful in the rear-view mirror is completely different than investing with a money manager who earned his or her returns in real-time. NOTE: At times there are innovative strategies that are developed that require investors to accept a back-tested analysis of possible returns. In such cases, investors should fully understand the time horizon that is back-tested, whether the test is done "in" or "out" of sample, and note how clearly the back-test is disclosed to investors.

When considering the risks of both core and satellite investing, it is no wonder that the predominant allocation is typically to the core portfolio, with the satellite assets serving as a hedge. However, we have discovered that both core and satellite strategies have their share of dangers. In the post-Lehman era of huge systemic risks, is there a better way to manage a portfolio that allows investors to take advantage of the best of both core and satellite investment strategies?

## Risk Budgeting and "Go Anywhere" Portfolio Construction

If you think about it, Modern Portfolio Theory is a complicated method of managing portfolio volatility where volatility is defined by the type and allocation of asset classes used to build the portfolio. The way it is typically used, portfolio optimizing models based on MPT assume that asset classes have mean reverting returns, correlations, and standard deviations; so that when you put them together in a diversified portfolio you have a reasonable expectation of achieving historical average levels of portfolio returns and volatility regardless of market values at the time of purchase.

If you don't target the *asset allocation* of the benchmark portfolio based on historical parameters of risk and return for each *asset class*, but instead target a level of *portfolio volatility* based on the real-time *volatility* of a multi-asset class benchmark portfolio, then something interesting happens: Suddenly you can focus on the *current value proposition* of the asset classes you own in the portfolio, instead of mechanically rebalancing to a fixed-mix of asset classes that are determined based on past performance. As long as the volatility of the portfolio meets your target, you are now free to own any asset classes that you want, based on your assessment of value. We call this "go anywhere" portfolio construction, meaning the portfolio manager is not constrained by asset allocation targets in selecting the asset classes in the portfolio at any point in time.

The notion of targeting a fixed amount of volatility for a managed portfolio is called, "risk budgeting." The investment industry also calls it risk parity. It is a style of portfolio management that acknowledges that investors define risk as volatility, so targeting a specific level of volatility (instead of a specific asset allocation) directly addresses the issue of risk management.

Using a risk parity approach, active and tactical investors are free to buy and sell asset classes if they choose to do so based on value characteristics as opposed to asset class targets. On the other hand, more traditional buy and hold investors employ risk parity as a method to build portfolios that are nothing more than strategically owned core and satellite portfolios. Using a risk budget as part of our tactical portfolio strategy gives us the freedom to find and exploit value opportunities throughout the year. At the same time, the risk budget assures investors that a conservative portfolio will remain conservative, a moderate portfolio will remain moderate, and a growth portfolio will remain a growth portfolio, at least as measured by portfolio volatility.

As you might expect, risk budgeting presents investors with a unique set of concerns. One concern is that risk budgeters must find a way to measure volatility in real time so that they know what the actual risk-reward parameters of their portfolio is at any given time. Perhaps more importantly, risk budgeters must decide if they will "buy and hold" volatility relative to their benchmark, or actively manage volatility versus the benchmark. As we will see, both issues are critical in evaluating how to properly use risk budgets to manage portfolio volatility.

## Actively Managing Portfolio Volatility

My observation is that investment managers live in fear of making an investment mistake. In fact, I devote an entire chapter to the subject in Chapter 13 called, "The Psychology of Making Investment Mistakes." As mentioned earlier, buy and hold investing, or traditional strategic asset allocation, offers advisors and their clients the illusion that they can't make an investment mistake. This suits all parties just fine as clients only want to lose money when everyone else is losing money, and investment advisors want the same. The buy and hold method of using risk parity to construct portfolios offers the same comfort to all parties. Instead of calculating portfolio volatility using traditional asset classes, investors can use alternative or satellite investments with low correlations to arrive at benchmark volatility using a seemingly far more sophisticated portfolio construction. Instead of just owning stocks and bonds the portfolio now additionally owns hedge funds, private equity, managed futures, etc. Although the portfolio asset allocation now offers more sex appeal *it is important to note that the underlying percentage weighting to each asset class is fixed.* At no time will the investor change the asset allocation because changing the allocation changes the agreed upon risk/reward parameters of the portfolio. Sound familiar? This is exactly the same agreement between advisor and client that we saw when we discussed the popularity of core portfolio construction.

Unfortunately, any time a portfolio is constructed with a fixed allocation to any asset class, whether it is owned in the core or the satellite portfolio, the investor is now at risk that things could change in the future. Why fix the core allocation or the satellite allocation if it's possible to imagine a scenario where either becomes a poor value proposition in the future? As it turns out, constraining the selection of asset classes in a portfolio by total portfolio volatility does not solve the problems of passive portfolio management. To put it bluntly, risk parity alone can be just as risky as buying and holding a fixed allocation of traditional asset classes, especially if the alternative investments in the satellite allocation of the portfolio betray you in the same way they did in the 2007—2009 bear market.

## Portfolio Policy and Tactical Risk Budgeting

The risk budget for Pinnacle's tactical portfolios is determined by using the same tools we used years ago to develop portfolio policy for strategic buy and hold investors. The amount of risk in the policy is defined by the range of returns that portfolios should experience based on past benchmark performance. To define the range of returns that a portfolio strategy is likely to experience, we utilize the historical volatility of the returns of a blended benchmark of traditional asset classes that is rebalanced on a monthly basis from January 1972 to the present. (I presented a sample of this test portfolio in **Figure 2.1** in Chapter two.) The reader may recall that we demonstrate a moderate growth portfolio benchmark invested in a five asset-class portfolio consisting of 38% large-cap U.S. stocks, 10% small-cap U.S. stocks, 12% International stocks, 30% U.S. bonds, and 10% cash. The average return of the portfolio over the entire time period is 9.29%. However, from the perspective of understanding a risk budget, the more important data is the volatility, or standard deviation of the portfolio, which is 8.99%.

From the standpoint of portfolio policy, investors have the information they need to form the basis of a *long-term* expectation for portfolio volatility. Based on the historical data, the returns on this portfolio should fall in a range between +0.30% and +18.28% approximately two-thirds of the time, when the portfolio is positioned for neutral, or benchmark, volatility. However, looking at average standard deviation is no different from looking at average portfolio returns. When markets are overvalued and systemic risk is high, investors should expect volatility to be higher than average, and consequently the range of returns (negative returns) is likely to be higher than average as well. Of course, when markets are extremely undervalued and systemic risk is low, higher volatility can be associated with higher than average positive returns.

The blended benchmark for each strategy becomes a real-time target for portfolio volatility. Since the benchmark will have different levels of volatility in different investment regimes, the benchmark is actually a moving, rather than a fixed target. Instead of targeting a standard deviation of 8.99% as a fixed volatility target, the comparison is relative and portfolio standard deviation can move up or down and still be neutral on a relative basis.

Notably, there are strategies that do target a fixed volatility target, selling volatile assets when it peaks and buying it when it falls so investors know exactly how much volatility the portfolio will have at all times. The problem with these strategies is that risk asset volatility tends to peak in extreme bear markets when the last thing you want to do is sell risk assets. Instead, peaks in market volatility, often measured by the Chicago Board of Options Exchange Volatility Index (VIX), have been tremendous opportunities to buy risk assets, thereby adding, rather than selling, at the peaks in overall market volatility. The opposite is true when volatility falls to extremely low levels. When markets get very complacent as measured by a low level on the VIX index, investors should beware. It is often a good time to reduce volatility instead of buying it to meet a fixed volatility target.

The key is flexibility. Pinnacle has the ability to manage the portfolio to more or less volatility than the benchmark depending on our view of the market cycle, market valuation, investor behavior, quantitative analysis, and independent research. When we have low conviction in our forecast of the markets, or when the weight of the evidence doesn't lead us to a strong conclusion about where we are in the market cycle, we are content to manage the portfolio to the same amount of volatility as the benchmark. We call this being neutral to the benchmark's volatility or risk. As stated above, all parties, including our clients and our advisors, are familiar with the risk and reward to be expected, on average, by holding the benchmark portfolio. Therefore when the portfolio is positioned at neutral volatility the relative volatility of the portfolio should be similar to the benchmark. At neutral volatility relative outperformance comes from sector rotation within asset classes and from security selection. Changing the overall volatility of the portfolio by changing the asset allocation is called a "beta trade." Trades that add value without changing the overall portfolio volatility are called "alpha trades."

While neutral volatility implies a low level of conviction in our forecast, when we have high conviction that we are either in a bull market or bear market cycle, we can manage the portfolio to a higher or lower amount of volatility than the benchmark. This relative approach to risk budgeting allows us to resolve the conundrum of buying and holding a fixed amount of volatility, regardless of market conditions. And by having a volatility budget instead of an asset allocation target, we can be a "go anywhere" portfolio manager with the mandate to only own securities that have a good value proposition in the future, and not just when the portfolio is originally constructed. We offer a *tactical* risk budgeting strategy, where our tactical asset allocation is constrained by the amount we want to deviate from the volatility of our benchmark.

Pinnacle portfolio policy statements actually have no constraints in terms of how little or how much of any single asset class we can own in any particular market environment. We have an unlimited amount of choice in how we construct portfolios within the constraints of our volatility budget. However, in practice we are constrained by the career risk that comes with making large market-timing bets with our asset allocation. To date, our biggest tactical call was implemented in January of 2008 when we forecast a recession and a bear market. At that time we positioned the portfolio to have 40% of the volatility of our unmanaged blended benchmark. Our actual realized portfolio volatility was a little higher than the target due to the disappointing performance of certain hedge funds we owned in our alternative asset class allocation.

## Measuring Portfolio Volatility

Now that we have successfully dealt with the problems of actively versus passively managing portfolio volatility, the next concern is the problem of measuring volatility in real time. One of the benefits of traditional buy and hold investing is that by owning a fixed mix of asset classes, the investor is presumed to have built a portfolio where the parameters of portfolio volatility are clearly defined based on the past performance of the asset classes in the portfolio. If markets are unexpectedly volatile, it is agreed that there is nothing to be done about it other than to rebalance the portfolio to the target asset allocation in hopes that volatility will regress to the historical mean. In this regard consumers of investment management and their investment managers agree; so long as the investment manager clings to the agreed upon asset allocation, then presumably portfolio volatility and subsequent investment returns will eventually return to expected ranges determined by historical performance.

However, when investors use risk budgets, they are free to own *any* asset class that is presumed to have good value. With no constraints on what to own, how do you know how much risk and volatility you have in the portfolio at any point in time? At Pinnacle we measure portfolio volatility using two different methods. The first method, called a "pro-forma analysis," uses our current portfolio holdings and analyzes how they would have performed over a defined historical time period, as if we owned the current portfolio during that period. We then use this information to extrapolate how volatile the current portfolio will be in the present. The second method is an analysis of actual portfolio volatility over a recent time period to test if actual portfolio volatility is in line with our pro-forma expectations.

## Pro-forma Volatility Analysis

We compare portfolio volatility to a benchmark using two different methods. One method is to measure the total volatility of the portfolio compared to the volatility of the benchmark, and the second is to estimate how much of portfolio volatility can be *attributed* to the benchmark. (We discuss the second method, which is a measure called portfolio beta, in some detail in **Figures 3.3, 3.4, and 3.5** in Chapter 3.) We use both methods because beta might not explain all of the portfolio's volatility at any point in time. For our analysis we use pro-forma volatility and beta, which answers the question: "Had we held the same portfolio we hold today over some trailing time period, what would our volatility and beta have been?"

The answer is typically an accurate estimate of the kind of volatility and beta the same portfolio will experience going forward. The pro-forma allows us to estimate the risk profile of virtually any portfolio composition, and is a very useful tool in assessing whether we are staying within the boundaries of our relative risk budget. It tells us if we're likely to meet our targets of having more, less, or the same volatility as our benchmark.

## Historical Volatility Analysis

In addition to our pro-forma analysis, we have developed two very short-term measures of volatility and beta based on our actual daily portfolio returns, which we routinely compare to the pro-forma estimates to make sure the portfolios are behaving as we expected.

Sauro Locatelli, CFA, Pinnacle's quantitative analyst, describes our methodology in some detail.

The first measure [of historical volatility] is called *one-month time-weighted trailing volatility* and starts with the calculation of the equal-weighted average of the portfolio's daily volatility over trailing 5 days (1 week), 10 days (2 weeks) and 20 days (4 weeks). This number is then divided by the same average volatility calculated for the portfolio's benchmark. The ratio gives us a measure of how volatile the portfolio is behaving relative to its benchmark:

**Ratio = 1 (neutral)**: the portfolio is experiencing the same volatility as the benchmark;

**Ratio > 1 (above neutral or aggressive)**: the portfolio is experiencing more volatility than the benchmark;

**Ratio < 1 (below neutral or defensive)**: the portfolio is experiencing less volatility than the benchmark;

The other measure is called *one-month time-weighted trailing beta* and uses the same approach to calculate the beta of the portfolios versus their respective benchmarks. Both measures are based on 1 month (4 weeks) of data, but since they are the equal-weighted average of three overlapping time frames, they give more weight to recent data. Specifically, the trailing 5 days are accounted for 3 times, the previous 5 days are accounted for twice, and the previous 10 days are accounted for only once. Because of their short-term nature, these measures can be particularly volatile at times, which is why we introduced a one-month moving average to better gauge the direction of the trend.

To put all of that in simpler terms, we compare our *estimates* of portfolio volatility and beta to our *actual historical* volatility and beta.

Accurately estimating the volatility of the portfolio in real time is no easy matter. However, without a systematic approach to measuring volatility it is impossible to know if you are investing within the constraints of your benchmark volatility target. Put another way, traditional investors rely on forecasts of asset class correlations to forecast overall portfolio volatility for clients. The parameters of volatility are defined using past data. The risk, of course, is that risk today is more "wild" than it has been in the past and correlations can peak along with systemic market events. On the other hand, for risk budgeters, one of the risks is that the measurement of real time portfolio volatility is inaccurate. In either case, forecasting volatility is a messy affair.

## Summary

The investment landscape has become more dangerous since the Lehman Brothers collapse. With systemic risk becoming an increasingly important concern for investors, the old risk management tools of diversification and rebalancing are now considered to be only one part of the sophisticated investor's arsenal of strategies for managing volatility. Wall Street's solution to managing the risks of a traditional core portfolio is called core and satellite investing. The core portfolio is invested in traditional asset classes and is designed to capture the returns of the financial markets. The satellite portion of the portfolio is designed as a hedge to the core and is often invested in alternative investments like hedge funds, private equity, managed futures, real estate, commodities, and other asset classes and investment strategies with a low correlation to stocks and bonds. We have discussed how both the core and the satellite positions are subject to a number of risks. In the case of the core portfolio investors are at risk to the misbehavior of markets. In the case of the satellite portfolio the risks include unforeseen correlation peaks with alternative asset classes, unreliable returns due to market arbitrage for alternative investment strategies, and superstar managers who suddenly lose their hot hand as stock pickers.

Instead of core and satellite, investors might consider a portfolio that borrows the best attributes of both. By crafting a go anywhere portfolio that tactically budgets risk relative to a blended benchmark, investors can focus on owning asset classes with excellent value characteristics while at the same time taking a systematic and structured approach to managing portfolio volatility.

If investors do construct a core and satellite portfolio, they should make certain that the result is suitable as a core holding, meaning that the satellite allocation isn't so large as to leave the investor with a major portfolio bet that unnecessarily adds to risk. Investors should also consider the satellite strategy in the context of more than just hypothetical and back-tested returns. They should also analyze the methodology, technology, capacity, and depth of management of the firm providing the satellite investment.

Now that we've explored risk-budgeted portfolios, it's time to answer many practical questions about how to go about constructing a portfolio that is different from the buy and hold, status quo portfolios of the past. In the following chapters we will explore how to become an investment expert, how to make top down and bottom up portfolio decisions, how to use sector rotation, how to make good security selection decisions, and how to account for investor psychology and tax issues.

Let's begin by discussing how active and tactical management requires a different kind of investment acumen in order to succeed.

# 9 BECOMING AN INVESTMENT EXPERT
## (or, How To Be Right For The Right Reasons)

I t was February 2003 and the U.S. stock market was in the middle of a failed rally after setting the bear market lows in October of the previous year. With the second Gulf war brewing ominously on the horizon and investors still reeling from the horrible bear market that had begun in early 2000, pushing the S&P 500 Index down by 48%, investors in blue chip tech stocks were facing unimaginable losses. I was participating in a breakfast meeting in Bethesda, Maryland, sponsored by Charles Schwab, that was attended by a variety of investment advisors who custodied assets at Schwab. These events were excellent opportunities to find out what was going on with other independent investment advisors, and so I found myself in conversation with a gentleman who ran a small financial planning firm in the area. As was usually the case at that time, I was once again complaining about the performance of our well-balanced strategic portfolios, railing about how we could have done better if only we would have given ourselves permission to do more than just rebalance the portfolio through the prior two-year decline.

My breakfast companion looked at me with some surprise and announced that his portfolios had actually gained 11% per year over the past two years. I was somewhat staggered by his claim and suggested that perhaps he meant his portfolio had a total return of 11% from the market top, which would have resulted in a much more believable annual return of +4% to +5% per year, which to my mind would still have been a remarkable achievement.

No, he assured me, he meant an 11% annualized return for the past two years, creating a total return of 22%. Like fishermen, when investment advisors get together they may tend to stretch the truth a little here and there about the size of their portfolio performance. Over the years, I, myself, may have been guilty of a little exaggeration between friends, and so I couldn't be certain on this cold winter morning that this gentleman, who I had just met at breakfast, was telling me the truth. So I began to inquire more earnestly about how he managed to generate such amazingly good returns in such a horrible investment environment. He proceeded to tell me that his portfolio owned 20% gold, 30% real estate, 20% pipeline partnerships, and 30% high-quality bonds. I was amazed. If we could have the benefit of knowing the future, and if it was possible to go back in time to pick only those securities that would do the best through the bear market, then this was the portfolio to pick.

Stunned, I asked my new friend how he had managed to construct a portfolio with so few asset classes, with so much success, and that looked so different from any traditional portfolio construction that I was aware of at the time. He looked at me and quite sincerely offered the following reply, "I just pretend that I am one of those Swiss bankers, you know what I mean? And then I pretend that I have one of those super rich Arab clients, who only invest with Swiss bankers, who wants me to invest his money. And then I just do what I think one of those Swiss bankers would do."

As I said, I am used to a little kidding when it comes to discussing investment results, so I naturally assumed he was pulling my leg. It took several minutes for him to convince me that he was telling the absolute and sincere truth. (To be honest, I still wonder if he isn't telling this story to this day and laughing about the gullible planner he met that morning who believed the story that he was spinning about Swiss bankers.)

Back at my office, I immediately convened a meeting with Pinnacle's investment analysts. Imagine their surprise when I announced that henceforth we were going to invest our clients' accounts as though we were "one of those Swiss bankers" and our clients were some of "those rich Arabs." The laughter in the room was well worth the time to tell the tale.

The moral of this story is that, even though I believe that it is important for investors to incorporate their judgment and experience in making forecasts necessary to actively manage portfolios, it is absolutely critical to question the difference between good investment judgment and plain old good luck.

Exactly what constitutes good investment judgment and how does one obtain it? I would have given anything to deliver our clients 11% annualized returns through the bear market of 2000-2002, but could anyone have known that the portfolio I heard about at breakfast that morning represented good judgment *before the fact*? Remember that Woody Brock gives us two criteria for any defensible strategy that is the basis for superior price forecasting:

1. The strategy must be consistent with a satisfactory descriptive and explanatory theory of how the markets work in reality, and not based on unrealistic or idealized assumptions.
2. The strategy must be defensible after the fact so that an investor can claim, "I was right for the right reason." In other words, it can't just be dumb luck.

The challenge for any investor that wants to evolve from strategic (passive) asset management where price forecasting is typically a process of projecting past asset class returns into the future, to tactical (active) asset allocation where price forecasting involves "a satisfactory descriptive and explanatory theory of how the markets work in reality," is that investors must find a way to gain the knowledge about markets necessary to be successful. How much knowledge is needed to succeed? According to Brock, the answer is the amount of knowledge necessary to "be less wrong than the consensus." As we will see, there is an interesting difference between the investment expertise needed to be a strategic (passive) investor and the investment expertise that is needed to be an active, tactical asset allocator.

## Judgment and Expertise Needed for Strategic (Passive) Decision-Making

Strategic market knowledge tends to be *explanatory*. It is the knowledge base strategic, buy and hold investors need to explain why events in the investment world are occurring. If a particular fund manager is underperforming, investors need a level of knowledge to understand why and to be able to explain it. The same can be said for the performance of an asset class. Strategic investors need a knowledge base to explain, *after the fact*, why the asset class performed above or below expectations. In fact, this level of knowledge is not a necessity at all since the only tactic to be pursued in the ongoing asset allocation of a strategic portfolio is rebalancing. Finally, financial advisors who pursue strategic asset allocation strategies must know the often complex and baffling language of Modern Portfolio Theory and the basic tools of modern finance. They must be able to explain concepts like efficient frontiers and capital asset pricing models and factor-based style analysis to their clients. Knowing this language and this "science" allows financial advisors to been seen as experts in the eyes of their clients, and just as importantly, allows them to properly communicate the main message of strategic allocation, which is patience. The mantra of strategic buy and hold investors remains the same: expected portfolio returns are likely to appear "over time," perhaps many years in the future.

To gain the knowledge base to explain MPT is relatively easy. As I have pointed out, MPT is functionally the only investment methodology accepted by the financial planning and money management community and there are hundreds of books and papers on the subject. The good news for investors is that learning about MPT is for all practical purposes a one-time affair. The rules for strategic asset allocation have not changed for 50 years, so once an investor has invested the time and effort to learn it, they don't need to spend any additional time on the subject. Since, as we all know, time is a precious commodity, not having to spend it on an ongoing basis to keep current with portfolio management theory is a blessing. I can speak about efficient portfolios with the same authority today that I did twenty years ago, and little has changed in the explanation for clients.

The second body of knowledge needed to be a successful strategic, buy and hold investor, which is the knowledge needed to *explain* market events and security performance, as opposed to Modern Portfolio Theory, can be gained in two ways. General market knowledge sufficient to understand the investment climate is readily available through any of the daily investment newspapers. An investor who reads the *Wall Street Journal*, the *Financial Times*, *Business Week*, *The Economist*, and other well-known daily and weekly publications, will have more than enough information to explain the financial markets to themselves or to their clients.

A second method for obtaining an explanatory level of knowledge about the markets in general and the performance of specific managed funds in particular, is to call the mutual fund companies to get the relevant information. Investors can either speak to a marketing specialist, the fund manager, or a senior analyst at the fund to get their views on the markets and specific fund information. In addition, Morningstar and other independent services offer analysis of mutual fund performance. To keep current with the various funds in a diversified portfolio does take an ongoing investment of time, but not enormously so. Professional advisors who provide quarterly performance reporting may decide to provide this type of explanatory security information with their reports. Therefore, once a quarter they must check in with the fund managers that they own to find out the story or the narrative that explains the fund's recent performance. On the other hand, many firms believe that their clients shouldn't focus on short-term investment performance and may not provide this information except for once a year, if at all.

## Judgment and Expertise Needed for Tactical (Active) Decision-Making

While strategic asset allocation requires professional financial advisors to explain the performance of the portfolio *after the fact*, it is only necessary in order to maintain strong client relationships. An advisor who can explain portfolio performance in an intelligent and authoritative fashion can do much to calm the nerves of client's that are experiencing less than expected returns. However, this ability has little to do with the ongoing rebalancing of the portfolio, which is the only tactic that is applied in strategic and passive portfolios in bear markets. After all, the rebalancing process has nothing to do with the "why" of market movements, and only depends on the "how much" markets have moved away from the buy and hold, strategic percentages that are set in stone at the beginning of the investment engagement. On the other hand, tactical (active) asset allocation requires investors to have the expertise needed to *forecast* the performance of asset classes *in the future*.

Readers may recall that Woody Brock gives us three general strategies for accurately describing reality and for being right *before* the fact. The first strategy is to exploit non-stationarity. Brock explains, "An investor who invests time and money to understand (forecast) structural change should possess and will possess an edge. Specifically, he will better forecast future news than will other investors—in particular those who stick their head in the sand and ignore structural change." Some well-known investment strategies that take advantage of structural change include fundamental analysis, sector rotation, and demographic and political "macro" bets.

The second strategy suggested by Brock is to exploit "endogenous risk." This refers to the degree to which asset prices change in response to the behavior of market participants. Successful investment strategies that are based on the idea of exploiting endogenous risk include arbitrage strategies predicated on convergence of price spreads, momentum investment strategies, and all market-timing strategies that exploit long-term bull and bear markets.

The third strategy suggested by Brock is to exploit logical errors of inference. This strategy suggests that there are often non-intuitive relationships between economic variables that can be misinterpreted by the market. Having a better understanding of how these fundamentals apply in the real economy can allow investors "to be less wrong" than the consensus and subsequently outperform other investors.

Readers will have their own preferences as to which of these strategies appeal to them. Not all investors will be comfortable implementing all of them, and I suspect that their preferences will have much to do with their individual beliefs and training in terms of their understanding of financial markets. For example, Pinnacle's approach to tactical asset allocation originally focused on the first strategy, which is to exploit non-stationarity—meaning we strive to better forecast future news and its impact on markets. Here the emphasis is on fundamental research, sector rotation, and macroeconomic bets. However, over the years we have fully incorporated the elements of Brock's other two strategies into our investment process as well. There are times (like the current market environment) when issues of exploiting endogenous risk become very important. Monitoring market "internals" like investor sentiment indicators or evaluating price overshoots versus various indicators of long-and short-term price trends can be very important. In addition, we are also constantly on the lookout for opportunities that are uncovered from focusing on counterintuitive relationships in the financial markets. In our particular case, we rely on independent research to point out these possible opportunities when they arise. Investors should carefully explore all three strategies to see which ones fit their view of financial markets and to determine their own comfort level in executing tactical (active) portfolio construction. I know of several investment firms whose investment process is entirely technical in their approach to financial markets, and they rely almost 100% on Brock's second strategy for successful market forecasting, which is to exploit endogenous risk. By focusing on market internals, investor sentiment, measures of momentum, and other tools of technical analysis, they attempt to beat the markets and add alpha to their performance.

Because Pinnacle's initial approach to tactical asset allocation was based on fundamental research about asset classes, sector rotation, and macro-bets, and then subsequently branched off into market internals and technical analysis, our professional education was originally focused on gaining the expertise needed to succeed at fundamental analysis. Today, the solution to the problem of gaining a high level of investment knowledge has evolved over the years into two critically important pieces of our investment process. The first was to hire professional security analysts and the second was and continues to be our reliance on independent research. To do this, two questions had to be addressed: 1) What are the qualifications of a great investment analyst, and 2) How do you manage the overwhelming amount of information about the financial markets in order to make good investment decisions? The answers to these questions should be of interest to any individual investor or professional financial advisor who is considering the move to active portfolio management.

## Investment Analysts

Individual investors must find a way to manage their time to properly implement whichever investment strategy they prefer. For all of its drawbacks, strategic, buy and hold investing offers the benefit of requiring the absolute minimum commitment of time in order to successfully implement the strategy. On the other hand, successful active portfolio management takes more of an investor's time, and individuals need to decide whether to spend their own time to implement the strategy or decide to retain the services of a professional investment advisor that specializes in active management. Interestingly, financial advisors face the same time issues when choosing their investment business model. Most financial planners pride themselves on being financial "generalists" who serve their clients by having expertise in many different areas of personal finance. Traditional areas of expertise include tax, cash flow, retirement planning, estate planning, life, disability and long-term care insurance, elder-care issues, education planning, philanthropic planning, qualified retirement plan construction, and investment planning. The newest exciting area of expertise for financial planners is "life planning," where the advisor's role is to counsel clients in the psychology of money, retirement lifestyle issues, etc. If a typical successful planner works with 50 or more clients, then depending on the model they use for delivering these services, it is easy to see how they must manage their time well if they are to succeed in professionally addressing all of these issues with their clients. So it is fair to ask, in the middle of remaining current on all of these other important areas of financial planning expertise, how can professional planners, or any investor, find the time to focus on gaining the investment expertise needed to forecast asset classes?

While I will leave it to my readers to answer this question for themselves, at Pinnacle we decided that the answer to the question was that individual advisors could not succeed at being the best financial planners and still be the highest quality investment analysts. Our particular solution was to create an investment team of full-time professional analysts whose sole responsibility is to do the research necessary in order for the firm to make informed asset allocation decisions. Obviously individual investors must act as their own analyst which requires them to personally have a unique skill set if they are to successfully meet the challenges of actively managing portfolios in a systematic and rigorous fashion. Fortunately for them, unlike the analysts at Pinnacle, they don't have to answer to the boss. They are the boss! And while that fact frees them to make investment decisions with impunity, it raises the bar in terms of how investment decisions get made and how they are implemented in an individual investor's portfolio.

We began to focus on the job responsibilities of our investment analysts after we made the commitment to implement a tactical asset allocation strategy during the 2000-2002 bear market, and the role of our analysts in our investment process has continued to evolve over the past nine years. Here are a few of the key lessons we've learned about how they do their job. Once again, these lessons apply to all investors, regardless of whether or not they are professionals who invest for clients or individuals who invest for their own account.

The primary role of an investment analyst where the investor is actively managing the portfolio is not to explain performance. Instead, their primary responsibility is to *forecast* performance. While this sounds like a simple statement, in fact, it is *the* critical attribute that is necessary to succeed where the investor is implementing an active investment strategy. For example, intelligent, motivated analysts who are at ease explaining why small-cap stocks outperformed large-caps during the past quarter, become tongue-tied when asked about the prospects for the *future* performance of small-caps versus large-caps over the next 12 months. To articulate such a forecast requires a high level of intelligence and self-confidence, as well as an environment that allows such an individual to be "wrong for the right reasons." It is very difficult to find people who are intelligent, motivated, fearless, and humble. In my opinion, all of these attributes are necessary to be a successful analyst.

The standard professional education for investment analysts is to either earn an MBA in Finance or to become a Chartered Financial Analyst®. For those unfamiliar with the CFA® curriculum, it requires that students pass a rigorous and difficult series of courses focused on investment analysis. It is a highly respected professional designation in the financial community. Achieving this level of higher education is a fantastic achievement and gives an analyst a strong base of knowledge to apply to their research. I would certainly encourage anyone interested in the field to actively pursue either professional designation. However, readers may be relieved to know that it isn't absolutely necessary to earn a professional designation in order to be a successful investment analyst. Investors simply need to develop the analytical skills necessary to succeed on their own.

In addition, there are personal attributes, other than analytical skills, that are also required for success. For example, to employ Woody Brock's third strategy for better forecasting, which is to exploit logical errors of inference, an analyst must not only have excellent analytical skills, but also be able to "think outside of the box." They must be able to look past the consensus and see the world differently from everyone else. Just as importantly, they must have the courage of their convictions if their view is outside of consensus opinion.

This ability is even more important for individual investors or analysts at small firms where the investment palette literally includes every possible investment category and global market. This is in stark contrast to larger firms where analysts are typically assigned to cover only one area of the market. Finally, in a professional environment, analysts must have the determination to keep advancing their investment ideas, even if past recommendations were not approved, or were approved but didn't work out in the portfolio. That is why independent thinking, courage, and determination are equally important as attributes for successful analysts, along with earning the industry's advanced professional designations.

Another vital skill for a successful investment analyst is to be able to create order out of chaos. In the case of individual investors or analysts at small firms, they must cover many different market sectors and industries, asset classes, and individual investments that are either already owned, or are being considered for ownership, in the actively managed portfolio. Analysts must create structure in an investment arena that is typically chaotic. They must have the ability to prioritize their work, especially when volatile markets can change priorities in a hurry. One day they may be working on researching an alternative investment for the portfolio only to find that bond yields crashed the previous day and they need to shift their focus to the fixed income markets. Not everyone can function well in such a hectic, changing, unstructured environment. However, this is a requirement when the job description is something other than explaining last quarter's portfolio results. The ability to compartmentalize life's other challenges and organize the research effort for the portfolio is obviously a necessary skill for individual investors who must manage their money in addition to managing the responsibilities of a family and a full-time job.

Analysts need to be passionate about their work because the "burnout factor" of the job is very high. The financial markets continue to throw curveballs at any investment theory that they might advocate. In addition, the news that impacts the market arrives on a daily basis through the mass media and through other sources of research. It is not easy to wade through the daily reading that is required of analysts and maintain a level of enthusiasm about the job. For most small firms, this is the hard work that becomes the "secret sauce" that creates success in a highly competitive market place. There is no doubt that analysts must love their jobs if they are to thrive in such a high-pressure work environment.

## Independent Research

The second step in becoming an investment expert is to read and understand a carefully selected menu of independent investment research. Independent research provides a much deeper level of analysis about financial markets than is available through the daily financial press and investors can learn from the expertise of independent analysts in order to develop their own accurate forecasts of economic and market direction. If the list of attributes that are necessary to be a successful analyst discussed previously is somewhat intimidating, it is something of a relief to know that many of the best analysts in the business are available for hire at the cost of their investment letters and research services.

Sell-side research is typically generated by brokerage firms for the benefit of their clients. Because there is an obvious conflict of interest inherent in an arrangement where analysts are recommending stocks that the firm's brokers are trying to sell, there is a presumed "glass wall" between the research department of brokerage firms and the brokers that sell financial products. Today there are some terrific sell-side analysts that are worth reading. Of course, with the recent collapse of the investment banking industry, it will be interesting to see what happens to the research departments of many of these firms now that they have been consolidated into traditional banks, or have gone out of business entirely.

On the other hand, buy-side research is research conducted by institutions that do not sell investment products. Buy-side firms are completely independent which eliminates any conflicts of interest about their recommendations. The good news is that there is an amazing amount of independent information available about the financial markets. With the advent of the Internet, there are hundreds of bloggers writing every day about the financial markets. Or, for those who are so inclined, there are many firms with long and distinguished track records that provide independent analysis and opinion about the markets for a fee. Of course the bad news is that there is too much information available about the markets to be useful. It is impossible to process all the facts, statistics, and opinions that are available to investors for free, forgetting for a moment the further avalanche of information that is available for a fee.

The key to being an investment expert is buried somewhere in this unimaginably confusing whirlwind of investment information. It seems so simple. Investors must find those investment experts who are considered to be the best in their respective fields, and then simply do what they tell us to do. To find the best research available we (Pinnacle) systematically asked every fund manager we knew about the research that they were reading. We also began to notice when certain research firms began to be referenced by more than one commentator or money manager. We also noticed which firms were mentioned by other analysts that we were reading. We compared notes as we read, trying to ascertain which of the analysts seemed to present the clearest points of view about the markets, and which offered the clearest recommendations about how to execute their point of view in our portfolio construction.

As the process evolved, it became obvious that the investment ideas of certain research firms were resonating with us more than others. We also began to understand the nuances of individual analysts at different research firms, as well as the nuances of how they reached their opinions about the markets. For example, some analysts tend to be more bullish than others. Some are driven more by technical considerations at certain points in time than by fundamental considerations. We found some firms we could rely on for their global macro opinions and others that we liked better for sector rotation in the U.S. market.

Another benefit of using independent research is that many of the firms use quantitative models that they have developed over the years to help with their investment recommendations. For individual investors and smaller firms that can't hope to match the resources of large investment firms with in-house "quant" departments, it levels the playing field by allowing the little guys to see the results of different quantitative approaches that have been very successful over the years.

The more we read, the more we began to realize that one aspect of our original strategy for becoming investment experts was not going according to plan. As we continued to add more well-known analysts to our reading list, and as we became more assured that the analysts that we were reading were not only the best in the business, but were the analysts that other successful money managers were reading, too, we became more and more discouraged. The reality was that instead of finding that the analysts were giving us uniform views about how to construct our portfolios at any point in the market cycle, we found that typically most of the analysts disagreed with each other most of the time. It was very disconcerting to read the views of the best and brightest analysts that we could find, with years of experience in their field, offering diametrically opposite opinions about just about everything.

Inevitably, the process of making forecasts began to subtly change from following the recommendations of any one analyst, to developing our own point of view based on our convictions about the viewpoints of many analysts with differing opinions. We found a way to make better forecasts; it just turned out to be a lot harder and a lot messier than we thought it was going to be. I suspect that the reader who is intent on achieving a higher level of investment expertise will experience a similar level of disappointment that the process isn't as easy as you might think it should be. Hopefully, all investors interested in active management will ultimately find themselves emancipated from depending on the views of any one particular analyst, or research firm. On that day, they will graduate to truly being an investment expert and join other active managers in embarking on a lifelong journey of trying not to be humbled by the markets every single day.

It is worth reiterating that the availability of independent research allows individual investors and small firms to leverage investment information so that they can compete with much larger firms. It may have been true in the past that you needed to have dozens of analysts, each specializing in a specific area of the markets, to compete in relatively efficient investment markets. However, with the benefit of the Internet and the resources available through the best research providers, investors can obtain all of the information they need to compete in the investment strategies they choose to implement. A high quality of independent research can lead to high-conviction beliefs, which can lead to excellent investment decisions for investors.

## Research as the Foundation for Active Strategy

Investors should rely on independent research for three important building blocks of any active management strategy. The first is that research helps to develop a point of view about the markets. Having a point of view allows investors to have a big-picture narrative that guides them in positioning the portfolio. A change in an investor's point of view over time is an important catalyst for making changes in an actively and tactically managed portfolio. The following statements are all random examples of points of view about the investment landscape that may require investors to change their portfolio construction based on the conviction of their belief:

- The U.S. stock market is in the end stages of a mid-cycle slowdown.
- The weight of the evidence suggests that we are either in a recession or soon will be in a recession.
- The Fed will be forced to cut the Fed Funds target rate to 1%.
- The emerging markets will not "decouple" from the developed world's economic growth.
- Deflation is a much bigger problem than inflation for the foreseeable future.
- The dollar is in a secular decline and will create inflation pressures well into the future.
- Yield spreads are likely to continue to widen over the next six months.

The second important goal of reading research is to develop a high conviction about your point of view. At any point in time, depending on the subject, the analysts that we read will agree on a particular market scenario.

When they do it helps investors to have more conviction about an investment idea, which ultimately translates into a security actually making it into their portfolio. Conviction is especially important in volatile markets where the changing news of the day can whipsaw market opinion faster than you can imagine. For investors who try to invest in longer-term themes, a high level of conviction allows them to sleep at night, even if the markets might not be validating their point of view at any particular moment in time.

The third important goal from studying independent market research is to obtain new and interesting investment ideas. You can find, at the touch of a keystroke, more investment ideas than you can possibly implement swirling around the Internet and other sources of news. This cacophony of information is often called "market noise." Research helps investors to cut through some of the noise to find better ideas proposed by analysts that they respect. These ideas often become the starting point for Pinnacle's analysts to conduct their own research to see if we agree that the idea has merit.

The following list is a sampling of the analysts and research companies that we currently read at Pinnacle. This list is constantly changing as we add and subtract individual analysts and independent research firms, either because our confidence in them has changed for better or for worse, or because of budgetary constraints. Some of the firms on the list are relatively expensive and constitute what we feel are excellent sources for fundamental research. Other firms offer technical research that we follow as part of our investment process. Other names on the list are periodicals and journals that most readers are already familiar with. For example, each week Jim Cooper at *BusinessWeek* writes an excellent column called *Business Outlook* that offers insightful comments on the economy. I hate to miss Jim's column, and it's yours for the cost of a subscription. John Mauldin's e-newsletter, *Thoughts from the Frontline*[41], offers one of the most insightful and clearly written newsletters on investment topics that you could possibly hope to find, and it's free. In addition, Mauldin's newsletter introduced us to many of the other analysts we now read, including the work of Ed Easterling, whom we have referred to several times in this book. There are literally hundreds of institutional quality sources of research that are not on this list, perhaps because we decided not to use them, or more likely because we haven't gotten around to reading them yet. Any investor interested in learning more about active management would do well to start here.

BCA Global Investment Strategy, BCA Research
BCA Equity Sector Strategy, BCA Research
The Bank Credit Analyst, BCA Research
Ned Davis Research
John Kosar, Asbury Research
John Mendelson, Stanford Research Company
Liz Ann Sonders, Charles Schwab and Co., Inc.
John Roque, Natexis Bleichroeder, Inc.
Jim Bianco, Bianco Research
Brian Reynolds, MS Howells
Bill King, M. Ramsey King Securities, Inc.
Steven Roach, Morgan Stanley
Dick Berner, Morgan Stanley
John Maudlin, InvestorsInsight Publishing, Inc.
Jim Grant, Grant's Interest Rate Observer
Gloom Boom & Doom report, Marc Faber Limited
Ken Tower, Cybertrader
Bill Gross, PIMCO
Paul McCulley, PIMCO
Van R. Hoisington, Lacy H. Hunt, Van Hoisington Investment Management
    Company
Ed Yardeni, Oak Associates, ltd.
*Business Week Magazine*

## Summary

In an earlier chapter, I mentioned the strange contradiction created when investors choose strategic management because they believe that they can't forecast the

---

41    John Mauldin, "Thoughts from the Frontline," e-letter, InvestorInsight Publishing Co.

future returns of asset classes, and yet they often choose active fund managers to manage the specific asset classes that they strategically hold in their portfolios. These investors seem to believe that active fund managers have some innate ability to beat the markets while strategic buy and hold investors mysteriously do not. Having spent thousands of hours reading investment research about a wide variety of investment topics, I feel confident that we have acquired the skills we need to be investment experts and we are more than qualified to actively manage portfolios and utilize our judgment, experience, and expertise to build the most efficient tactically managed portfolios. I believe that any investor, regardless of their prior experience or training as a strategic asset allocator, can make the same conversion. Apparently the difference between active fund managers and strategic asset allocators isn't as mysterious as it appears to be. The answer to the riddle lies in doing the work. Given that investors make a significant investment of their time and money, they too can move past the level of skill necessary to *explain* asset class returns, and obtain the level of expertise necessary to *forecast* asset class returns.

One last thought on this topic: Investment expertise, as it is utilized in the pursuit of the highest "subjective" efficient frontier as explained by Woody Brock, is as much an art as it is a science. In this higher level of portfolio construction investors can't solely rely on past data to make tactical portfolio adjustments, and they can't entirely rely on quantitative models to make asset allocation decisions. By deciding to add *qualitative* decision-making to the investment process, investors commit themselves to a *lifetime learning process*. The financial world is extraordinarily complicated and the goal of trying to make better forecasts is indeed a tough goal to meet. It requires a passion for the markets, and a high degree of humility. However, the payoff is very clear. Dedicated investors can achieve the goal of making fewer mistakes than the consensus and earning higher investment returns.

# 10 THE INCREDIBLE, AMAZING P/E RATIO

I t all seems so simple: Buy low and sell high. As we saw in Part One, buying the S&P 500 Index when the P/E multiple (the same as P/E ratio) was relatively low and likely to expand led to long-term 20-year stock market returns that were much higher than expected. And we saw that buying the market at P/E multiples that were high and likely to contract over time led to much lower than average returns over long-term 20-year time periods. (Remember, the P/E multiple is a measure of how much investors are willing to pay for the earnings of an individual company or a market. The more investors are willing to pay for earnings, the more expensive the company or market is considered to be.)[42] So what is all the fuss about? Why can't investors simply be buyers at low prices and sellers at high prices?

The first and most obvious answer is that the classic method of portfolio construction based on Markowitz's portfolio optimization process does not require any consideration of fundamental value as measured by P/E ratios. Since most investors who practice strategic investing use either past market returns or past risk premiums as the assumptions for portfolio returns, they have no need to consider a fundamental measure of market value, such as P/E. They begin the asset allocation

---

42   Readers should note that P/E is but one of many accepted measures of market value. The most obvious other techniques include price-to-book value (P/B) and price-to-sales value (P/S). While this chapter focuses on P/E ratios in order to make a point about the difficulties in determining market value, I don't mean to imply that P/B and P/S are not subject to similar difficulties. I believe that P/E is the most popular measure of market value and so I chose it as the focus for this chapter.

process with the assumption that markets are efficiently valued, so the very idea of determining whether or not markets are "expensive" or "inexpensive" is considered to be irrelevant, or even worse, unprofessional.

However, for investors who desire to own asset classes based on their fundamental value characteristics, and who believe that value considerations are an important driver of asset class returns, it turns out that reaching a conclusion about market valuation by calculating the P/E ratio is more challenging than it would seem to be at first glance. Even though the math only requires a P and an E, the E is a surprisingly elusive number that is subject to a great deal of interpretation among investors. In fact, the more we learn about the P/E ratio the more it seems that we are entering an "Alice in the Looking Glass" world where up is down and down is up, or more to the point, cheap is expensive and vice versa. Once again, the need for investors to exercise good judgment becomes very important. Today's volatile markets may be changing the conclusions that investors are reaching about market valuation, and subsequently changing how they are approaching the construction of their portfolios. As we will find out, different investors will reach different conclusions when trying to resolve the puzzle of interpreting P/E ratios. Successfully solving the valuation puzzle will have a dramatic impact on whether or not investors will earn excess returns.

## Stalking the Elusive "E" in P/E

The "P" of the price to earnings ratio is easily knowable: it is simply the price of the security or the asset class you are analyzing. For now, we will focus on the S&P 500 Index as a proxy for the stock market. Therefore "P" is the price of the index, which is calculated by taking the sum of the individual market values of each stock in the index (shares * price) and then using a divisor (currently 8703) to adjust for stock splits, new members to the index, etc. For the most part, there isn't much room to have an argument about the price of the market. You can see what it is on a tick-by-tick basis throughout any trading day.

The "E" of the P/E ratio also seems simple enough. The earnings for the index is calculated similar to the price, where the earnings are the sum of the number of shares times the earnings per share of each company in the index, and then adjusted by the divisor. This calculation of the index earnings becomes the denominator of our P/E fraction. Unfortunately, calculating the E in the P/E is a lot more complicated than it seems. The first complication is that there are at least three well-known ways to measure corporate earnings. If you choose to value a company's earnings in the same way that corporate accountants do, then you would use Generally Accepted Accounting Principles (GAAP) earnings, also known as As-Reported earnings, as the denominator for your P/E ratio.

This measure includes all of the conventional write-offs that companies must take for all expenses under the FASB accounting rules (Financial Accounting Standards Board), even if the expense is only a one-time event. Investors who use GAAP earnings in their P/E calculation have the advantage of using a relatively conservative earnings number that is subject to FASB-approved accounting conventions. You would think that there would be no room for controversy when using GAAP or As-Reported earnings.

Unfortunately, you would be wrong. For some, GAAP or As-Reported earnings can be misleading, resulting in a company's reported earnings being higher than the company's actual operations would warrant. (Warning: we are about to descend into a short discussion of accounting rules. Readers should prepare themselves accordingly.) One of the biggest problems raised by critics of GAAP accounting rules has to do with how pension expenses and income are handled under the FASB conventions for pension accounting. Under GAAP accounting, FASB combines the pension fund with the company's overall business by calculating the net gain earned by the pension fund after all pension-related expenses, and then includes this gain in the company's net income. Further, because the net pension gain depends on the stock market, and market returns are volatile, FASB replaces the actual pension funds returns with an expected return. While using the expected return reduces the volatility of company earnings, critics maintain that it results in distorting the actual core business condition of the company which must ultimately fund the plan based on actual, not expected, market returns.

In 2002 Standard and Poor's introduced a new measure for calculating earnings, called Core Earnings, that dealt with this issue, as well as other perceived problems with the GAAP accounting standard. S&P Core Earnings takes a different approach to defined benefit plan accounting. Using the Core Earnings approach, the costs of the plan are calculated using actual versus expected plan earnings, and the costs are included in company expenses. However, the assets in the plan are only available for paying pension benefits, so the earnings are not included in the company's net income. For older companies in the information technology and industrial sectors of the U.S. economy that still offer defined benefit plans for their employees, this difference in accounting for plan expenses and earnings can make a dramatic difference in a company's bottom line, and have a major impact in the perceived valuation of the company. Generally speaking, the Core Earnings method is not widely used, but it usually results in more conservative estimates of E than the GAAP methodology.

Unfortunately, the options for trying to determine the "E" in P/E don't end there. Some analysts use an entirely different measure called Operating Earnings, also referred to as Pro-Forma Earnings or Adjusted Earnings. The purpose of this measure is to try to determine what the actual month-to-month earnings of a company might be, not counting extraordinary expenses. This is similar to determining your family's annual budget without counting the all-cash auto purchase you made this year. It makes no sense to assume that you will purchase a car every year for cash, so there's no point in including it in your projected cash expenses for every year in the future. Companies do much the same thing. Analysts don't count certain expenses from GAAP earnings in order to get a clearer picture of what ongoing earnings are likely to be. These adjustments have different names, including non-recurring charges/gains, one-time items, extraordinary items, or adjustments. This measure of earnings is likely to give a much higher E for our P/E ratio than either GAAP earnings or Core Earnings because certain deductions to earnings are not being counted. Remember that in our admittedly simplified view of P/E calculation, a higher E creates a lower P/E ratio, therefore making the stock (or stock market) seem less expensive. A statement of reconciliation usually accompanies the statement of Operating Earnings to GAAP earnings showing where the adjustments occurred. With the passage of the Sarbanes-Oxley legislation, corporate CEO's are personally responsible to make certain that adjusted earnings are not fraudulent and meet accepted accounting principles.

At this point, you may ask, which of these varied approaches to determining the E in P/E is the correct measure to use? Unfortunately, there is no "right" answer. For example, it is generally true that analysts that have little confidence in management's projections of corporate earnings tend to emphasize either Core or GAAP earnings more than operating earnings. Their assessment of *earnings quality* becomes all-important. A well-known measure of earnings quality is to simply compare the ratio of operating earnings to GAAP earnings. The wider the ratio becomes, the lower the earnings quality is assumed to be. Some analysts will evaluate all three methods of calculating earnings, but may emphasize one more than the other, depending on the specific industry. Other analysts may claim that operating earnings are a more accepted measure of earnings by the majority of investors, so they may focus their efforts there. In its simplest form, investors who use operating earnings may conclude that the stock market is less expensive than when using the other methods, because the E in the ratio tends to be higher than it is with either GAAP or Core. This can lead to more bullish opinions about market valuation, but as we will see, such conclusions are not necessarily correct. Investors who are interested in active management should pay attention to the valuation of the market based on all three types of earnings calculations. With experience, they will become comfortable using the different methods in combination or separately, depending on the condition of the market.

## Relying on the Past or Future

If the choices regarding the mysterious E aren't already confusing enough, there are even more judgment calls that must be made. In addition to the choice of using GAAP, Core, or Operating Earnings, the next decision to make is whether to be forward looking when determining the E or backward looking. If you believe that investors are discounting the *future value* of earnings to determine the valuation of the stock market, then you might conclude that the E in the P/E ratio should be based on estimates of future earnings. However, if you believe that future earnings estimates are so unreliable that they are essentially worthless, then you may wish to choose an E for the P/E ratio that is based on past earnings, which are not subject to analyst interpretations. Both methods have their benefits and drawbacks. Since we've already introduced the idea of using trailing 10-year GAAP earnings in calculating P/E multiples in a previous chapter, let's start by looking at the past in order to determine market value.

There are several excellent reasons to use trailing and normalized (averaged) earnings when calculating the P/E multiple. The reason to use trailing earnings is that forward or future earnings will always be an unknown since they haven't been earned yet. Trailing earnings have the benefit of actually existing, which is no small consideration, and they are not subject to changing opinions, market conditions, or revisions. The reason to use averaged, or normalized, earnings is that if you use a

| YEAR END | S&P 500 INDEX GAAP EARNINGS |
|---|---|
| 1997 | 39.72 |
| 1998 | 37.71 |
| 1999 | 48.17 |
| 2000 | 50 |
| 2001 | 24.69 |
| 2002 | 27.59 |
| 2003 | 48.74 |
| 2004 | 58.55 |
| 2005 | 69.93 |
| 2006 | 81.51 |
| 2007 | 66.18 |
| Trailing 10 Year Earnings for 2007 Sum of 10 Year Earnings/10 or $552.79/10 or $33.279 | |

**Table 10.1**

Source: Pinnacle Advisory Group, Inc.

long enough period of time to calculate the E on an average basis you can smooth out the cyclical swings in earnings that make analyzing market values so difficult. To calculate the normalized or trailing 10-year earnings number, you simply add the previous 10 years of earnings data and divide by 10. **Table 10.1** shows the calculations for 2007 PE-10 using GAAP earnings.

Using this methodology, the very high level of earnings that followed the boom years in 1998 and 1999, as well as the very low level of earnings that followed due to the recession of 2001-2002, are smoothed out by the calculation. The chart above shows the cyclical nature of earnings over the years. By averaging the earnings numbers over time, the boom and bust quality of earnings are smoothed and the E becomes a more reliable number. Depending on where you are in the earnings cycle, the normalized number can either be higher or lower than current earnings data might indicate. In addition, corporate earnings tend to be "mean reverting," meaning that earnings data tends to not deviate from its long-term trend for extended periods of time. By normalizing or averaging past earnings data, analysts can acknowledge the mean reverting nature of earnings, which may otherwise significantly deviate from the trend for short periods of time, depending on where we are in the economic cycle.

Another reason to use trailing earnings is the very practical consideration of the amount of data available for analysis. While there is a relatively small amount of data available about forward earnings projections, the data pertaining to trailing earnings is available going all the way back to the 1800's. Different analysts use slightly different methodologies for normalizing or averaging trailing earnings. For instance, Steve Leuthold of the Leuthold Group prefers to use five years of trailing earnings in his calculations (Leuthold actually uses 18 quarters of trailing earnings and two quarters of forward earnings). Robert Shiller of Yale University and others prefer to use 10 years of inflation-adjusted trailing earnings. John Hussman, portfolio manager of the Hussman Funds, prefers to use the current price over the highest earnings per share figure for the index to date. However, they all conclude that looking backward is better than trying to look forward for determining market value.

Finally, another reason to use trailing and normalized earnings is that there are a number of academic studies showing that using long-term average trailing earnings in calculating the E in the P/E multiple is highly effective in accurately predicting long-term market performance compared to using forward earnings. It may be that trailing earnings are used in these studies for the simple reason that there is much more data available to researchers. Perhaps as more data are available, forward earnings will turn out to be a reliable indicator of long-term returns. However, it appears that most of today's research depends on using trailing normalized earnings.

We already explored some of this research when we reviewed Ed Easterling's (Crestmont Research) data on normalized P/E ratios in Chapter Two to conclude that buying and holding stocks for 20-year periods can be a high risk strategy when purchasing stocks at high P/E multiples. We will look at some additional research on this subject later in this chapter when we discuss the Fed Model.

## Using Forward Earnings

Analysts who use projected forward earnings in order to determine the E in the P/E ratio readily acknowledge the risk of forecasting future earnings. They make the very powerful argument that investors pay prices for stocks based on the outlook for the company's future earnings, not the past. If stock prices represent the discounted value of future corporate cash flows, expressed as dividends or earnings, then it makes no sense to base the conclusion about a stock's value, or the stock market's value, on trailing earnings. These investors view trailing earnings as completely irrelevant to the prices that investors should be willing to pay for the shares based on the discounted future cash flows from the company. If investing in stocks has risk, then clearly the risk has much to do with investors' inability to know exactly what earnings will be in the future. Since investors won't know the "true probability law" governing earnings, then once again it is judgment and experience that is required to make the most accurate forecast possible. Advocates of using forward earnings would point out that in the real world, it is the changes to analyst's forecasts of forward earnings that actually move market prices on a day-to-day basis, and therefore concentrating on any other type of earnings measure may be interesting, but ultimately a waste of time.

For investors in individual stocks, there is much to learn about how to analyze and forecast what an individual company's earnings might be in the future. Graham and Dodd's book, *Security Analysis*, is still a highly recommended book for determining the intrinsic value of individual companies. For top-down investors who actively manage portfolios by investing in asset classes, sectors, industries, and countries, rather than in individual equity issues, a broader set of tools can be utilized to analyze and forecast the trend of future earnings. Using the S&P 500 Index as our example, the starting point for most investors should be to study the consensus earnings estimates of the analysts who cover the stocks in the Index. There are several different independent services that publish earnings estimates, including Zacks, Thompson Financial, Standard and Poor's and First Call. Each of these services surveys numerous professional analysts to get their opinion about an individual stock's forward earnings estimates. They then publish the total projected earnings for all of the stocks in the Index. This is called a "bottom-up" approach to earnings forecasts. Other economists use econometric models of the broad economy to make "top-down" estimates of future earnings. Both methods can be useful for investors who are interested in learning what the consensus estimates are for the stock market.

## Value Traps

There are several problems with analyzing consensus forecasts of S&P 500 earnings. The first problem is that at any point in time the consensus earnings estimate from any one of these services will be different from the others. On the other hand, critics would point out that the earnings estimates are guided so much by the companies that the analyst consensus estimates represent a "herd mentality" where the estimates don't vary as much as they should. The second problem is that analysts have a tendency to extrapolate trough-to-peak earnings gains or peak-to-trough earnings losses far above or below their relatively stable, long-term trend channel. At the top of the economic cycle when enthusiasm about future business prospects is at its highest, analysts tend to reflect that enthusiasm in their estimates. This is understandable because at this point in the earnings cycle actual earnings are typically very strong, and corporate CFO's are optimistically guiding analyst estimates higher, which causes earnings estimates to soar. Conversely, at the bottom of the earnings cycle analysts tend to be too pessimistic and earnings estimates overshoot to the downside.

When earnings and earnings estimates rise at a faster rate than stock prices, they often present what is known as a "value trap." The trap is set because the high E at the peak of the economic cycle makes the market seem to be inexpensive, when in fact the market is actually very expensive. In this case, the E is a mirage that can disappear in an instant at market tops. When the cycle turns, the E can plummet and investors find out that the market was much more expensive than they thought at the peak. The reverse problem appears at market bottoms where the market can appear more expensive than it actually is because investors and analysts are too pessimistic about the earnings outlook.

**Figure 10.1** from Ned Davis Research illustrates historic "peak" earnings growth from 1930 to the present using trailing 1-year GAAP earnings and shows the P/E multiples that investors will pay at the peaks and troughs of the earnings cycle. The chart shows that investors typically recognize peak earnings by awarding them comparatively low P/E multiples, which turn out to be an average of only 12.9 times earnings for the 14 EPS growth peaks shown in the chart. On the other hand, investors pay relatively high P/E multiples for the market at troughs in earnings growth throughout the earnings cycle. At the troughs in the earnings cycle, investors pay a much higher multiple, an average of 19.09 times earnings. If the reader is thinking that the market should be expensive at the top of the earnings cycle and that the P/E multiple should be high, then the lower multiples at earnings peaks could be confusing. The reverse is also true at the bottom of the cycle. Clearly "Alice in the Looking Glass" applies at the peaks and troughs of market cycles.

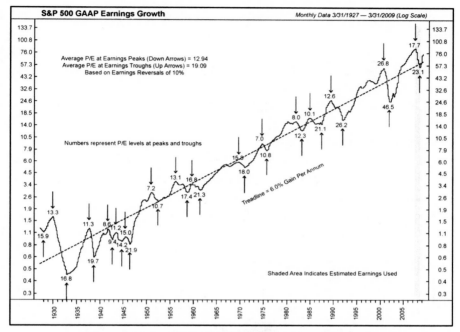

**Figure 10.1—S&P 500 GAAP Earnings Growth**
Source: Ned Davis Research

For the unwary or uninformed investor who listens to a pundit declare that the market is cheap or expensive based on the current P/E multiple, the problem is obvious. If the market is deemed to be cheap at 12.9 times earnings and then earnings growth plunges, the investor who was a buyer based on this one assessment of market value is likely to be disappointed with subsequent market returns.

Another problem is that the forward operating earnings estimates change over time as professional analysts change their minds about the economic fundamentals of the companies that they follow, or they simply get caught up in the herd mentality of other analysts changing their minds about the company's future earnings prospects and so they change their minds as well. David Dreman, the well-known proponent of contrarian value investing, and author of several well-known books on the subject like *Contrarian Investment Strategies: The Next Generation*[43], offers compelling

---

43   David Dreman, *Contrarian Investment Strategies: The Next Generation*, Simon and Schuster, New York, N.Y., 1998

evidence that analysts' estimates of future earnings are often so wrong that investors who invest opposite to their recommendations can consistently beat the markets.

Fortunately, investors have several tools to help them track changing consensus opinions about earnings. One well-known method is to track earnings revisions. As analysts change their forecasts for the different stocks in the index, the revisions to their forecasts are tracked by a variety of research services. Ed Yardeni is a well-known market analyst who provides excellent insights into consensus forward earnings estimates. **Figure 10.2** from Yardeni Research shows how earnings revisions plunged during the bear market of 2000-2002 and again in the 2007-2008 bear market. Generally speaking, it is the direction of the revisions, the rate of change of revisions, as well as the number of revisions that investors focus on when evaluating what operating earnings will be in the future. Investors will either conclude from this data that stock market earnings will continue to head lower based on the dramatic number of negative revisions shown, or they may reach the conclusion that the percentage of negative revisions is so low that the earnings revisions numbers are likely to turn higher soon, helping them to reach a bullish forecast for the stock market.

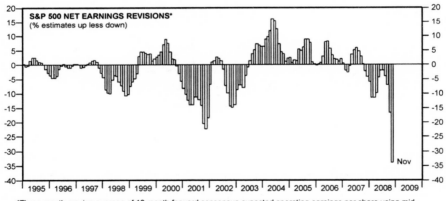

*Three-month moving average of 12-month forward consensus expected operating earnings per share using mid-month consensus forecast.

### Figure 10.2—S&P 500 Net Earnings Revisions
Source: Yardeni Research

For investors who are interested in following the revisions in analysts' opinions about forward earnings, Yardeni provides a unique chart he calls "earnings squiggles." His earnings squiggles chart tracks annual analyst earnings estimates from 25 months prior to when earnings are reported all the way through to when the earnings are actually reported (the dotted line on the chart). Looking at the squiggles tells you whether analysts were underestimating or overestimating earnings as they approached the actual report date. By looking at whether the squiggles are trending higher or lower you can see whether or not analysts had to revise their forecasts either higher or lower as the year progressed. If earnings were coming in above consensus and analysts were revising their forecasts higher, then that was a tailwind for the stock market that potentially contributed to higher market prices as investors responded to the more positive earnings outlook. If the squiggles were disappointing and the consensus forecast was moving lower, then the stock market was likely trending lower on the disappointing earnings news. The solid black line on the chart reflects 12-month rolling forward earnings estimates, which Yardeni defines as the time weighted average of current and next year's consensus earnings estimates. As time passes the annual estimates (the dotted line) converges toward the coming year's expectations (the solid line), and becomes identical to the coming year's consensus forecast at the end of the current year (December). By comparing the end of the dotted line, which ends at the actual reported earnings for each year, to the point where it crossed the solid line, which represents the previous 12-month forward forecast for end of year earnings, you can see if analysts were overly optimistic or pessimistic in their outlook each year. **Figure 10.3** obviously shows that analysts are overly pessimistic in bull markets (2004 through 2006) and overly optimistic in bear markets (2000-2002 and 2007-2008). It is also interesting to note that at the end of each calendar year on the chart, where the dotted lines end, the next year's forward estimates are almost always significantly higher. The only exception appears to be 2001 where the forward estimates for 2002 are actually the same as year-end 2001 earnings.

*Time-weighted average of current and next year's consensus earnings estimates. Numbers above time line are annual growth rates

**Figure 10.3—S&P 500 Index Operating Earnings Per Share**

Source: Yardeni Research

**Figure 10.3** shows that 2009 estimates have been crumbling as we reach the 2008 year-end. As always, investors are busy disagreeing about whether or not analysts are overly pessimistic about the prospects for corporate earnings for the coming year.

As you may have guessed, investors who are specifically interested in earnings surprises can find that data published, as well. Several research firms track earnings surprise, which is the amount that company earnings either outperform or underperform consensus estimates for each quarterly reporting period. Once again, it is the number of earnings surprises, as well as the degree of earnings surprise that moves the markets. Of course companies know how to guide analyst expectations lower as earnings season approaches so that they can then announce a positive earnings surprise, even though the actual earnings number is poor.

**Table 10.2** from Standard and Poor's[44] shows earnings surprise data from the 2nd quarter 2008 earnings season. The third table column shows that most of the companies had reported so far in the period. Not so surprisingly, the biggest negative earnings "surprise" at the time was the financial sector reporting 46.5% negative surprises, with negative median reported earnings growth of -17.4%. The most positive earning surprises were in the industrials and health care sectors with 82.4% and 72.5% positive surprises respectively. In retrospect, it is clear that the earnings surprises in the financial sector were a preview for investors of even worse news to come. Investors who follow this data would agree that companies (or markets) that deliver negative earnings surprises lose the benefit of the doubt about future earnings estimates until they actually begin to consistently deliver positive earnings surprises.

There is another method of evaluating earnings that can reveal some interesting insights into the possible value of future S&P 500 operating earnings. By evaluating the stock market earnings by individual sectors of the stock market, instead of just looking at the projections for the total earnings for the entire market, investors can see where the earnings growth and disappointments are coming from. The recent volatile market environment provides a good example of how analyzing earnings on a sector-by sector basis can lead to different conclusions about the prospects for future earnings growth, and how quickly investor perceptions can change. **Table 10.3** was created using numbers provided by Standard and Poor's in August 2008 and shows the earnings growth of each of the S&P 500 sectors as well as the forecasted earnings growth for each sector 12 months in the future. A review of the chart shows how much of the S&P 2008 earnings growth estimates were attributed to massive losses in the financial sector, as well as the consumer discretionary sector of the market. Considering the news about the huge losses to

---

44  Standard & Poor's®, S&P® and S&P 500® are registered trademarks of the McGraw-Hill Companies, Inc.

| SECTOR | "QTR 2 MEDIAN REPORTED GROWTH %" | "QTR 2 MEDIAN SURPRISE %" | "% REPORTING EARNINGS" | "% POSITIVE SURPRISE" | "% NEGATIVE SURPRISE" | % IN-LINE |
|---|---|---|---|---|---|---|
| Energy | 27.4% | 2.6% | 100.0% | 66.7% | 28.2% | 5.1% |
| Materials | 6.6% | 4.2% | 100.0% | 65.5% | 24.1% | 10.3% |
| Industrials | 13.9% | 5.0% | 92.7% | 82.4% | 11.8% | 5.9% |
| Consumer Discretionary | -4.0% | 3.7% | 71.1% | 62.1% | 25.9% | 12.1% |
| Consumer Staples | 10.1% | 2.6% | 82.9% | 63.6% | 21.2% | 15.2% |
| Health Care | 14.3% | 4.7% | 96.2% | 72.5% | 11.8% | 15.7% |
| Financials | -17.4% | 0.0% | 98.9% | 48.8% | 46.5% | 4.7% |
| Information Technology | 21.4% | 4.2% | 83.3% | 61.7% | 25.0% | 13.3% |
| Telecomm Services | 15.5% | 3.9% | 100.0% | 66.7% | 11.1% | 22.2% |
| Utilities | 8.1% | 4.4% | 96.8% | 56.7% | 36.7% | 6.7% |
| S&P 500 | 9.4% | 3.1% | 89.8% | 63.5% | 26.7% | 9.9% |

**Table 10.2**

Source: Standard and Poor's

banks and brokerages due to the systemic problems in the financial markets, as well as the sharp downturn in the housing industry and auto sales, it should be no surprise that these two sectors were and still are responsible for the large percentage of earnings declines.

| | 2008E | % CHG | 08 P*/E | 2009E | % CHG | 09 P*/E |
|---|---|---|---|---|---|---|
| S&P 500 | 80.79 | -2% | 15.96 | 108.43 | 34% | 11.89 |
| S&P 500 Consumer Discretionary (Sector) | 11.61 | -13% | 20.93 | 15.56 | 34.0% | 15.62 |
| S&P 500 Consumer Staples (Sector) | 17.39 | 11% | 17.08 | 19.12 | 10.0% | 15.53 |
| S&P 500 Energy (Sector) | 61.18 | 32% | 8.68 | 72.99 | 19% | 7.27 |
| S&P 500 Financials (Sector) | 6.37 | -72% | 44.62 | 27.51 | 332% | 10.32 |
| S&P 500 Health Care (Sector) | 25.58 | 10% | 15.11 | 29.23 | 14% | 13.22 |
| S&P 500 Industrials (Sector) | 22.71 | 7% | 13.95 | 24.96 | 10% | 12.69 |
| S&P 500 Information Technology (Sector) | 19.89 | 15% | 18.7 | 24.44 | 23% | 15.22 |
| S&P 500 Materials (Sector) | 17.27 | 8% | 13.8 | 19.39 | 12% | 12.3 |
| S&P 500 Telecommunication Services (Sector) | 9.61 | 16% | 13.63 | 11.73 | 22% | 11.17 |
| S&P 500 Utilities (Sector) | 12.81 | 10% | 14.6 | 14.35 | 12.0% | 13.04 |

**Table 10.3**

Source: Standard and Poor's

A careful study of the August 2008 data reveals that the earnings growth for the non-financial and non-consumer discretionary sectors of the S&P 500 Index was forecast to remain surprisingly strong. No other sectors in 2008 were estimated to have negative earnings growth, and all of the S&P 500 sectors were projected to have positive growth in 2009. In this example, when looking at the 12-month earnings growth estimates, you can see that at the time, analysts were projecting a huge earnings increase for the financial sector in 2009 of 332%, perhaps because the earnings growth was coming off of such a low base after all of the write-offs in the first half of 2008. Obviously, with the benefit of hindsight, bearish investors were proved correct. They believed that analysts were too optimistic in their forecasts of financial earnings and therefore total stock market earnings were likely to disappoint. In addition, they concluded that the weakness in the financial sector would create a recessionary environment that was not yet being reflected in the earnings expectations for other market sectors. Bearish investors were convinced that the projected P/E of 11.89 for the S&P 500 in 2009 was a value trap. They believed that the high E in the ratio is a mirage and the 2009 earnings estimate of $108 would simply not materialize.

Interestingly, at the same time that bearish investors were finding reasons in the data to sell stocks in preparation for a continuing bear market, bullish investors were finding reasons for optimism in the same data. Their thesis was that if most of the losses had been written off by CEO's in the financial and consumer discretionary sectors earlier in the year, and if the rest of the market sectors continued to perform well from an earnings perspective, then they could conclude that S&P earnings were likely to surprise to the upside as the financial and consumer discretionary sectors would outperform the consensus. For bullish investors, the same chart that supported the bears showed a buying opportunity at hand. For these optimistic investors, the E was viewed as being dramatically understated making the P/E ratio seem higher or more expensive than it should have been if earnings actually materialized based on the investors' bullish forecast. Clearly investors who accept the E in the P/E ratio at face value without understanding how it is derived do so at their own peril.

So far we have examined the E in the S&P 500 Index P/E ratio and discovered that there are many judgment calls to be made when determining how to calculate the E. We have seen that there are actually three methods of calculating E, including Core earnings, GAAP or As-Reported earnings, and Operating or Pro-forma earnings. Each has its benefits and drawbacks and each has its proponents and critics. In addition, we've learned that earnings can be evaluated on a trailing basis or a forward basis. Once again, each method has its own constituency of users who can be sharply critical of other valuation methods. Finally we have seen that looking at the earnings for each underlying sector of the stock market can give us useful insights into the validity of the consensus view on earnings. As we stated earlier, there is much to be said for using all of the different methods for calculating E in reaching a decision about market valuation using a comprehensive approach to the data. Table 10.4[45] shows the different P/E multiples that can be calculated currently based on the metrics we have reviewed so far. The range is startling,

---

45  P/E estimates are calculated as of December, 2008. GAAP data is updated through 6/30/2008. Forward earnings data is current through 9/30/09.

from a P/E as low as 11.61 to a high estimate of 22.04. Obviously investors could conclude that the stock market is either cheap or expensive depending on how they choose to view the data.

| METHOD | EARNINGS | MARKET VALUE | P/E |
|--------|----------|--------------|-----|
| Trailing 10 year GAAP | 51.36 | 904 | 17.6 |
| Trailing 5 Year GAAP | 63.73 | 904 | 14.18 |
| Trailing 1 Year GAAP | 68.3 | 904 | 13.24 |
| Forward Operating | 77.85 | 904 | 11.61 |
| Forward GAAP | 41.02 | 904 | 22.04 |
| Trailing 10 year GAAP | 51.36 | 904 | 17.6 |

**Table 10.4**

Source: Pinnacle Advisory Group, Inc.

## Comparing P/E Ratios - Absolute Valuation

Given all we know about the variability of the E in the P/E ratio, how should investors analyze the P/E data they obtain so that they can reach an opinion about market value? One method is to compare the current P/E multiple of the stock market to the market's P/E multiple in the past. With this method, investors are trying to identify the absolute value of the stock market. Absolute value is an assessment of the valuation of an asset class by comparing current valuation data to past valuation data. This methodology does not compare the asset class to any other asset classes, and it can be used to determine whether today's P/E multiple is cheap or expensive compared to past data.

Let's look at the absolute valuation of the stock market using a variety of the earnings measures reviewed above. Figure 10.4 shows the S&P 500 P/E multiple based on 12-month forward operating earnings. We also show the average or median forward earnings number calculated using data that go back to 1978. Based on this calculation we find the market's current P/E of 12 to be somewhat inexpensive relative to the historical average of 14. For investors using this data series, the concern is that the historical data only goes back to 1978. Therefore, the mean or the average may be skewed either by the huge spike in market values that occurred at the height of the tech bubble in the year 2000, or by the persistently low P/Es that were recorded towards the end of the last secular bear market in the late 1970's and early 1980's.

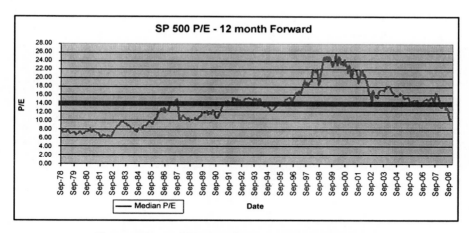

**Figure 10.4—S&P 500 P/E: 12-Month Forward**
Source: Pinnacle Advisory Group, Inc.

**Figure 10.5** shows the trailing 5-year normalized P/E multiple for the S&P 500 Index. This series is calculated by Steve Leuthold and The Leuthold Group and use 18 quarters of trailing As-Reported earnings and two quarters of estimated forward earnings. The data in this series goes back to the mid-1940's. Using this methodology the market P/E multiple as of January 2, 2009 was 13.44X, which was well below the historic median measure of 17.3X. What is interesting about this measure is that Leuthold's research shows that most bear markets make a bottom when stocks retreat to their 5-year median valuation level. The only exceptions were the 1949-1953 periods (recession concerns) and the 1974-1984 periods (high inflation and high interest rates). Based on this valuation metric the stock market would be considered to be inexpensive, if not downright cheap. Leuthold's methodology would conclude that downside risk in stock prices from these valuation levels should be minimal.

**Figure 10.6** shows the P/E ratio using a 10-year normalized methodology, which is very similar to the Robert Shiller trailing 10-year method. This method uses Shiller's data and goes all of the way back to the late 1800's. Using the 10-year normalized method the P/E multiple of the index is currently 17, which is slightly higher than the historic median multiple of 15.5. Because the trailing 10-year methodology uses the median of 10 years of data, it would take a massive change in current As-Reported earnings to have a significant impact on the P/E multiple. It is usually the change in price that has a short-term impact on the multiple when using this methodology. Of course, the market has recently experienced record volatility

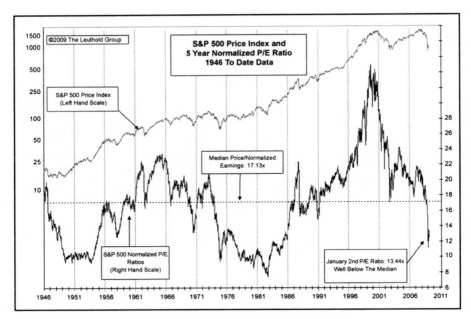

### Figure 10.5—S&P 500 Price Index and
### 5 Year Normalized P/E Ratio: 1946 to Date Data
Source: The Leuthold Group

in price changes which are reflected in the steep decline in PE-10 ratios on the chart. In fact, at the current market bottom of 741 on the S&P 500 Index the PE-10 was as low as 14.

For investors focusing on this data series, their conclusions about market valuation have changed in a relatively short period of time. Instead of concluding that the market was expensive based on this valuation metric, they would now consider it to be fairly valued. As we saw from Ed Easterling's work in Chapter 2, the good news is that the probability of investors earning expected returns over the next twenty years is much higher than it has been for more than a decade. The bad news is that secular bull markets have never started from a "fair" market value in the past. PE-10's have always been 10 or below before the secular bull began.

We can now take a second look at our various methods of evaluating absolute P/E multiples using data through August of 2008. The last column in **Table 10.5** shows that there is only one method showing the stock market to be expensive, which is using estimated forward GAAP earnings. The PE-10 methodology of using normalized 10 years of trailing GAAP earning shows the market value is still slightly above its median historical value. However, all of the remaining valuation metrics show the stock market to either be fairly valued or to be cheap on an absolute basis.

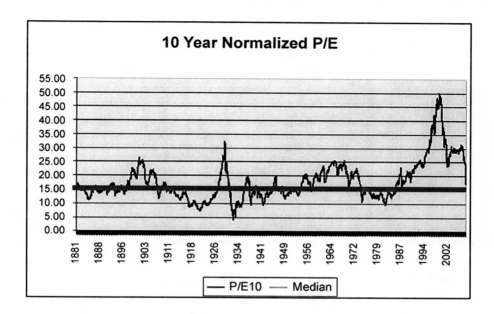

**Figure 10.6—10 Year Normalized P/E**
Source: Pinnacle Advisory Group, Inc.

It is a rare event when all of the methods show the stock market to be either cheap or expensive, but when they do, investors should be prepared to accommodate valuation in their portfolio construction decisions. In this case, investors should consider that the recent crash in market prices has created a valuation environment that is favorable to earning historical average long-term stock market returns. If the PE-10 ratio falls to 12 or below, investors should understand that for the first time since the early 1990's market valuation may become a tailwind for long-term stock market returns in the future. However, as skeptics might say, "in the long-term we will all be dead." In fact, they might question if investors will come back to the stock

| METHOD | P/E | VALUATION |
|---|---|---|
| Trailing 10 year GAAP | 17.6 | Fair/Expensive |
| Trailing 5 Year GAAP | 14.18 | Fair |
| Trailing 1 Year GAAP | 13.24 | Fair/Cheap |
| Forward Operating | 11.61 | Cheap |
| Forward GAAP | 22.04 | Expensive |

**Table 10.5—The Cobweb Model**
Source: Pinnacle Advisory Group, Inc.

market even at historically low multiples, having been devastated by serious bear markets twice in the past decade. In which case, buying and holding stocks could still be a failing strategy, even from historically low measures of valuation.

## Turning P/E Upside Down

Each of the market valuation measures we have reviewed so far compares the current value of the stock market to its long-term valuation levels. We consider each of these to be measures of absolute value because we don't compare the valuation to any other asset class, or use any other data, like interest rates, to make our valuation assessment. However, in a classical sense it is difficult to value the stock market without considering interest rates. After all, when valuing individual stocks, the present value of dividends, cash flows, and earnings, are all determined by using current interest rates as the discount rate for the present value calculation. It makes sense that the stock market would be considered more or less expensive based on the environment for interest rates. If bonds were paying investors very high yields with much less relative risk than stocks, then we would expect that investors would favor bonds over stocks, and all things being equal, stocks would be considered more expensive. On the other hand, when interest rates are very low, as they are today, then it makes sense that stocks would seem more favorable to investors, if for no other reason than the dividends paid by stocks would seem favorable compared to the low yields of bonds and cash. One of the simplest relative valuation measures is to compare the dividend yield of the S&P 500 to the yield of the Ten Year U.S. Treasury Bond, and for the first time since the 1950's the dividend yield of the stock market is actually higher than bond yields. Comparing the prices of stocks to the prices of bonds introduces the idea of *relative valuation* versus absolute valuation, and perhaps the most well-known method to relatively value the stock market using interest rates is the Fed Model.

## The Fed Model & Earnings Yields

Former Federal Reserve Chairman Alan Greenspan introduced the Fed Model in Congressional testimony in 1997, just a few months after Greenspan made his famous "irrational exuberance" comments about the stock market. The Fed Model basically compares the reciprocal of the P/E ratio, called the Earnings Yield, to the yield of the Ten Year U.S. Treasury bond. The methodology is really just a simplification of a standard valuation equation that states that:

$$Value = E/(T+R-G)$$
(E=earnings, T=10 Year U.S. Treasury Bond yield, R=risk premium, and G=earnings growth)

If you make the simplifying assumption that the risk premium for the stock market (the amount that stocks will outperform 90-day T-Bills in the future) is equal to the growth rate of corporate earnings (R–G = 0), then the equation becomes:

$$Value = E/T$$

The last part of the thought process is that in order to compare the earnings of the stock market to the yield of U.S. Ten-Year Treasury Bonds, investors should express earnings as a yield as well. Therefore, the earnings of the S&P 500 Index get expressed as E/P, rather than P/E. With this information in hand, we can use the same shortcut made famous by Alan Greenspan to calculate the valuation of the stock market.

To calculate the earnings yield, the Fed Model methodology uses 12-month forward operating earnings and divides them by the current market price, or E/P. If the forward estimated earnings for the S&P 500 Index are $80 per share, and the current index price is 900, then the earnings yield is 8.9% ($80/900). Today's 10-year U.S. Treasury Bond yields are at historic lows. Let's assume that the current yield of the 10-year bond is 3.0%. Comparing the bond yield of 3% to the current earnings yield of 8.9% would indicate that stocks are dramatically undervalued versus bonds. In this case you would say that stocks are 66% undervalued relative to bonds. Or, even more simplistically, you would conclude that given the choice, you would choose the investment that yields 8.9% (stocks) versus the one that yields 3% (bonds).

**Figure 10.7** from Ned Davis Research shows the historic valuation of the stock market using the Fed Model. As of 8/11/2008 the model showed the S&P 500 Index to be 46.6% undervalued. They also show the sensitivity of the model to forward earnings projections, so if projected operating earnings fall to $50 the model would show the market to be 4% overvalued, and at $75 it would be 30.6% undervalued.

There are many criticisms of the Fed Model and investors should be aware of them. Critics complain that comparing the earnings yields of stocks to the yields of the safest possible credit securities, U.S. Treasuries, is unfair. For those that subscribe to this thought process, corporate AAA bond yields can be substituted for U.S. Treasury yields to provide a rate that is not risk-free. Some other models use price-to-sales (P/S) rather than P/E multiples in order to come up with the numerator in the equation because sales data are less subject to manipulation than earnings data. Other criticisms involve the same old problems of using forward earnings in the calculation and the obvious concerns with using earning

**Figure 10.7**

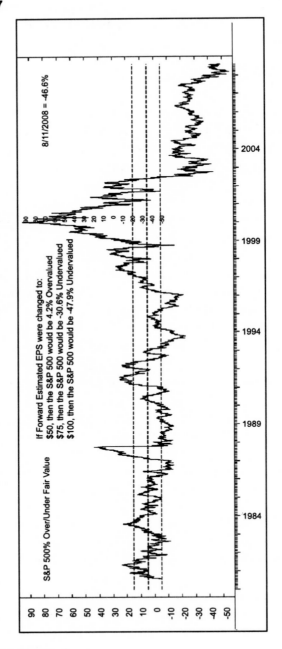

Source: Ned Davis Research

projections. Regardless of the critics, in the current interest rate environment, any comparison of earnings to interest rates would show the stock market to be extraordinarily inexpensive.

There are other problems with using the Fed Model. One major concern is that the work of Leuthold, Hussman, and others seems to show that the model only worked for a specific period of time in the 1980's to 1990's. When the model is analyzed over longer periods of time, it is shown to have little predictive value. In a recent study by the Leuthold Group, the Fed Model was shown to have little predictive power over long-term 10-year time horizons. In their study they abandon the idea of using 12-month forward operating earnings as proposed by Greenspan, because of the cyclical nature of the earnings discussed earlier, and because of the lack of historical data about analysts' forward earnings estimates. Instead, Leuthold uses their preferred method of using five-year normalized GAAP earnings to calculate the earnings yield for the stock market. **Figure 10.8** is a scatter chart that shows the subsequent returns of the stock market 10 years after the calculation of the earnings yield for the period from 1930 to 2008. The results are almost totally random, meaning that the measure had very little predictive power.

It is interesting to note that Leuthold did the same study without adding in the comparison to bond yields. They simply looked at the predictive ability of earnings yields (P/E ratios expressed as a yield) over the same 10-year periods. After tweaking the data to eliminate the results of the earnings dislocations of the Great Depression, they ran the analysis from 1935 to 2007. The results shown in **Figure 10.9** are startling, and not at all dissimilar to the data presented in Chapter 2 from

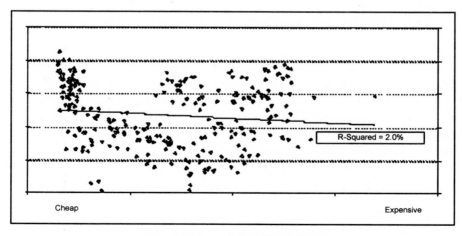

Figure 10.8—The Leuthold Group

Ed Easterling. Using five-year normalized earnings, the model explains almost half of the subsequent ten-year returns.

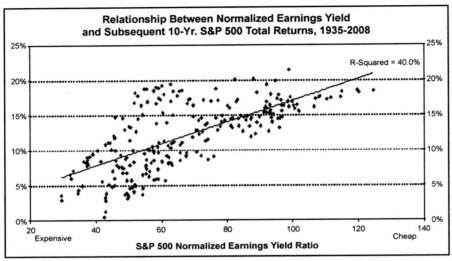

**Figure 10.9—Relationship Between Normalized Earnings Yield and Subsequent 10-Yr. S&P 500 Total Returns, 1935-2008**

Source: The Leuthold Group

Hussman's work seems to corroborate the research from the Leuthold Group. Hussman concludes that "Historically, readings from the Fed Model explain just 3% of the variation in S&P 500 total returns over the following year, 2% of the variation in 7-year returns, and just 1% of the variation in subsequent 10-year returns. In contrast, the simple raw operating earnings yield explains 8% of the variation in subsequent 1-year returns, 41% of the variation in 7-year returns, and fully 52% of the variation in subsequent 10-year returns.[46]

There are many more concerns about the Fed Model that need not be addressed here. Virtually any valuation technique has its passionate advocates and its critics. Investors must use their judgment to sift through the often conflicting conclusions about valuation to reach their own high-conviction point of view about market valuation. Despite all of the concerns mentioned above, the Fed Model, or at least the idea of comparing earnings yields to bond yields, is still used by many smart institutional investors. In a more general sense, most respected analysts still use some form of interest rate comparisons to reach conclusions about relative stock market valuations around the world. Considering that using this methodology indicates that the current stock market

46    For more of Hussman's discussion regarding earnings yields and the Fed Model, go to http://hussmanfunds.com/wmc/wmc070820.htm.

is extremely inexpensive, it is worth adding these considerations to an investor's "war chest" of valuation options.

Once again it seems that judgment and experience are required in order to value the market. The simple statement, "buy low and sell high," no longer seems so simple. Students of active management should know that there are many other approaches to determining relative value, the most obvious being the comparison of the P/E multiple of the S&P 500 Index to the P/E multiple of other asset classes. For example, it is worthwhile to compare the P/E multiple of large-cap U.S. stocks to small-cap U.S. stocks, or value stocks to growth stocks, and so on. It may be possible to find pockets of relative value in the stock market that can be exploited even when the overall market appears to be expensive. As we saw earlier when analyzing S&P data, interesting and investable relative valuation conclusions can be reached from studying different sectors of the market.

Another form of evaluating P/E ratios is to consider the P/E ratio versus the growth rate of earnings. This relationship is known as the PEG ratio or the ratio of P/E to earnings growth. Typically a ratio of 1 is considered to be fairly valued. This ratio allows investors to buy stocks with very high P/E's as long as their earnings growth rates are high as well. Momentum investors often invoke the PEG ratio to justify purchasing stocks as they soar above their moving averages. Once again, the investor's judgment will prevail. While growth investors will be perfectly comfortable buying stocks with high P/E ratios and high earnings growth rates, traditional value investors might very well have a heart attack. We will leave it to the reader to further explore the many comparisons that can be made in order to find good relative values.

## What Do We Do With All of This?

The famous economist John Maynard Keynes said that the stock market can remain irrational for longer than you can remain solvent. The point is that investors who depend on market valuation in order to determine the short-term direction of the stock market are often disappointed. In the short run, many would argue that investor psychology and herd behavior have much more to do with market direction than fundamental value. Momentum is a powerful force that seems to take market prices well above and well below any reasonable measure of fair value. Yet, the statistics showing how market values impact long-term investment returns can't be ignored. We have learned that historical average market returns do not materialize from any purchase price, but instead are driven by market valuation at the time the investor buys the market.

In addition, in this chapter we have observed that fundamental measures of value, like the P/E ratio, can be tortured to reach many possible conclusions with the same data. Investors will have their own biases regarding operating versus GAAP earnings, forward versus trailing earnings, and absolute versus relative valuation. Strategic investors would use this variety of choice to reach the conclusion that it isn't possible to make an informed decision about valuation, so therefore the best solution is to forget the whole thing and simply assume that investors will earn historical average returns if they buy and hold, regardless of the valuation of the market, and wait long enough for the returns to materialize. However, we suggest that investors who are interested in active, tactical management take a more constructive approach to the valuation challenge.

The first strategy to consider is the most obvious. When a comprehensive approach to looking at a variety of valuation techniques leads the investor to the same conclusion, then the investor should strongly consider valuation in the construction of the portfolio. We are beginning to see just that occurring with several analysts that we follow at Pinnacle Advisory Group. Analysts, who were previously bearish based on economic fundamentals or technical analysis, are now becoming bullish based on their assessment of market values. In their assessment, cheap market values trump any other considerations. However, investors should beware. Once you establish stock positions based on inexpensive valuation, it is difficult to sell them. The only tactic left is to continue to add to positions from that point, since presumably the market is getting even cheaper. As the saying goes, hopefully the investor can remain solvent while the market comes to its senses.

Perhaps the best approach is to include market valuation as one of three important metrics to be considered in portfolio construction. As we will learn in subsequent chapters, how an investor evaluates the market cycle and how they evaluate the technical condition of the market are also very important elements of the portfolio construction process. Both the market cycle and technical analysis are likely to be more rewarding to investors in the short-term. However, market valuation, as we've discussed it in this chapter, deserves special consideration. It is the most powerful and predictable force for long-term market returns. Investors who are willing to be patient will find valuation to be a powerful headwind or tailwind, depending on whether markets are cheap or expensive.

More specifically, it seems that using any of the normalized or trailing average earnings methods for valuing the market is likely to help investors reach a high-conviction conclusion about long-term market direction. Using forward earnings is more likely to give better insights into short-term market direction. Various methods of relative valuation may help investors find opportunities where the performance of one asset class may be significantly better than another. What mix of these valuation techniques is the "best" mix to use in order to reach a conclusion about market valuation? The answer is up to the individual investor. How should your active, tactical portfolio construction change based on your conclusions about market valuation? You guessed it. Unfortunately, there is no single correct conclusion to be reached about the tools and techniques of active management. That is why I believe it is art as well as science, and that is why the best practitioners will be rewarded by earning excess returns.

Having reviewed market valuation as one method to identify opportunities for profit, in the next chapter we will consider top-down market analysis as a method to identify opportunities for profit.

# 11 DEVELOPING A POINT OF VIEW WITH TOP-DOWN ANALYSIS

A ctive portfolio managers do not believe the stock market is perfectly efficient. The stock market is, however, pretty darn good at discounting the news of the day, and at a minimum it is a good leading indicator of the economy. In fact, the stock market is one of the Conference Board's series of leading economic indicators, and while its record of predicting recessions isn't perfect, wise investors pay attention to what the market says about the world around us at any point in time. That being the case, the question for active managers becomes, how do you best forecast a leading indicator? If the stock market leads the economy, then what indicators lead the stock market? In this chapter we will discuss some of the methods that investors might consider when attempting to make accurate forecasts about the stock market, or other asset classes.

In the last chapter we proposed using a traditional fundamental measure of value, the P/E ratio, as a means of determining when it is likely to be profitable to invest in the stock market for the long-term. For those few investors with the luxury of being able to invest based on a long-term 10 to 20 year time horizon and who don't have to worry about the returns and volatility of the stock market over shorter periods of time, we showed that using PE-10 (a P/E measure that uses normalized trailing 10-year GAAP earnings) is an outstanding method of forecasting future returns.

However, we also learned in the last chapter that P/E ratios are subject to a tremendous amount of subjective evaluation by analysts and investors, and can be used to support dramatically different conclusions about market valuation. For example, at the time of this writing, the U.S. stock market is fairly valued based on PE-10, inexpensive based on 5-year normalized earnings, very inexpensive based on forward operating earnings (if you believe the analysts' consensus earnings forecasts), and incredibly inexpensive based on the Fed Model of comparing earnings yields to bond yields. Clearly, investors need to be aware of the pitfalls of using P/E, or any other fundamental measure of value, as the only method they might consider in forecasting markets. For these reasons, investors should include P/E and market valuation in general as part of a multi-faceted approach to determining portfolio construction.

As we move beyond fundamental measures of value, such as the P/E ratio, the next important step in the process of tactical investing is to determine where we are in the stock market cycle in order to forecast shorter-term market direction. While PE-10 is useful in determining whether the market offers good value over 10- to 20-year secular market cycles, it is less helpful in determining if there are investment opportunities to be exploited within the short-term bull and bear markets that are found within the typical secular cycle.

**Figure 11.1** shows the secular bear market for the Dow Jones Industrial Average for the period beginning in 1965 and ending in 1982. Contrary to what investors might think when they hear the term secular bear market, which might conjure up a picture of a long and relentless stock market decline, this chart shows how the stock market actually staged many significant and investable rallies during this particular secular bear. In fact, during the period shown, the stock market actually produced seven rallies of more than 20%, many of which lasted for more than a year. Of course, these rallies were followed by significant market declines, and the end result was that the Dow Jones Index basically traded sideways for a period of 16 years. Yet even though buying and holding the index for the entire period was not profitable, there were many tradable shorter-term rallies that provided significant opportunities for profit. For those investors who are willing to trade the short side of the market, there were many tradable bear market declines that also provided significant opportunities to earn excess returns.

Considering the amount of inflation over this period, investors who chose to buy and hold the market for the entire time period actually lost a great deal of money net of inflation. However, investors who correctly focused on being either long or short the Dow Jones Industrial Average during any of the shorter-term cyclical price peaks and troughs during the period obviously generated significant excess returns compared to simply buying and holding. The critical point here is that during secular bear markets, investors have to make a choice about how to manage future portfolio returns. They can choose to risk their financial future by passively owning the market for the entire secular bear market period and accept

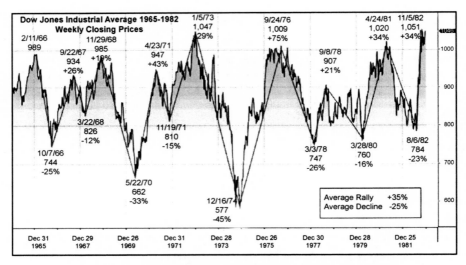

**Figure 11.1—Dow Jones Industrial Average 1965-1982,
Weekly Closing Prices**

Source: Pinnacle Advisory Group, Inc

whatever returns the market will offer, or they can choose to engage in actively managing the portfolio to take advantage of the cyclical market moves within the secular bear.

Which approach is riskier? Assuming the stock market is characterized by high P/E ratios and other fundamental measures of value at the beginning of the period, the greater risk is buying and holding since there is no evidence that the stock market has ever delivered historical average returns for extended periods of time beginning at a point of high market valuation. Clearly, actively managing the portfolio to try to capture excess returns during shorter-term market cycles also involves risks, but at least there is the opportunity for profit. Investors can choose the virtual certainty of investment disaster in secular bear markets by buying and holding the stock market and hoping that historical average returns will magically appear, or they can choose the possibility of properly forecasting shorter-term market cycles, where an average forecasting performance is likely to result in better than market returns. Many investors misperceive the risks involved in choosing between the two choices, because up until now buying and holding has been accepted by investors as the status quo for traditional institutional investment management, regardless of the results. However, today's investors have patiently waited for more than a decade for stocks to outperform cash, and the industry will soon find that their patience is at an end. I believe that there is actually no choice at all for investors who require their risk capital to achieve historical average returns in order to achieve their financial goals, because there is absolutely no evidence that buying and holding during a secular bear market offers any possibility of success.

All long-term market trends can be broken down into shorter cyclical bull and bear markets. An analysis of the most recent secular bear market that began in March of 2000 reveals three major cyclical moves within the secular bear. **Figure 11.2** illustrates the S&P 500 Index for the period and shows that the first cycle was the bear market that began in March of 2000 (or October of 2000, depending on how you want to treat reinvested dividends) and ends in October of 2002. The next cycle was the powerful bull market that began in October of 2002 and lasted for exactly five years until October 2007. And the current cycle is another cyclical bear market that began in October 2007 and continues as of this writing.

**Figure 11.2—S&P 500 Index**
Source: Pinnacle Advisory Group, Inc.

An investor who correctly forecast the beginning of the secular bear cycle because of extremely high market valuations in March of 2000 and owned cash for the entire period has added tremendous value compared to buying and holding the stock market for the entire eight year and eight month period ending in November 2008. However, staying out of the market for the entire period based on market valuation was actually a costly strategy compared to investing in a shorter-term market cycle approach. Investors who relied on market valuation alone might not have forecast the beginning of the next bullish cycle that began in October of 2002 because the 10-year normalized P/E of the stock market was still approximately 25 times earnings. Since a 25 multiple is much higher than the long-term median of 15.8, value investors might have missed the next cyclical 5-year bull market even though the stock market had already suffered a vicious 48% decline. I agree with many analysts who feel that the 2002-2007 cyclical bull market was one of the most powerful bull markets in history by virtue of the fact that every asset class, including all domestic and international stock sectors, U.S. and international real estate, commodities and other hard assets, rallied to new highs. The S&P 500 Index gained an astounding 102% during this period. Investors who properly forecast the many macroeconomic factors that drove this five year cyclical bull were amply rewarded.

The message is clear. If the reader concludes that market valuation drives long-term secular market cycles, then the next consideration should be to consider how to invest the shorter market cycles within the long-term secular trend. Cyclical bull and bear markets typically last for several years, and astute investors can position their portfolios to earn added returns during these periods, regardless of where they are in the longer-term secular market cycle.

## Top-Down Analysis

Before investors can begin the process of investing in shorter-term market cycles, they must first understand where they are in the broader economic cycle. This type of analysis attempts to discern what factors impact the global and U.S. economy under the premise that investors who can better forecast changes to the economy will better forecast changes in the financial markets. The goal of this strategy for active management is for investors to develop a "top-down" point of view about the global economy, which leads to a point of view about the likely behavior of financial markets and ultimately to decisions about which securities to own in their portfolio to maximize profits.

Let's consider how having a point of view about the U.S. and global economy might impact portfolio construction at any point in time. For investors pursuing this strategy, the process of finding investment opportunities that will work in shorter cyclical time frames begins by developing a qualitative point of view about current economic conditions. By definition, a point of view is an opinion. It is an informed forecast about what the investor considers to be the most likely outcome for economic or market direction. As we discussed in the previous chapter, independent research is a vital ingredient for investors who want to formulate an investment point of view. Based on their research, the investors' points of view then take the form of economic or market themes that they can invest in their portfolios in order to earn excess returns. Once investors identify a theme, they should begin a rigorous process of exploring the contrarian opinions to their point of view with the objective of reaching a high level of conviction about their investment thesis. Investors can count on there being opposing viewpoints regarding any investment theme, and it is not easy to achieve the goal of developing a strong conviction about any particular investment idea or point of view.

Once an investor is reasonably convinced that a particular investment theme has a high probability of coming to fruition, their research efforts can switch to discovering those investments that best support their top-down theme. At that point, moving to a "bottom-up" approach to security analysis helps to find the best security to actually invest in based on the economic/investment theme being considered. The process of bottom-up security evaluation is the subject of the next chapter.

## Examples of Economic Points of View and Investment Themes

The following is a list of 10 hypothetical investment ideas. They are presented as examples of the kind of top-down investment themes that might offer investors an opportunity to change their portfolio construction through active and tactical asset allocation in order to earn excess returns. These are hypothetical examples and readers should not consider them to be timely or accurate based on current market conditions.

- Small-cap U.S. stocks are overvalued versus large-cap U.S. stocks.
- The economy is entering a "normal" recession that would typically last for at least 4 quarters.
- The dollar will continue to weaken against Asian currencies, but will strengthen against the Euro.
- Yield spreads will continue to widen, as systemic risk is not fully priced in the fixed income markets.
- The emerging market countries' economic growth will decouple from the developing world, helping to support commodity prices.
- Industrial companies that earn a large percentage of their earnings from overseas operations will out-perform, relative to other sectors of the U.S. economy.
- The Federal Reserve will continue to lower interest rates even though we already have negative real (inflation-adjusted) interest rates.
- 2015 earnings estimates are too high because the earnings projections for the financial and consumer discretionary sectors of the market are too optimistic.

- The European Union will eventually be forced to lower interest rates because, among other things, the Euro has rallied excessively against the dollar.
- The commodity complex is not immune from a slowdown in global economic growth and will suffer a nasty correction in prices as the year progresses.

Each of these ideas could be obtained from reading independent research, and analysts with opposing points of view can and will disagree about every idea on this list. Assuming that an investor's qualitative research leads them to a high level of conviction about any one of these themes or points of view about the market or the economy, they can then implement a change to portfolio construction in order to add value and/or reduce portfolio volatility. Here are some sample investment ideas that could accompany each theme listed above:

1. Rotate the U.S. equity allocation out of small-cap stocks in favor of large-cap stocks.
2. Reduce the risk or volatility in the portfolio, perhaps by selling stocks and raising cash, or rotate from high beta to low beta investment ideas.
3. Buy European government bonds that are fully hedged to the U.S. dollar. Sell European stocks in favor of U.S. stocks.
4. Begin to rotate out of high-quality U.S. government bonds in favor of U.S. corporate bonds and eventually U.S. high-yield bonds.
5. Overweight emerging market stocks in the portfolio. Consider investment ideas like the U.S. materials sector and the industrials sector, or owning direct commodity investments and energy stocks that benefit from the continued growth in emerging markets.
6. Consider investing in large-cap stocks versus small-cap stocks. Rotate the portfolio to the industrial, materials, and energy sectors of the U.S. market.
7. Extend the duration on high-quality U.S. Treasury Bonds because yields are likely to fall.
8. Avoid the U.S. financial and discretionary sectors of the stock market and overweight non-cyclical sectors like healthcare and consumer staples.
9. Sell the European bonds and buy back the European stocks that you sold in number 3 above.
10. Reduce commodity positions but be prepared to buy them back if the commodity markets overshoot to the downside.

Each of these ideas can be invested using Exchange Traded Funds (ETFs), managed funds, individual fixed income securities, etc. The resulting portfolio can be diversified with investments that hedge the overall point of view held by the investor. The best hedges are the ones that are most likely to have low correlations and high diversification benefits in case the investor is wrong in his or her view of the markets. Finally, each of these ideas is subject to change based on changes in market conditions. As market conditions change, or if the investor's conviction in any of these ideas changes, then each of these investment ideas can be trimmed, sold, or bought. The portfolio construction is not static, but reflects the investor's changing point of view about economic conditions and the financial markets.

In no case are the investments owned because the investor is trying to capture the average historical return that these asset classes have earned in the past in the same way that a strategic buy and hold investor might approach forecasting future returns. In addition, investors are not adding these investments because an optimizing model suggests that the portfolio will be more efficient. Instead, they are trying to find excellent investments out of a whirlwind of possible investment ideas, evaluate them through qualitative and quantitative research, and then express them in the portfolio through appropriate investments. In combination with the fundamental valuation analysis in the preceding chapter, they are attempting to invest the portfolio with investments that represent "good value," however they may define it.

As Woody Brock explained in an earlier chapter, one way for investors to succeed at active portfolio management is to expend the time and money necessary to interpret and forecast the news better than the consensus. As I see it, the goal is not to be error-free but to be "less wrong" than the average investor by adding value through fundamentally-based, top-down, active management strategies.

## Where to Look

As I've already pointed out, it takes a special kind of financial analyst, as well as high quality independent research, to formulate a confident point of view about the financial markets. Fortunately, or perhaps unfortunately, there is an immense amount of information available about the financial markets. Investors should focus their research efforts on those areas that they believe to be the most important in order to correctly forecast the economic environment. There are hundreds of different economic and market indicators to be considered by investors who want to develop a high degree of conviction about their market forecasts, and evaluating each of them can help to concentrate their research effort in an effective manner. Different investors will reach different conclusions about the validity of the various economic data relative to making accurate forecasts, but the time invested in order to be able to focus on those indicators that seem to have the best ability to lead the market is time well spent. **Figure 11.3** is a sample list of broad domestic economic data that Pinnacle Advisory Group follows in developing our top-down viewpoint about the economy. This list is not all-inclusive and is subject to change as we continue to explore fertile new areas of research. In addition, this list does not contain any of the technical indicators that we follow as part of our comprehensive research effort. However, this list should give an investor who is considering active, tactical asset allocation a head start in determining how to best spend their time on fundamental qualitative research.

**CONSUMER SPENDING**

1 Personal Consumption Expenditures

2 Real Wages

3 NAHB Index

4 New Home Sales

5 Building Permits

6 Ned Credit Conditions Index*

7 Fed Funds

**CORPORATE**

1 Investment Grade Credit Default Swaps

2 High Yield Credit Default Swaps

3 Corporate Option Adjusted Spreads

4 High Yield Option Adjusted Spreads

5 10 Year U.S. Dollar Swap Spreads

6 30 Day Nonfinancial Commercial Paper

7 LIBOR minus T-Bill Yield

8 Deliquency Rates on C&I Loans

9 Debt/Net Worth of Nonfinancial Corp.

10 Net Interest/Corporate Cash Flow

11 Short Term Debt/Credit Market Debt

12 Liquid Assets/Short Term Liabilities

13 Senior Loan Survey - Lending Standards

**THE FED**

1 Tips Spreads

2 NDR Timing Model

3 OER

4 ECRI - FIG

5 Money Supply

6 Utilization

7 Unit Labor Costs

8 Labor Mkt

9 Debt

10 Dollar

11 Taylor Rule

12 Yield Curve - Fed Study

**LEADING INDICES**

1 Conference Board LEI

2 Coincident to Lagging Indicator

3 ECRI WLI

4 ISM Mfg Index

*NDR Consumer Credit Conditions index includes 9 components

** Components of NDR Business Credit Conditions index

**Figure 11.3**

Source: Pinnacle Advisory Group, Inc.

This list implies that investors could divide their research efforts into four major categories. The first category is U.S. consumer spending. Because consumer spending represents more than 70% of U.S. gross domestic product (GDP), if investors can forecast a turn in consumer spending it will allow them to forecast changes in U.S. economic growth. There are many economic indicators that provide insights into the health of the U.S. consumer. Investors can focus on the spending data itself, or they can focus on wage data if they believe that changes in real wages tend to lead changes in consumer spending. **Figure 11.4** shows the data on real wages and consumer spending, smoothed over three-month periods. The data clearly shows the current devastation in both wages and spending as the economy is fully in the throes of a severe recession.[47]

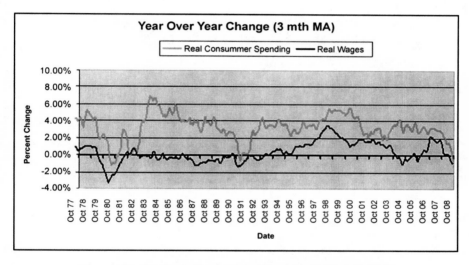

**Figure 11.4—Year Over Year Change (3 Month MA)**
Source: Pinnacle Advisory Group, Inc.

Investors should also follow the data on the U.S. real estate markets because studies show that consumer spending is greatly influenced by changes in U.S. housing values. Important housing data include housing starts, permits, new construction, existing and new home sales, home equity withdrawal, and other indicators of the health of the U.S. real estate market. **Figure 11.5** shows new home sales in the U.S. basically falling off the chart. As this is written, virtually all of the housing fundamentals are negative, which could lead investors to conclude that further weakness in consumer spending should be anticipated. Investors

47 Investors who want to learn more about wages and spending as leading indicators should read Joseph H. Ellis's essential book on the topic, *Ahead of the Curve: A Commonsense Guide to Forecasting Business and Market Cycles*, Harvard Business Press, 2005.

should focus on charts showing rates of change in the data for early signals that the data may be improving. Another data point that may have an impact on this data series is the lower mortgage rates that are the result of direct purchases by the Federal Reserve of mortgage-backed securities in the open market. The chart also suggests that the data on U.S. new home sales accurately forecasted the problems in the subprime mortgage market, and the subsequent bear market in U.S. equities.

**Figure 11.5—New Home Sales**

Source: Bloomberg, New Home Sales

Another important data point to monitor is credit conditions for U.S. business and consumers. Several research sources offer insightful and proprietary measures of credit conditions, including interest rates, bank-lending standards, default rates, and retail sales data. It is also worth monitoring consumer attitude surveys. While it is true that attitudinal surveys tends to follow, rather than lead consumer spending, they are part of the process of determining a point of view about the likely direction of consumer spending in the future. The bond market is another excellent indicator to follow to gain insights into credit conditions, as well as the general health of corporate balance sheets and profitability. **Figure 11.6** shows the current high-yield corporate bond spreads to Treasury yields. (The spread is the difference in yield between high-yield or less-than-investment-grade bonds and U.S. Treasury yields.) High-yield spreads that are tight reflect investor confidence in corporate profitability, while wider spreads are a good measure of investor fear about corporate profits, and in today's economy fears about corporate solvency. The chart shows the recent dramatic increase in high-yield spreads over U.S. Treasuries. Today the spread can be attributed to the massive flight to safety that has caused

Treasury yields to move lower as well as less-than-investment-grade bond yields moving to new highs. In any event, some investors might believe that the current fear in the junk bond market has resulted in attractive values for this asset class and consider this a good opportunity to sell high-quality U.S. bonds in favor of low-quality, or junk bonds.

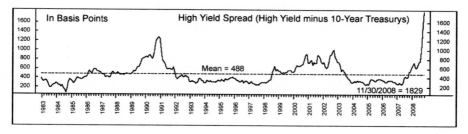

**Figure 11.6**
Source: Ned Davis Research

A third major category of economic information to follow in order to formulate a point of view about the economy is to analyze those data series that we believe impacts the Federal Reserve in their decisions to raise or lower the Fed Funds rate. The absolute value and direction of interest rates are very important to the evaluation of where we are in the economic cycle. Some of the data, like the Taylor Rule or the yield curve, allows investors to draw inferences about whether or not current rates are restrictive or accommodative to the economy. Other data, like unit labor costs, capacity utilization, or the Economic Cycle Research Institute's (ECRI) future inflation gauge, give insights into whether or not inflation is rising or falling. Inflation data is critical when trying to forecast the direction of short-term and long-term interest rates. Of course, in today's market environment many of the traditional metrics for evaluating interest rates are broken, and investors need to add more current data points to their research arsenal. For example, studying the Fed's balance sheet, understanding the various liquidity facilities that have been put in place, and focusing on the velocity of money and the impact of quantitative easing, are all recent, but critical, focuses of Pinnacle's top-down research. Reaching an opinion about the Fed's ability to sterilize the recent gigantic increases in the money supply in the future will have an important impact on an investor's views on future inflation, and the future direction of interest rates. This is but one example of how an investor's approach to top-down research must be flexible and can change with the news.

**Figure 11.7** shows the recent data for owner's equivalent rent (OER), which is one of the largest components of the CPI inflation index. Total shelter expenses comprise about one third of the CPI and OER is a large percentage of shelter expenses, roughly 24% of the total CPI. The measure is used in the index as a proxy for housing costs and is the subject of much debate among pundits about its usefulness. Instead of trying to track actual changes in housing values, OER assumes that the cost of housing is relatively stable for most Americans who either have a mortgage or pay rent. Therefore, the Bureau of Labor Statistics conducts surveys to determine the 6-month changes in economic rent, which are essentially rents paid by tenants and received by landlords. This data becomes a proxy for the cost of housing in the CPI calculation. As you might imagine, the critics who feel that promiscuous Fed policies led to unsustainable asset inflation that is not measured in CPI, but is responsible for the vicious deleveraging cycle that is currently devastating the financial markets, feel that the OER calculation has been a total disaster.

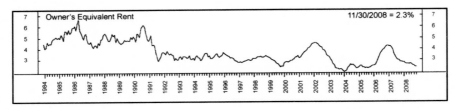

**Figure 11.7**

Source: Ned Davis Research

The chart shows that owner's equivalent rent seems to be well contained, perhaps because of the increase in supply of rental properties due to increasing foreclosures on new and existing housing, or perhaps because landlords simply can't raise rents in a weak economic environment. A rise in OER is significant because the Federal Reserve has indicated that it watches this indicator closely in its assessment of inflation expectations. In fact, the Fed favors another inflation indicator, the personal consumption expenditures deflator (PCE deflator), in part because it has a lower exposure to OER than the CPI.

The fourth area to evaluate when forming an investment point of view is to analyze the leading economic indicators themselves. The most well-known of the leading economic indicators (LEI) is published by the Conference Board, an independent business organization that has been in existence for almost 100 years. The Conference Board also publishes a Coincident Index and a Lagging Index. In addition, they also publish Leading Indexes for global investors. **Table 11.1** shows the components of the LEI and their weighting in the index.

| | Leading Index | Factor |
|---|---|---|
| 1 | Average weekly hours, manufacturing | 0.2552 |
| 2 | Average weekly initial claims for unemployment insurance | 0.0307 |
| 3 | Manufacturer's new orders, consumer goods, and materials | 0.0773 |
| 4 | Index of supplier deliveries—vendor performance | 0.0668 |
| 5 | Manufacturer's new orders, nondefense capital goods | 0.0183 |
| 6 | Building permits, new private housing units | 0.0271 |
| 7 | Stock prices, 500 common stocks | 0.0391 |
| 8 | Money supply, M2 | 0.355 |
| 9 | Interest rate spread, 10-year Treasury bonds less federal funds | 0.1021 |
| 10 | Index of consumer expectations | 0.0284 |

**Table 11.1—U.S. Composite Indexes:**
**Components and Standardization Factors**
Source: The Conference Board

A close look at the LEI reveals several interesting components. First, as mentioned earlier, stock prices for the S&P 500 Index are themselves a leading indicator of the economy. Although they represent only 3.9% of the index, it is worth noting that when investors attempt to forecast the direction of the stock market they are attempting to find those components that lead a leading indicator. Second, the two biggest components of the index by a wide margin are M2 Money Supply at 35.5% of the index (M2 is a measure of money supply that includes all currency, checking accounts, savings accounts, and non-institutional money market funds) and average weekly hours manufacturing at 25.5% of the index. Third, investors can evaluate many of these same components in other areas of their top-down research, which makes perfect sense since, like the Conference Board, they are also trying to forecast turns in the economy and financial markets. For example, investors can review weekly unemployment claims, building permits, interest rate spreads, and consumer expectations in other parts of their research model. Figure 11.8 shows a current view of the LEI. The steep slope of the data reflects the deep recession that the economy is facing. Although the NBER (National Bureau of Economic Research) has only recently announced that the current recession began in December of 2007, the LEI had been flashing a recession warning for months for investors who are trained to look at this data series.

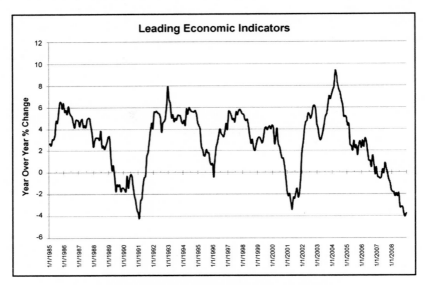

**Figure 11.8—Leading Economic Indicators**
Source: Bloomberg, LEI Year Over Year Change

## Quantitative Methods

Although one of the premises of this book is that observation, judgment, and experience are all necessary to actively manage multi-asset class portfolios, and that qualitative analysis is just as important as quantitative analysis in portfolio construction, we believe that there are many benefits to quantitative decision-making. As we discussed in an earlier chapter, there are several excellent reasons to use quantitative methods to assist in the decision-making process. Chief among them is that humans seem to be genetically predisposed to reduce complex issues into simpler narratives that may be easier to understand—but may also be wrong. Behavioral finance research has shown that humans are subject to a variety of heuristics and biases that make it difficult for us to make rational decisions based on the facts. And we learned from James Montier that there are many examples in the "real world" where the simplest quantitative models perform as well as the "experts" in decision-making.

Of course, we also discovered from Nassim Taleb's *The Black Swan* that a single observation can invalidate years of beliefs which form the basis of inputs to quantitative models. And, like his Thanksgiving turkey on the day before Thanksgiving, one additional observation can lead to a major "revision of belief." Nonetheless, the money management profession has had a deep and abiding love affair with quant models that began with Harry Markowitz and continues to this day, although the relationship may be a little strained recently as the entire investment banking industry has been destroyed and quantitatively managed hedge fund strategies continue to make news with occasional high-profile "blow-ups," in large part due to a misplaced reliance on quantitative models.

Having made the case that quantitative models should be used with caution in the decision-making process, it's time to review some of the quantitative approaches that can be used to help formulate a point of view about the economy and the stock market. While the details of most quantitative approaches today involve an understanding of advanced mathematical models, the basic issues and questions regarding how to go about building a quant model apply to all investors.

For most investors, the first and best sources for quantitative opinions about the market environment are research provider(s). Many of them have been building and fine-tuning their quantitative models for decades, and they update these models on a routine basis. Today virtually all buy-and sell-side research operations make the conclusions of their quantitative research available to their subscribers and clients. In some cases the firms are surprisingly open about the composition of their models. For example, the Leuthold Group publishes their monthly Green Book that shows investors the more than 180 factors they include in their model. Each week they alert subscribers to changes in the model's score and provide insights into what sections of the model caused the scores to change. Leuthold tracks just about every kind of fundamental and technical data about the market imaginable. Investors who either pay for their research or invest in their funds get a good look inside of the Leuthold quantitative process, although as you might imagine, they don't get everything. Not surprisingly, the different quantitative approaches used by the various research firms for modeling the economy and the markets offer different conclusions about the state of the market at any point in time, so once again, observation, judgment, and experience are necessary to interpret the quantitative recommendations that an investor obtains through research.

In addition to following the quantitative models provided by independent research, investors can develop their own approach to quantitative decision-making. For example, Pinnacle Advisory Group attempts to evaluate all of the factors that we consider in our qualitative top-down economic analysis on a quantitative basis. We have found that the biggest limitation to building our model is the availability of data. Many of the data series that we follow were simply not available more than 20 years ago. The lack of historical data raises the concern that the model may be accurate only for the time frame that we are considering, and not in all economic scenarios. Nevertheless, there is a surprising amount of data available for many of the factors that we do consider, and the limitations of the data can be dealt with by either finding proxies for the data series that seem to make sense, or by keeping them in the model but recognizing the limitations of the data for any one particular factor, or by dropping the factor altogether if a suitable proxy can't be found.

A second problem relates to what we are trying to forecast with the models that we build. For example, studying U.S. capacity utilization may be very helpful in analyzing the direction of the Fed Funds target rate 12 months in the future, but it may be less helpful in forecasting 12-month stock market returns. In our subjective, qualitative process we look at all of the factors in the context of what they tell us about consumer spending, corporate health, central bank policy, and the future direction of U.S. and International economic growth. We then use our judgment to form a point of view about the markets (or other asset class that we are analyzing). However, when we build our quantitative model we focus on how each factor might predict the future direction of the stock market only. We relate the data for each of the factors to the price of the S&P 500 index 12 months later, and try to evaluate the predictive qualities of each factor based on how they did historically.

Once again, subjective decisions must be made. Should we focus on stock market returns six months in the future, or six years in the future? What if a particular factor works well for predicting six-month returns but doesn't do well for predicting 12-month returns? And, what if the factor worked very well for the decade of the 1990's, but didn't work nearly as well in the 1970's and 1980's? Should more weight be given to the recent performance of a particular factor in the model in predicting future stock market returns, or should all data be treated the same? Is it possible that so much structural change has occurred in the workings of the economy over the past three decades that the results of the model in the 1950's through the 1970's should be discounted? If it should be discounted, then by how much? These questions are the types of questions that should be considered by investors who are developing a quantitative approach to global macroeconomic models, or who rely on the models of others to reach a high conviction about an investment point of view.

Examining one factor in our quantitative model as an example will help illustrate this aspect of the quantitative decision-making process. **Figure 11.9** shows the year-over-year percent change in money supply (M2) as a three-month moving average. Given that money supply had a large weighting in the Conference Boards LEI index, it should be no surprise that it appears in Pinnacle Advisory Group's quantitative model, as well. When the money supply is low it generally means that the Federal Reserve has had tight monetary policy (high interest rates). As the change in money supply increases, it generally means that the Fed is cutting interest rates, which is stimulative for the economy and good for the stock market. Today changes in the money supply are one of the hottest topics for investors to consider as the Federal Reserve has recently flooded the economy with excess reserves through various emergency liquidity facilities, but the money supply as measured by M2 has not increased as much as the Fed would expect due to a falling velocity of money in the economy.

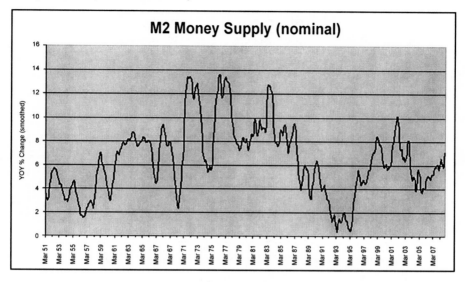

**Figure 11.9—M2 Money Supply (Nominal)**
Source: Pinnacle Advisory Group, Inc.

**Figure 11.10** shows the quantitative scoring for this particular factor as we analyze the percentage changes in the money supply versus the subsequent 1-year returns of the S&P 500 Index. In this case we score the data in a somewhat counterintuitive manner. Investors might consider a scale of 1 to 10 where the highest year-over-year percentage increase in the money supply is ranked as a 10 (the Fed is presumably cutting interest rates) and the largest year-over-year percentage decrease in the money supply is ranked as a 0 (the Fed is presumably raising interest rates). However, we reverse the scoring process for this factor because we believe that it is a contrary indicator. As the money supply is plummeting, indicating that the economy is slowing, it gets higher and higher scores. We believe that when it reaches an extreme it is very bullish because it signals a market bottom. The resulting data looks like this:

With a little practice you can see why this data point is so important to our model. **Figure 11.10** shows the money supply score from 0 to 10 on the vertical scale and the subsequent 12-month returns of the S&P 500 Index on the horizontal scale. Remember that the score is inverted so a score of 10 means the percentage change in the money supply is low. In this case we have ample data for the series which goes all the way back to the early 1950's. Notably, the data series never actually goes

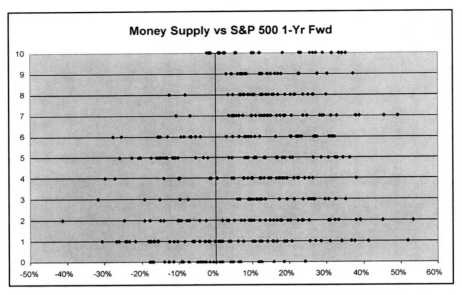

**Figure 11.10—Money Supply Versus S&P 500 1-Year Forward**

Source: Pinnacle Advisory Group, Inc.

negative. For this time period, whenever the increase in the money supply has been very low, the subsequent one-year returns for the S&P 500 Index have been almost uniformly positive, with only one data point showing a small negative return for a subsequent 12-month period when the score is 10. The scores are similar from 7 and higher on the scale. However, in a somewhat counterintuitive manner, when the money supply growth is high (lower scores on the scale), subsequent stock market returns are more ambiguous with equal data points for positive and negative market returns one year later. This type of unexpected result may be one of Woody Brock's "logical errors of inference" where the expected result just doesn't show up in the data. It is a classic benefit of adding a quantitative approach to a qualitative decision-making process.

Once we have scored the individual factors in the model, we go through a process of optimizing the factors to see what mix of factors best predicts future market returns. Optimizing is the mathematical process of testing all of the data points against the market's past returns to see what percentage weights of all of the factors best forecast the market. Care must be taken to avoid "data mining," or constructing a model that best explains past market moves but has little predictive ability. In this case, we believe that data mining is unavoidable and so we treat the model results with a healthy amount of skepticism. Another problem is that the optimization process tends to reduce the number of factors that are in the model. For example, we have found that the leading economic indicators themselves get little weight in the model, probably because we are already including many of the individual components of the LEI separately in the model.

The end result of the optimization process allows us to form opinions about the future direction of the stock market based on objective, quantitative decision-making. The model gives us a score of 1 to 10 where low scores are bearish and high scores are bullish. Both the trend of the scores, as well as the absolute score may be useful as we continue to add factors to the model and test it in real-time. The aggregate score allows us to compare our qualitative, human judgment-based point of view about the market cycle against a quantitatively scored conclusion. We include the quantitative score as part of our overall multi-faceted approach to decision-making.

## Sector Rotation

Our discussion of top-down decision-making would be incomplete without a discussion about sector rotation. Sector rotation is an investment strategy that recognizes that certain sectors of the stock market tend to perform better than others as the economy goes through the cycle of business expansion to contraction and back again. Generally speaking, when the economy is in the expansion phase, businesses whose sales are tied to economic growth tend to outperform. Conversely, when the economy is contracting businesses whose sales are less dependent on economic growth tend to outperform. For today's investors, it is relatively easy to identify the companies and sectors of the equity markets that belong to each group of businesses.

In 1999 Standard and Poor's, in conjunction with MSCI, created the Global Industry Classification Standard (GICS) that sorts more than 26,000 companies and 29,000 industries worldwide into sectors, industry groups, and industries. According to MSCI, their system covers more than 95% of the world's equity market capitalization. In the U.S., the GICS system divides the companies in the S&P 500 Index into ten different major sectors of the stock market. The sectors are: health care, consumer staples, utilities, financials, consumer discretionary, technology, materials, industrials, energy, and telecom services. Each sector is further subdivided into 24 industry groups and 64 industries. MSCI determines what group each company or security belongs to by analyzing the revenues, earnings, and the market perception of each.

Not only is it now possible to easily identify the various sectors and industries in global markets, it is also easy to invest in them using exchange traded funds (ETFs). ETFs are available through many different financial companies and some of them have become recognizable brand names for both institutional and retail investors. Today some of the most well-known brands for ETF investors are iShares, SPDRs, Rydex shares, Powershares, HLDRS, Market Vectors, Wisdom Tree, and ProShares. Essentially, ETFs are investment companies that own baskets of stocks, much like mutual funds. However, there are some dramatic differences between ETFs and mutual funds. ETFs are priced throughout the trading day as opposed to mutual funds, which are bought and sold at their Net Asset Value (NAV) at the end of the business day. In addition, the structure of ETFs is typically much more tax efficient than actively managed mutual funds. It is rare for an ETF to pass-through capital gains to investors in the same manner as mutual funds. Additionally, most ETFs tend to be less expensive than a typical actively managed mutual fund because ETFs are passive baskets of stocks that conform to a specific index or GICS classification, as compared to the typical mutual fund that is actively managed by a fund manager who is paid a fee for his or her management services. Finally, for investors in hedge funds and funds using hedge fund strategies, ETFs can be shorted, just like a stock in the portfolio, and in many cases options can be written on them. Investors can create pair trades by being "long" one market ETF and then selling short another ETF in an effort to earn money on an arbitrage between the two. Or, inverse ETFs which are constructed to offer investors returns that are opposite of the direction of a specific asset class, can be used as a short position against a portfolio of individual stocks.

All of the S&P U.S. sectors can be purchased with ETFs, as can many of the underlying industries. In addition, virtually all of the other well-known U.S. equity indexes, including all of the different investment style indexes such as growth and value and small-cap and large-cap categories, are available as ETFs through the various providers mentioned above. In addition to U.S. sectors and indexes, many individual foreign country ETFs are available as well as international index ETFs. Finally, there are a growing number of ETFs available that offer some element of active management that may be of great interest to investors.

## Following the Cycle

The following charts in **Figures 11.11** and **11.12** are stylized views of the economic cycle and the sectors that tend to outperform during different parts of the cycle. **Figure 11.11** from Standard and Poor's shows the economy moving from contraction to expansion and back again and the progression of market sectors that tend to do well at each point in the cycle. Notice that during the contraction phase the sectors that would seem to be least tied to economic growth tend to lead. For example, the health care sector is considered a "defensive" sector of the market that usually outperforms during economic contractions. The companies that comprise the health care sector include pharmaceutical companies, managed care providers, medical equipment manufacturers, biotechnology companies, and hospitals. For the most part, when people get sick they will purchase their medicines, visit their doctors, and go to the hospital if necessary, regardless of the broader economy. On the other hand, the health care sector is subject to many other different types of risk, such as the risk of adverse government regulation that can impact the profitability of the sector.

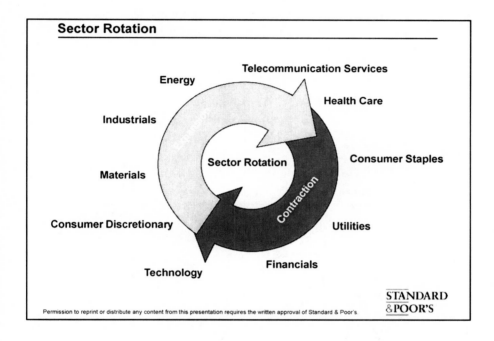

**Figure 11.11—Sector Rotation**
Source: Standard and Poor's

By contrast, the industrial sector, which is considered a "cyclical" group of stocks that include industries such as industrial conglomerates, aerospace and defense, machinery, air freight, building products, etc. are very much dependent on the state of the economy. When the economy is expanding, consumers are employed and happily spending and corporations are profitable. The industrial sector directly benefits from this state of affairs as they provide equipment and services for industries both in the U.S. and around the world, and their profits benefit from the economic expansion.

**Figure 11.12** from BCA Research shows a similar view of the economic cycle, but includes three important new elements to our analysis. BCA shows the market cycle, beginning with the liquidity in the economy, which is a function of central bank interest rate policy. As a central bank cuts interest rates in response to a slowing economy, the liquidity line moves higher as more liquidity is available to businesses and consumers due to low interest rates. As the economy moves from contraction to expansion, the central bank begins to raise interest rates to a neutral level. And as the economy moves to a later stage of the expansion cycle, the central bank continues to raise rates to a point where rates become restrictive and economic growth begins to slow. At this point the liquidity line begins to roll over as the amount of liquidity in the economy is reduced by tight monetary policy, and the cycle repeats itself.

The second element of the cycle is corporate profitability. In BCA's stylized view of the economic cycle, corporate profits follow the liquidity cycle. As the amount of liquidity expands in the economy, companies increase their sales as the economy expands. Increasing sales leads to increasing profit margins and productivity growth.

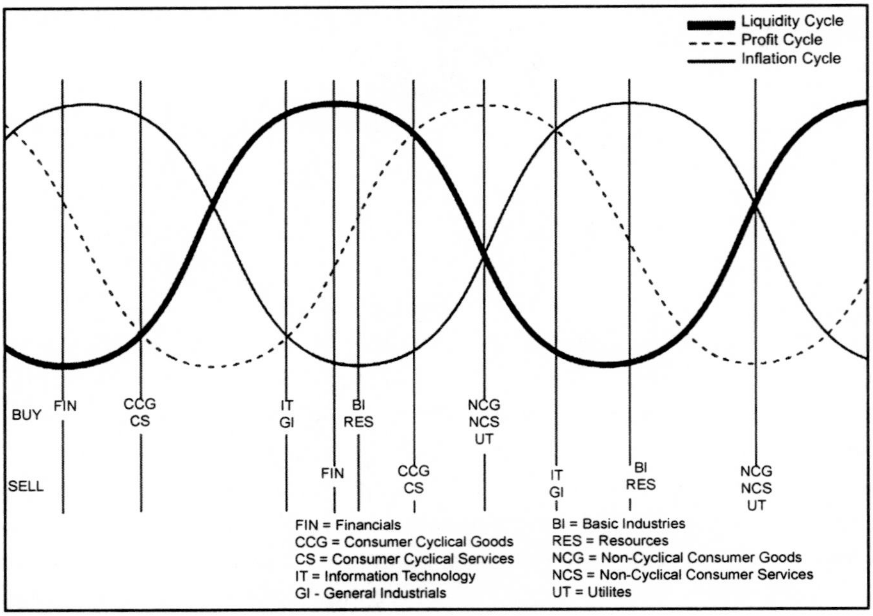

**Figure 11.12—Market Timing Sequencing**

Source: bcaresearch.com

Corporate profit margins tend to peak about 12 to 18 months after the peak in the liquidity cycle.

The profit cycle is followed by the inflation cycle. As profits continue to grow, fueled by a strong economy, at some point excess demand or constraints on supply create pricing pressures. Many economists believe that inflation is a monetary phenomenon caused by the central bank providing too much liquidity at this point in the cycle. In a classic inflation cycle, the pricing pressures are relieved by the central bank raising interest rates and corporate profits moving to a contraction phase. Prices then fall until interest rates have been lowered enough to stimulate the economy again and corporate profits once again begin to increase. In this diagram, inflation lags the liquidity cycle by about 36 months.

In this stylized view of the liquidity, profit, and inflation cycle, the chart illustrates which sectors should outperform as the economy goes from contraction to expansion and back again. As the liquidity cycle peaks and the Federal Reserve begins to raise interest rates, the chart suggests that healthcare, consumer staples, and the utilities sectors should outperform. As the liquidity cycle approaches the trough at the beginning of a new expansion phase, they show financials, technology, and consumer discretionary sectors outperforming. This is the same rotation shown in the Standard and Poor's chart we reviewed earlier.

For investors, this rotation from sector to sector represents an interesting opportunity to create value and manage risk. First of all, for those investors who don't like being "out of the market," sector rotation allows them to defensively position their equity exposure without selling stocks and moving to cash. The investor's risk management decision becomes a decision about relative risk, comparing the risks and reward opportunities of one sector or industry of the market to another. This strategy may be very attractive to skeptical buy and hold investors who would prefer to stay invested in the stock market at all times. The volatility of the equity allocation can be managed by "hiding in the market" using the health care, consumer staples, and utility sectors. When properly implemented, investors can significantly reduce downside volatility in their equity allocations. On the other hand, it is possible to load up on "high beta" sectors of the market at the beginning of cyclical bull markets by investing in the consumer cyclical, financial, and technology sectors of the market.

It is also possible to manage volatility within certain sectors by rotating to less cyclical industries within a particular sector. For example, if an investor feels that an economic slowdown is likely, they may wish to rotate from an economically sensitive industry like semiconductors in the technology sector in favor of a position in the software industry, which is often considered to be a more defensive industry within the technology sector.

## Implementation

Sector Rotation, as it is commonly practiced, can have much in common with pure market timing strategies. Typical sector rotation strategies almost always use technical momentum indicators to determine which sectors are performing the best at any point in time. Investors then "ride" a specific sector or sectors until their relative performance declines, and then "rotate" to the next hot performer. However, investors should be cautious in relying solely on technical analysis for decision-making. If improperly implemented, the portfolio can be concentrated in only one sector at the worst possible time, leading to unnecessary portfolio declines. Creating a "win-lose" proposition based on correctly owning the single best market sector at any point in time may not be a wise long-term strategy and may actually increase the risk in an investor's portfolio.

As an alternative, investors can invest the time and energy to forecast the current position of the liquidity, profit, and inflation cycle. They can then combine their global macro fundamental analysis with technical trading tools in order to reach a more comprehensive opinion about where they are in the market cycle. Then they can use a variety of ETFs to express their fundamental, value-driven, view of the market. Owning specific market sectors and specific industry groups can add value to portfolio performance *as long as the strategy is implemented in the context of a well-diversified portfolio.* Investors should consider hedging their market view by owning sectors that will perform in a different market environment than their base case view of the market cycle. For example, they might own industrials and technology at the same time that they own the classic defensive sectors like health care and consumer staples, specifically as a hedge against the possibility that they are wrong in their market forecast. The amount of the hedge should be determined by their level of conviction about their "base case" view of the market. Investors will not always have a high-conviction view, and in fact one of the benefits of experience is recognizing high conviction when you experience it. For most investors, most of the time, hedging the base case should be the rule rather than the exception. Of course, if the base case plays out as expected, the hedge positions will probably underperform, leading investors to question why they hedged the base case in the first place. We will discuss this problem in the chapter on investor mistakes.

Even with all of its benefits, top-down analysis is no panacea. There may be times when investors should invest opposite a purely cyclical view of industry or sector selection due to structural or other reasons. And it is certainly possible to get the top-down call correct and still not be rewarded with excess returns. However, more often than not, investors are playing the game with a tailwind at their back if they understand the cyclical nature of the markets and invest accordingly.

The last step in the investment process is to evaluate the securities that investors must utilize to implement their portfolio construction. To better understand how an investor can choose sector and industry ETFs for the U.S. allocation of their portfolios, as well as the securities they should use to invest the remainder of their portfolios, the next chapter focuses on methodologies for bottom-up security analysis.

# 12 BOTTOM-UP INVESTMENT ANALYSIS: A CASE STUDY

O nce investors reach a high level of conviction about their market outlook, based on the ideas discussed in the previous chapters, the next step is to decide which security or securities will deliver the best performance and earn excess returns based on the investor's investment forecast. We characterize this part of the investment process as "bottom-up" analysis because investors are no longer concentrating on broad macroeconomic themes, but instead are analyzing very specific investments relative to a particular security, sector, industry, region, or country.

All investors have to go through the process of marshaling and analyzing the facts in order to decide if their investment ideas merit inclusion in their portfolios. One good way to approach this task is to take on the role of a professional investment analyst who is required to thoroughly research an investment idea and persuade the rest of the investment team (especially the Chief Investment Officer or Portfolio Manager) that his or her investment idea deserves a place in the actively managed portfolio. Individual investors would be well served to conduct research, prepare documentation, and build a strong investment case, just as they would have to do if they were a professional investment analyst with the responsibility of convincing a portfolio manager to accept their investment recommendation.

The following hypothetical case study is offered to give investors a detailed, practical example of bottom-up investment analysis. In this case, we will meet a rather sophisticated hypothetical investor, Tom, and learn how he goes about putting together his top-down views of the economy along with his bottom-up research of specific investment ideas in order to add a new security to his portfolio. Of course, the case is presented for educational purposes only and the example presented may be completely inappropriate for any individual investor. The reader will note that Tom's outlook for the markets, which was formulated in early 2008, turned out to be prescient. Interested readers will have to find out for themselves how Tom's hypothetical investment actually performed during the market crash that evolved for the remainder of the year.

The semantics of top-down versus bottom-up analysis can be confusing for different investors. For example, investors who concentrate on picking individual stocks might consider many of the elements discussed in this chapter to be part of their top-down analysis. I believe that for investors who utilize actively managed funds or ETFs to invest their portfolios, the ideas that we cover in this chapter are as close to a bottom-up analysis as they are likely to get. Regardless of the label, the following important elements of portfolio construction must be addressed by active managers.

Bottom-up security analysis can be divided into four parts:

- Valuation
- Story
- Technical analysis
- Security construction

It is worth mentioning that in the 1930's, Benjamin Graham discussed story, valuation, and momentum in his important book on value investing, *Security Analysis*, so the ideas presented here are not new by any stretch of the imagination. While Graham generally applied his ideas to one asset class, U.S. stocks, investors who are building globally diversified, multiple asset class portfolios can certainly use similar value-based concepts for investing in different asset classes, sectors, industries, and countries.

In the following case study, our hypothetical investor—let's call him Tom—works his way through the bottom-up decision-making process leading to the acquisition of a biotechnology exchange traded fund, ticker FBT. In late 2007, Tom chose the biotech industry for possible inclusion in his portfolio because at the time of the analysis it fit his top-down view of the macroeconomic environment. As stated earlier, an investor's point of view about the market cycle can lead to high-conviction beliefs about the probable performance of asset classes and the best opportunities to identify value and earn excess returns. At the time of this particular analysis, Tom's macroeconomic "top-down" outlook was as follows:

1. He believed the U.S. economy was in recession, although he was still unclear about how deep the recession would be.

2. Tom thought that the recession was primarily caused by a vicious downturn in the U.S. housing market. The housing downturn contributed to a credit crisis which was caused by a number of factors, but a major consideration was that speculative and unregulated mortgage-backed structured investment products were routinely being written down to the point that they had little to no value. As a result, major financial institutions were being forced to recapitalize their balance sheets and the subsequent result was a significant tightening in credit standards and a slowdown in credit creation. Tom believed that the credit crisis was going to result in a deleveraging cycle in the U.S. financial system that could take years to unwind.

3. The U.S. Federal Reserve, under Chairman Ben Bernanke, had taken extraordinary steps to battle the deflationary result of the credit bust by significantly lowering interest rates and creating several new and innovative lending facilities for financial institutions. Tom believed that the Federal Reserve would not be able to fully resolve issues of credit solvency with the use of monetary policy tools, and expected significant intervention in the economy through fiscal stimulus policies, regardless of which candidate won the election that was being contested at the time.

4. Tom expected U.S. economic growth to remain slow until the real estate market began to stabilize, which he thought in a worst-case scenario could take several years.

5. The U.S. dollar had declined dramatically as U.S. monetary policy had largely decoupled from the European Central Bank (ECB) and the Bank of England. While U.S. central bankers believed that the risks of slow economic growth (full employment) and inflation (price stability) were balanced, European Central Bank policy still seemed tilted towards inflation as the greater risk. Tom believed the dollar would stabilize as the year progressed, as European Central Banks would be forced to lower interest rates. He thought that the ultimate impact of the soaring Euro versus the dollar would be slower European growth in the future. The U.S. was ahead in the monetary cycle of providing liquidity.

6. In Tom's view, global growth was expected to slow from its record high levels, but the secularly weaker dollar would continue to provide support

to U.S. companies that had large percentages of their sales and earnings from overseas. Tom was skeptical that the emerging markets of China, India, and South America would completely decouple from the developed world and continue to grow at their current pace in the face of a slowdown in the U.S., Europe, and Japan.

7. Tom believed that U.S. earnings estimates for 2008 and 2009 were wildly optimistic and that the consensus of analysts was likely to have overstated earnings in the face of a significant slowdown in global growth. He believed that the U.S. financial and consumer sectors were still under great duress, and that the remaining U.S. stock market sector earnings could potentially come under pressure by the end of 2008 and into 2009.

8. Tom believed that the combination of higher oil prices, tighter lending standards, falling real estate values, and higher unemployment, significantly increased the risk that U.S. consumer spending would slow considerably in the near future. He expected that the economy would remain in recession well into 2009.

With a high degree of conviction in this top-down macro outlook, our hypothetical investor, Tom, had already defensively positioned his portfolio in the prior year in anticipation of a slowdown in U.S. economic growth and an increase in U.S. stock market volatility. The two largest U.S. stock market sector weightings in his portfolio were Consumer Staples and Healthcare, both of which are considered to be "defensive" sectors that have historically performed relatively well during recessions. Tom owned all U.S. sector positions by investing in exchange traded funds which afforded him great flexibility in rotating market sectors based on his changing views of the economy and the market cycle. His position in Consumer Staples had performed very much as expected and had significantly outperformed the broad market through the beginning stages of the downturn, which Tom had correctly forecasted. However, his position in the Healthcare Sector SPDR, ticker XLV, had been relatively disappointing. Even though the fundamentals of the sector were attractive, including strong forward earnings growth coupled with excellent valuations on a relative and absolute basis, the sector had only been a "market" performer, meaning that it had declined as much as the broad market in the current bear market. Tom surmised that the poor recent performance was due to the "headline risk" created by the presidential election campaign, where it seemed that both political parties promoted policies that would not necessarily be favorable to the health care industry. Therefore, Tom decided to either trim the current Healthcare SPDR position or sell it outright in favor of a more attractive investment idea.

## Why Biotechnology?

Tom focused on the biotechnology industry because he believed that it would outperform the broad market based on his top-down economic outlook. Some of the unique characteristics of the biotech industry that Tom found attractive included:

- Biotech typically performs well in recessionary environments.
- Biotech has previously performed well deep into Fed rate cutting cycles.
- Biotech tends to perform well when the industrial sector is slowing.
- Biotech is a higher beta (greater volatility) investment at a time when Tom was trying to earn excess returns in a difficult market environment.
- Biotech companies were viewed as takeover targets of big pharmaceutical companies that were struggling with ailing pipelines of new products.

With this general framework for the analysis, Tom took a closer look at the biotech industry itself and tried to determine if this investment idea met his criteria for story, valuation, technical analysis, and security construction, and what the risks of this investment might be if he purchased it.

The first step in the research process was to determine the size of the biotech industry relative to the health care industry and the S&P 500 Index as a whole. The question was what companies make up the biotech industry and how big were they. Tom also wanted to know what these companies produce.

One easy way to determine the size of an industry compared to the size of the broad market as measured by the S&P 500 Index is to use the Standard and Poor's/ MSCI Global Industry Classification Standards (GICS) industry classifications. **Table 12.1** shows that the biotech industry represents a rather small 1.35% of the S&P 500 Index.

| SECTOR/INDUSTRY | % OF S&P 500 |
|-----------------|--------------|
| Biotechnology Industry | 1% |
| Pharmaceutical Industry | 6.20% |
| Healthcare Equipment Industry | 1.90% |

**Table 12.1**

Source: Pinnacle Advisory Group, Inc.

| COMPANIES IN BIOTECH SECTOR | SYMBOL | % OF S&P 500 |
|---|---|---|
| Gilead Sciences | GILD | 40% |
| Amgen | AMGN | 39% |
| Celgene | CELG | 23% |
| Genzyme | GENZ | 17% |
| Biogen Idec Inc | BIIB | 16% |

**Table 12.2**

Source: Pinnacle Advisory Group, Inc.

As a comparison, two other industries within the health care sector, pharmaceuticals and healthcare equipment have a 6.2% and a 1.9% respective weighting in the broad market. Of some concern was that the entire GICS industry group for the biotech sector contained only five companies, as shown in **Table 12.2**, although Bloomberg and AMEX maintained broader biotechnology groups. Even though a few of these companies are large and mature businesses, Tom typically liked to see more businesses represented in any one industry group, if only to reduce the business risk inherent in investing in so few individual stocks.

The next question was what does the biotechnology industry produce? The biotech industry produces products for multiple uses, including:

- Agricultural uses—such as modifying crop seeds to withstand herbicides and resist pests.
- Medical/Human uses—including genetic engineering that prevents medical disorders, as well as having non-medical uses like changing eye color.
- Pharmaceuticals—diagnostics, vaccines, antitoxins, antibiotics, therapeutics, genetic testing, gene therapy.
- Industrial Biotechnology—using enzymes to enhance fuels and detergents.

While many of these biotech products could lead to large increases in future revenues, it seemed to Tom that the promise of pharmaceutical products developed by the biotech industry leading to investor-friendly acquisitions by large pharmaceutical companies was a wonderful opportunity to exploit for future profits.

## The "Story"

The next step in Tom's bottom-up research process was to consider the fundamental "story" for this particular industry. The story is the narrative that explains why investors would want to own a particular industry, within the context of their top-down view of the markets. It supplies the reasoning for why this particular investment could outperform a sector or industry. The story is subjective in nature and is a significant part of the total qualitative analysis.

As we learned in previous chapters, humans have a propensity to develop a story *after the fact* to simplify and explain our experiences. The world is a complicated place and simple stories are fraught with the risk that investors are oversimplifying a complicated subject. Nevertheless, stories are critical to the development of an investment outlook and they can help investors to build their base case that may *prove to be accurate before the fact*. To paraphrase Woody Brock, the story can help us show that we have been right for the right reasons. Investors can develop stories by reading various sources of investment research, or they can compare the views of

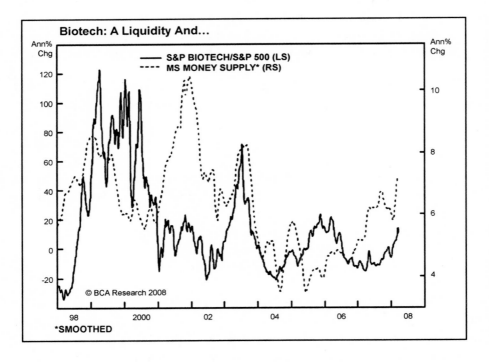

Figure 12.1—Biotech: A Liquidity And...

Source: bcaresearch.com

different independent analysts to see if there is a consensus among them about any one specific investment opportunity. In this case, there was a favorable consensus among several of Tom's favorite research analysts, from both the buy-side and the sell-side, which was collectively favorable to the biotechnology industry. The following charts by BCA Research -U.S. Equity Strategy helped to illustrate the fundamental story for the biotechnology industry.

The biotech industry historically performs well during periods when the money supply is expanding. **Figure 12.1** juxtaposed two data sets on top of one another. The dotted line is a chart of the M2 money supply, which is essentially physical money (coins, currency and demand deposits) plus savings and checking accounts as well as non-institutional money market funds.

It is notable how the money supply soared after the Federal Reserve responded to the bursting of the tech bubble early in 2001 with several interest rate cuts, and the Bush administration's first round of tax cuts were enacted in the spring of 2001 with the first tax rebates appearing in July.

The solid line in the chart is the performance of the S&P biotech group of stocks relative to the S&P 500 Index (read on the left scale on the chart). When the solid line moves higher the biotech industry is outperforming the S&P and when it moves lower the relative performance is worse than the broad market. With the exception of the Bush tax cuts in 2001, investors can see a correlation between increasing money supply and relative outperformance by the biotech sector. Since, generally speaking, increasing money supply is a knock-on consequence of falling interest rates, it appeared to Tom that recent Federal Reserve interest rate cuts would provide a tailwind for the biotechnology sector's future relative performance.

In another panel of charts, shown in **Figure 12.2**, BCA provided further data that the biotech sector could perform well in the current market cycle. The top chart in the panel once again shows the relative performance of the biotech industry versus the S&P 500 Index. In this case, they juxtapose the relative performance of the biotech industry versus the S&P 500 with the ISM Manufacturing Composite Index. The Institute of Supply Management (ISM) manufacturing composite is based on a survey of more than 300 purchasing executives from across the country. They provide monthly data about changes in production, new orders, new export orders, imports, employment, inventories, prices, and the timeliness of supplier deliveries in their companies, comparing the current month to the previous month. The ISM is an excellent top-down indicator that can help investors to assess and estimate where they are in the business cycle.

In **Figure 12.2**, the ISM data is inverted, so the dotted line that represents the ISM Composite indicates that manufacturing data was weakening. A quick check of the right scale confirms that the scale is inverted. Looking at this chart, our hypothetical investor, Tom, saw that the biotech industry's relative performance generally improves when the manufacturing sector is weakening. This conclusion also made sense with his observation about biotech outperforming whenever the money supply is increasing, since money supply tends to increase when the Fed cuts interests rates, and the Fed cuts interest rates when manufacturing conditions are weakening. The "story" was starting to come together.

To increase his confidence in the narrative for Biotech, Tom dug a little deeper. The second chart in **Figure 12.2** showed him that pricing power, as represented by the producer prices for the biotech drug and pharmaceutical companies, was strong. Pricing power is a prerequisite to keeping profit margins high and should result in higher future earnings growth. The research also mentioned that inventories at the manufacturing and wholesale levels were lean, which helps to keep prices high.

## Valuation

The third chart in **Figure 12.2** showed the consensus of analysts' earnings expectations for 12-month forward operating earnings based on data from Thomson Financial. The data clearly showed that analysts were very pessimistic about the earnings growth potential for the biotech industry. At the same time, the bottom panel indicated that the relative forward P/E estimates for the biotech industry versus the S&P 500 Index were also well below their historic average. The last two panels showed that even though the top-down economic picture seemed to favor the companies in the biotech space, analysts were still pessimistic in their views. This was the first building block for supporting a case for biotech that said that the stocks in the sector were inexpensive relative to the broad market. Analysts were extremely pessimistic and there was plenty of room for investor expectations to improve, allowing the P/E multiple for the sector to expand.

Tom was familiar with the work of Ed Yardeni, a well-known market analyst with Yardeni Research, who provides a wealth of data on industry groups and sectors in his research work. **Figure 12.3** shows the consensus of analysts' earnings expectations for biotech by showing the forward P/E multiples for biotech versus the S&P 500 Index. Tom noted that even though the S&P 500 traded to P/E multiples of 25 times earnings using Yardeni's methodology in the 1999-2000 bubble years, the biotech industry, like other technology related industries, soared to extraordinarily high multiples. The industry peaked at 65 times forward earnings in early 2000 and valuations had been falling ever since. Compared to the height of the tech bubble, investors no longer seemed to be giving biotech any credit for having the ability to generate higher than average earnings growth. Of course, investors could also interpret the data as saying that the prior earnings peak was so abnormal that current

## Figure 12.2

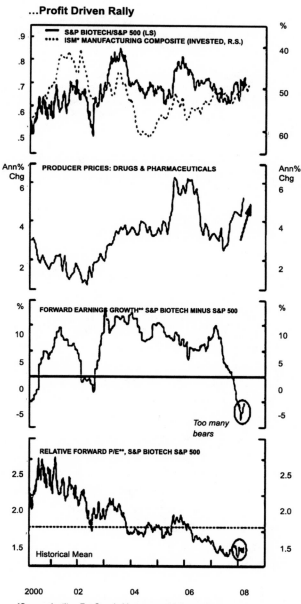

...Profit Driven Rally

*Source: Institue For Supply Management Advanced
** Source: Thomson Financial  EE$ Based on 12-Month Forward EPS

*Source: www.bcaresearch.com*

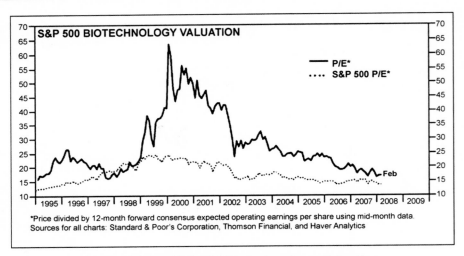

**Figure 12.3—S&P 500 Biotechnology Valuation**
Source: Yardeni Research

valuations simply reflected normal valuations. In that case, perhaps the sector was not as cheap as it appeared to be.

**Figure 12.4** showed that current profit margins in the industry remained high. This seemed to corroborate BCA's view that margins would remain well supported as industry pricing power remained strong due to, among other things, lean inventories at the manufacturing and wholesale level.

In **Figure 12.5**, Tom considered the following chart from Ned Davis Research (NDR) in order to compare the relative performance of the NDR biotechnology group of companies versus the equal-weighted S&P 500 Index.

Because NDR often uses an equal-weighted approach to market performance, as opposed to the more widely followed capitalization-weighted view of index performance, their work can reveal different insights into valuation than those available through other sources. The top chart in this series showed the year-over-year relative performance of biotech versus the S&P 500 since 1982. Tom could easily see the huge spike in relative performance in 2000, followed by a "regression to the mean" where the relative performance of the industry was worse than the broad market starting in 2001, and with the exception of a few small blips, had stayed negative through the current period. (Regression to the mean is a way of saying that the data will revert to the long-term average. It is important to note that not all data series are mean-reverting. However, because the economy seems to operate in a cycle, many economic data series are mean-

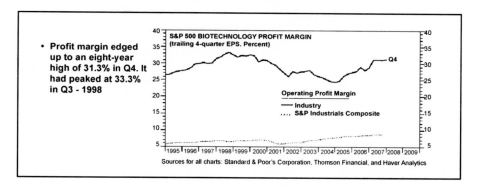

**Figure 12.4—S&P 500 Biotechnology Profit Margin**
Source: Yardeni Research

reverting.) In this case many analysts agree that data about valuation and profits are mean-reverting.

In the bottom chart of the same analysis, instead of using year-over-year performance data, NDR used three-year performance data. This longer-term analysis makes the relative performance of biotech even easier to see. If the top-down assessment of the economic cycle proved to be correct, and if the biotech industry performed as expected, Tom believed that there was plenty of room for the industry to outperform the broad market. If the industry revisited prior peak valuations then value could become a tailwind for the sector returns for the foreseeable future.

## Cycle Analysis

Cycle analysis also played a role in Tom's assessment of sectors and industries and helped to guide his decisions about how to rotate sectors. Using **Figure 12.6** from Ned Davis Research, Tom analyzed the historic composite performance of the NDR biotechnology-major group versus the S&P 500 equal-weighted performance from 12 months before a recession until 12 months after the start of a recession. The data is based on the composite performance of the sector over four previous recessions. The chart shows the start of a recession as the vertical black line. In this case NDR used 1/31/1980, 7/31/1981, 7/31/1990/, and 3/21/2001 as recession starting dates in order to compile their performance data. The chart also includes another vertical line on the rights side of the chart, which is the 9 1/2-month period after the start of a recession that has historically (since 1980) been the beginning of the next economic expansion.

**Figure 12.5**

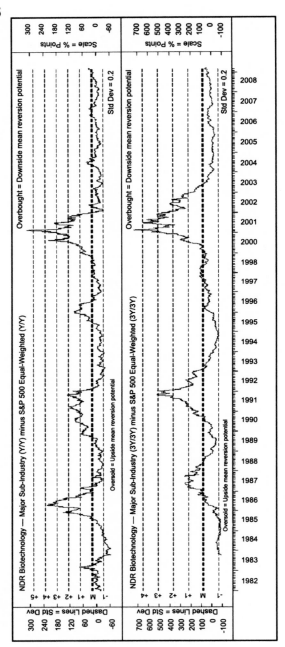

Source: Ned Davis Research

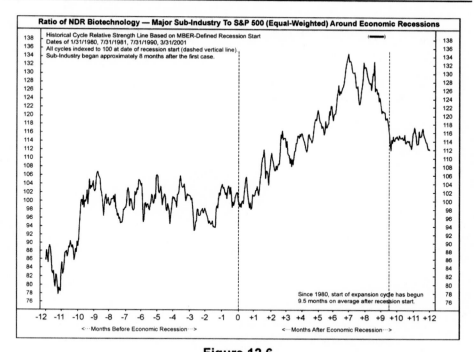

**Figure 12.6**

Source: Ned Davis Research

The rising black relative strength line shows that historically the biotech sector has performed very well relatively in recessionary environments. It appears that investors begin to rotate out of biotech a few months before the next economic expansion begins. Tom believed that the U.S. was at the beginning stages of a recession, and the data showed that biotech still had a ways to run relative to the broader market.

Ned Davis presented another cycle chart that was equally helpful. In this analysis, they illustrated how the biotech sector performed during the Federal Reserve rate cutting cycle. In **Figure 12.7**, they showed the performance of the NDR biotech industry group versus the equal-weighted S&P 500 for the 12 months prior to and after the Federal Reserve's sixth rate cut. Since the Federal Reserve began cutting interest rates in this cycle in October of 2007, and had subsequently cut rates an additional six times, Tom found the historical view of how the biotech industry had performed since the sixth Fed rate cut in a series of rate cuts to be especially interesting. If the composite of the 1982, 1986, 1989, and 2001 rate cuts was any guide, then Tom concluded, the biotech industry had many more months of positive relative performance ahead.

**Figure 12.7**

Source: Ned Davis Research

## Technical Analysis

Having analyzed both the story and the value characteristics of the biotech industry, Tom's next step was to focus his research effort on technical analysis. For aspiring value investors, the concept of technical analysis can be counterintuitive. Technical analysis is generally based on the idea that the price of a security reflects all of the market's knowledge about the fundamental information available about the particular investment, and so the movement of the price reflects whether or not the prospects for a company, industry, sector, or the broad market, are improving or deteriorating. If the assumptions of technical analysts are correct, then there is no need to learn about a company's market share, products, competition, balance sheet, management, or earnings, because all of this information is already assumed to be included in its stock price. For value investors who spend a lifetime studying the fundamentals of companies and industries, the idea of simply studying the action of prices may seem ludicrous. However, many active managers and independent analysts include at least some elements of technical analysis in their investment process, and Tom believed that at a minimum, he could use technical analysis to help him with the timing of his transactions.

Technical analysis is too broad and complicated a field of study to delve too deeply into here. However, investors can evaluate attitude and sentiment indicators, trend and momentum indicators, and contrarian indicators that point to short-term oversold or overbought conditions in the course of their analysis. There are many different technical tools available to do this type of analysis, including relative strength, rate of change, MACD (moving average convergence divergence), stochastics, and Bollinger bands. In terms of sentiment indicators, it is helpful to evaluate put-call ratios, volume, the CBOE VIX (Chicago Board of Options Exchange index of implied volatility for S&P 500 Index options over the next 30 days), changing percentages of market capitalization, and surveys of investor attitudes. Investors who are unfamiliar with these technical strategies for evaluating securities will find that learning more about them will allow for a more comprehensive approach to their active management decisions.

One of the best-known strategies for technical analysis involves momentum investing. Momentum investors believe prices will continue to move in the direction of the trend as investors extrapolate future performance based on the current price direction. The price can continue to move in the direction of the trend for reasons that have little to do with the fundamentals of the investment itself. It is the emotional reaction of investors who are fearful of "missing a move" in an investment in either direction that often creates momentum in the shares. They believe that if the price of the security really does represent all of the existing knowledge about the underlying business, then rising prices must indicate improving prospects for the business. This is one manifestation of the old investment saying, "buy the rumor and sell the news." The market is determining the nature of the news based on the direction of the trend. Once the news is actually released, traders would then sell because the price is already presumed to have adjusted for that news. Momentum is the ultimate indicator of the herd mentality at work. Some of the most widely used tools for momentum analysis include drawing trend lines on price charts, measuring the relative strength of the price versus its own past performance or other securities, and measuring the rate of change of price to determine the strength of any particular trend.

In Tom's case, a series of charts from Ned Davis Research, shown in **Figure 12.8**, provided an interesting start to his momentum analysis. The charts in **Figure 12.8** compared the relative price strength of two different components of the healthcare sector (pharmaceuticals and biotech) to the healthcare sector as a whole. In this relative strength chart, when the line is going up it means that the industry is outperforming the broad sector, and when it is moving lower it means that the industry is underperforming. NDR presents the data along with a 200-day moving average of the relative strength line. (The 200-day moving average simply adds the past 200 days of data and divides by 200 to get the next data point on the 200-day line. It has the effect of "smoothing" the data so that very short and volatile movements in relative strength are minimized when viewing the chart. The 200-day moving average is a well-known and often-used tool to determine long-term trends.)

In this case, the charts led Tom to some interesting observations. First, the two industries with the best momentum based on a strong move above the 200-day moving average were Biotechnology—Major (top chart) and Pharmaceuticals—Other (bottom chart). In both cases the relative strength line had made a meaningful move above the moving average since the beginning of 2008. Since Tom was considering an investment in biotech, he recalled that the GICS industry classification only included five fairly large and mature businesses in the biotech industry, and all of those companies were likely to be in the NDR Biotech-Major group.

On the other hand, the second chart shown was the NDR Biotech—Other group. This group of biotech companies was likely made up of companies that were much more speculative and had much smaller market capitalizations than the Biotech—Major group. It was clear that investors had not yet discovered this group

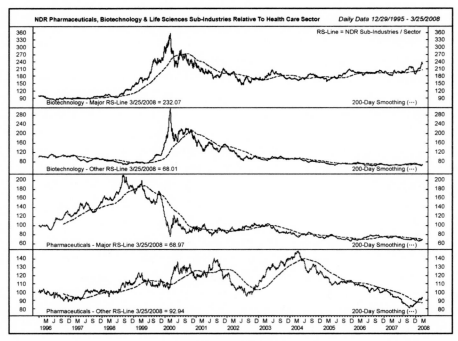

**Figure 12.8**

Source: Ned Davis Research

of biotech stocks since the relative strength line hadn't moved relative to its 200-day moving average. It was also notable that the Pharmaceutical—Major group also hadn't shown any price momentum in the past year. This was no surprise to Tom. His disappointment in the recent performance of the Healthcare sector SPDR, which was composed of approximately 50% pharmaceutical companies, was one of the reasons he was researching biotech in the first place. In this view, the downward sloping 200-day moving average of the relative strength line indicated very little momentum in the shares versus the healthcare industry, with the exception of the Biotechnology—Major group shown in the top panel.

Another aspect of Tom's momentum study of the biotech group was to analyze the short-term momentum characteristics of the industry. At the time there were five exchange traded funds (ETFs) that specialized in owning biotech companies. Tom observed that the earliest date that all five of the ETFs were first available was on 6/26/2006, and the correlation between the five ETFs was approximately 85%. Therefore, he arbitrarily chose FBT, the First Trust Amex Biotech ETF, for his analysis. FBT owns 20 stocks in the Amex biotech index that are equally weighted. Without making any judgments about the investment merits of the security itself, he could now evaluate the short-term momentum characteristics of FBT.

Tom's momentum analysis included a combination of relative strength analysis, trendline analysis, and consideration of price moving averages and the slopes of price moving averages. In this case, he examined the relationship between the security price and the short and long moving average of the price to see if a positive price trend was developing. **Figure 12.9** showed the performance of FBT versus its 50-day moving average and its 200-day moving average over the prior twelve months. The biotech industry, as shown by FBT, had been volatile for the period. However, using this particular form of relative strength trend analysis, FBT had only given one signal, which was to sell on 1/29/08 when the 50-day moving average crossed below the 200-day moving average.

When using short-and long-term price moving averages, Tom often looked for price to fall below the 50- and the 200-day moving average, AND the 50-day to confirm the new trend by following the price through the longer 200-day trend line. From that day on 1/29/08 to the low on 3/17/08, FBT lost 11.3%. However, it then made a bottom and had experienced a very strong rally closing on 4/4/08, up 16% from the low. Even though the price had rallied back through the 200-day and the 50-day moving average, the 50-day moving average had not confirmed the move so the new trend had not been fully established. Of course that is why the technique is called trend following. There can be dramatic price movements in either direction before the trend is firmly established. Tom made one last important observation which was that the 200-day price moving average had rolled over and was moving lower, indicating downside price momentum, but recently had shown signs of stabilizing.

**Figure 12.9**
Source: Investors FastTrack—fasttrack.net

Notably, other types of momentum analysis revealed a different conclusion. Tom observed that the movement of the price rising above both the 50-day and the 200-day moving average could be considered a positive buying signal. Tom also drew a trend line across the price peaks in October, December, and January to conclude that the price was just breaking through an important resistance point. For him, the outcome of the analysis was that the momentum picture was mixed and did not result in a buy recommendation for FBT based on short-term price momentum alone. In fact, the very strong price move from 3/17/2008 to the date of Tom's analysis on 4/4/08 (+15.76%) actually created some strong short-term concerns regarding the possible timing of this acquisition.

Tom's conclusion was that the biotechnology industry was an interesting diversification to his current health care sector positions. Tom was persuaded by the story, valuation, and many of the technical indicators for the industry, even though he remained concerned about the impressive vertical short-term price movements for the ETFs he was considering.

At this point, Tom could move on to the last part of his bottom-up analysis, which was to determine which biotech ETF was the best security for him to own in his portfolio.

## Security Construction

As mentioned earlier, there were five available ETFs in the biotech space. Tom always considered the total number of holdings in an ETF since he was interested in the actual amount of diversification offered by a particular ETF. Depending on the underlying index used to build the ETF, there can be a significant difference in the number of holdings. Investors should also consider the allocation percentage to each underlying stock in their ETF analysis. In some cases the underlying index can allocate a large percentage of ETF assets to relatively few stocks, which once again jeopardizes the diversification that some investors hope to achieve. If so, investors might favor ETFs with more equal percentage weightings to the holdings versus large capitalization weighted differences in the holdings based on the construction of the underlying GICS classification. In this case, the actual GICS biotech sectors only had five stocks, which Tom thought was unacceptable. **Table 12.3** is a quick list of the available ETFs and the number of holdings in each at the time Tom did his analysis:

After studying the top holdings in each of the ETFs, Tom felt that FBT met his requirement for a relatively equal weighting in the securities that comprise the index. He also considered the number of shares that trade on a daily basis in each ETF, which is known as the trading volume. Because of the size of the average new positions that he trades in his managed accounts, Tom wanted to be assured that there were enough shares in the ETF traded each day in order to have confidence that he could execute transactions in the ETF without having an undue impact on price movements on any given day. After considering all of the details of the security-specific analysis for his biotechnology investment idea, Tom eventually chose FBT as the ETF to acquire for his very successful portfolio.

The last part of Tom's analysis centered on the risks of potentially trimming the Healthcare SPDR in favor of adding FBT to the portfolio. Tom identified several major risks to this trade, including:

- He could be *wrong* in his forecast of slower economic growth and investors would be selling biotech in favor of more cyclical, growth-oriented U.S. investments.
- He could be *correct* in his forecast of slower economic growth, but the market could be so close to the bottom of the economic cycle that investors would still sell biotech in favor of more growth-oriented U.S. investments.

| NAME | SYMBOL | INDEX | # OF HOLDINGS |
|---|---|---|---|
| SPDR Biotechnology SPDR | XBI | S&P Biotech Industry Select Index | 30 stocks |
| Powershares Dynamic Biotech | PBE | Actively Rebalanced | 30 stocks |
| iShares Biotechnology | IBB | Nasdaq Biotech Index | 176 stocks |
| First Trust Amex Biotech | FBT | Amex Biotech Index | 20 stocks |
| Biotechnology HLDRS | BBH | None | 18 stocks |

**Table 12.3—Biotechnology ETFs**

Source: Pinnacle Advisory Group, Inc.

- The biotech industry had, in the preceding weeks, experienced a rash of positive news having to do with mergers in the industry, which had driven the shares significantly higher. There was a risk related to the timing of the purchase if the shares retraced a significant percentage of their recent gains.
- It was possible that the Healthcare SPDR would be discovered by investors for all of the reasons that Tom owned it in the first place, and that the biotech SPDR would be a relative underperformer. In other words, perhaps Tom wasn't being patient enough with his Healthcare SPDR position.
- Biotech was a relatively high-beta industry to invest in. If the base case forecast underestimated the severity of the economic slowdown that was being forecast, then biotechnology could significantly underperform other asset classes like cash and bonds, and potentially other defensive sectors like consumer staples, general healthcare, and utilities.

After considering the various risks to his forecast, Tom decided to trim the Healthcare SPDR position in his portfolio in favor of adding a new position in FBT. However, his purchase was contingent on waiting for FBT to retrace some of its recent price gains in order for Tom to have a better entry point.

## Summary

In this chapter we examined a case study in order to better understand the process of security analysis that investors should consider when conducting bottom-up security analysis. Investors should analyze each element of story, valuation, technical analysis, and security construction as an integral part of their decision-making process in an actively managed portfolio. We have now become an investment expert, determined our point of view about where we are in the market cycle as well as market valuation, and chosen a specific security to invest in, in order to earn excess returns. Presumably the job is done and we can get on to planning the family vacation. However, before we leave there are other hurdles to cross in our journey to becoming an expert at tactical asset allocation.

Having had a front row seat to observe Tom's very thorough bottom-up analysis, it is time to consider another important and practical issue for any investor considering active portfolio management, the psychology of making investment mistakes.

# 13 THE PSYCHOLOGY OF MAKING INVESTMENT MISTAKES

I n March of 2003, Pinnacle Advisory Group (where I am currently employed as Chair of the Investment Committee) concluded that the 2000-2002 bear market was effectively over. With the second Gulf war recently underway and the bullish model of the market's performance during the first Gulf war on our minds, we decide to change the asset allocation of our portfolios to reflect our bullish base case for the economy and the financial markets. The S&P 500 Index had made its low in October of 2002 at a price of 770 and had subsequently rallied through year-end, only to rollover again and re-test the lows in the first few months of 2003. By the time we decided to buy, the S&P 500 was trading at 880, more than 14% above the lows set the previous year. We added a full 10% to our U.S. equity positions in that transaction, even though many of us were worried that it was too late to buy. We feared that we were emotionally and unprofessionally chasing the market after it had already made a nice gain from the prior low. I distinctly remember being so worried about the buys we made that day that I felt physically ill for the remainder of the afternoon. Of course, we could not know that the stock market was embarking on a very powerful bull market which would eventually last for almost five years and see the market more than double from our purchase price.

We all know that the best investors are supposed to be robotic, unemotional decision-making machines, who should never experience anxiety, fear, joy, or jubilation as the markets move for or against them. To be "worried sick" is the antithesis of what investors should strive for in their quest to make unemotional and unbiased decisions. Perhaps nothing in the theory or practical reality of actively managing portfolios is more emotional than the fear of making an investment mistake. No one likes to make a mistake, and professionals (in any profession) certainly don't want to make mistakes when working with clients. Professionals pay exorbitant sums for errors and omissions insurance to insure against the possibility that they will make an error that will cost their clients money. So to purposely pursue an investment philosophy that virtually guarantees that we will make mistakes seems foolhardy. To entertain such a mistake-ridden investment philosophy when there is a competing philosophy that seems to offer the potential to be error-free is, well, almost unthinkable.

Passively and strategically managing portfolios *seems* to offer investors the magic elixir of never making an investment mistake. This mirage is made possible by a clear and unambiguous strategy of only looking at portfolio results over a very long-term time horizon. For financial advisors, buying the stock market when P/E ratios are high and likely to contract will almost certainly result in dramatically less than expected returns over the client's life expectancy, but by the time the disappointing results of buying and holding become obvious, the advisor may very well have retired and moved on to other pursuits. Every objection about portfolio returns in the interim can be met with the clear reminder that "professional" investors are patient. The idea of changing the portfolio's asset allocation to increase short-term investment returns is traditionally thought to be a classic investment mistake made by amateurs.

The strategy recommended in this book, the strategy of actively managing the portfolio asset allocation in order to find good investment values throughout the investor's investment time horizon, is certain to result in some investment mistakes. This is because the task of forecasting the future is an uncertain business with only one guarantee, which is of course, that no one can perfectly forecast the future. Making mistakes is the inevitable and unavoidable side effect of active management. An investor simply cannot pursue active portfolio management without making mistakes. Therefore, active management offers investors the best opportunity for achieving needed returns in secular bear market environments. However to do so, investors must learn to deal with making mistakes.

Based on my informal conversations with investors across the country, I would say fear of making a mistake is the single biggest reason that many investors don't incorporate active management strategies into their investment process. When they do try to change their asset allocation based on their assessment of market conditions and they turn out to be too early, too late, or just plain wrong, they immediately conclude that successful active management is impossible and that accurate forecasting is a fool's game. Confronted with an investment mistake, they are sometimes willing to embrace any investment philosophy, no matter how flawed, that will allow them to avoid making another mistake. The psychological pain is obviously too great for them to bear, as is (for professional investors) the potential risk to their professional relationships with their clients. With this in mind, it may be helpful to shine some light on the issue of investment mistakes. Perhaps if investors realize that "everyone makes them," they will be able to approach active management strategies with less emotion and more professionalism. It's time to get investment mistakes "out of the closet."

## Getting Investment Mistakes "Out of the Closet"

We know from our study of behavioral finance that investors are subject to a number of biases and heuristics that cause them to make decisions that seem to be less than rational. Biases and heuristics are "rules of thumb" or simplifying strategies that investors use when making decisions in the face of overwhelming data. Heuristics are innately human and universal to everyone. That investors are less than rational should be no surprise to active managers who believe that markets are inefficient and that investors routinely make mistakes. If we are to believe Mordecai Kurz and Woody Brock, who write that it is possible to earn excess returns by making fewer mistakes then the consensus, then learning about how investors make mistakes should be an important part of any investor's education. Notably, Kurz is careful to point out that making mistakes is the obvious result of not being able to predict the future, and not necessarily the result of being irrational. Rational investors believe that past returns will repeat in the future, and investors are considered to be rational in his pricing model called The Theory of Rational Beliefs. However, Kurz concludes that such investors, while rational, are doomed to be wrong in their forecasts if there is any kind of structural change. Brock's work adds other important considerations for how investors make mistakes. He points out those same investors don't necessarily have to miss the impact of structural change; they can also make improper inferences about how the markets work in reality. Investors can make mistakes without structural change entering into the equation at all. In other words, farmers (investors) don't need to misunderstand the impact of global warming (structural change) to still make mistakes about how the weather will impact a farmer's crops (investor's portfolio).

Of course, none of this information about irrational investors and investor mistakes is covered in the current education for professional advisors because strategic buy and hold investors theoretically cannot make mistakes. It is presumed that average historical returns of asset classes will be earned at some time far in the future, and therefore advisors don't need to make active management decisions about asset classes that could lead to a mistake. This paradigm, which is so convenient for the investor-client relationship, makes studying investor mistakes unnecessary for strategic investors. Unfortunately, we have already discovered that the idea of "efficient" asset class performance is a myth and that investors who buy asset classes when they are dearly priced will almost certainly have made an investment mistake, at least if we define a mistake as a very high probability of not earning anticipated returns over a long period of time.

Therefore investors must either passively accept whatever market returns are offered by strategically owning asset classes, or they must engage in a more active money management strategy that requires them to make forecasts about asset class performance that could result in adding value to an investor's account, but will almost certainly lead to making at least some mistakes.

I believe that one of the best ways to get this idea of mistakes "out of the closet" is to talk openly about them. In the same spirit that skiers can always top each other with stories about how they wiped out on a black diamond hill, or boaters do the same when they talk about their close call in bad weather or in a crowded harbor, I now present a case study of a classic investment mistake in order to illustrate how they occur, and how to learn from them.

Before diving into the details of this case study, it is important to be clear about a few essential truths regarding the basic rules of successful active investment management. First and foremost, the portfolio should always be properly diversified so that the impact of an investment mistake is minimized. Ironically, the "proper" amount of diversification is not the same for active managers versus buy and hold investors. According to Modern Portfolio Theory, the proper amount of diversification is the amount necessary to build an efficient portfolio that lies on an efficient frontier of all possible portfolios that can be constructed from the pool of asset classes available to the investor. On the other hand, proper diversification for active and tactical investors is that amount of diversification needed to hedge an investor's base case about the investment markets. Investors with strong convictions can have less diversification, and investors who are unsure of their forecast should have more diversification. No single transaction or series of transactions should put an investor in a win-lose situation with regards to his or her financial plan. In addition, the portfolio should always be managed within the constraints of an investment policy that is coordinated with the overall financial planning objectives of the investor or client. By investing within these policy constraints, the impact of any investment mistakes will be minimized. With these stipulations in mind, I now humbly present the somewhat painful history of Pinnacle Advisory Group's run-in with owning gold in 2004.

## An Investment Mistake Case Study: Viewing Gold as an Alternative Currency Rather than a Hedge Against Inflation

In 2003 the dollar was falling versus most international currencies, and Pinnacle was concerned about a secular bear market in the dollar. Our investment thesis was based on a great deal of research by our analysts regarding the structural nature of the U.S. trade deficit. We were convinced that the dollar would fall in value over time, and we decided to invest this weak dollar theme in several different ways in our managed accounts. First, we increased the international stock exposure of our managed portfolios on the theory that the falling dollar would make our foreign shares more valuable for our U.S. investors. Second, we took a position in an international bond fund, the American Century International Bond Fund (BEGBX), which owned European government bonds without being hedged to the dollar. We believed that as the Euro rose against the dollar, it would create a headwind for European growth that would be European bond–friendly, and the unhedged structure of the fund would allow us to benefit from the falling dollar. The third part of our strategy was to take a position in a mutual fund that invested in gold mining stocks. We chose the American Century International Gold Fund (BGEIX). At the time, there was a rumor that the gold bullion ETF (GLD), which allows investors to buy the bullion in an ETF format, was going to be approved for investors sometime later in the year, but it was unavailable to us at the time. The point was moot because our analysis concluded that we should buy the gold mining stock shares because historically gold shares had outperformed bullion in bull markets for gold. This made sense because the economics of gold mining companies make them a leveraged play on gold prices.

For us, our gold position was to be a classic hedge against the falling dollar. We took a 3% position in the fund in our Dynamic Moderate portfolio in January of 2004. At the time, we were not at all concerned about inflation as an investment risk, but felt that gold would benefit from dollar weakness. Gold was trading at $380 per ounce at that time.

In 2004 international stocks outperformed the U.S. stock market and analysts agreed that the weak dollar contributed to positive investor perceptions of international markets. Our allocation to international equity funds added tremendously to client returns. Our forecast for the dollar was right on the money and we earned large gains in our international bond fund position as well. In fact, our bond fund outperformed the S&P 500 Index in a decent year for the stock market, which was an added bonus to returns.

But our gold shares lagged our expectations. During the year gold stocks struggled versus the performance of gold bullion and the shares of our fund gyrated wildly, *even though the dollar was weakening versus other currencies*. After initially paying $13.32 per share for the fund in January, the shares fell 29% in just 5 months and we added an additional 1% to our position in May. While we were prepared for the position to be volatile, we expected to be rewarded for getting our dollar forecast correct and we were not. As the year progressed several of the analysts that we followed that had been bearish about the dollar changed their minds and offered high-conviction forecasts that the dollar was now oversold and by the fourth quarter of 2004 we began to look for opportunities to sell the gold position and change the asset allocation of our portfolio to reflect our new bullish short-term outlook for the dollar.

We decided to leave our overweight positions in international stocks in place and to sell our positions in international bonds and gold with the assumption that both would underperform if the dollar rallied. We sold the international bond fund for large gains, and sold 1% of the gold fund in September at $11.73 per share and the remaining 3% of the position at $11.03 per share in February of 2005. As shown in **Figure 13.1**[48], the net result for our clients was small losses on the overall gold position because of our timely May 7 buy at $9.43 per share.

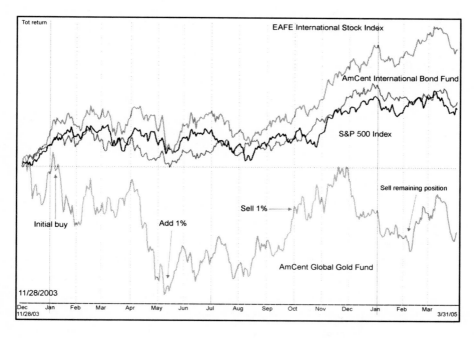

**Figure 13.1**

Source: Pinnacle Advisory Group, Inc.

48   This chart is created using software by Investors Fasttrack, http://www.fasttrack.net

Once again our forecast proved to be correct and the dollar did rally against international currencies throughout 2005. International bonds had a relatively poor year versus domestic bonds, and our bond sale added value to client portfolios. Gold didn't do much in the beginning of the year and our sale worked fine through the spring. However, in May of 2005 both the fund shares and the bullion began to move higher, even though the dollar was rallying as we expected. We sold our gold shares in February, and it seemed that the minute we did so, the price of gold bullion began to skyrocket. Even though the dollar was rallying and even though bullion had presumably been trading as an alternative currency for many years, once we sold the position a somewhat surprising change occurred. According to the analysts, gold stopped trading as an alternative currency and began to trade in its more traditional role as a hedge against inflation. It was almost as if we had flicked a switch after we exited the position that caused bullion prices to go vertical.

It is important to note that our base case regarding inflation had not changed. We did not believe that structural inflation was going to be a problem for the global economy at the time and in fact, we were probably more concerned about structural deflation. Historically gold had not performed well when inflation was contained. In addition, gold pays little in the way of dividends or interest so there is a cost to carry it in the portfolio. We also believed (and still believe) that assessing the value of any individual commodity is difficult, and gold's status as "gold" made it even more difficult as random central bank selling could scuttle the value of the metal seemingly at any time. Finally, the volatility of the position was a concern. We felt we had survived quite a scare in the price of the shares the previous year and we were not anxious to get back on that rollercoaster again. It seemed that without high conviction in the story for gold, it was not worth chasing the shares higher. We simply didn't believe that inflation was a problem, and we thought that the dollar would continue to rally throughout the year, and so we let it go.

To put it in direct terms, not buying back into the gold fund or the gold ETF was a mistake. Gold was trading at $450 per ounce when we sold the fund, and as bullion prices began to climb past $500 and upwards of $600 per ounce, the pain of that sale began to increase dramatically. How could we have held the shares through the volatile roller coaster ride of 2004 only to sell them just three months before they began to really take off? We kept questioning whether or not it was too late to jump back into the position, but every time we considered a purchase we concluded that both the gold shares and the bullion had appreciated too far and too quickly to represent a good value for our clients.

The higher the shares traded the more it reinforced our thinking that the shares were too expensive to buy. A large part of the story for the gold ETF was that it would unlock a huge wave of investor demand for gold, since without the ETF it was difficult to actually physically own the metal. With institutions now free to pile into gold as an asset class, we feared that maybe gold would be the new investment mania, and we were missing it! Several of the bearish analysts that we follow changed their opinion on gold by the end of 2005 and early 2006 and became bullish on the metal as the momentum of gold stocks and gold bullion became obvious. Even so, we still didn't want to buy back the position. Even when we changed our mind and thought that we should buy back in, we thought we would find an entry point when the price of gold convincingly dipped below its 200-day moving average. Unfortunately, it never did.

**Figure 13.2** shows the performance of GLD since the day we sold our gold position in February 2005. Note that except for a brief period in 2006 the ETF has consistently traded above its 200-day price moving average until its very recent severe price decline. The "rest of the story" is that we eventually reestablished our gold position in 2008 by buying GLD at prices below $800.

**Figure 13.2**
Source: Investors FastTrack

## Investors Make Mistakes

Behavioral psychologists have studied literally hundreds of cognitive biases and heuristics that can contribute to investment decisions, including investment mistakes. Some of the most relevant ones include:

- The Bandwagon Effect: the tendency to believe things because many other investors do.
- Bias Blind Spot: the tendency not to compensate for one's own cognitive bias.
- Choice-Supportive Bias: the tendency to remember one's choices as better than they actually were.
- Confirmation Bias: the tendency to search for or interpret information in a way that confirms one's preconceptions.
- Extreme Aversion: the tendency to avoid extremes, being more likely to choose an option if it is the intermediate choice.
- Framing: using too narrow an approach or description of the situation or issue.
- Illusion of Control: the tendency for human beings to believe they can control or at least influence outcomes that they clearly cannot.
- Outcome Bias: the tendency to judge a decision by its eventual outcome instead of based on the quality of the decision at the time it was made.

There are two biases that deserve special mention because I believe they are pervasive in the behavior of all investors. The first is risk aversion, or more accurately, loss aversion.[49] Simply put, risk aversion is a bias that means that investors do not approach decisions about gains and losses equally. Bernstein quotes Tversky in *Against the Gods* on the topic:

> Kahneman Tversky interprets the evidence produced by these experiments as a demonstration that people are not risk-averse: they are perfectly willing to choose a gamble when they consider it appropriate. But if they are not risk-averse, what are they? The major driving force is loss aversion, writes Tversky (italics added). It is not so much that people hate uncertainty, but rather, they hate losing. Losses will always loom larger than gains.

Kahneman and Tversky also found that the valuation of a risky opportunity depends far more on the reference point from which the possible gain or loss will occur than on the final value of the assets that would result. It is not how rich you are that motivates your decision, but whether that decision will make you richer or poorer. As a consequence, Tversky warns, "Our preferences… can be manipulated by changes in the reference points." This is an important point for wealthy investors

---

49  Note: I strongly recommend that readers read Peter Bernstein's chapter "The Failure of Invariance," in his essential book on the history of risk, *Against the Gods*, for an excellent discussion of loss aversion and decision regret.

to consider. From both a psychological and financial perspective, losses matter more than gains for these investors.

Investors hate to take a loss. It is an admission that we have made an error in judgment. Our ego does not allow us to accept such a proposition. We see this behavior often with clients who honestly believe that they have not lost money until a position is sold. Until then they are in perfect denial that they have any kind of investment loss, and are often willing to take large and unnecessary gambles in holding loss positions in the hopes that they will turn into gains in the future. Ironically, as we will soon see, for professional investors, dealing with clients who are loss-averse often makes it difficult to execute investment strategies that are designed to minimize risk and volatility in their portfolio.

The second special bias that is worth discussing is decision regret. Decision regret is the result of focusing on the assets that you might have had if you had made the right decision. In the case of the Pinnacle gold position, as long as the price remains above where we sold gold in February of 2005, we could theoretically experience decision regret that we sold it when we did. For all investors, decision regret is especially important to understand and guard against when actively managing a portfolio.

Another important point about decision regret is for investors to remember the correct investment decisions that they did make. In the case of our gold sale, while we didn't buy the bullion, we did eventually take a large position in a commodity index fund. The fund essentially owns the Dow Jones-AIG commodity futures index, which includes oil, natural gas, industrial and precious metals, and agricultural commodities. While it is easy to fixate on the one investment idea that was within your grasp and "got away," it is important not to do so out of context. In my experience, the best active managers will find a way to avoid decision regret and move on to their next investment decision with as much objectivity as possible. Once again, experience and wisdom have much to do with successfully executing an active management strategy.

One last point about decision regret is that it seems to be closely related to "hindsight bias." As the name implies, hindsight bias is the tendency to see past events as being predictable. This "I knew it all along" perspective is pervasive among investors who believe, with perfect 20-20 hindsight, that they could or should have known what a particular security or market would do in the future. I see it most often with investors who point to stock charts that show a defined range of returns, and want to know why they didn't buy and sell at every trough and peak. These investors must train themselves to understand that stock charts always look simple when viewed from the perspective of 20-20 hindsight. In real time, looking forward into the unknown future, no one can possibly know what the price of the security will do in the short-term. However, financial advisors should beware. They must be prepared to explain why they don't have this special ability to those few clients who perceive this inability as inexcusable.

As we close our discussion about Pinnacle's checkered past with gold investments, let me share our internal analysis of the gold trade. In our opinion, both the purchase of the security and the sale of the security were made for the right reasons. The purchase offered our clients good value since we had high conviction that the dollar would fall in value. We give ourselves high marks for our well-timed add to the position after the significant decline in price, but question our conviction of not adding more than 1% to the position since our base case had not changed. Our sale in February 2005 made perfect sense given our forecast that the dollar was oversold and ready for a rally. We had no reason to believe that gold would begin to trade as an inflation hedge, and even if it did, inflation was simply not on our worry list at the time. The sale was timely and appropriate and under the same circumstances, I would do it again. Missing the run in gold prices after the sale was the result of our conviction that structural deflation was the theme of the day, and that central banks had too much credibility as inflation fighters for structural inflation to be a problem. Not owning gold under these circumstances made perfect sense.

However, once we decided to buy back into the gold position, it is fair to question our strategy of waiting to buy a dip in the gold price. It is possible that we were unduly influenced by the volatility of gold after our first purchase in 2004, or it is possible that we are simply too value-oriented and had an irrational fear of chasing prices higher. While hindsight tells us we should have waded in and bought regardless of where the price was relative to its long-term trend, I am perfectly comfortable having missed the entry point while waiting for a better time to buy. Sometimes good ideas will run away from you, and this was one of those times.

## Coping with Uncertainty

Learning to deal with the psychology of decision-making under conditions of uncertainty is one of the most difficult aspects of transitioning from a strategic buy and hold money management philosophy to a more active, tactical management strategy. Here are several lessons investors should learn about good decision-making.

**Keep retesting your base case:** A good defense against decision regret is to review the facts and circumstances that formed the basis for your original investment decision. If the fundamentals that drove your decision haven't changed, then the likelihood is that you haven't made a mistake. Try to find solace in the data, especially when the markets are moving against you in the short-term. John Mauldin, in his book *Bulls Eye Investing*[50], calls it "finding your inner Spock" (Spock being a fictional character from the planet Vulcan where they have no emotions). Focusing on the facts is a great way to minimize biases and heuristics.

**Encourage dissenting opinions:** This is closely related to retesting the base case. In a professional environment, investment analysts, like any other group, can sometimes foster a congenial urge to compromise on points of view. Instead, encourage analysts to feel free to disagree with the consensus and express an opposing view. If the base case still withstands this scrutiny, then you can go on to fight another day. Individual investors can turn to other investors, family members, and friends to discuss their ideas. Investors should actively seek out an opposing view to their investment thesis.

**Try not to be too dogmatic in your point of view:** There is a fine line between having the high conviction in your beliefs necessary to take a contrarian view of the markets, and being too dogmatic about your views in the face of structural change. Be open to new ideas and new data.

**Learn from your mistakes:** You are going to make mistakes if you actively and tactically manage portfolios. The best investors are able to turn an analytical lens on themselves to learn more about how they make good and less good decisions. Don't make the error of trying to forget an investment mistake without first dissecting it to find out if you can avoid it in the future.

**Think longer-term:** Match your evaluation of the performance of an investment to the proper time horizon. While tactical investors typically don't get the luxury of 10- to 20-year time horizons, they often make decisions that should play out over shorter market cycles, which may be a year or longer. Don't get overly emotional over weekly or even monthly returns if they don't meet your investment time horizon.

**Turn off the TV:** The drumbeat of daily news coverage can make it more difficult to focus on one's investment themes, and encourages a more emotional response to data that may not be significant to your investment thesis. TV news is a great source of timely information, especially when newsmakers are breaking news on the air. However, the opinions that are expressed are generally biased towards whatever is the most sensational at the moment. Of course, breathless headlines create higher ratings. Because TV is a visual medium, it tends to be more persuasive than other sources of information, and can lead to emotional decision-making. Every once in a while, turn off the TV.

**Don't dwell on losses:** Our review of our investment mistake in gold is the product of our (hopefully) objective internal analysis of what happened in that particular transaction. If you make a mistake, allow yourself all of the traditional

50   John Mauldin, *Bull's Eye Investing, Targeting Real Returns in a Smoke and Mirrors Market*, John Wiley and Sons, Inc., Hoboken, N.J., 2004

steps of the grieving process as determined by Dr. Elisabeth Kubler-Ross: shock, denial, anger, bargaining (with God), depression, and acceptance. Just try to get through the process in about five minutes and get on with the analysis of your next great investment idea.

**Take credit for your victories:** One of the lessons that was hardest for me to learn is that hard work and great research *does* lead to excellent investment forecasts. Allow yourself the benefit of the doubt. It turns out that beating the consensus is not as hard as you think it will be. When you can professionally and dispassionately evaluate the data that moves the broad market, and have better insights into how the markets work than the consensus, it gives you an edge that will allow you to deal with investment mistakes in a more positive frame of mind. Do not attribute the results of your hard work to good luck!

**Take a break:** There is an endless grind of investment research to be read. Give yourself a chance to step away from it for a while and clear your head. Take a walk. Talk to your spouse and kids. Get a life. When you are trying to find the important signals in the emotion of all of the daily investment noise, it helps to step back from the fray and decompress for awhile.

## Transparent Portfolios (A Note for Investment Advisors)

The term transparent portfolio refers to a managed account where investors can see the individual holdings in their account. Many types of widely-owned securities are not transparent at all. The most common security with a lack of transparency is a mutual fund. When investors buy a mutual fund they are buying shares of a special type of investment company that hires an investment manager to actively manage a portfolio of securities on the investor's behalf. The portfolio is priced every day and the Net Asset Value of the fund is posted at the end of the business day. However, the investor has no idea what securities are owned in the fund on any given day. The fund manager is bound to follow the general guidelines that are described in the prospectus for investors, but the details are often kept secret, if for no other reason than the fund manager doesn't want speculators trading against his or her positions. The actual positions owned by the fund are spelled out in the annual and semi-annual fund report, but by the time the report is actually printed and published the underlying fund portfolio could have changed dramatically.

Another type of managed funds that are not transparent is hedge funds, which are also very secretive about their holdings. Like mutual funds, the day-to-day investment strategies that are executed by these fund managers remain a mystery to the fund owners.

In contrast, most investment advisors manage client portfolios in a way that is completely transparent. The assets are typically held by a custodian in the client's name, and the positions are reported each month by the custodian on the client's portfolio statement. In addition, virtually all custodians offer on-line access to accounts so that clients can see their holdings at any time during the business day.

This is excellent news in many ways for both the client and the advisor. From the advisor's perspective, the client can feel like they have access to their account, giving them a sense of comfort, which is always helpful in building trusting relationships. For the client, they can see their portfolio holdings which gives them a sense of control over the account, even if they have given their investment advisor the discretion to trade the account. In addition, the transparency of the account allows for better tax planning for all parties since clients can see the unrealized gains and losses that are in the portfolio and plan for the tax implications of trading strategies that are executed throughout the year.

Transparency is generally a good thing, but in the context of discussing investor psychology, transparent portfolios can pose many problems for investment advisors who want to execute state-of-the-art risk management strategies for their clients. Many clients are notoriously loss-averse, which can significantly impact the investment process. Here is a hypothetical portfolio statement of performance. Which security do you think the client will want to discuss at their next portfolio review?

| | |
|---|---|
| Security A | + 8% |
| Security B | +12% |
| Security C | - 9% |
| Security D | +23% |
| Security E | +9% |
| Security F | +11% |
| Security G | +4% |
| Total Return | +13% |

If you guessed Security C you are probably correct. What went wrong with the analysis for this security? Who was responsible for this mistake? While the portfolio result is excellent and the rest of the securities made money, human nature seems to draw clients to want an explanation for the loser.

Another example is the use of perhaps the simplest and most effective risk management tool, a stop-loss strategy. A stop-loss effectively puts a floor under the amount of money that an investor can lose on a position. Professional investors use stop-losses in many situations. One example might be if a security is currently trading well below its purchase price and the investor is no longer willing to suffer further losses. The stop-loss allows the investor to hold the position with the expectation that it will rally due to either fundamental or technical reasons, yet at the same time avoid the emotional rationalization of the hold or sell decision if the security value continues to fall. It is a simple mechanical tool designed to minimize the loss aversion of selling by predetermining the sale price. Another example of using a stop-loss might be when entering a new, speculative position in the portfolio. If the security is trading at a technical support level, the stop-loss might be used to make certain that the security is sold if the price falls through technical price support.

However, once the investment advisor implements such a strategy in a transparent portfolio, and if the stop transaction is executed below the initial purchase price (the security is sold at a loss) then every one of his or her clients will see this transaction if they care to look. At that point it is not only the heuristics and biases of the investment advisor that matter, it is the collective biases of hundreds of non-professional investors who may experience loss aversion or decision regret. It can be a daunting task to realize an investment loss on hundreds of investors' statements where any one of them might be thinking they wouldn't have lost money if only the advisor hadn't sold the security. At that point perception might become more important than reality, and even though an excellent strategy for risk control was implemented, the biases of the client become all important.

Another example of possible loss aversion and decision regret in transparent portfolios occurs if the investor puts on a "pair trade." A pair trade is a transaction where advisors invest in one security that represents their highest-conviction forecast for the market, and then hedge that position with another security that could enhance portfolio returns if their base case is incorrect. Generally the objective of a pair trade is to reduce the overall market's impact on portfolio performance and increase the impact of security selection. A classic example would be an investor who believes that large-cap U.S. stocks will outperform small-cap U.S. stocks. In its simplest form, the investor could be "long" in the S&P 500 Index and "short" the Russell 2000 Index. Shorting involves borrowing shares at the current market price and then selling them, hoping to repurchase them at a lower price in the future, effectively reversing the idea of buying low and selling high. Short sellers attempt to sell high and then buy low. Today's investors can easily build short portfolio positions by using inverse funds and inverse ETF's, which essentially give you the opposite return of whatever index you want to short.

"Pairing" the long position with the short position allows the investor to attempt to earn additional returns on the arbitrage between the long and the short returns, and minimizes the impact of the movement of the broad market. Obviously, if both positions earn the same returns the investor cannot have a gain or a loss since the return on each position offsets the other. However, if the long position gains more than the market and the short return equals the inverse of the market, the investor earns the difference. Sophisticated investors use pair trades to manage portfolio volatility and defend the portfolio in bear markets. **Table 13.1** shows a stylized example of a pair trade using our example of the long position being the S&P 500 Index and the short position being the Russell 2000 small-cap index, where the S&P 500 Index gained 8% and the Russell 2000 gained 4%.

| ASSET | $ INVESTED | RETURN | INVESTMENT GAIN/LOSS |
|---|---|---|---|
| S&P 500 Index | $10,000 | 8% | $800 |
| Inverse Russell 2000 Index | $10,000 | -4% | -$400 |
| Total Gain/Loss | | | $400 |

**Table 13.1**

Source: Pinnacle Advisory Group, Inc.

In this case the inverse fund lost 4% which is the opposite of the 4% gain in the Russell 2000 Index. For the advisor, this gain may be more than acceptable because the structure of the transaction defends against the worst case scenario for investing in these two indexes, which is that they both trade lower in a bear market. Sophisticated investors realize that large-cap and small-cap stocks often do trade in the same direction, so defending makes sense if market conditions are uncertain.

By reversing the direction of the stock market in the previous example, we can see the benefit of the pair trade in a bear market. In this case the S&P 500 Index loses 8% and the Russell 2000 Index loses 4% as shown in **Table 13.2**.

| ASSET | $ INVESTED | RETURN | INVESTMENT GAIN/LOSS |
|---|---|---|---|
| S&P 500 Index | $10,000 | -8% | -$800 |
| Inverse Russell 2000 Index | $10,000 | 4% | $400 |
| Total Gain/Loss | | | -$400 |

**Table 13.2**

Source: Pinnacle Advisory Group, Inc.

The pair trade transaction lost $400 when the result could have been a bear market loss of $1,200 in a long-only portfolio. However, if an advisor implements this transaction in a client account then the advisor risks a client perceiving these two results in a dramatically different manner. In the first example, the client may experience decision regret that the advisor chose to short the small-cap stocks in a bull market. The opportunity cost is the difference between making $400 by being long small-caps and losing $400 on the short position, a significant "loss" of $800. The client (or the advisor for that matter) could experience hindsight bias and believe that they should have known that small-cap stocks would increase in value.

Finally, since the "loss" is due to a short-term trading strategy, they may consider the loss of $400 in the pair trade shown in **Table 13.2** to be "worse" than the loss of the long-only trade, because 1) "everyone" knows that you should buy and hold for the long run, and 2) if the advisor was long on the small-cap index and it was trading below its purchase price, and the advisor doesn't sell the position, then they never would have lost any money in the first place. All of the above may be considered by the client to be an investment mistake by the advisor, which adds to the risks of an advisor choosing to implement certain risk management strategies in actively managed accounts.

Ultimately, transparent portfolios demand that advisors take the time to properly educate their clients about the realities of actively managing portfolios. Or, in the case of individual investors, these are important points they may want to review for themselves. Some of ideas about making mistakes in actively managed portfolios that they may want to cover include:

- I am making decisions based on my best estimate of the highest probability of future events. That does not rule out the possibility that low probability events will actually occur.
- For affluent clients, the opportunity cost of missing out on a gain is usually less of a threat to the success of their financial plan than the risk of fully participating in a market loss. This is because you already have enough assets to retire. We are going to defend against losses in your portfolio strategy.
- I am going to be using hedging techniques that will require me to sell securities at a loss. This is part of our overall portfolio strategy. Realizing the losses does not mean that we are failing to achieve your investment objectives.
- There will be times when we sell a security soon after we buy it for you. When that happens, the sale will probably be a part of our risk management strategy. We do not acquire any securities for you with the intention of a quick sale, but sometimes it happens.
- There will be occasions when we make a mistake in our forecast because we are not gods and we do not know the future. The mistakes will always

be made in the context of a portfolio that is properly risk managed so that we will not jeopardize your overall investment objectives.

- If we do make a mistake in our forecast, you will be the first to know. Making investment mistakes is a part of the process, and over time we will make our share of them.

## Transparent Portfolios and Strategic Investing

Loss aversion and decision regret are not at all confined to active managers when discussing transparent portfolios. Investors concerned about transparency issues should consider the fact that any diversified portfolio, regardless of whether it is actively or strategically managed, will own several asset classes. One of them will be the winning performer and the rest of the asset classes will trail. In virtually all cases, investors will wonder how they (or their advisor) could have owned the losing asset classes when they were smart enough to own the winning asset class. This is the perfect combination of hindsight bias, decision regret, and loss aversion. Of course, no one minds if a portfolio is poorly diversified as long as all of the asset classes go up in value at the same time. However, if the portfolio is properly diversified in the strategic approach and performs as expected, then the conclusion could be that someone should have been smart enough to sell the losers and buy the winners, before the fact.

Here is a favorite story of mine in explaining the psychology of transparent portfolios to clients:

If we are managing a balanced portfolio for you, then in a bull market the portfolio will go up in value, but it will probably trail the broad stock market indexes and you will almost certainly be disappointed. If we manage the same portfolio in a bear market, then the portfolio will decline in value and the portfolio will trail the performance of cash and you will almost certainly be disappointed. Therefore, in bull markets or bear markets, you are certain to be disappointed, which means that you will be disappointed with your portfolio performance all of the time. As long as you are OK with that, then we have a good basis for a long-term relationship!
(Note: It is very important that the client laugh after you tell them this story.)

I believe that active management requires an even higher degree of professionalism from both investment advisors and their clients as it relates to the psychology of managing risk. All parties must understand that the risk of owning overvalued asset classes is much greater than the risk that the advisor will make a mistake in the execution of a portfolio strategy designed to outperform in any short-term investment cycle. This is because there is a *virtual certainty* that the asset class will not perform as expected if purchased at a high price. The cost of such an investment mistake can be catastrophic and result in the complete destruction of a retirement plan. If an investor makes a mistake in the assessment of asset class performance in a shorter-term investment cycle, where long positions are taken with care that the value characteristics of the asset classes meet the requirements of value, story, and technical analysis, then both the chance of a mistake, as well as the cost of a mistake, are greatly reduced.

If properly implemented, the tactical investment strategy of active portfolio management is by far the lower risk strategy of the two, but it asks a lot of the participants. Mistakes are an ongoing part of implementing the tactical strategy. How investors deal with them will determine whether or not they will ultimately succeed in achieving their financial planning goals and earn excess returns.

# 14 THE TAX TAIL AND THE PORTFOLIO DOG

Many investors know the old saw, "don't let the tax tail wag the investment dog," meaning that tax considerations should not determine one's investment decisions. Nonetheless, one of the most cherished beliefs held by strategic, buy and hold investors is the false idea that taxes and expenses keep actively managed funds from outperforming passive investment strategies. As we saw in the previous chapter on Active Share, this is not necessarily the case. For strategic investors who have a limited arsenal of tactics to employ in a bear market, the idea of minimizing both taxes and expenses becomes critical since they literally have no other tools to generate alpha in their portfolios, unless they employ active fund managers to invest individual asset classes. In which case, they must hope that their particular fund managers outperform their passive indexes, even though, as strategic investors, they presumably believe in efficient markets. In this context, the idea that active management can result in higher taxes and subsequently result in lower returns becomes one of the strongest objections to active, tactical portfolio strategies. Hopefully, by this point in the book, the case for actively managing portfolio asset allocation has been made. Therefore, the issue of taxes becomes important. If we are actively buying and selling asset allocations as part of our tactical investment strategy to maximize value in our portfolio, then it follows that we will be paying taxes on these transactions, which leads us to a very practical question: How big of a role should taxes play in the decision-making process of a tactical investor?

## The Rules of the Game

Rest assured, I have no intention of reviewing in detail the tax code as it relates to investing or anything else. I suspect that the reader is already wondering whether or not to skip this chapter and go on to something (anything!) more interesting than taxes. But wise investors know that we are stuck with the current tax system, or something similar to it, for the foreseeable future. So it is necessary to at least review the basics of portfolio-related taxes before we get into the meat of the chapter, which is to correct a number of misimpressions and misunderstandings about the actual tax cost of active portfolio management.

The basic rules regarding the taxation of investments include the following:

- The buying and selling of most securities are considered capital transactions. The tax code divides these transactions into gains and losses, and I assume by now we all know which is which.
- Investors only pay taxes on "realized" capital gains. Securities can appreciate year after year without the investor paying taxes on the gain. Only when the security is sold is the capital gain realized and the investor is required to pay the tax. The ability to not pay tax on the appreciation of a security until it is sold amounts to a wonderful opportunity to defer taxes. If a security appreciates in value but it has not been sold, it is considered to have "unrealized" capital gains.
- The amount of gain or loss is measured by the value of the sale price of the security relative to the cost basis of the security. Simplistically, the cost basis of a security is what you paid for it. The basis can be adjusted over the holding period depending on a variety of circumstances. Perhaps one of the most common adjustments to cost basis relates to mutual fund investors who reinvest dividend and capital gain distributions by using these distributions to buy additional shares. Because they pay tax each year on the dividend and capital gain distributions, even though they simply turned the money around and reinvested it back into the fund instead of taking it as cash, they get to add the dividend and capital gain reinvestment amount to their cost basis.
- The tax rules apply different tax rates to a sale depending on how long you hold a security before you sell it. If you hold a security for longer than one year then you pay income taxes at the long-term capital gains rates which are currently 15% of the gain for Federal taxes. (State taxes will vary.) Capital gains can be as low as 0% for taxpayers in the lowest tax brackets. If the security is held for less than 12-months, the gain is considered short-term and is taxed at a less favorable ordinary income tax

rate. For our purposes we will assume short-term gains are taxed at a 28% rate. While tax rates can and will change in the future, generally speaking it is considered a public good to encourage capital investment by keeping long-term capital gains rates lower than ordinary income tax rates.

• The government does not tax you on taxable losses. If you sell a security for less than the cost basis, in most cases no taxes are due. In addition, capital losses can be used to offset an unlimited amount of capital gains on other transactions, or they can be used to offset ordinary income up to a limit of $3,000 per year. So, if you make money on one transaction, and lose an equal amount on another transaction, the government says that you didn't earn any capital gains in the aggregate so you owe no tax. And if you can't use your capital losses to offset gains in the current tax year, you have the option of carrying them forward to use against realized capital gains in future years.

• Another method of avoiding capital gains taxes is to own securities with large unrealized capital gains when you die. Upon your death, assets owned in your name currently get a "step-up" in basis so that your heirs will inherit these securities with no unrealized gains. Generally speaking, the cost basis of these appreciated securities for your heirs is the value of the securities upon your date of death. (Under current law, this provision of the tax code is scheduled to change in 2010.) Estate tax rules are impossibly complicated, but for our purposes the main point here is that you can either sell appreciated securities during your lifetime and pay capital gains taxes, or you can offset the gains with losses from other securities that you own during your lifetime, or you can hold the securities with unrealized gains until you die and your heirs will get a step-up in basis, eliminating the capital gains liability under the current rules.

The bottom line is that unless you happen to die, or unless you lose money on your investments equal to the amount of money that you made on your investments, then whenever a security is sold for any reason, you *will* pay capital gains taxes. Thus, the only tax questions for most investments are about what the capital gains tax rate will be in the future, how long in the future it will take for you to sell the security, and how much can you earn on the security in the meantime. In fact, beyond sales that occur as a part of the investment process, the only way the appreciated assets can ever actually be spent to support an individual's standard of living is through a sale where the capital gain is realized.

There are many more tax rules, actually more than I care to count, but I think we can move on to how these rules are applied in actively managing portfolios.

## Paying Portfolio-Related Taxes

Perhaps the biggest problem that investors face in portfolio tax planning is that they don't understand the basic economics of paying taxes. We all tend to think about paying capital gains taxes in simple terms. "If I sell this security I have to pay the tax, but if I don't sell the security then I don't have to pay the tax." Or, "if I have a big gain in a security I will have to pay a lot of tax, so the bigger the unrealized gain in my portfolio the better it will be not to sell." Both statements are true, but only up to a point. These simple statements must be qualified by several other comments. For example, it is true that if you don't sell a security with an unrealized capital gain this year then you won't owe capital gains taxes, but is also true that unless you die or the security loses all of its gains, you will have to pay the tax someday in the future. Or, to put it another way, no matter how big your unrealized capital gain is, if you ever want to spend any of that money you are going to have to sell the assets and pay the associated tax sometime in your life.

While it is true that large capital gains involve large capital gains taxes, another important consideration is that securities with large gains tend to have other risks associated with them. For example, the security may no longer be fairly valued, or it may have grown to the point where owning it results in a lack of diversification in the investor's portfolio. Both of these represent investment risk, and as we will see, investment risk can have ramifications that are far greater than the psychological risk of paying taxes. Both ideas, that gains will probably be realized during your lifetime, and that large gains are usually associated with other investment risks, deserve closer scrutiny.

## The Surprisingly Small Value of Tax Deferral

Most investors have at least an intuitive understanding of the benefits of tax deferral. It is better to pay Uncle Sam tomorrow than it is to pay today because keeping those dollars in your pocket allows you to earn money on those tax dollars now that you will eventually have to pay later. Because the tax code states that we don't have to pay tax on unrealized capital gains, the appreciation of the securities that we own seems to be free of tax. Of course we are only *deferring* the tax to a later date when the security will eventually be sold. Nevertheless, there is some value to the deferral of taxes. The question is how much is tax deferral really worth.

To find out, let's imagine that our balance sheet has one asset and one liability, where the asset is the one security that you own and the liability is the tax you owe on the unrealized capital gain in the position. If we own a $10,000 security with almost no cost basis, where our hypothetical $.01 investment grew to be worth $10,000, and the capital gains tax rate is 15%, then the tax that we owe is $1,500 ($9,999.99 gain x 15%). **Table 14.1** shows how it would look on our balance sheet:

| ASSET | | LIABILITIES | |
|---|---|---|---|
| Stock A | $10,000 | Unrealized Tax | $1,500 |
| Total Assets | $10,000 | Total Liabilities | $1,500 |
| | | **NET WORTH** | $8,500 |

**Table 14.1**

Source: Pinnacle Advisory Group, Inc.

What happens if we sell the Stock A, pay the $1,500 tax, and use the net to buy Stock B? Our new balance sheet would look like this as shown in **Table 14.2**.

| ASSET | | LIABILITIES | |
|---|---|---|---|
| Stock B | $8,500 | Unrealized Tax | $0 |
| Total Assets | $8,500 | Total Liabilities | $0 |
| | | **NET WORTH** | $8,500 |

**Table 14.2**

Source: Pinnacle Advisory Group, Inc.

How could our net worth be the same $8,500 if we lost $1,500 in taxes? Didn't we lose the $1,500 in taxes that we paid when we purchased Stock B? The answer is no! Stock A had a tax liability associated with it, even if it is a liability that we don't see when we look at our investment statement which only shows our "assets" but not our net worth. In realizing the gain you are simply swapping a security with an unseen tax liability for a security that does not yet have any tax liability. Unless you intend to die owning stock A, or unless you lose some or all of your gains by having the value of the stock decline to zero (a far greater loss than paying taxes), then you will always have that tax liability. *The only loss that you have when you pay a capital gains tax on the sale of a security is the opportunity cost of the earnings that you might have received on the capital gains tax you hadn't yet paid.*

Remember, unless you die with the asset and get a step-up in your cost basis on behalf of your heirs, you will pay this liability when you sell the stock sometime in your lifetime. It doesn't matter whether you hold the position for one year or for forty years; you will always owe the tax on the gain. Therefore, when you choose to pay the tax today versus paying it in the future, your loss is the possible future earnings from the amount of the tax liability that was otherwise still invested.

| YEAR | CUMULATIVE $ (END OF YEAR) | NET ADDITIONAL GROWTH @ 8% | NET ADDITIONAL GROWTH AFTER TAXES | ANNUALIZED% | CUMULATIVE NET ADDITIONAL GROWTH | CUMULATIVE% |
|---|---|---|---|---|---|---|
| 0 | $1,500 | $0 | $0 | 0% | $0 | 0% |
| 1 | $1,620 | $120 | $102 | 1.20% | $102 | 1.20% |
| 2 | $1,750 | $130 | $110 | 1% | $212 | 2.50% |
| 3 | $1,890 | $140 | $119 | 1% | $331 | 3.90% |
| 4 | $2,041 | $151 | $128 | 1% | $460 | 5% |
| 5 | $2,204 | $163 | $139 | 1% | $598 | 7% |
| 6 | $2,380 | $176 | $150 | 1% | $748 | 8.80% |
| 7 | $2,571 | $190 | $162 | 1% | $910 | 11% |
| 8 | $2,776 | $206 | $175 | 2% | $1,085 | 13% |
| 9 | $2,999 | $222 | $189 | 2% | $1,274 | 15% |
| 10 | $3,238 | $240 | $204 | 2% | $1,478 | 17% |

**Table 14.3—Opportunity Cost Assuming 8% on the Earnings**

Source: Pinnacle Advisory Group, Inc.

It is easy enough to figure out what the opportunity cost is of paying the tax. Let's go back to our example. Remember that we will pay the $1,500 of tax now or in the future, so if we pay $1,500 of tax on January 1 of Year 1, then the amount that we would earn if we could invest the taxes in a side fund earning 8% is shown in **Table 14.3**.

In this table, the first column of numbers (after the year) is the $1,500 tax bill growing at our assumed 8%. The next column assumes that we will owe the $1,500 in tax this year or in the future, so we subtract it from the first column to get the true cumulative benefit of the deferred tax amount. The third column calculates how much of this additional growth increases our net worth, since it, too, must be taxed. The fourth column shows the annualized annual return created by the additional tax deferral growth, based on the new investment amount of $8,500 (our net worth available after taxes). The last two columns calculate the cumulative total values of columns 3 and 4.

The analysis assumes the absolute worst case scenario of having no cost basis in the security that we are considering selling, which is very unlikely. Even in this gloomy scenario, over a ten-year period we would only need to earn an additional 1.62% per year on our new investment to "break even" for the lost opportunity cost of the taxes that we paid today instead of deferring to a future date ten years down the road. It is worth noting that most economic and business cycles last three to eight years, so a ten-year holding period is generous if the investment objective is to maximize returns by utilizing tactical management.

Let's consider the same investment choice, to keep security A or to sell it and buy security B when the cost basis of our $10,000 investment is $7,500. In this example we will assume an investment of $7,500 exactly 12 months and 1 day ago, and now have a fantastic new investment idea to be purchased. Of course, having earned 33% in 366 days is a hard act to follow, but as a prudent investor we are no longer comfortable with the value proposition of our current position since it has appreciated by so much in such a short period of time. Now let's consider the opportunity cost of selling security A and buying security B. Remember, as in our previous example, our balance sheet doesn't change when we pay the capital gains tax. We are simply exchanging one security with an unseen tax liability for another security that has not yet earned a tax liability. We will pay the tax on the gain on Stock A, presuming we still have a gain in the position, as long as it is sold during our lifetime. In this case our tax liability is $375 ($2,500 x 15% capital gain tax rate.) As shown in **Table 14.4**, our balance sheet then looks like this:

| ASSET | | LIABILITIES | |
|---|---|---|---|
| Stock A | $10,000 | Unrealized Tax | $375 |
| Total Assets | $10,000 | Total Liabilities | $375 |
| | | **NET WORTH** | **$9,625** |

**Table 14.4**

Source: Pinnacle Advisory Group, Inc.

Or, we can sell Stock A to purchase Stock B with the after-tax proceeds of our sale. **Table 14.5** shows our resulting balance sheet.

| ASSET | | LIABILITIES | |
|---|---|---|---|
| Stock B | $9,625 | Unrealized Tax | $0 |
| Total Assets | $9,625 | Total Liabilities | $0 |
| | | NET WORTH | $9,625 |

**Table 14.5**

Source: Pinnacle Advisory Group, Inc.

Once again, the only money to "lose" on this transaction is the opportunity cost of the future earnings we can't receive on the $375 capital gains tax liability because we paid it today instead of at some future date. Using the same methodology as before, we end up with the following analysis as shown in **Table 14.6**.

Consider what we've just learned. If you are an investor and you don't sell a security with a long-term capital gain of 33.3% because you are concerned about taxes, then you are effectively saying that the value characteristics of your current holding are so good that you could not earn an additional annual return of 0.38% per year on a subsequent investment over the next ten years. Or, you could not earn an additional total return of 3.84% over the next ten years.

We know that many investors get upset when they have to pay taxes on realized gains in their portfolio. The irony is that the greater the gain is in the position, the more likely it is that it should be sold because it is priced above its intrinsic value. Yet for these investors, as their tax liability grows they become more and more tax-phobic. These investors seem to believe that the tax on their gain will never have to be paid in the future. Or they believe that the value of deferring the tax to a later date is so great that no amount of risk that they will lose their gain as the security reverts to fair value would justify the sale.

| YEAR | CUMULATIVE $ (END OF YEAR) | NET ADDITIONAL GROWTH | NET ADDITIONAL GROWTH AFTER TAXES | ANNUALIZED% | CUMULATIVE NET ADDITIONAL GROWTH | CUMULATIVE% |
|---|---|---|---|---|---|---|
| 0 | $375 | $0 | $0 | 0% | $0 | 0% |
| 1 | $405 | $30 | $26 | 0% | $26 | 0% |
| 2 | $437 | $32 | $28 | 0% | $53 | 1% |
| 3 | $472 | $35 | $30 | 0% | $83 | 1% |
| 4 | $510 | $38 | $32 | 0.30% | $115 | 1% |
| 5 | $551 | $41 | $35 | 0% | $150 | 2% |
| 6 | $595 | $44 | $37 | 0% | $187 | 2% |
| 7 | $643 | $48 | $40 | 0% | $228 | 2% |
| 8 | $694 | $51 | $44 | 0% | $271 | 3% |
| 9 | $750 | $56 | $47 | 0% | $318 | 3% |
| 10 | $810 | $60 | $51 | 0% | $369 | 4% |

**Table 14.6**

Source: Pinnacle Advisory Group, Inc.

Just for fun, let's examine the excess returns that would have been realized in what is probably the most obvious value-related transaction we are likely to be presented with in our lifetime. At the top of the tech bubble in the Year 2000, large-cap growth stocks had appreciated to the point that their P/E multiples reached unprecedented levels. At the time, investors justified the impossibly high valuations by believing that the U.S. was in the middle of a technology-led boom that required new metrics for assessing fair value. During the preceding five-year period, small-cap and mid-cap value shares were almost completely ignored by investors. The relative difference in value between the two asset classes was so great that no investor who was looking for relative value could miss it. I have met dozens of investors who didn't sell their large growth positions because of the large tax liability associated with the sale. In retrospect it is easy to see their tax problem.

As shown in **Table 14.7**, let's consider the relative performance of a $10,000 investment in the Russell 1000 large-cap growth index versus the S&P 500 Index versus the Russell 2000 small-cap index for the five-year period prior to 1/1/2000 (all adjusted for dividends):

| ASSET CLASS | ANNUAL RETURN % | TOTAL RETURN % | ENDING VALUE |
|---|---|---|---|
| Russell 1000 Growth | 32% | 307% | $40,700 |
| S&P 500 Index | 28% | 250% | $35,000 |
| Russell 2000 Small-cap | 13.10% | 85% | $18,500 |

**Table 14.7**

Source: Pinnacle Advisory Group, Inc.

By 1/1/2000 the investor had fallen in love with his investment in large-cap growth. Through his brilliance, or his luck, he now had an astronomic gain of $30,700 in this position over the original $10,000 cost basis. If he sold it, which was difficult to do because he either felt that markets were efficient and large-cap growth was always fairly priced, or because he believed in the "New Economy" and believed that P/E ratios greater than 100 were justified, then the sale would result in a tax bill of $4,605 (a rate of 15% on a gain of $30,700). (For investors with larger portfolios, substitute this number with the emotional pain of 10 times larger tax liabilities). In either event, for many investors the tax on their gains was large enough to help rationalize a decision not to sell.

Table 14.8 shows what happened in the subsequent five-year period for each of these asset classes, from 1/1/2000 to 1/1/2005:

| ASSET CLASS | ANNUAL RETURN % | TOTAL RETURN % | ENDING VALUE |
|---|---|---|---|
| Russell 1000 Growth | -9% | -39% | $6,140 |
| S&P 500 Index | -2% | -11% | $8,894 |
| Russell 2000 Small-cap | 17% | 121% | $22,100 |

**Table 14.8**
Source: Pinnacle Advisory Group, Inc.

Using our previous methodology, if the investor assumed that he would earn 8% on the value of the tax bill that he was going to have to pay in the future, but was reluctant to pay in the 2000 tax year, then the return he would have needed to earn on his "Security B" after selling his large-cap growth position in order to break even would have only been an annual return of 1.0%, or a total return of 5.09% over 5 years. In this case, the sale would have resulted in an annual return of 17.29% and a total return of 121%. If it was the tax bill that caused the investor not to pull the trigger on this transaction, you can see that perhaps they misunderstood what the tax implications of the sale really were. In this case, the investor gave up $12,100 of extra return over the next five years in order to save the 5-year potential tax deferral benefit of only $1,837 ($36,095 of available after-tax proceeds x 5.09%). And of course, because the markets didn't actually go up 8% (or at all), the investor didn't even receive the $1,837 tax deferral benefit! Unfortunately, at the market top in 2000, this erroneous approach to tax planning cost many investors a staggering amount of money.

## What about Short-term Capital Gains?

There is always a complication or two or a thousand when dealing with the tax code. One obvious problem for investors is that the tax rate for short-term capital gains is much higher than for long-term capital gains. Is it possible that the benefits of tax deferral are significantly different for short-term transactions? After all, there are many sector rotation strategies that assume an investor is rotating among asset classes on a quarterly basis, or even more frequently. If an investor chooses to invest in a shorter-term time horizon than the one-year holding period required to obtain the favorable capital gains rate, what happens?

The answer is surprisingly little. The break-even rates of return for subsequent investments, even after paying the higher short-term capital gains tax rates, are still very low. Michael Kitces, a nationally recognized expert on taxation and Pinnacle Advisory Group's Director of Financial Planning Research, offers a creative way of looking at the problem of short-term versus long-term capital gains. He begins by asking an excellent question. If there is investment risk in holding on to a security once it has reached an extended valuation, then during the time period that you have to wait to satisfy the one-year holding period for long-term gains, the security could suffer a decline in value. Thus, the critical question becomes how much of a decline in the security's value during the waiting period would completely offset the tax savings of paying the lower tax rate for long-term rather than short-term capital gains?

Assuming that the long-term capital gains tax rate is 15% and the short-term capital gains tax rate is 28%, Kitces derives the breakeven tax table shown in **Table 14.9**.

| GAIN | 5% | 10% | 15% | 20% |
|---|---|---|---|---|
| BREAKEVEN | 1% | 2% | 2% | 3% |

**Table 14.9**

Source: Pinnacle Advisory Group, Inc.

Take, for example, an investor who purchased a security that has gained 10% in less than 12 months and wished to sell it because it has reached its fair value and he or she wanted to protect their profits. If the security is sold now, the investor will recognize a short-term capital gain taxed at 28%. However, the breakeven formula reveals that if the security declines in value by as little as 1.53% while the investor is waiting to reach the required 12-month holding period for long-term capital gains, the entire tax savings attributable to the lower tax rate would be lost by this relatively minor decline in value. If the gain were 20%, the security would only have to decline by 3.06% during the holding period to lose the tax savings of being taxed at the long-term gain rates. In volatile markets, where securities can experience declines of this magnitude in a matter of weeks, days, or sometimes even hours, it is sometimes too risky to hold an unwanted security in order to get long-term gain treatment on the sale. Once again, investors who refuse to sell a security because they will realize a short-term capital gain may not fully understand the economics of paying the tax.

## Capital Losses

As mentioned earlier, capital losses can be used to offset capital gains. Unfortunately, the lesson here is that using the losses to offset capital gains isn't as valuable as it appears to be, for exactly the same reason that paying the capital gains isn't as costly as they appear to be. For informed readers, using portfolio losses to offset capital gains is a year-end ritual that is crucially important to good tax planning. As we will see, it simply isn't as important as owning securities in the portfolio which represent good value.

There are some complications to offsetting gains with capital losses and it is worthwhile to review them here. It is often good planning to sell investments with unrealized losses to offset gains, with the provision that doing so does not compromise the investment strategy of the portfolio. For example, let's assume that even though our research indicated that Security A offered excellent value and had an excellent story, we purchased it too early and the current market price is now 20% below our cost. However, we still like the story for Security A and now the valuation seems even more attractive. We might even want to add to our position in Security A instead of selling it to realize our tax loss. One solution would be to sell Security A and realize the loss for tax planning purposes, but to then buy Security B, which is similar to Security A, in order to continue to own this particular investment theme in the portfolio, while offsetting other gains in the portfolio.

The IRS has special rules governing these types of transactions, called "wash sale" rules, which do not permit selling a security at a loss and then buying it back within 30 days. Thus, selling Security A to realize a loss, just to buy back Security A, would disallow the loss. The key, instead, is to take the loss when you can while still owning the investment story in a security that is similar enough to be consistent with the story, but without being "substantially identical" to meet the criteria for avoiding a wash sale. On the other hand, the risk here for investors is that the similar but not the same security that they invest in may not exactly track the performance of the security that was sold. The difference in performance, or "tracking error" between Security A and Security B, is a risk that the investor takes for a short period of 30 days in order to harvest the loss for tax purposes.

There is an interesting bit of investor psychology involved with this transaction. Many investors do not feel that they have lost money until a security is sold. They may have purchased a position for $10,000 and it may be sitting on their balance sheet at $3,000, but to them the $7,000 loss doesn't count… yet. Even though the government is willing to essentially allow them to earn the value of the tax deferral on the gains that they can offset with their capital loss, for many investors the act of selling is just too painful. It confirms that they have made an investment mistake and that somehow the investment itself has betrayed them. We discussed the psychology of investment mistakes in some detail in the previous chapter. Once again investor loss aversion becomes a problem. It is psychologically much easier to hold the position and wait for it to rally back to its original value so they don't have to confront the emotional pain of the sale. Often the pain is so great that investors are incapable of rationally evaluating the investment merits of a security once it is in a loss position.

There is another problem of misperception that investors face when taking losses to offset gains. We can call this psychological problem extreme tax aversion. It is manifest in investors who believe that if they don't use a tax loss to offset a capital gain, regardless of the investment merits of the securities involved, that they have suffered significant economic harm by overpaying the government in the year that they didn't use their losses. Since I personally suffer from this particular psychological ailment, it may be instructive to look at an example to prove the point. Let's use the example of our loss averse investor whose investment in Security A of $10,000 is now worth $3,000. The math seems rather self-explanatory. If we can use the capital loss from the sale of Security A to offset other capital gains that have been realized during the tax year, then the value of the sale would appear to be $1,050. ($7,000 capital gain offset x 15%).

However, here is where the reality of the transaction is slightly different then it first appears. Let's execute the sell transaction and purchase Security B with the proceeds. We now own Security B with a cost basis of $3,000. Additionally, let's assume that we still liked the story for Security A so we made certain that our purchase of Security B avoided the wash-sale rules, but nevertheless kept us invested in the same industry as Security A. Now let's assume we get the market rally that we were hoping for. If we had not sold Security A and held it at its value of $3,000, and then the stock market rallied and the security appreciated back to our original costs basis of $10,000, then the appreciation of $7,000 would have been tax-free since there is no tax due on securities with no capital gains. However, the story is different for Security B. Here our new cost basis is $3,000, and if the security participates in the same rally as Security A and appreciates to $10,000, we would have an unrealized capital gain of $7,000 in our $10,000 position. Of course, the liability associated with this unrealized gain is the same $1,050 we saved from the sale of Security A in the first place.

Once again it appears that the value of the transaction is not the value of the $1,050 tax that was deferred when we sold Security A to offset other capital gains in the portfolio. All that actually happened was that we swapped one security with a cost basis of $10,000 for another security with a cost basis of $3,000, which means that we will eventually have to pay the tax. The value of the transaction is not $1,050. Instead it is the value of the earnings on the $1,050 of tax that is now deferred, but not eliminated. We still have the taxes to pay when we eventually sell Security B. As we saw earlier in this chapter when we examined the value of the tax deferral on capital gains, the deferral value from using capital losses to offset capital gains just isn't what it appears to be at first glance.[51]

Perhaps the best way to think about the benefits of realized tax losses is to think of them as accelerated benefits from tax deferral. Once again, the comparative economics of Security A versus Security B are the most important issue. In all cases, the benefits of realizing capital losses, like the costs of realizing capital gains, are very small compared to possible investment benefits of a better investment idea.

There is one more thought on the psychology of tax losses that is worth consideration. Many investors actually hope for tax losses to offset capital gains. They feel that the emotional pain of paying taxes is so great that they will go to any lengths to avoid it. They forget that even after they pay capital gains taxes, they still keep 85% of all of the increases in their wealth. This is very good news! They made money. Tax losses feel good when they are available to offset capital gains, but they are not good news for investors. It means the investor has lost money on the transaction, and the tax loss only helps recover a percentage of the total economic amount lost. While it is foolish to forgo what amounts to a government subsidy to sell your losers, no one should confuse having an equal amount of gains and losses as being good news.

## Mutual Funds

Investors have had a several-decades-long love affair with mutual funds in their portfolio construction because mutual funds are liquid, have small minimum investment requirements, are professionally managed, and allow investors to choose among an enormous number of investment ideas. Tactical and active portfolio managers may find that mutual funds provide a wonderful alternative for investing in certain asset classes and other investment themes.

But from a tax perspective, mutual funds can be problematic. Care must be taken when owning managed funds in taxable accounts to maximize the tax benefits of mutual fund ownership. Here are a few of the mutual fund basics for tax planning purposes:

Mutual funds must distribute capital gains to their investors, but may not distribute capital losses. Fund managers can use fund losses to offset gains in the mutual fund's portfolio (which does ultimately reduce the amount of gains that must be distributed in the future). However, since many mutual fund investors are investing in mutual funds with assets from pension and profit sharing plans, IRA accounts, charitable accounts, and other tax-qualified accounts, some fund

---

51  Readers might consider that capital gains tax rates may increase in the near future. If so, the proper strategy would be to hoard your capital losses and not use them against current capital gains at today's lower tax rates. Instead, investors should carry their losses forward to use them when capital gains tax rates are higher, which will increase the value of the strategy.

managers are less concerned about tax consequences (while others are more "tax aware"). In some cases, the fund managers may ignore taxes altogether in their pursuit of the highest possible fund returns, especially since they cannot know the tax circumstances of thousands of shareholders who own their fund.

When an investor buys fund shares, they purchase the current embedded gains and losses in the fund portfolio. Even though they didn't own the fund at the time that the gains were earned, they will pay their pro-rata share of the taxes due when the gains in the mutual fund portfolio are actually realized and distributed to current shareholders. Notably, investors also receive their pro-rata share of losses and the associated tax benefits, even though they didn't have to experience the financial loss.

For example, Manager A makes a correct bet on the technology sector in his growth fund and the underlying technology stocks gain 400% in value over a period of many years. An investor who is infatuated with Manager A's past performance buys the mutual fund at the current net asset value, which includes the appreciated value of the technology shares owned in the fund. Soon after the investor buys the mutual fund, Manager A changes his mind about the investment merits of technology stocks and decides to sell his positions in the fund in order to protect his gains in a falling market. TßΣted that this has the effect of converting favorable capital gains taxes to unfavorable ordinary income taxes when the assets are eventually distributed from the tax-qualified plan. The variables include how long the assets will stay in the plan, what the growth rate of the asset might be in the future, how long the asset will stay in the plan on a tax-deferred basis, and most importantly, what tax bracket the investor will be in when they take the taxable distribution in the future. The best advice is for retail investors to consult with their financial planner or tax advisor on this issue.

Investors should maintain a tax hierarchy of securities that they own so that they can constantly evaluate the tax-efficiency of their investments and own them in the appropriate accounts. Investors, who have the same asset allocation in each of their accounts, where some of them are tax-qualified and some are not, should reevaluate the location of the securities that they own. They may have to consider a "swap and switch," which means that they sell a security in an IRA account in order to repurchase it in a taxable brokerage account, and then sell a security in the brokerage account in order to make room for the IRA asset, and repurchase it in their IRA account. Even if the sale in the brokerage account results in realizing a capital gain, it may be a good tax strategy for the long-term.

## Summary

One of the big objections to active portfolio management is that it can result in realizing more capital gains taxes than the passive strategy of buying and holding securities. Strategic investors, who have little opportunity to add value in strategically managed, buy and hold portfolios, must cling to the benefits of diversification, rebalancing, reducing portfolio expenses, and reducing portfolio taxes, as their means of adding value. In this context, it is no wonder that strategic, buy and hold investors are tax-phobic.

However, as we have seen, there is much truth to the old saying about not letting the tax tail wag the investment dog. The data amply prove that the benefits of actively managing portfolios far outweigh any drawbacks having to do with the cost of the resulting taxes. While prudent investors should take all of the appropriate steps to reduce their tax liabilities, we have attempted to show that most of the available tax planning techniques ultimately involve tax deferral, and that the benefits of tax deferral are surprising small relative to the risks of passively owning securities. If investors ultimately want to be able to spend their money during their lifetime, then capital gains will be realized and taxes will be paid. Investors should choose their investment strategy based on the one that will ultimately result in accumulating the most assets. In most market environments that means actively managing portfolios to take advantage of value opportunities as they present themselves throughout the market cycle.

# 15 DECISIONS, DECISIONS, DECISIONS

nvestors who have managed to make it this far in the book should now have a working knowledge of the fundamental problems with buy and hold investing, as well as the rationale for active management and the basic tools and techniques for actively and tactically managing a portfolio. The final steps, dear reader, are up to you. Only you can answer the subtle and not so subtle questions that must be addressed before implementing an active management strategy. There are no correct responses to the questions I am about to pose and without a doubt active investors will disagree about their answers. Any investment approach will be based on an investor's own beliefs and experiences, and is uniquely their own. The "art" of money management makes it personal and the "science" of money management should make it repeatable. In the end, the only way to develop a high conviction in your specific investment process is to put brush to canvas and begin.

Investors who wish to actively manage their portfolios must answer six important questions:

1. What types of securities will you use to invest the portfolio?
2. Will you use alternative investments?
3. How will you choose your benchmark?
4. How far will you deviate from your benchmark? (Absolute versus relative return investing.)
5. What is your investment time horizon?
6. Will you use passive or active managers to invest each asset class?

Before we answer these questions, we need to compare and contrast our mission as portfolio managers from that of money managers. As we will see, there are some crucial differences between the two job descriptions. Portfolio management is the process of constructing multiple asset class portfolios. This is distinctly different from money managers, who specialize in managing one asset class. Portfolio managers must engage in all of the issues that we have covered in this book, including deciding what asset classes to own in a portfolio, whether to be strategic or tactical in their ownership of asset classes, whether to be passive or active in their investment of asset classes, and what types of securities to use to invest in asset classes. Virtually all financial advisors in the life insurance, brokerage, and independent financial planner industry fall into the category of portfolio manager versus money manager.

Money managers, on the other hand, are professionals whom portfolio managers "hire" to manage specific asset classes in their portfolio by investing in managed funds. Money managers are typically experts at investing in one particular asset class. They also typically specialize in only one specific investment style. You can find money managers to invest virtually all of the institutionally accepted asset classes, including all of the U.S. equity categories found in the Morningstar Style Boxes, all of the developed and emerging international markets, and all of the various categories of fixed income, from high quality U.S. Treasury and Agency securities to junk bonds to emerging market debt. In addition, today you can also find money managers that invest in "alternative" investment strategies, such as commodities, international real estate, hedge funds, and more.

Money managers generally manage two different types of managed funds: mutual funds and separate accounts. In many cases financial advisors, in their role as portfolio managers, "sell" their services by claiming that the particular mutual fund or separate account money managers whom they utilize to invest their portfolios are "better" than those used by their competitors.

Readers of this book who are interested in actively managing their portfolio must focus on building a diversified, multi-asset-class portfolio to meet their specific financial goals and objectives—which brings us to that list of questions that only you can answer.

## What Type of Securities Will You Use to Invest Your Portfolio?

Today investors have a wide array of choices to invest the asset classes in an actively managed portfolio. Popular choices include mutual funds, ETFs (exchange traded funds), separate accounts, variable annuities, and of course, individual bonds and stocks. While each of these has its own benefits and drawbacks, the choice that is often the most problematic for portfolio managers is in individual stocks. Here's why.

Typically, portfolio managers who build multiple asset class portfolios choose not to exclusively use individual stocks to invest the equity allocation of their portfolio. The reason for this has little to do with whether or not stock picking is better or worse than owning industries, sectors, or general asset classes, like large growth or large value, in mutual funds, separate accounts, or ETFs. In fact, several studies (including the Active Share study discussed in Chapter 7) show that small, concentrated, professionally managed portfolios of individual stocks do consistently deliver benchmark-beating returns. The reason that many portfolio managers avoid individual stocks is that mathematically they make it virtually impossible to properly diversify a portfolio and they make it very difficult to actively manage a portfolio at the asset class level. To get a better look at this, let's consider a typical $1 million portfolio and do the math.

First, let's assume that we have a typical balanced allocation of 60% in equities and 40% in fixed income, with our 60% equity exposure divided into 40% U.S. stocks and 20% international stocks (i.e., $400,000 U.S. and $200,000 international). Next, let's divide the U.S. equity allocation into a rough approximation of the stock market by market capitalization, and agree to own 70% of the U.S. allocation in large-cap stocks, 20% in mid-cap stocks, and 10% in small-cap stocks. In addition, we will further equally diversify the allocations by investment style into value stocks and growth stocks. Based on a $1 million account, our U.S. equity allocation would appear as shown in **Table 15.1**.

| ASSET ALLOCATION | $ ALLOCATION | # SECURITIES | $ PER HOLDING |
|---|---|---|---|
| **Large-Growth** | $140,000 | 15 | $9,300 |
| **Large-Value** | $140,000 | 15 | $9,300 |
| **Mid-Growth** | $40,000 | 20 | $2,000 |
| **Mid-Value** | $40,000 | 20 | $2,000 |
| **Small-Growth** | $20,000 | 30 | $666 |
| **Small-Value** | $20,000 | 30 | $666 |
| **Totals** | $400,000 | 130 | |

**Table 15.1—U.S. Portfolio Holdings**
Source: Pinnacle Advisory Group, Inc.

There are several obvious problems with this approach. The first and most obvious challenge is that we would need the knowledge and experience to pick stocks in each of these asset classes. Presumably, the companies in each style category have many characteristics that are different from each other, which is of course why we consider them in different style categories in the first place. We would potentially need substantial additional analytical resources to cover all of these asset classes properly. A second major problem is the sheer number of stocks in this part of the portfolio. In this case, the chart includes a conservative estimate of the number of stocks that institutional money managers would say are needed to properly diversify a portfolio in each of these style categories. Once again, we would need to allocate a significant amount of resources to properly cover this many stocks in the portfolio. And this is just our U.S. equity allocation. If we were to include picking stocks for the international allocation, the number of stocks would dramatically increase, including selecting a large number of individual holdings in Europe, Japan, and a variety of emerging markets in India, Asia, and Latin America.

Another problem with our portfolio is the cost of the transactions needed to actively manage it. Remember, as active managers we are constantly looking for value opportunities to present themselves that will require changes to our portfolio construction. For example, if we want to sell 5% of the U.S. small-value position in order to rotate the portfolio to large-growth, how many transactions would be required? Given a pro-rata approach to each allocation of the portfolio, we might need 30 sells and 15 buys to execute this one trade. At $9 per trade, that's $405 just for one change in portfolio construction. It is easy to see how this could add up to a lot of dollars by year-end if we actively manage the portfolio. The worst case is to feel restricted in the tactical changes you want to make to your portfolio due to a lack of flexibility and the cost of investing in individual issues.

For these reasons, many portfolio managers stick to managed funds, ETFs, and separate accounts when investing the equity allocations of their portfolios. (Remember that portfolio managers are distinctly different from money managers who typically specialize in owning the individual stocks.) Some investors will buy a few individual large-cap stocks for the portfolio in order to attempt to add value based on their stock picking skills. These investors feel that since the remainder of the equity allocation is already properly diversified by owning funds or ETFs, there is no diversification problem due to "cherry picking" a few individual stocks for the portfolio. Others will invest the large-cap U.S. allocation with individual stocks as a core allocation and use managed accounts for the mid-cap and small-cap allocations.

A second choice for investing the portfolio that deserves special attention is the use of separate accounts, or "wrap accounts" as they are known in the industry, to invest a tactical, actively managed portfolio. (These are called wrap accounts because the advisory fees, management fees, and trading costs are all "wrapped" into one fee for the retail investor.) Some financial advisors actively sell the benefits of separate account management as the unique value proposition of their firm. Separate accounts can seem more sophisticated than mutual funds, if for no other reason than mutual funds are so widely available to investors due to their low investment minimums.

Separate account managers generally come in two different flavors for investors. The first type of separate account manager is found on a menu of managers that choose to serve the retail market using the separate account model. The menus are offered by many different stockbrokers, insurance broker-dealers, and independent custodians, all of which want to serve the wrap-fee market of affluent investors. The fees for these managers tend to be pre-negotiated and the investment story for the managers is packed in a glossy, highly professional marketing kit.

The second type of separate account manager is not usually found in a prepackaged menu of managers. They typically are willing to custody money on different independent platforms, which makes them available to a variety of investment advisors. Advisors must search for these managers using independent databases typically used by institutional pension investors, or through other sources provided by custodians and broker-dealers. The fees for these managers are negotiable, and the money management firms in this group are often smaller and more eclectic in their approach to style than the larger and more well-known separate account firms. As a practical matter, both types of separate account managers offer similar benefits to investors, including:

**Separate accounts are transparent.** Because the individual holdings of separate accounts are owned in the investor's personal account, investors can see the securities currently held in the portfolio as opposed to mutual funds where the information about individual fund holdings are unavailable until after the publication of the annual or semi-annual mutual fund report.

**Separate accounts offer lower fees** for higher investment amounts than the average mutual fund. For super-wealthy investors who may invest $1 million or more in each asset class of their portfolio, the fee savings can be significant. However, for typical wrap account investors who allocate $100,000 to $200,000 to each separate account manager, care should be taken to check the actual value of lower fees. The fee differential is often not that significant at lower investment amounts, especially when comparing fees to some of the lower-cost mutual fund choices and ETFs.

**Separate accounts allow for better tax management** than mutual funds. Mutual funds cannot pass-through losses to investors and can only use tax losses at the fund level to offset gains. On the other hand, clients actually own the individual holdings of a separate account in their portfolios and can use tax losses to minimize their taxes. In addition, mutual funds are inflexible in requiring investors to choose one method for fund accounting, which could be average cost, FIFO (first-in, first-out), or specific lot accounting, when they do their tax planning.

Although separate accounts are much simpler and transparent to deal with from a tax perspective, there are some practical drawbacks to doing tax planning with separate accounts. The separate account manager, who typically has thousands of accounts set up for retail investors, manages separate accounts to a portfolio model. They (the separate account managers) are not eager to take a small "retail" account off of their investment model. They may strongly argue that the investment merits of the sale don't make sense, even if the tax benefits do. For example, the simple transaction of realizing a tax loss and repurchasing a substantially similar security that qualifies for the wash sale rules, and then buying back the original security after 31 days, can be very difficult to execute depending on the firm providing the separate accounts. Keep in mind that a single position in a $100,000 separate account with 50 stocks could be less than $2,000. If the position is currently trading at $1,500, how much time and attention will this potential realized loss of $500 actually receive from the advisor and the wrap account manager?

Finally, portfolio managers may find that even though separate accounts have the potential to be more tax-efficient than funds, they are much less nimble in terms of how they are owned in a portfolio. It is typically not easy to quickly add or trim positions in separate accounts in the tactical management of a portfolio. If a separate account manager owns 70 different stocks in their portfolio model and you want to sell 5% of the account in order to change your portfolio construction, the manager is faced with either selling 5% of every stock in the portfolio (70 transactions) if they want to stay on their investment model, or trying to figure out which securities in the current portfolio to sell outright.

For tactical investors these discussions can be frustrating. However, separate accounts can work very well for strategic portfolio managers who tend to buy and hold asset classes for many years. In this case, the issue of trimming or adding to separate accounts only comes up in the context of rebalancing the portfolio, and that can be managed more easily than tactically reallocating the funds. From the point of view of active managers, who put a premium on liquidity and flexibility, wrap accounts can be problematic.

## Will You Use Alternative Investments?

Alternative investments are typically considered to be investments in asset classes that have low correlations to the traditional asset classes of stocks and bonds. For strategic investors who rely on diversification as their only risk management technique beyond the choice of portfolio policy, the rise in popularity of alternatives investments has been timely. They can presumably rely on these new alternative asset classes to deliver the kind of diversification and additional returns needed to buoy the portfolio in difficult markets when traditional asset classes like stocks and bonds cannot. Many of the large endowment funds, like Yale and Harvard, have popularized the alternative investment asset class due to the fact that they have invested more than half of their portfolios in the alternative space, including hedge funds and private equity, with spectacular results over the past decade.

Perhaps the most well-known alternative asset classes are real estate and commodities, both of which offer long-term investors some degree of portfolio diversification. However, with the advent of hedge funds and private equity, there are now a bewildering number of choices in the alternative investment space that offer the promise of high returns and low correlations to stocks and bonds. Specifically, investors can now invest in a wide variety of hedge fund strategies in a mutual fund or exchange traded note format where the investment minimums are very low, the holding is liquid, is held on a custodian's platform and is priced daily, and the fees are reasonable. Long-short, market-neutral, convertible arbitrage, distressed securities, hedge fund of funds, as well as other well-known hedge strategies can now be utilized in investor portfolios using mutual funds and exchange traded notes.

Another recent trend has been the use of structured notes to creatively invest in selectively targeted specific underlying indexes or investment themes. These securities are called structured notes because the underlying investment is literally in the form of a note backed by an investment bank. The note is typically not liquid and matures on a specific date in the future. Structured notes typically use derivatives and swap arrangements with counterparties to match the returns of underlying asset classes or specific investment themes. For example, a note could be structured that earns a positive return to investors if the yield curve inverts or steepens. Or, a note can deliver returns based on the divergence of performance of different currencies. Today a popular category of notes offers principal protection to investors. The note terms deliver a fractional share of the upside of a particular stock index, in exchange for a guarantee of principal if the note is held to maturity. In fact, the main limitation to the construction of these notes is often the creativity and imagination of the investor, as well as the liquidity and optionality of the underlying indexes used to structure the note.

However, tactical and active investors need to be very careful when considering the use of alternative investments, and in the current market environment they need to be especially careful when considering the use of hedge fund strategies or structured notes in their actively managed portfolios. From a tactical perspective, investors should realize that traditional alternative investments like commodities and real estate have been highly correlated to the stock market since the bottom of the bear market in 2002. Highly stimulative fiscal and monetary policies have created conditions where the prices for stocks, bonds, real estate, and commodities were all supported by excessive liquidity, which fueled global growth. Now that this asset bubble is bursting, investors are finding that commodities and real estate positions are collapsing along with global equity positions. The question for tactical investors is whether or not to buy and hold alternatives in the same manner as strategic investors, or whether they will trade them along with other investments in the portfolio as they change their views about the market cycle.

As this is written, many hedge funds are collapsing due to a lack of liquidity because their assets are frozen due to the bankruptcy of Lehman Brothers. The cascading selling in the hedge fund space has created a situation where the underlying arbitrage models for a variety of hedge fund strategies do not work, and the losses are significant for investors who thought that the hedge fund portfolio was actually "hedged." In addition, the limited "window" that hedge fund investors have to liquidate their positions is causing additional stress because the funds no longer have access to lines of credit needed to cash out frightened investors. The discovery of the extent of the exposure of hedge funds to systematic market risk is a relatively new development, and active portfolio managers may want to consider using more traditional hedges, like cash and bonds, when they want to reduce the equity exposure of their portfolio. Even if the hedge fund space recovers, active and tactical investors will still have to decide if they want to buy and hold these types of funds while actively managing the rest of the portfolio.

Finally, structured notes, which have been offered to investors by investment banks, are also currently problematic for investors. The guarantee of the note itself is only as good as the credit rating of the bank creating it. A further problem for the notes is the counterparty risk of the underlying swap agreements that are often used to create the note's return. Once again there is now an element of systematic risk that investors must be aware of if they want to take advantage of the creativity offered by the note structure. The very nature of structured notes makes them illiquid in nature, and active portfolio managers should be careful in how they utilize these securities in their portfolio. Active managers who want to invest in structured notes might consider using them as a core position within their overall alternative investment allocation, and then actively manage other segments of the portfolio.

## How Will You Choose Your Benchmark?

This subtle question is vitally important for active and tactical managers. To the extent that they are asked to "prove" that they are adding value or alpha due to the implementation of a tactical portfolio strategy, the choice of passive benchmark that is used for comparison purposes becomes critically important. Ironically, there is little science to support the choice of a benchmark for an actively managed portfolio. The situation is completely different for money managers who typically manage a style-specific portfolio that is designed to invest in only one asset class.

For them, the choice of a benchmark is relatively easy and is usually not subject to any controversy. For example, a small-cap value manager can choose to either benchmark to one of many general small-cap indexes like the Russell 2000 small-cap stock index, or one of several small-cap value indexes. But for a portfolio manager the benchmark choice is completely arbitrary. How should professional and non-professional portfolio managers go about making such an all-important decision?

There are many questions that must be considered when constructing the benchmark for a diversified portfolio. Some questions for investors include:

- Should the benchmark portfolio be globally diversified? If so, should you use a global index or a mix of U.S. and international indexes? Should the mix be a market weight of U.S. and international stocks (the U.S. is currently about 40% of the world's market capitalization), or should it reflect a more U.S.-centric weighting of U.S. stocks? For non-U.S. investors, their benchmark will probably reflect their own country-centric view of the global markets.
- What U.S. equity index should be chosen? For example, should the benchmark include large and small U.S. stocks, or is it OK to just show large U.S. due to their large capitalization weighting in the total U.S. stock market? Perhaps a comprehensive index of the entire stock market, like the Russell 3000 Index, is most appropriate.
- What fixed income proxy should be used in the benchmark and what should be its duration and credit exposure? Should you include international bonds in the benchmark?
- Should you include alternative investments like real estate or commodities in your benchmark? If so, how do you change the percentage allocation to stocks and bonds in the benchmark to accommodate them?
- Should the benchmark be constructed for simplicity so that investors and retail clients can better understand it, or should it be complex to better represent the variety of asset classes available in today's global market place?

Interestingly, the construction of the benchmark may ultimately say more about the motivations of the investor constructing the benchmark than it does about the active portfolio strategy that investors are trying to measure. Pinnacle Advisory Group recently completed a study of benchmark construction to better understand the implications of constructing a benchmark. With the help of Ned Davis Research, we created four institutional quality benchmark portfolios. Each of them had different qualities that could be considered favorable for the purpose of using them to evaluate the returns of professionally managed accounts. We then back-tested the performance of the benchmark portfolios for a period of twenty years and divided the performance into individual 4-year periods. We analyzed the performance of the benchmark portfolios for each of the individual time periods as well as the total time period. Our goal was to see which of the benchmark portfolios had the highest return for each period. High returns are considered to be the "worst" for active managers because it is more difficult to beat the passive benchmark return with actual portfolio performance. In this context, the "best" benchmark is the benchmark with the lowest return, consequently making investment performance comparisons easier for active managers.

We chose 4 year return periods because we felt that 4 years was the longest possible period that sophisticated investors would allow their advisor to trail a reasonable institutional quality benchmark. (It is notable that many advisors would maintain that the 4-year period is much longer than the average investor would allow them to trail the returns of the portfolio benchmark.) It is also important to note that professional investor returns are reduced by management fees and trading expenses, both of which are avoided when owning the benchmark portfolio. We used four arbitrary benchmark portfolios for our study:

1. 60% S&P 500 Index, 30% Barclays Capital US Aggregate Bond Index, 10% T-Bills
2. 10% Russell 2000, 12% EAFE, 38% S&P 500 Index, 30% Barclays Capital US Aggregate Bond Index, 10% T-Bills
3. 60% MSCI World Index, 20% Barclays Capital US Aggregate Bond Index, 10% CRB Commodities, 10% REITS
4. 20% S&P 500, 20% MSCI World, 10% Mid-Cap, 10% Small-cap, 40% Global Bond

The first benchmark portfolio is the simplest of the four because it is constructed using only three asset classes, stocks, bonds, and cash. The obvious issue with this particular benchmark is that it is U.S.-centric and does not own any international asset classes. If the actual managed portfolio was constructed in a manner that included an allocation to international securities and the international stocks subsequently outperformed the U.S. stock market, the portfolio manager would have earned positive alpha. If the international securities underperformed, then the manager would have negative alpha.[52]

The second benchmark portfolio is less U.S.-centric since it contains a 12% allocation to the EAFE Index of international stocks. It also divides the U.S. stock market by market capitalization, with 38% of the portfolio in U.S. large-

---

52 Readers might recall that alpha is the amount of risk-adjusted return a portfolio manager earns above the expected benchmark return.

capitalization stocks (S&P 500 Index) and 10% in U.S. small-capitalization stocks (Russell 2000 Index.) The fixed income benchmarks are the same as in the first benchmark portfolio, and they are invested in U.S. bonds and cash.

The third benchmark portfolio is conspicuous due to its global theme. The equity allocation is 60% MSCI world index, which includes the U.S., but is obviously not U.S.-centric. However, the fixed income benchmark remains U.S.-centric since the Lehman Aggregate Bond Index is constructed using U.S. bonds. This benchmark adds 10% in each of two "hot" institutional asset classes that, until recently, have been performing well over the past several years. These asset classes are commodities and real estate investment trusts.

The fourth benchmark portfolio makes several subtle changes to the preceding benchmarks. The large-cap allocation of the benchmark is split 50-50 between the U.S. and global stocks. We added a position in U.S. mid-cap stocks, which have performed relatively well over the past ten years, as well the U.S. small-cap position. However, we changed the fixed income benchmark in this portfolio to be a global index rather than a U.S. index.

The following charts (**Figures 15.1 through 15.6**) show the performance of each of the 4 benchmark portfolios as well as their standard deviation (volatility) for the five distinct 4 year periods that we studied, as well as for the entire period beginning in 1986 and ending in 2006.

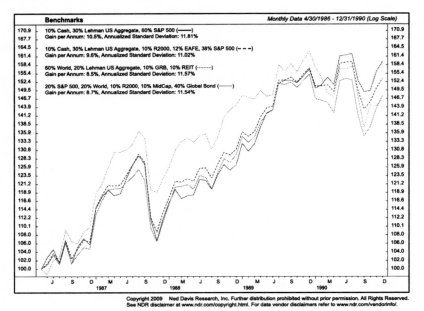

**Figure 15.1**

Ned Davis Research

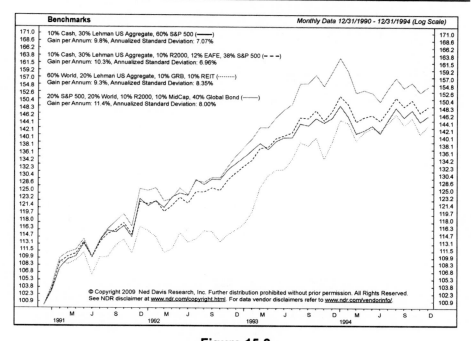

**Figure 15.2**

Source: Ned Davis Research

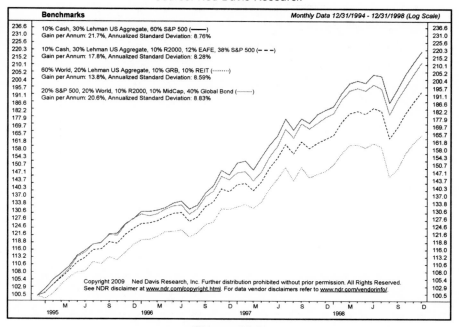

**Figure 15.3**

Source: Ned Davis Research

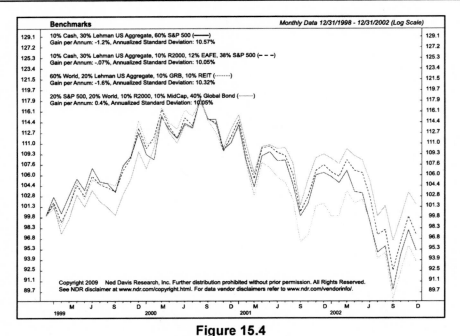

**Figure 15.4**

Source: Ned Davis Research

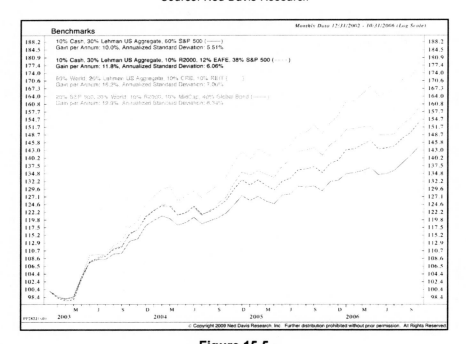

**Figure 15.5**

Source: Ned Davis Research

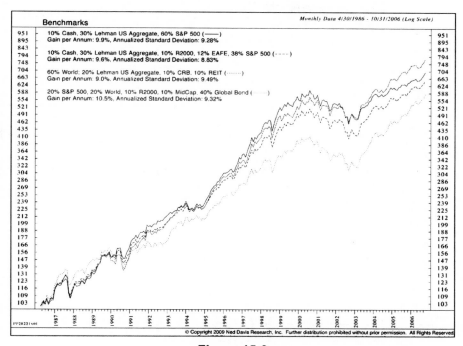

**Figure 15.6**
Source: Ned Davis Research

The study reveals a surprising amount of variability in the performance of the different benchmark portfolios over relatively short 4-year time frames, even though the annualized total return of the benchmark portfolios was similar for the entire twenty-year period. For the entire period, the difference between the best and worst performing benchmark portfolio was only 1.5% per year. The difference between the highest and lowest standard deviation for the entire 20-year period was only 0.66 per year. Based on these results, we made the following observations:

1. There was at least a 2% annualized difference in return between the best and worst performing benchmark portfolio for each four-year period, which is significant. We consider a 2% "miss" to be a matter of concern in our internal evaluation of portfolio performance. This occurred despite the fact that the difference between the best and worst annualized return for the entire cumulative time period was only 1.5%

2. If a professional portfolio manager hypothetically invested their portfolio so that they strictly bought and held the same asset classes as the worst-performing benchmark portfolio for each four-year period, at a minimum

| | BENCHMARK 1 | BENCHMARK 2 | BENCHMARK 3 | BENCHMARK 4 | BEST TO WORST |
|---|---|---|---|---|---|
| **1986-1990** | | | | | |
| Annual Return % | 10.5 | 9.6 | 8.5 | 8.7 | 2 |
| St. Deviation | 11.81 | 11.02 | 11.57 | 11.54 | 0.79 |
| **1990-1994** | | | | | |
| Annual Return % | 9.8 | 10.3 | 9.3 | 11.4 | 2.1 |
| St. Deviation | 7.07 | 6.96 | 8.35 | 8 | 1.39 |
| **1994-1998** | | | | | |
| Annual Return % | 21.7 | 17.8 | 13.8 | 20.6 | 7.9 |
| St. Deviation | 8.76 | 8.28 | 8.59 | 8.83 | 0.55 |
| **1998-2002** | | | | | |
| Annual Return % | -1.2 | -0.7 | -1.6 | 0.4 | 2 |
| St. Deviation | 10.57 | 10.05 | 10.32 | 10.05 | 0.52 |
| **2002-2006** | | | | | |
| Annual Return % | 10 | 11.8 | 16.2 | 12.9 | 6.2 |
| St. Deviation | 5.51 | 6.06 | 7 | 6.34 | 1.49 |
| **1986 - 2006** | | | | | |
| Annual Return % | 9.9 | 9.6 | 9 | 10.5 | 1.5 |
| St. Deviation | 9.28 | 8.83 | 9.49 | 9.32 | 0.66 |

### Table 15.2—Benchmark Comparisons
Source: Pinnacle Advisory Group, Inc.

they would have trailed the best benchmark by 3% annually in each time period, after adjusting for a 1% annual management fee. The worst spread in returns, net of fees, would have been an unacceptable 8.9% per year during the 1994-1998 period. If an investor who believed in passive strategic investing happened to buy and hold Benchmark 3 during that particular period, the negative relative performance compared to Benchmark 1 could not be attributed to poor active management decisions. *Instead the performance would correctly be attributable to either passively owning the wrong strategic portfolio, or comparing to the "wrong" or best-performing benchmark.*

Active portfolio managers are often asked to prove that they can actually add to portfolio returns through tactical or active management strategies. Our study revealed that if the answer to the question depends on comparing the returns of an actively managed globally diversified portfolio to the returns of a passively constructed benchmark portfolio, then the answer may have little to do with active management strategies at all, and everything to do with the choice of benchmark.

The most ardent, buy and hold, strategic investor could choose to own any one of these benchmark portfolios by buying the indexes in the benchmark, which will minimize fees and taxes for the investor. If after 4 years of underperformance our hypothetical strategic investor changed to a different passive portfolio construction that matched another of our benchmark portfolios, and if they owned the "wrong" passive portfolio, they would have trailed the benchmark (if they were unlucky enough to have chosen the best-performing benchmark) by as little as 3% per year over a 4-year period and by as much as 8% per year. It would be asking a lot of a typical investor to accept that amount of persistent underperformance over time.

In reviewing the results of the study, it is obvious that choosing the "correct" benchmark is an arbitrary process for active managers with diversified portfolios, and that the choice of benchmark will have a dramatic impact on whether or not the active manager is considered to earn positive alpha. Ironically, the benchmark decision also impacts strategic investors in exactly the same way, with catastrophic results if they choose the "wrong" benchmark. So much for taking on additional business risk if professional investors choose active management. It appears that strategic investors have the same risk when it comes to relative benchmark performance. For consumers of investment advisory services, they must learn to beware. While comparing a managed portfolio to a fixed benchmark seems to be the right thing to do for a concerned and discerning consumer, it may not tell them as much as they might think about the probable performance of an active manager in the future.

## How Far Will You Deviate From Your Benchmark?

The choice of benchmark is inextricably linked to a decision about what the benchmark return ultimately means to the investor. It would be nice to wave our magic wand and have all investors focus on portfolio tactics and strategy instead of past returns, but I'm afraid that rational people who are trying to be good consumers of portfolio management services will always require some kind of benchmark performance comparison. Active managers being held to a skeptical standard of performance that demands that they "prove" their performance versus benchmark returns will be heavily incentivized not to stray too far from the benchmark allocations in their managed account. Trailing the benchmark for an extended period of time will be considered to be a business risk by professional investors who must publish performance results for clients. (Ironically, delivering negative absolute returns due to strategically buying and holding the market is considered to be free of business risk, a somewhat amazing state of affairs considering the length of the current secular bear market.) For individual investors, trailing the benchmark will at least cause them to question the active management tactics and strategy that they are employing.

Another important question raised by employing benchmarks to evaluate performance is the question of absolute versus relative performance. Let's assume the investor has properly concluded that a severe bear market lies just ahead, and the proper tactical response is to reduce the equity exposure of the portfolio and add to the fixed income allocation. If we assume that the investor has a balanced portfolio policy and the benchmark equity allocation is 60% of the portfolio to stocks and 40% to fixed income, then what is the proper response in terms of asset allocation, assuming that the investor has high conviction in the market outlook? By reducing equity exposure by 10%, to a total equity exposure of 50% versus the benchmark weighting of 60%, the investor can be assured that the portfolio should outperform the benchmark portfolio on a relative basis. In addition, the relatively small adjustment in total equity assures that the investor can't be too wrong in their market outlook because they retain a 50% exposure to the stock market.

However, the portfolio will still decline dramatically in value in absolute terms, and the investor will still experience losses in portfolio value that could have been mitigated with a more aggressive tactical strategy. Given that the investor had high conviction in the market outlook, they could have reduced the equity exposure of the portfolio to 20% (or less) from 60%. This dramatic reduction would have a major impact on absolute portfolio declines in a bear market, and if the investor is correct in the market outlook, the result will be a dramatic protection of capital in a significant market decline. In this case the investor wins both relatively compared to the benchmark, and absolutely in terms of total return. Of course, the risk of this strategy is that the investor can make a mistake in the market outlook causing him or her to miss a dramatic market rally due to an extreme asset allocation call in the wrong direction.

For most active managers, there is no worse kind of decision regret than making the correct macroeconomic call about market direction, but not investing the theme with enough conviction to gain all of the benefits of being correct.

On the other hand, wisdom comes in the form of recognizing that all investors will eventually be wrong, and making a very large tactical adjustment versus a benchmark can create business risk for professional investors, and return risk for all investors. Investors with a background in strategic investing are probably more likely to choose the more moderate portfolio asset allocation adjustments, and investors who do not have a similar background may choose to be more aggressive in their willingness to deviate from benchmark allocations. We leave it to the reader to decide which is best.

## What is Your Investment Time Horizon?

Depending on the tactical strategy being employed, and the choice that is made between absolute and relative returns, being an active and tactical portfolio manager can lead to having shorter investment time horizons. The impact of shortening the investment time horizon can be dramatic, and has an impact on virtually every aspect of the investment process, including what techniques are used to identify value, how often you evaluate performance, the amount of transactions and taxes that are generated due to the management tactics being utilized, and more.

Tactical investors can generally divide the time horizon for different active management techniques as follows:

| Technique | Time Horizon |
|---|---|
| Valuation-based | Long-Term (5-10 years or longer) |
| Fundamentals-based | Intermediate Term (1-7 years) |
| Technical Analysis-based | Very Short-Term (day-trading and longer) |

We discussed valuation techniques in some detail in Chapter 9 and concluded that valuation is a difficult methodology to use if the investor is concerned about short-term timing considerations. However, we have also seen that valuation has an impeccable record of forecasting future market performance over long time periods. In our example we studied the relationship between P/E multiples derived by using trailing 10 years of normalized earnings to subsequent 20-year S&P 500 returns and found that they led to highly accurate long-term return forecasts. On a less academic basis, in late 2008 Warren Buffett publicly announced that he was buying stocks in his personal account, based on finding value in stocks using a long-term ten-year time period. As of this writing, the short-term timing of these transactions doesn't appear to be immediately rewarding.

In either case, investors will be challenged to be patient enough to allow values to materialize over such a long period of time. As I have stated in earlier chapters, professional investment advisors will find their role is to manage client expectations more than changing portfolio allocations with such a long time horizon. Individual investors will also be challenged to "look through" current market volatility and portfolio declines that could take years to materialize, in order to actually be rewarded for this type of value investing. With the greatest respect to Mr. Buffett, this kind of patience is very hard to find.

It is worth noting that many professional investors do use valuation to make short-term asset allocation adjustments to their portfolio. Changes in earnings expectations can drive market performance during earnings season, and forward P/E multiples are quoted by traders with short-term investment time horizons. However, tactical investors with short-term time horizons should use these valuation techniques with caution and in combination with other techniques that we have already discussed in earlier chapters.

Changing portfolio construction using market fundamentals to determine where we are in the market cycle was discussed in detail in Chapters 10 and 11. The market cycle in the post-WWII period has typically lasted between 2 and 8 years with the longer cycles occurring during the last 30 years. The current decade is characterized by a 2-year bear market that lasted from 2000 to 2002, followed by a 5-year bull market from late 2002 to 2007, followed by the current bear market that began in October of 2007 and continues as of this writing. The longer time frame required to invest cyclical bull and bear markets allows the investor to comfortably rotate capital among sectors and industries, as well as countries. It also allows for changes in the fixed income portion of the portfolio as the investor adjusts the duration and credit of the bond portfolio to meet changing economic conditions. Fundamental-based investing typically is less stressful than using technical analysis techniques that require daily and weekly portfolio decisions.

The problem with using fundamentals to tactically change portfolio construction is that the market is likely to move in either direction well in advance of changes in economic fundamentals. The fundamental indicators that were listed in Chapter 10 are all "leading indicators" that presumably lead changes in the economy. However, the stock market is itself a leading indicator. Investors who insist on waiting for changes to appear in fundamental indicators must be willing to give up possibly significant market advances at the beginning of each cyclical bull market in exchange for greater certainty that they will not be drawn into the classic money-losing strategy of "buying the dips" in the stock market during a bear market.

On the other hand, focusing on fundamentals can provide investors with insights into changing economic conditions that will allow them to change portfolio construction well in advance of bear market declines, significantly preserving investor capital. In either case, investors must be prepared to appear "wrong" in their assessment of the market cycle over short periods of time. However, changing portfolio tactics based on fundamentals allows for significantly better timing decisions than relying on valuation indicators alone.

Investors who want to be immediately rewarded for correct market forecasts should utilize technical analysis to change portfolio construction. In today's record-breaking volatile markets, many active managers are relying on sentiment indicators like put-call ratios and the VIX Index of option volatility to help guide them in changing portfolio construction. The "extremely oversold" condition of the markets is determined by measuring the market price compared to various price moving averages, as well as by measuring the number of stocks trading above their 200-day moving average, and market breadth indicators like the number of stocks making new highs and new lows. There are too many technical analysis techniques to be mentioned here, but all of them can be used by active and tactical investors in their investment process.

The problem with using technical analysis techniques is that many of them tend to shrink the decision-making process to very short time periods. Analysts try to catch market trends that may last weeks or months, instead of years. Many of the indicators may work well for short periods of time, but then stop working at all leaving active portfolio managers on the wrong side of significant market moves. The benefit of technical analysis is that it promises investors that they can be "less wrong" in the very short-term, because the various techniques can capture very short-term changes in market direction. The difficulty is that having such a short-term investment time horizon requires extreme diligence regarding changing market conditions, and it requires that the investor make a lot of correct decisions over short periods of time. Both of these requirements can be very difficult to meet.

Some technical indicators can be utilized as part of a longer-term tactical approach. For example, an investor can add a simple criterion to their investment tactics that says that they will overweight the stock allocation of a portfolio when the S&P 500 Index trades above its 200-day moving average, and they will underweight stocks when the index trades below the 200-day moving average. If implemented, this simple rule should not result in undue stress or a high number of portfolio transactions. (Strategies like this leave an investor open to being "whip sawed" if the index oscillates above and below the average, throwing off numerous trading signals forcing the investor to continually trade in and out of the market. The other problem is that as the market trades to an overbought or oversold extreme, the requirement for the market to trade back to the moving average before adjusting the equity allocation can result in losing significant returns.)

On the other hand, sentiment indicators can be notoriously volatile and fickle. Trying to trade short-term changes in investor sentiment like the VIX, put-call and others, can result in a high volume of trading activity, and a lot of lost sleep. Once again, investors have to balance the amount of time they are willing to be "wrong" about market direction over relatively short periods of time with the amount of effort they are willing to expend changing their portfolio construction.

## Should I Use Passive or Active Managers to Invest Each Asset Class?

This is the traditional question that academics and strategic investors have been trying to answer since Bill Sharpe published the CAPM model. For strategic investors, the answer is full of hidden meaning about whether or not markets are efficient, and whether capitalization-weighted indexes really represent the best methodology to measure market returns. However, for active and tactical managers, these points are mute. They fully understand that markets are not efficient and that the CAPM model is based on such poor assumptions that it is virtually worthless as an investment tool in the real world of portfolio management. Hopefully by now the reader agrees that portfolio asset allocations should be adjusted to meet changing market conditions, and the question of strategically owning asset classes at the portfolio level has been answered to their satisfaction.

The question remains, however, whether or not an active and tactical manager should invest each asset class using passive investments like index mutual funds or ETFs, or instead use actively managed funds like no-load mutual funds or separate accounts to invest each asset class. In making the decision, investors should weigh a variety of considerations.

**Sector Rotation:** If the investor is comfortable with their market forecast and wants to pursue a strategy of sector rotation in actively managing the portfolio, then they will find that using active managers is very difficult. Obviously the managers themselves will make their own sector calls, and the structure of mutual funds makes it difficult to know the holdings of the funds in "real time." On the other hand, there is a large variety of sector specific ETFs and index mutual funds that will allow the investor to pursue a sector rotation strategy with complete confidence about what they actually own in the portfolio.

**Lack of Research:** There are many asset classes that demand a level of expertise that the typical investor or financial advisor will simply not be able to obtain. A typical example includes investing in international markets where the coverage of market sectors by country is either unavailable or too overwhelming in scope to be properly evaluated by investors with limited resources. A variety of fixed income markets also offer similar challenges. A tactical investor may be more comfortable choosing an active manager to invest in the junk bond asset class even though there are several ETF choices available to index that particular market. The same could be said for international fixed income investing, where active managers may be able to find value in inefficient markets and earn returns above the ETF or index returns.

In short, active managers must choose how to best use their research dollars and time to implement a tactical portfolio strategy. There will typically be asset classes in the portfolio that are simply too extensive, or too expensive, to manage tactically in-house. In these cases, choosing an active manager to invest in the asset class makes sense.

**Expenses and Taxes:** There is a difference in cost between utilizing ETFs and index funds versus actively managed funds to invest the asset classes in a tactical portfolio. While we have shown that both expense and tax considerations are significantly less important than maximizing portfolio returns through active management, at the margin investors should be diligent in their approach to both. ETFs are more tax efficient than most managed funds and should be located in taxable accounts. In addition, ETFs generally have significantly lower fees than actively managed funds, and the lower fee structure should be considered when choosing between a passive fund and an active manager to invest each asset class. However, as mentioned above, and in earlier chapters, ETFs have their own challenges in terms of the construction of the underlying index that they are built to mimic, and investors must beware of making a choice based on a simple criterion of low expenses or taxes, without doing the proper due diligence.

## Putting It All Together

Investors need to answer the questions listed above, and a host of other questions, based on their own experiences and observations about the financial markets. If you happen to be lucky enough to apprentice with an active portfolio manager, then the answers to these questions will be provided for you. But for the great majority of investors, the answers will probably come from trial and error, with a great deal of emphasis on the error. Financial planners know that it is difficult for investors to quantify their tolerance for risk before they actually experience a bear market together and the advisor can observe how the client reacts in a difficult market environment. The same can be said for active, tactical investors who find themselves trailing their portfolio benchmark because in the short-term the market is not performing according to their forecasts. How investors handle this uncomfortable situation will probably determine how far from a strategic benchmark they will allow themselves to tactically adjust portfolio asset allocations in the future. There is no substitute for experience in learning how to actively manage portfolios. The challenge is to answer the questions that are posed in this chapter in a way that is consistent with your beliefs about the markets, and the limitations of your abilities.

You are the only one who will know if the answers you reach are correct.

# 16 INDUSTRY FORECAST
## *(An Essay)*

Since much of this book is about making better forecasts, I thought it fitting to end with a forecast about the future of active portfolio management and briefly discuss the changes that are likely to occur in the money management and financial planning industry if investors embrace the need for change.

The first major change that I see will be changes in the curriculum for students studying to receive the academic designations associated with professional money management, including the MBA, CFP® certificant, and CFA® designations. As a practicing CFP®, it seems obvious to me that the course study required to pass the investment exam is dramatically skewed towards learning Modern Portfolio Theory and the Capital Asset Pricing Model. If the industry is going to evolve towards a more active style of management, several new and innovative ideas need to be added to the study materials. As you might suppose, many of the ideas are covered in this book. I don't see how we can properly train CFPs® to be investment professionals without adding significant new study information regarding market valuation and how it relates to long-term market returns. In addition, I think there needs to be more basic information about the intersection of the economy and the financial markets. Finally, there needs to be at least an introduction to technical analysis and the tools that investors use to measure the internals of the stock market. These three additions should be considered the most important elements of the curriculum, and Modern Portfolio Theory should be an interesting side note. As long as we are redesigning the text book, there should be additional chapters covering behavioral finance, the history of pricing theory, and last, but not least, the psychology of actively managing money.

The second major change I see is that the industry will have to create new actively managed investment products to meet the demands of consumers who want a more active approach to managing their wealth. Perhaps the biggest change would be in the way that investors currently demand that money managers invest their capital within a strictly defined style of management. Large-growth managers dare not try to find value in small-cap stocks, and U.S. managers dare not try and find value in international stocks. It is unthinkable that either manager would be free to find value in bonds. Instead of being fired for style drift, in the new paradigm of active management, investors would celebrate style drift, looking to reward managers that can tactically allocate funds to different asset classes. In essence, the industry needs to blow up the Morningstar Style Box approach to assessing manager performance, and find a better and more innovative way to determine if active managers are adding value. And yes, in this context it will be difficult to measure alpha in the traditional way since agreeing on a benchmark for managed accounts that own a variety of globally diversified asset classes will be nearly impossible. I will leave it to the bright minds in the industry to figure this out.

Along the same lines, I see the industry manufacturing new actively managed investment funds for individual investors. These tactical investment choices would be available in company 401(k) plans and for all investors that can meet the minimum investment requirements to buy a mutual fund or a separate account. While I am a passionate advocate for active and tactical portfolio management, I am also a financial planner with 25 years of experience in watching investors chase the most dangerous investment ideas and new fads. Having professionally managed choices available for smaller investors who cannot meet the minimums for financial advisors that specialize in active management will be profitable for the firms that pioneer the use of these funds, and a great benefit for the consumers who will want to invest in them.

As a member of the financial planning community for virtually my entire professional life, I would be remiss in not admitting the pride I feel at being associated with such an outstanding group of professionals. While this book points out the areas of disagreement that I have with my colleagues in the profession regarding the status quo of how we manage money, there is no doubt that the professional planning community is committed to providing the best possible service to our clients. In an era where investors are faced with the horrors of the Bernie Madoff's of this world, planning professionals still offer a wonderful standard of client service and responsibility. Fortunately, as I have mentioned throughout the book, I believe that there is a new level of concern among financial planners and investment advisors about the implications of buying and holding as the current secular bear market continues. There is a new paradigm in town, and a growing realization that the needs of investors and clients are not being met.

What should you do if you want to leave the strategic and passive asset allocation world behind and become a more active investor? Let's divide the readers of this book into two general groups. The first group is the investors who prefer to delegate the ongoing management of their wealth to either professional portfolio managers or investment advisors. These consumers will have to develop a new and different vocabulary to be excellent consumers of active portfolio management services in the future. Instead of being swayed by strategic asset managers whose unique value proposition is selling the idea that they have access to the "best" money managers, these more educated consumers will be asking advisors the following questions:

- Do you believe that the investment markets are efficient?
- At what point would you consider the stock market to be under or overvalued?
- How do you make your valuation decisions?
- How far do you deviate from your benchmark allocations?
- How much trading can I expect?
- What is your investment time horizon?
- How often will you communicate with me to discuss your active management strategy?
- What types of securities do you favor in order to implement your strategy?
- Do you incorporate technical analysis in your decision-making process?
- Do you employ investment analysts and what is their role in your firm?

These questions are new to consumers and new to most advisors as well. In addition, it is not hard to imagine that investors will be asking their trusted advisors, like CPAs and attorneys, to refer them to advisors that are experts at active management. The entire professional community will begin to learn a new way to approach portfolio construction that requires a different kind of due diligence in choosing an advisor as well as evaluating him or her on an ongoing basis. Obviously the answers to these questions will be critical to how financial advisors are hired by affluent individuals and referred-to by trusted advisors in the years ahead. Perhaps the greatest challenge will be for interested consumers to find advisors that will admit to being active managers at all. Such is the stigma that is put on those who are deemed to be "market timers" in the profession today that most advisors are still unwilling to be labeled as anything but a strategic investor. I believe that as the demand grows for active portfolio management, the industry will evolve in order to meet the demand.

If the first group of readers is delegators who prefer to pay for money management services, then the second group of readers is those who prefer to manage portfolios on their own, either as individuals or as professional investment advisors. For them, the first action step is to answer the questions posed in Chapter 15 of this book. The questions are not posed lightly and the answers are not easy. In Pinnacle's case, the answers are still evolving after eight years of concentrated effort. Nevertheless, for those who would like me to tell them exactly how to actively manage a portfolio, unfortunately I cannot help you. Part of the reason that the money management industry fell in love with quantitative approaches to money management in the first place is for precisely this reason, which is the insistence by practitioners that someone give them the magic solution for portfolio construction. Of course, MPT and CAPM perfectly fit the bill as a push-button approach to portfolio construction, and now investors are paying the price for never having to learn how to actually manage money. As long as we remain in a secular bear market, and even if we do not, the buy and hold—efficient markets crowd is in serious trouble. At some point, even these investors will have to consider leaving their antiquated model-based portfolio construction behind. If they choose to utilize a methodology of money management that integrates qualitative decision-making into the portfolio construction process, then they too will have to make their own decisions about what is the "right" way to actively manage money.

So, I'm forced to leave with you with the same exhortation that I made many times in the body of this book, which is to *do the work*. You will find that it is a fascinating and exhilarating venture to undertake. There really is an art to actively managing portfolios, and while I can't tell you what style of brush strokes will work best for you, I can tell you that the rewards of learning this new craft are well worth it. Instead of feeling helpless in the grasp of a continuing bear market with few tools at your disposal to earn excess returns, and even worse, being told that there is no such thing as excess returns, instead you can take control of your portfolio returns by excelling at active management. As long as you implement the techniques that you favor in the context of a well diversified portfolio with clear rules for managing risk, you will be well served. I believe that you really are embarking on a life-long journey towards marrying the analytical skills necessary to better understand the workings of the economy and the markets, with the art of knowing what constitutes a "high conviction" point of view, or knowing how far to deviate from a fixed benchmark.

In Chapter 13 I discussed the Psychology of Making Investment Mistakes, and it's worth repeating that you should be prepared to make mistakes. These mistakes are going to be unavoidable, and can't be attributed to your lack of skill, desire, intelligence, or hard work. Your mistakes will simply be the result of not being able to perfectly predict the future. As we learned from Kurz and Brock, all investors make mistakes. To be successful, you need to learn how to make fewer mistakes than the consensus. Follow the rules that are presented in Chapter 13 for dealing with mistakes, and then reread them again and again. Try your best to remember that every single investment strategy that you ever heard of involves making some kind of forecast. Some are wrapped up in fancy language like standard deviation, correlation, means-variance, and efficient frontiers. As an active manager, your forecasts will sound different, but be no less valid. Your forecast might be that the economy will remain weak, the stock market is still expensive but could rally by the end of the year, and there are currently large risks to your forecast that require you to hedge your base-case to a large extent. As someone who has made both kinds of forecasts in the course of my career, I can assure you that if you have done your homework, the second forecast rises to a much higher level of professional portfolio management then the first.

Finally, there are many places throughout the book where I leave it to you, the reader, to decide what works best. Don't be discouraged. The silence in the industry about active management is becoming strained, and there is a small group of individual and professional portfolio managers who are eager to share their experiences about active management. I hope that this book is one of the tools that you will refer to over and over again as you evolve your own process for active investing. If you end up with a process similar to ours, then you too can call yourself a tactical asset allocator, and perhaps after awhile, you will give me a call and we can compare notes.

Good luck.

# ABOUT THE AUTHOR

**Kenneth R. Solow, CFP®** is a founding partner of Pinnacle Advisory Group, Inc., a Registered Investment Advisor providing private wealth management services to more than 1,000 families around the world. Solow is the Chairman of Pinnacle's Investment Committee, which manages close to $2 billion in assets using the tactical asset allocation strategies he developed over the past fifteen years. With over 30 years of experience as a financial planner, Solow is nationally known for his views on active portfolio management, and his 2009 book, *Buy and Hold Is Dead (Again): The Case for Active Portfolio Management in Dangerous Markets*, is considered the definitive work on Tactical Asset Allocation.

A popular speaker at professional conferences across the U.S. and internationally, Solow appears regularly at events sponsored by the Financial Planning Association, National Association of Financial Planners, the Investment Management Consultants Association, and the AICPA. He has been published in *The Journal of Financial Planning, Smart Money, Financial Planning Magazine, The Baltimore Sun*, the *Globe & Mail*, and the *Wall Street Journal*. He has guest lectured on Quantitative Portfolio Construction at Frank G. Zarb School of business at Hofstra University and at the Smith School of Business at the University of Maryland, and serves on the Board of Trustees of the Howard Community College Education Foundation.

A graduate of Towson University, Solow lives in Maryland with his wife, Linda, and Connor the dog. He is a proud member of Rotary International, where he has served as District Governor. He enjoys golf, tennis, fishing, and boating.

For more information about Ken or his company, visit **pinnacleadvisory.com**.

# Index

CPSIA information can be obtained
at www.ICGtesting.com
Printed in the USA
FFOW05n0254180416

9 781630 472108